MW00997624

# The
# Journey

# The
# Journey

The oral Histories of 24
of the most Proficient American Kenpoists of Today

Foreword by
## Joe Hyams

("Zen In the Martial Arts")

Gilderoy Publications / Ojai, California

Gilderoy Publications titles are available at quantity
discounts for sales promotions, premiums or fund raising.
For information write to Special Sales Manager,
Gilderoy Publications, Post Office Box 1048, Ojai, CA 93024.

THE JOURNEY
Gilderoy Publications, Ojai, California
Copyright © by Tom Bleecker
All Rights reserved
First edition published 2001
Printed in the United States of America

05 04 03 02 01 00 99 98 97 96 5 4 3 2 1


Libary of Congress Catalog Card Number: 2001 135341
ISBN (Paperback): 0-09653123-4-7


Portrait Illustrations
Copyright ©2000-2001 by Edmund K. Parker Jr.

Front and back cover and book design plus illustrations:
Ed Parker, Jr.
2245 E. Colorado Blvd. #104-PMB 257
Pasadena, CA 91107


Printed by Bush Printing
Brea, CA   92821

Yaakov-Yossept took his defeat badly. He felt bitter, rejected by his colleagues, misunderstood, a victim of justice. His friend Pinhas of Koretz did his best to comfort him with a parable:

"When the king retires at night, his crown rests on a nail fastened to the wall."

"Why on a nail, which is nothing but a common object? Why not on the minister's head?"

"Because the minister might take himself so seriously and believe he is the king. No such danger with a nail."

*– Elie Wiesel,* **Souls of Fire**

# Contents

# *word from the* Publisher

My own journey began in August 1962 at the age of sixteen. Two months earlier when school let out for summer vacation, an older kid had threatened to beat me up if he saw me at any of the popular hangouts that included the bowling alley, record stores, hamburger joints, movie theaters, and beaches of southern California. I was scared, and after ducking this guy for two months I finally realized that if I didn't do something about learning how to fight, I would spend the rest of my life hiding out from one nasty character after the next.

Within days of deciding to take action, I appeared at one of only three karate schools listed in the Los Angeles phone book. The school was Ed Parker's Kenpo Karate Studio on LaCienega Boulevard. I signed up for a month of lessons, paid my dues of $20.00 and purchased a uniform and white belt for $12.50.

On January 28, 1963 I received my first promotion to one brown tip, which today would be the equivalent of an orange belt. My certificate, signed by Ed Parker, is proudly displayed on my office wall not far from the certificate that promoted me to the rank of first-degree black belt on October 4, 1965.

Over the next four years I continued training in Kenpo while attending city college and later transferred to UCLA as a premedical student. In

an effort to help pay my way through school I taught Kenpo at Ed Parker's WLA School in the afternoons and evenings.

In the summer of 1969 an event occurred that dramatically changed the course of my life. One of Ed Parker's students, director Blake Edwards, was bringing his adolescent son Geoffrey in for private lessons. We struck up a friendship and I soon began teaching Geoff, Blake, and his soon-to-be wife, Julie Andrews, private lessons at her Beverly Hills home.

In late 1969 Blake offered to teach me the film business and gave me the job of William Holden's stand-in and double on the MGM film "Wild Rovers, which Blake directed. Several movie bit roles followed, including an appearance on "The Julie Andrews Hour" television show with Chuck Norris, John Natividvad, and Steve Walton. We did the opening musical number with Julie, performing karate techniques as she moved cautiously among us singing, "Something's Gotta Give."

Over the next fifteen years I continued my Kenpo training and teaching as I pursued a writing career in the Hollywood film and television industry. Like so many of Kenpo black belts, I kept in touch with Ed Parker and others in the Kenpo community, but it wasn't until August 1987 that a major milestone occurred in my

Kenpo journey.

I had been living in Hawaii for five years, writing for several producers. Having finally been plagued with Island Fever, in the spring of 1987 I moved to Solvang, California where I soon opened a Kenpo Karate school under the IKKA banner while I continued my writing. As a result of opening the school, I took my students to the 1987 Long Beach Internationals. Late into Saturday I was sitting in the stands watching the competition when Ed Parker suddenly appeared in the aisle and practically fell into the empty seat beside me. He looked exhausted and I almost had the feeling that he had taken a back way into the stands and was hiding out. He stared down with mixed emotions at the sea of karate before him. Although he was proud of having in 1964 created what had since become the biggest and most prestigious martial arts tournament in the world, there was a sense of nostalgia about him. He stared down at the main floor and then said almost to himself, "Tom, wouldn't it be great to go back to the way things were back in the old days? You know, the old times at Chuck's – the barbecues and all those fun times with the old guys?" Suddenly he was besieged by a group of people who had located him and claimed he was needed in half the rings on the floor. There were phone calls and decisions to be made about Sunday night's seating and everyone seemed to be talking at once. Ed stood up, glanced at me and said, "Well, it was a nice thought, anyway. See you."

I sat in the stands and watched him walk away. Barbara Hale (an esteemed American Kenpo black belt) was sitting on the other side of me, and I turned to her and asked, "How difficult would it be to get together these old timers he's talking about and throw a barbecue like back in the old days?"

The following Monday Barbara and I talked on the phone. Together we compiled a list that amounted to about thirty people. We figured a time and place and a way that we could surprise the Old Man. By Wednesday, however, another ten people somehow were added to the list, and by Friday another ten. Soon it was no longer feasi-

ble to hold this Kenpo Memory Lane get-together at someone's house, so we agreed to rent a small banquet room at a Pasadena midsize hotel. That worked for about three days until the phones again began ringing. More people wanted to come to the event that was now being talked about as a surprise party for Ed Parker. It wasn't long before this casual surprise party buffet turned into a major event that made Kenpo history.

Along with my two associate producers, Barbara Hale and Mike Pick, I produced a Tribute to Martial Arts Grandmaster Edmund Parker, which was held at the Bonaventure Hotel in Los Angeles on February 27, 1988. Over a thousand friends, students and martial arts dignitaries sat down to a five-course dinner and were entertained throughout the evening. In addition, scores of television and film celebrities came from all over the world to pay tribute to Ed Parker, along with his entire immediate family, many of whom were flown in from Hawaii and Utah. It was truly a grand evening held on a grand scale.

There were so many great moments that evening. Ed Parker had seen the outpouring of love and camaraderie among his Kenpo family – black belts who shook hands for the first time in years, old grievances set aside as martial artists of many styles and systems came together in the uniquely nonpartisan setting. By the conclusion of the evening it was clear that bringing the Kenpo community close together, as we had been in bygone years, was paramount on the mind of our founder Ed Parker. In one of the most memorable moments of the Tribute, he walked to the podium and closed with his story about "Sam the wagon master." Many have heard this story, which essentially has to do with the strengthening of our brotherhood from the perspective of members of the Kenpo community, as well as members of the much greater community of martial artists. The seed had been planted.

Less than two years later Ed Parker died from a heart attack in his beloved Hawaiian Islands, bringing deep sadness to the martial arts world and sending shockwaves through the Kenpo community.

Not long after our founder was laid to rest, the reality that he had not named a successor created a sense of unrest and uncertainty within the Kenpo rank and file. This was similar to what had occurred after the passing of Bruce Lee and the Jeet Kune Do Society. As to why Ed Parker had not chosen to name a successor, one can only speculate. Regardless, over the next decade we have seen the results of our foundation's shifting sand. There have been many promotions to higher and higher degrees of black belt, as well as the establishment of over a dozen major newly formed American Kenpo associations.

Why the need for this book? As both a kenpoist and a publisher, I feel that this book will fill two needs. The first is that over the past decade, and as a direct result of our Kenpo community undergoing a restructuring, our vast membership has to one degree or another fallen into a general state of isolationism. From my point of view – as one who for the past decade has been more socially, rather than politically, involved with many of the individuals featured in this book, such isolationism has for the most part not been intentional. Rather it has been the result of the right hand not talking to the left. And so I felt this book would on a personal level reacquaint many of our family leaders with each other and help bring the brotherhood closer together while at the same time allow each of the individuals featured in this book to maintain his or her own independence.

The second substantial need I feel this book will fulfill has to do with the future generations of martial artists. From the standpoint of American Kenpo, it is my hope that this book will help the new student acquire a clear picture of the legacy of Grandmaster Ed Parker and Kenpo's basic historical roots, as well as the lineage of those esteemed individuals featured in this book. On a much broader perspective, the journeys described herein are representative of the basic journey shared by all martial artists regardless of which style or system one chooses to study. Personally, I wish this book had been available when I was coming up through the ranks, for it would have, by being both informative and inspirational,

helped me over many speed bumps, as well as a handful of major obstacles.

I personally did not select all of the individuals featured in this book. In order to get the wheels in motion, however, I did select the first ten. These were kenpoists I felt would have appeared somewhere on just about anyone's list of twenty-five prominent descendants of Grandmaster Ed Parker – for example, Chuck Sullivan, Dave Hebler, Frank Trejo, and Bob White. Moreover, it was vital that these ten were readily and easily accessible to each other because from that point the selection process became their responsibility. Once these ten were in place, I asked them to nominate and vote on five more inductees, making their total fifteen. Once in place, these fifteen repeated the process and selected another five, and then this resultant twenty brought the final total to twenty-five (in addition to three alternates). By the time of publication that number was fixed at twenty-four. As a footnote, with a few adjustments that had to do with the book's flow, the placement of the Honorees in this book is essentially by random order.

The Journey was never intended to be the biographies of those featured in the book. Nor was it meant to be a vehicle to promote which one stood on the tallest mountain, or had the most specialized and latest version of Kenpo knowledge, or could boast of the closest personal friendship with Ed Parker. By the same token, this book is not about accomplishments. From the outset it made no sense to me to feature a group of "prominent and proficient" individuals and then spend 350 pages explaining why they are "prominent and proficient." To focus on their accomplishments, which would have been self-serving, would be to focus on the destination rather than the journey. Also, I feel it is important to point out that no one associated with this book is taking the position that these featured individuals are the *most* proficient American Kenpoists. Rather they are twenty-four *of* the most proficient, and there is an enormous difference.

The process of how these featured individuals talked about their journeys was relatively simple.

Each was required to participate in a taped telephone or personal interview that amounted to approximately two hours. After this was done, a transcript was made of the interview and pared down to the essentials. A follow-up interview was then conducted, and the resultant 4500-word final text was then combined with photographs provided by each Honoree. While each Honorees had a redline veto and could delete anything that was written into his or her story, they were not permitted to freely add to their stories. Additions had to meet the basic ground rules that were established at the outset.

It seems like I've known Joe Hyams forever. I had heard about Joe for many years before first meeting him. Having received his black belt from Ed Parker back in the late 1950s Joe is my senior in Kenpo. In addition to having considerable respect for his accomplishments in the martial arts, I greatly admire, if not envy, Joe's profound writing talent. He is truly a gifted and prolific writer and renowned biographer. Because of his years of experience interviewing famous people, Joe has developed an uncanny knack for cutting right to the chase. In addition, while having the respect of the Kenpo community, Joe personally has neither an allegiance to any kenpoist in particular or any Kenpo association, nor does he have any axes to grind. Best of all he has years of experience working as a newspaper reporter and knows the meaning of meeting deadlines. For several years Joe and I had been searching for a book that we could work on together, and almost as if by divine providence *The Journey* turned out to be it.

My earliest recollection of Ed Parker Jr. (late 1960s) is that of jogging on the mats of the WLA school with him on my shoulders. Back then he was a young child. Two decades later I stood inside the California Ballroom of the Bonaventure Hotel in Los Angeles and watched him give a speech from the podium that moved the audience to tears and resounding applause. Truly our founder, Grandmaster Ed Parker, can be proud of his only son, not only as a man and a gifted kenpoist in his own right, but also as an artist whose talent is both unique and unparalleled. In addition to the book's cover and design, the stunning portraits of the Honorees featured in this book are the result of his hundreds of hours of Edmund's labor. I am both honored and grateful to have Ed Parker Jr. and his remarkable artistic talents associated with this book.

I would also like to mention Dr. Steve Walton, who wrote the Origins of American Kenpo section and the In Memorandum section on Elvis Presley. I first met Steve in the late 1960s when we were students at UCLA and living in the same apartment building. At the time, I was the head instructor at the WLA studio. One day Steve spotted my gi and belt, and questioned me. I invited him down to the studio and he was hooked. He earned his black belt in 1974 and today lives in Hawaii where he runs a health clinic as a Doctor of Chiropractic and is also an Elder in his church. His Kenpo experience spans various iterations of the system, and his long residence in Hawaii provides an added perspective on the origins of American Kenpo.

In closing I would like to thank all of the esteemed featured Honorees for giving generously and unselfishly of their time and efforts, without which this finished work could not have been possible.

— Tom Bleecker

# Foreword

*M*y journey in kenpo began in the mid-fifties. At the time I was a hotshot thirty-five-year-old Hollywood columnist, sedentary, overweight, easily bored and hostile. In an attempt to work off my anger I began studying fencing at Joseph Vince's salle (studio) in Beverly Hills. Vince had been a world saber champion in his native Hungary before coming to the United States. Every morning I went to the salle to work out with other students: Tony Curtis who was learning to fence in preparation for a film role; Cornel Wilde, film star and former college saber champion; Bronislau Kaper, an Oscar wining composer who was a world-class saber champion in his native Poland.

One day after a bout with Kaper he put away his weapon and made a few fast hand moves followed by a low kick to my knee which caught me by surprise.

"What was that all about?" I asked him.

"That's kenpo karate," he said.

At that time karate was new on the Hollywood scene and viewed merely as an exotic Asian way of hand-to-hand fighting.

"Where are you studying?" I asked.

Kaper arranged for me to meet with Ed Parker, who was teaching Kenpo to a few private students in the weight room of the Beverly Hills Health Club.

At our first meeting Mr. Parker reminded me of a huge tree, with arms like powerful boughs and bare feet rooted firmly on the floor. He was wearing an old loose fitting gi that, like his black belt, was frayed from repeated laundering. His face was serene and peaceful.

His first words to me were, "I am not going to show you my art. I am going to share it with you. If I show it to it becomes an exhibition, and in time it will be pushed so far into the back of your mind that it will be lost. But by sharing it with you, you will not only retain it forever, but I, too, will improve."

At that time Mr. Parker taught only about twenty-five techniques or katas, a series of parries, punches, blocks, a couple of low kicks, and some self-defense moves against a variety of attacks and weapons.

Although I was Mr. Parker's senior by eight years, we bonded, possibly because my name was Joe like his older brother who was my age. I liked Mr. Parker, not only for his abilities, but because during the lesson he always gave positive input first. Criticism included suggestions for improvement.

When he demonstrated the proper way to perform a technique it was with incredible but controlled power. One day when Mr. Parker was dummying for me I accidentally hit him. He shook his head and looked angrily at me. "If you can hit, you can miss," he said

Several months after I had started studying, I parked my new car in a Beverly Hills lot. When I came to get it I found the gears were locked. The attendant had put it in reverse without coming to a full stop. I berated the attendant who threw a punch at me. Without thought I made an outward block with full force and broke his arm.

When I told Mr. Parker what had happened he smiled. "You were curious to see if kenpo really works, weren't you?" he asked me.

I nodded sheepishly, and he continued.

"The only reason men fight is because they are insecure; one man needs to prove that he is better or stronger than another. The man who is secure within himself has no need to prove anything with force, so he can walk away from a fight with dignity and pride. He is the true martial artist – a man so strong inside that he has no need to demonstrate his power.

"The point of achieving proficiency in any martial art is to be able to walk away from a fight rather than to win it. But you will walk with shoulders erect, pride in your bearing, knowing inside what the outcome of the battle would have been had you wished to precipitate it. And this attitude of confidence will be communicated to your antagonist, who will realize that he narrowly escaped defeat. If you have nothing to prove, you have no need to fight."

During that first year of studying Kenpo my ability to play tennis improved. I had begun to apply Kenpo principles to my movements. My body mechanics were better. I was able to use torque to hit the ball harder and more precisely.

I was so enthused about Kenpo that I frequently wrote about Ed Parker in my column and magazine pieces. I talked up Kenpo whenever I met a star, producer or director, anyone who might be a potential student or want to use Mr. Parker in a film.

One day I arranged for Mr. Parker and several students to put on a demo at Gary Cooper's home. Cooper wanted to study, but unfortunately became ill and soon died.

Thanks in part to my help Mr. Parker, began to get work choreographing fight scenes in films. Due to his charisma, presence and ability, he also landed occasional acting roles.

He promoted me to black belt, not because of my ability I am sure, but because I was a diligent student and spokesperson for him and Kenpo.

Mr. Parker soon left the weight room and opened a school in Pasadena.

In my book, *Zen in the Martial Arts*, I write of the day when I was sparring in the Los Angeles studio with a more skillful opponent. I forgot about technique, began to improvise, and was trounced. After the lesson Mr. Parker took me into his office, a small sparsely furnished room with only a battered desk and a few chairs.

"Why are you so upset?" he asked me.

"Because I was so outclassed."

Mr. Parker got up from behind the desk and with a piece of chalk drew a line on the floor about five feet long. "How can you make this line shorter?" he asked me.

I studied the line and gave him several answers, including cutting the line in many pieces.

He shook his head and drew a second line, longer than the first. "Now how does the first line look?"

"Shorter," I said.

Mr. Parker nodded. "It is always better to improve and strengthen your own line or knowledge than to try and cut your opponent's line. Think about it?"

Some time later I told George Waite, one of Mr. Parker's black belts and my mentor in Kenpo, about my defeat. George recalled his brown belt days in Kenpo and how discouraged he became when he saw someone far better than he, although he considered himself good.

"When that happened I used to go into the studio and watch the white belts. I saw that, compared with them, I was good. But then I'd watch the black belts and become inspired all over again.

When I finally became a black belt I realized that I really knew nothing compared with Mr. Parker, and I was discouraged until he told me how great was William Chow, his teacher in Hawaii."

I continued studying Kenpo until the summer day in 1964 when I saw Bruce Lee perform at Mr. Parker's International Karate Tournament in Long Beach, California.

Bruce walked onto the floor of the Long Beach Municipal Auditorium wearing a simple, black, tailor-made kung-fu uniform. He spoke quietly for a few moments about his art and then began executing techniques with blinding speed, his movements as quick and as elegant as a bird in flight but with obvious power.

When he finished there was a moment of silence and then ear shattering applause.

I told Stirling Silliphant, my friend and an Oscar winning screenwriter, about Bruce's demonstration. We arranged for Bruce to give us private lessons in the driveway of my home.

One day over lunch in Chinatown I complained to Bruce about my limitations and lack of flexibility. He laughed and said, "I became a martial artist in spite of my limitations. My right leg is shorter than the left, which gives me an advantage with certain types of kicks, since the uneven stomp gave me greater impetus. That fact dictated the best stance for me – my left foot leading.

"And I'm nearsighted which means I have difficulty seeing an opponent when he's not up close. I originally started to study Wing Chun because it is ideal for close-in fighting. I accepted my limitations for what they were and capitalized on them.

"Instead of trying to do everything well, do those things perfectly of which you are capable. Although most martial artists have spent years mastering hundreds of movements and techniques, in a bout a champion may use only four or five techniques over and over again. Those are the techniques which he has perfected and which he knows he can depend on."

When Bruce learned that I was still fencing, he asked me to show him some of the techniques. I went into my house and returned with a foil. Bruce was especially impressed with the way fencers close the gap, subtly shuffling forward, then lunging toward an opponent at full speed with weapon hand leading.

Bruce took my foil and executed my movements perfectly. "There's something here I can use," he said. "The efficiency of extending the hand before the footwork is a great way of closing distance."

He put the foil down and told me to stand about ten feet in front of him. "I'm going to close your eyelids before you can," he said. And he did just that using the fencing technique he had just learned.

Bruce's dream at that time was to be an even bigger film star than his friend and student, Steve McQueen. Stirling wrote parts for Bruce in several films and television shows. I took Bruce to Warner Brothers to meet William T. Orr, studio head Jack Warner's son-in-law and a studio vice-president.

During the meeting Orr, who was sitting behind his desk smoking a cigar, asked Bruce to demonstrate his martial art. Bruce, who was standing in front of the desk, suddenly whirled around. His leg shot out fully extended over the desk as he kicked the cigar out of Orr's mouth. The meeting was ended.

Orr later called me and said that there had never been a Chinese star in Hollywood movies and Bruce's English was barely understandable: "He's wasting time trying to get into films." Years later, Bruce's smash hit "Enter the Dragon" would save the studio from financial disaster.

Although skilled in many martial arts, Bruce believed it necessary to truly master only a few simple moves and techniques to be formidable in hand-to-hand combat. But, he said, skill does not come easily nor can it be achieved by wishful thinking. He stressed that the only easy road lay through sustained hard work, lots of it. He drilled me until my reactions became automatic, without thought. He likened this to going into a dark room and turning on a light switch or hitting your brakes at the sight of a child in the road ahead.

He insisted that I practice every move for

hours, days, and weeks until I could react blindfolded responding only to his touch or what he termed sense-awareness.

Occasionally Bruce would wear a blindfold and challenge me to attack him. During more than two years of working out with him, I was never able to touch him. He claimed his ability to anticipate an attack came through his development of a sixth sense that enabled him to grasp an assailant's intentions.

At the conclusion of every lesson Bruce suggested that I replay in my mind everything I had learned before going to sleep at night. "If you can think it, you can do it," he once told me. That simple suggestion kept me awake many nights in which I visualized various scenarios in which I was sometimes victim, and occasionally the victor. It is no surprise to me that anyone with a true passion for a martial art constantly rethinks lessons learned whether sleeping, driving on the freeway, or attending to business.

Despite his size Bruce was undoubtedly the strongest man I have ever met: he could do one-finger pushups with either hand. But he rarely used his power. As he once told me, "The Buddha expects us to be like a body of water, flowing downhill. When you reach a tree or boulder, you go around it rather than try to use force against it."

Bruce, a cha-cha dance champion as a youngster in Hong Kong before coming to America, believed that there was one prerequisite to excelling at a martial art. "If you don't have rhythm, you can't learn karate," he once said. Sad news for me since I seem to have been born with two left feet.

Bruce's tactics that apply to all confrontation were to always dominate the opponent physically and psychologically in space and time. "Victory comes to the man who knows how to take the initiative of the attack and knows how to manipulate his opponent," he said. "In short, attack when your opponent attacks and prevent him from carrying out another attack or from considering one."

One day in 1965 Bruce told Stirling and me that he had a chance for a big break. He was going to Hong Kong to make films. At this, our last lesson, he wanted to test our abilities.

Stirling and I wore full padding as we sparred for three two-minute rounds. Next, we crossed hands and did leg and hand trapping techniques. Then we broke boards with waist high punches and kicks. Our final test was to break a brick on the ground suspended over cinder blocks. Bruce congratulated us and gave us Jeet Kune Do certificates.

The question arises: why discuss Bruce Lee when he was not a kenpoist? Bruce exchanged ideas with Mr. Parker, and took as much from Kenpo as he gave to it. And, he was an integral part of my journey.

Over the decades since I first met Ed Parker and Bruce Lee I have studied a dozen different styles of martial arts (ranging from Aikido to Wing Chun) in England, South Africa, Germany, Japan, and Sweden. I earned black belts in some and certificates of achievement in others. Foolishly I was always searching for the magic style that would defeat all opponents. I had forgotten what Mr. Parker once told me: "It's not the style, it's the man."

In time I came to realize that technical knowledge about the martial arts is not enough. A martial artist must transcend technique and develop intuitive action so that the art becomes an artless art, not only a way to physical excellence, but as a way to spiritual enlightenment.

I'd had some hints of Zen from some of my instructors and began to take notes after each lesson. Within a few years I realized I had the basis for a book about Zen in the martial arts.

Now that I am nearing the age of eighty and I reflect back on my journey starting with Kenpo, I have come to appreciate a story told about Mas Oyama, arguably the greatest of last century's karataka. Oyama believed that brain will beat brawn in karate.

To prove his point he chose two new students who were as evenly endowed with natural talents as possible. One he trained only on calisthenics and workouts and taught him a few simple but practical moves. To the other he gave less physical training, but made him meditate for half an hour when he awoke and again before his evening workout, squatting like a Buddha, forcing all his internal organs into proper alignment, breathing down to his toes and clearing his mind. After six months, both men came up for their black belt test. One had beefed up and put on ten pounds. The other was wiry. The thinker made mince meat of the muscle man.

Great news for us old-timers and good news for young people starting to study Kenpo. I recently visited some Kenpo tournaments in Los Angeles and realized again how much Kenpo has to offer.

Kenpo cannot be practiced as a form of entertainment or self-defense. It cannot be approached tentatively or with superficial layers of thought or heart. It would be better never to become involved, but if you begin the journey it is essential to carry on to the end, until one's being is rejuvenated to the point of being complete. As soon as you set your bare feet on the mat, you have entered forever. If you waver or quit, one day you will realize something essential is missing from your life.

There is a Zen saying that, "When the student is ready, the teacher will appear." It is no coincidence that in the stories of each of the kenpoists profiled here Ed Parker appeared only when they were ready for him.

Many of the men were angry as youngsters and studied Kenpo for the wrong reason, to beat up on a bully or unleash aggression. Kenpo taught them discipline, self-restraint, and respect for others. Another common denominator fascinated me. Many black belts were dancers, performers, or gymnasts when they were children. Every movement on the mat rhythmically expresses proportion, balance, and universal order. A powerful man is graceful. A graceful woman is powerful.

The immediate goal of Kenpo study is to build a healthy mind in a sound body thus breeding confidence and strength. A person possessing these elements never need be concerned about the outcome of confrontation, whether on the street, the office, or in personal relationships.

Some Kenpo instructors today have adapted Ed Parker's original system and created new principles of their own. There are more than a thousand Kenpo studios throughout the world: a vast brotherhood dedicated to keeping the Kenpo flame burning brightly.

This book cannot accurately portray a life lived. Instead we have attempted to provide an opportunity for kenpoists of all ranks to compare their own journeys with that of some of today's most prominent American Kenpo masters. Theirs has been a fascinating journey in terms of attitude and performance during which each individual came to realize that the spiritual, mental and physical must be integrated into one.

– Joe Hyams

# The Origins of American Kenpo

## by Dr. Stevan Walton D. C.

*A*ll creatures have an innate drive to survive. This instinct for self-preservation is expressed in the marvelous variety of nature: from the predator's fang and claw to the more passive defenses of quill, shell and camouflage. Physically, mankind suffers by comparison with the natural weaponry and defensive attributes found in the animal kingdom. Still, we have survived, thrived and become the dominant predators on the planet based on the gift of intellect, which allows us to observe, learn, problem-solve, fashion tools, and pass on the accumulated knowledge to following generations as a foundation for further progress. This is the history of the transmission and evolution of that body of knowledge currently known as American Kenpo.

Violent conflict is older than mankind. Despite our relative paucity of natural weaponry, humans are violent creatures beneath a thin veneer of civilization. As early man watched animals to discover sources of food and water, he would also observe how to procure game or escape predators. In the process, early hunters watched and learned from their competition in the animal kingdom. Hunter-warriors learned practical lessons in the strategic value of stalking, concealment, ambush, and surprise. They could learn the tactical wisdom of choosing a suitable battleground, and the timing of an attack. They saw the benefits of the attributes of speed, power, and accuracy. They learned that attacking at the most vulnerable point insured success, whether it is the weakest member of a group or the most vulnerable anatomical target of an individual. All these lessons were derived from observing the hunting behavior of predators, and they applied equally to conflicts with other men. Shamanistic attempts to absorb these desirable attributes were made through imitation of totem animals in ritual dance.

When hunting and gathering was replaced by the domestication of herd animals and development of agriculture, more stable territorial boundaries were required. Agricultural surpluses could support a specialized warrior class. This ruling group could protect the territory and the peasants, while at the same time focusing on development of martial skill. When tension grew between ruler and ruled, there would be uprisings and the peasants would be disarmed, which led to improvised weaponry and the secret practice of fighting arts.

These general patterns of development were played out in China, Okinawa, and Japan. The rhythms of war and peace, trade and isolation, subjugation and rebellion, experimentation and cross-training all combined to stimulate the development and evolution of an amazing variety of systems of technique and training. The various systems began to be categorized as internal and external styles, hard and soft styles, family or temple styles, Taoist or Buddhist styles, or northern (kicks) and southern (fists) styles. Colorful origin myths, including those involving Bodhidharma and the Shaolin Temple, were devised and passed down, products of that genre of Asian literature known as yeh-shih ("wild history").

## Hawaii: the melting pot

By the time of first western contact in 1778, the Hawaiian islands had well-developed indigenous martial arts honed by centuries of incessant warfare. While a form of boxing and wrestling (mokomoko) was practiced (matches were held to entertain Captain Cook), the deadliest martial art was known as lua. A lua master was adept with a variety of weapons, particularly the spear (regarded as the "king of weapons" by the Chinese). The huge Hawaiian warriors had correspondingly large weapons; the Hawaiian spear ranged in length from nine to eighteen feet! A favorite training method was to practice spear-dodging (a practical skill), and there are eyewitness accounts of agile ali'i dodging spears thrown by as many as eight

warriors, grabbing some out of the air to deflect others, and returning others at their throwers in one fluid move. In addition to the spear, the lua fighter learned to use the club, wooden dagger, sling, and other specialized weaponry like the 'ikoi, a tripping stone thrown with a cord attached to entangle the enemy, and the lei-mano, a hardwood knuckle-duster studded with shark's teeth. Keeaumoku used a lei-mano to disembowel one of Kamehameha's rival chiefs (Kiwala'o) early in Kamehameha's campaign to conquer the Island chain. But, above all, the lua practitioner was feared for his deadly hand-to-hand expertise. Lua literally translates as "pit" or "two," and the name may refer to fighting pits, the principle of duality (similar to the Chinese yin-yang), or the tactic of giving two strikes for one. The loose translation of lua, however, is "the art of bone-breaking." This was no art of self-defense, but an aggressive war art designed to maim and kill the enemy. Tales abound of Kamehameha and his martial art instructor Kekuhaupi'o striking fear into enemy troops by breaking a man's back, and then dislocating the helpless man's joints, perhaps to save him for later sacrifice to the war god Kukailimoku. King Kamehameha had conquered the Islands by 1810 and died in 1819. Many of his warriors lived well into the 19th century.

By 1850 the sugarcane plantation era had begun in the Islands. Plantation owners looked to Asia to import cheap labor. First the Chinese were brought in. Then the Japanese, and next the Filipinos. Each group brought their own martial arts.

In 1906, sixteen-year-old Seishiro Okazaki emigrated from Japan to Hawaii. Okazaki worked on sugarcane plantations and by 1909 became sickly, "pre-tubercular." In his quest for health he began working out at the Hilo Shinyu-kai, the jiu-jitsu dojo of Master Kichimatsu Tanaka. Within a year, Okazaki had regained robust health, and he was hooked. While continuing his study of jiu-jitsu, Okazaki also studied the other martial arts available in this mid-Pacific melting pot, including Hawaiian lua, Okinawan karate, Filipino knife, and Kung Fu from Master Wo Chong. Wo

Chong referred to Hawaii as "Danzan" or "Sandalwood Islands," in reference to the early Hawaiian sandalwood trade with China. When Okazaki eventually created his own eclectic amalgam of martial arts, he named it "Danzan Ryu Jiu-jitsu."

In April of 1922, a friend of Okazaki's named "Speed" Takahashi challenged a boxer, Carl "Kayo" Morris. Morris lived up to his nickname and knocked Takahashi out in the first round. Okazaki immediately issued a challenge to "Kayo" Morris and trained for the next six weeks for the match. The boxer versus jiu-jitsu expert match was held on May 19, 1922 at the Yuraku-Kwan Theater. Okazaki had his nose broken halfway through the first round. In the second round, Okazaki found an opening, closed under Morris's jab and threw him with an arm lock. Morris's arm was injured and he was unable to continue. On Saturday, May 10, 1922, The Hilo Daily Tribune carried the headline: "Morris Has No Chance Against JuJitsu Expert." Okazaki's fame spread all the way to Japan. He toured Japanese dojos for six months in 1924, and was awarded Sandan rank at the Kodokan.

Okazaki spent seventeen years in Hilo developing his approach to martial arts, and also his system of therapeutic restorative massage. During his lifetime Okazaki was more famous as a physical therapist than as a martial artist, living out the Asian archetype of the combined martial arts master and healer.

As early as 1922 Okazaki began teaching non-Japanese, for which he was severely reprimanded by his teachers. By the time he moved to Oahu in 1930, (by now adopting the name "Henry") his Honolulu dojo was open to all races, and indeed, the inheritor of his system, Sigfried Kufferath, was Caucasian. After moving to Oahu in 1930, Henry Okazaki established his Sanatorium and dojo, working with his life's passions until he died in 1951. Seishiro "Henry" Okazaki set the tone of the martial arts environment in Hawaii; a tone of eclecticism and willingness to teach anyone of any race who desired to learn.

James Masayoshi Mitose was born in Hilo,

Hawaii in 1916. At the age of five, he was sent to Japan for education. He remained in Japan from 1921 until 1936, when he returned to Hawaii.

On December 7, 1941 the Japanese attacked Pearl Harbor, and Mitose knew he had to make a choice. He was born and lived as a citizen in the U.S. territory of Hawaii, yet he spent his formative years in Japan. Mitose made his choice: the next day, he enlisted in the Hawaii Territorial Guard.

After his honorable discharge from the Territorial Guard, Mitose felt such gratitude for

*Seishiro Okazaki*

3

the kind treatment he had received while in the service that he decided to openly teach his self defense art of Kosho-ryu ("old pine tree style") Kenpo. He founded the "Official Self Defense Club" in Honolulu in 1942 and, like Okazaki, opened instruction to all races. Mitose left the club in the hands of Thomas Young when he left for California in 1953.

In 1953, Mitose published his book, *What Is Self Defense?* He subtitled it "Kenpo Jiu-Jitsu," probably due to the popularity of Okazaki's Danzan ryu jiu-jitsu; in fact, in the text, Mitose takes great pains to explain the difference between Kenpo and Jiu-jitsu. (Mitose had compared techniques with top Danzan-ryu stylist Sig Kufferath and taught in the same locale as Okazaki). The text expounds a philosophy of self-defense drawn from a combination of Buddhist and Christian sources, promoting humility, self-restraint, and a respect for all life. Both Bodhidharma and Abraham Lincoln are held up as role models possessing ideal Kenpo character traits. Photographs illustrate the basics of punching, kicking, maki-wara training, stances, and approximately ninety self-defense techniques against punches, kicks, grabs, and weapons. While basic joint locks are incorporated, striking combinations are empha-sized, and kicks are kept low. Mitose wrote, "Punching, striking and kicking are the best methods of self defense . . . Locks should be used only when the opponent is not dangerous." Mitose also expresses the following wish, "Recalling the old adage "When in Rome do as the Romans do," the author hopes that eventually Kenpo will be Americanized."

James Mitose ultimately proved to be an enig-matic and controversial character. In *What is Self Defense?*, Mitose says, "Daruma was the founder of the Shorinjiryu Kenpo, and this art was slightly changed by the author's ancestors to a method suitable to the Japanese people." This general statement is consistent with the theory that the "ancestor" who taught Mitose Kenpo was none other than the Okinawan Kempo master, Choki Motobu. Some have asserted that Motobu was Mitose's uncle. Add to that the fact that both men

were in Japan from 1921 through 1936. Mitose's techniques are similar to the techniques utilized by Motobu, and Mitose clearly emphasizes maki-wara training, a uniquely Okinawan method. In the beginning of Mitose's book, there is a sequence of photographs: Bodhidharma first, Zen master Rinzai next, Choki Motobu next, and then James Mitose, strongly implying a lineage. The caption under Motobu's photo reads, "Choki Motobu, The great master of Karate Kenpo." Mitose's crest is also the same one used by Motobu. Finally, there are reports that Mitose was familiar with the Naihanchi kata, the same one practiced by Motobu. This is all highly suggestive but ultimately circumstantial evidence.

In later interviews in California (published in "Karate's History and Traditions," by Bruce Haines), Mitose, dressed as an ordained Christian minister, gives a different and more elaborate pic-ture of Kenpo's origin and nature. First, he asserts that Kosho-ryu Kempo is a complete way of life, studying Buddhism, human anatomy and physiol-ogy, fencing, archery, flower arranging, swimming, tree-climbing, horsemanship, blowgun, and Shaolin chuan-fa. (In *What is Self Defense?* Mitose says, "Among the arts of self-defense in which weapons are not used, no other can surpass the art of Kenpo." Now, the sword, bow, and blowgun are included.) He then asserts that the art was brought to Japan in the late sixteenth century, and there shaped and modified by generations of his ancestors. No mention is made of Choki Motobu. We can speculate that the possible motive for Mitose to distance himself from Motobu was Motobu's unsavory reputation as a brawler. Motobu had left a Russian boxer bleeding on the mat in Japan in 1921, and was denied entrance to Hawaii in 1932 to engage in similar contests.

By the late seventies, Mitose provided still more details: his family art was now called "Kosho Shorei-ryu Kenpo," and he identified himself as the 21st Zen-master and inheritor of the system, brought to Japan by Daruma (Bodhidharma) and taught to family members at their Buddhist tem-ple, which housed hundreds of monks.

Unfortunately, it is well known that Daruma

never traveled to Japan and died in China about one thousand years before Mitose claimed that Kenpo was introduced to Japan. In addition, Japanese yoga (qigong exercises) and ninja arts are claimed to be part of Kenpo.

Mitose's story becomes more elaborate, detailed, fantastic and grandiose over time. Is this increasingly complex and detailed story the result of improved memory over the decades, lifting of a veil of secrecy, or progressive embellishment ("wild history")?

Much depends on Mitose's credibility. Unfortunately, he was convicted of first-degree murder and died of a stroke serving a life sentence in California's Folsom prison (1981). A black belt student of Mitose viciously attacked an elderly Japanese couple at home in the night. Armed with his knowledge of Kosho ryu and a screwdriver, the assailant managed to kill the elderly man, but the wife survived. If Mitose taught him any of his "ninja arts," they didn't take well, because the whole break-in and assault was poorly executed and left a trail straight to the killer. Once in custody, the killer turned state's evidence, and investigators unraveled a story of fraud and extortion: Mitose had been selling the old couple his secret "cancer cure" for an exorbitant fee, they had gone into debt with no results. They demanded their money back, and Mitose warned them to keep silent. They told him to repay or they were going to the police. This was the testimony of the surviving widow. The actual perpetrator told of a meeting at Mitose's house with Mitose and his wife, where the attack was planned. In return for his testimony (the only way to unravel the conspiracy and directly connect Mitose to the killing) the killer received a reduced sentence.

Ironically, Mitose himself wrote in *What Is Self Defense?* "A person who violates the laws of society, instead of protecting himself, is actually destroying himself, both physically and mentally, and sooner or later the law will curtail his freedom." The fall from grace is a story as old as man. However it is interpreted, James Mitose's life story is a cautionary tale for martial artists.

During his ten years of teaching prior to leaving Hawaii, James Mitose had trained five men to the level of shodan: Thomas Young, Bobby Lowe, Paul Yamaguchi, Arthur Keawe, and William Chow.

Chinese-Hawaiian William Kwai Sun Chow was born in Honolulu on July 3, 1914. His mother died when he was eleven years old, and three years later his father returned to China, leaving young William in Hawaii. Circulating between different family members, William dropped out of school to find work. At five-feet-two-inches, Chow was not a big man, but years of hard labor on the streets and docks of Honolulu had made him strong.

During the manpower shortage of World War II, Chow had no trouble finding work. When James Mitose opened his Official Self Defense Club in 1942, Chow became a dedicated student of the art. In addition to learning Mitose's Kosho-ryu Kenpo, Chow also acquired a knowledge of Kung Fu from his father, who had returned from China and remarried. In addition, one of Chow's half-brothers, John Chow-Hoon, was a top student in Okazaki's Danzan-ryu jiu jitsu, and when William wasn't practicing his Kenpo, he would often spend time at Okazaki's Honolulu dojo.

William Chow was a training fanatic. He had a gift for remembering every technique he was shown and he would perfect each one against a variety of opponents. Each day, he would drill the basics, lift weights, and train on the makiwara. Early photos reveal the conditioned knuckles characteristic of regular makiwara practice. He developed his speed and power to such high levels that he acquired the nickname, "Thunderbolt!" The streets of WW II Honolulu, teeming with military personnel, provided an ideal laboratory for testing the practicality and street effectiveness of Chow's techniques. In addition, there are apocryphal tales of Professor Chow meeting visiting martial arts dignitaries at the Honolulu airport for a contest of skills. Facing Chow was like being forced to answer the question, "Where do you want to be hit with this sledgehammer?" Many had a very short stay in the Islands.

Chow was featured in Mitose's book, *What is*

*Self Defense?* (Kenpo Jiu Jitsu). When Chow left Mitose in 1949 and began to teach on his own, he took the title "Professor." After Okazaki's death in 1951 and Mitose's departure for California in 1953, Professor Thunderbolt Chow became a key figure in the development of the Hawaiian martial arts scene. Chow took a more pragmatic approach than the philosophical Mitose. His ad in the Honolulu phone book read, "Learn from the Foremost Karate Master in Hawaii!" And in the early sixties he listed himself as the founder and head instructor of the "Dian Hsuhe Go Shinjutsu Kenpo Kai Karate Association."

Over the years, his art was known by a variety of names: at first, it was simply "Kenpo Karate;" later, he called it "Goshin-jitsu (art of self-defense)," then "Shaolin Kenpo," and finally "Kara-ho Kenpo." Whatever the name, it was a system that was first and foremost practical and street effective. Professor Chow followed the pattern established by Choki Motobu and James Mitose: development of powerful basics on the makiwara, practice of techniques with a partner, and little or no kata practice. One of his students relates how Chow had him spend his first year developing one kick and one punch! The "Professor" was a simple man, but his simplicity was also his virtue. His philosophy can be summed up: learn what you can, use what works, and train hard.

Though Professor Thunderbolt Chow devoted his life to teaching Kenpo, he made only a meager living as a martial arts instructor. Still, his impact was great. Perhaps due to his modest formal education, and unlike Motobu or Mitose, Chow left no written record of his art. But, when he died on September 21, 1987, what he did leave behind was even more impressive. Consider this: the small man with the nickname "Thunderbolt" demonstrated such single minded purity of purpose that he motivated numerous students to found impressive systems of their own and to devote their lives to teaching martial arts. Among others, the Emperado brothers' Kajukenbo, Ralph Castro's Shaolin Kenpo, Sam Kuoha's Kara Ho Kempo, and, of course, Ed Parker's American

Kenpo all trace their origins back to the teachings of Professor William Kwai Sun "Thunderbolt" Chow.

## Ed Parker and American Kenpo

Edmund Kealoha Parker was born in Hawaii on March 19, 1931, the sixth child in a family of seven. As a great-grandson of King Kamehameha, he was born from the lineage of Hawaiian warriors. By the time he was attending Kamehameha High School in Honolulu, he had studied judo and boxing. Parker's mischievous antics caused one high school teacher to pronounce, "Ed Parker, you will never be a success in life!" Young Ed took it to heart and developed a deep resolve to prove the teacher wrong.

Parker was raised a devout Mormon, and one day in church a thinly-built friend named Frank Chow related how he had subdued a local bully. Sixteen-year-old Parker was in disbelief until Chow showed him the Kenpo technique that he had used. Parker was immediately intrigued and began to study with Frank Chow.

Streetfights were common in the tough Kalihi district of Honolulu. One in particular made a lasting impression on the young developing martial artist; during the fight, one participant had most of his nose bitten off, but was so tough that he came back and defeated his opponent. Parker

*Ed Parker holding boards for William K. S. Chow*

realized what sheer mental toughness and a refusal to admit defeat could accomplish.

After a few years, Frank told Ed that he had taught him all he could and introduced him to his older brother, William Chow, who had just started teaching independently from Mitose at the Nuuanu YMCA (1949). There, Parker would appreciate the benefits of training with a variety of partners and with Chow himself. Parker recalled, "From the moment I witnessed William Chow move and appraised the ability of his students, a strong and spiritual feeling penetrated the very depth of my soul communicating to me that Kenpo would become my life's work."

Certain strategies remain consistent in Kenpo from the time of Choki Motobu: an overall emphasis on self-defense techniques utilizing fast hand combinations (with both strikes and joint locks) with low kicks. Parker credits Chow with re-introducing the circular movements of the Chinese arts back into Kenpo and also with giving him some "master keys." Parker developed an appreciation for the combination of circular and linear motion, strong basics, hard training, and common-sense analysis from his training with Professor Chow. Parker later wrote, "It was William Chow who cultivated the seed of American Kenpo . . . I followed him, questioned him, bugged him, and it paid off. He explained and stressed the need for modifications and additions and introduced me to master key movements, which set me on the road to becoming a creative innovator . . . Chow . . . felt there was a need to change the art to meet the needs of the American people at this time . . . I cannot thank him enough for setting me on a path of logical and realistic thinking."

In Kenpo the open left hand covering the closed right fist has several meanings, one of which is the union of the scholar and the warrior. Ed Parker showed amazing prescience when he actualized the Kenpo scholar-warrior ideal by pursuing a college degree at Brigham Young University. He felt that higher education was an essential prerequisite to embarking on his career as a martial arts instructor. During his second year at

BYU Parker began training seven days a week in anticipation of earning his black belt.

Parker's college education was interrupted in 1951 when he was drafted during the Korean War. He joined the Coast Guard and was stationed in Honolulu, and was able to continue his Kenpo studies with Professor Chow. By the time he was honorably discharged in 1953, he had earned his black belt from Chow. Before resuming his education at BYU, Parker brought up the idea of opening Kenpo Karate schools on the mainland, after he had completed his education. Chow favored the idea, but when the time came, he declined to leave his familiar Island home. Parker resumed teaching in 1953 in Utah, teaching other

college students and, after an impressive demo during a UCLA vs. BYU basketball game (1954), local law enforcement officers, including prison guards, police officers, sheriffs, and FBI agents.

During this period a freak hunting accident took the life of a friend. Parker's hunting companion shot a deer, and when they approached the dying animal it delivered a fatal kick to his throat. This tragedy taught Parker that the failure to consider unintended consequences could snatch defeat from the jaws of victory. Parker began to explore the principle of checking.

Late one night while driving with his wife Leilani, pregnant with their first child, they were cut off by another vehicle. Four men got out of the car, and Parker met them. He dropped two of

*Perhaps the earliest photograph of Ed Parker teaching Kenpo in the United States. With Charles Beeder in the BYU wrestling room. 1954-55*

them within a few seconds. His mind went into overdrive and he experienced the encounter in slow motion. He had time to consider the deterrent effect of breaking the first man's nose with a hammerfist, covering his white T-shirt in blood. A second assailant hesitated, and a handsword to the back of his neck popped the cigarette out of his mouth and put him out of action. The first man went down hard, motionless on the ground. Parker was actually relieved when the attacker regained consciousness. The assailants fled, and Parker gained a healthy fear of the consequences of utilizing his skills.

In Utah, Parker's assistant instructor at Roy Woodward's BodyBuilding Gym, Charles Beeder, became his first official black belt. Parker graduated from BYU 1956 with a B.S. in sociology and psychology, and a minor in political science. After he graduated from college, Wally Jay, a Hawaiian jiu-jitsu practitioner from Parker's old Kalihi neighborhood, asked him, "You're teaching martial arts. Did you go to college for that?"

Parker replied, "No, I went to college so I

could talk to people, on any level."

Roy Woodward also managed a gym in Pasadena in Southern California and offered Parker the opportunity to move there and teach. Parker accepted, but after he had relocated to California the gym was sold and Parker found himself unemployed.

Ed Parker's 1956 move to Pasadena was a providential turning point. Being thousands of miles from Hawaii reinforced his independence, while the challenges of a new environment stimulated his creativity. Southern California was, and still is, a major center of the entertainment industry. In addition, California has large Chinese, Japanese, and Filipino communities, each with its own traditional martial arts. All three cultures are well represented in Hawaii, and many of these martial artists had emigrated to the mainland through the Islands. This nexus of the entertainment and martial arts communities required someone who could bridge the gap and relate equally well in both arenas; Ed Parker was that man.

Parker's intelligence, education and charisma enabled him to move well in Hollywood circles, while his Hawaiian heritage, Chinese instructor, and skill opened the traditionally closed doors of the California Chinese martial arts community. He could satisfy his drive to learn more, to go deeper into the martial arts, and then expose what he had discovered to a wider audience. Ed Parker was the right man, in the right place, at the right time.

When the gym job fell through, Parker was motivated to open his Pasadena Kenpo Karate Studio. Also, in line with the vision of opening a number of Kenpo Studios, he laid the organizational foundation by forming the Kenpo Karate Association of America (in 1960 the KKAA became the International Kenpo Karate Association, with the new crest showing the increased Chinese influence on the art).

Woodward invited Parker to a Hollywood gym to meet Terry Robinson, physical director of the Beverly Wilshire Health Club. Terry Robinson had taught "Kill or be Killed" techniques during WW II, but when he saw Parker's Kenpo, he immediately acknowledged its superiority.

Robinson, who became Parker's life-long friend, invited the young Hawaiian to the Beverly Wilshire Health Club and introduced him to his elite clientele. Soon Parker began to meet and teach businessmen, professionals, and celebrities, including television and motion picture actors and directors, thereby gaining exposure in the entertainment and print media.

In 1960 Terry Robinson arranged for Parker to demonstrate Kenpo at the Beverly Wilshire Hotel. In Parker's words, "The demonstration was exceptional. Energy flowed with all of the intensity of a life or death combat." Elvis Presley was staying at the hotel and humbly introduced himself to Parker after the demonstration, beginning a long friendship and association between the two men. Around that same time, Parker also published a series of articles in *Iron Man*, a prominent body building magazine.

The series in *Iron Man* led to the publication of his first book in 1960, *Kenpo Karate; The Law of the Fist and Empty Hand*. Parker's open mind and progressive attitude toward training methods is evident in his first book. In addition to traditional training (makiwara), he devotes much of the first part of the book to modern physical conditioning methods, including progressive resistance weight training, even in light of the prevailing "wisdom" among athletic trainers of that era that weights should be avoided because they would cause the athlete's muscles to be tight. Today every sport has a supplemental weight-training regimen. This text also contains what is still one of the best charts of vulnerable areas of the human body, and a wide variety of natural-weapon hand formations demonstrating the increased Chinese element of the art. The base moves of many techniques still practiced in American Kenpo (through Form 6) are contained in this first book. Following Chow, who had replaced much of Mitose's idealistic philosophy with a pragmatic attitude, Parker replaced religious creeds with a simple ethic of self-defense,

summed up in the Kenpo Creed:

*"I come to you with only karate, empty hands, I have no weapons But should I be forced to defend myself, my principles or my honor, should it be a matter of life or death, of right or wrong; then here are my weapons, karate, my empty hands."*

This was backed up by the observation that when one has confidence based on self-defense skill, he can walk away from trouble, not because he is afraid of what an assailant can do to him, but of what he can do to his assailant!

Things began to happen fast. In 1961 the first issue of *Black Belt* magazine included a big article on "Ed Parker, the Black Belted Mormon," featuring Parker teaching actor Nick Adams. That same year, *Time* magazine ran an article on the growing popularity of the martial arts and referred to Parker as the "High Priest of the Hollywood sect."

The increased popularity of Kenpo and a broader and more sophisticated clientele stimulated innovations in Parker's approach to teaching. Parker began developing his unique teaching tools: the clock principle, the three stages of learning (primitive, mechanical, and spontaneous), the printing/script/shorthand sequence of development, analogies and terminology in the English language, all which facilitated the learning process of Kenpo students.

While Kenpo was gaining more public exposure, Parker was taking advantage of the opportunities in California to increase his knowledge and skill. He was always looking for ways to refine his art, and he would travel all over California seeking out other martial artists to work with. During the early sixties Parker exchanged ideas with martial artists of the caliber of James Lee, James Wing Woo, Bruce Lee, Ben Largusa, and Gene LeBell.

In 1960 Parker took a road trip to San Francisco's famous Chinatown to visit martial art schools. While there, he met a young kung fu master, James Wing Woo, who taught both Tai

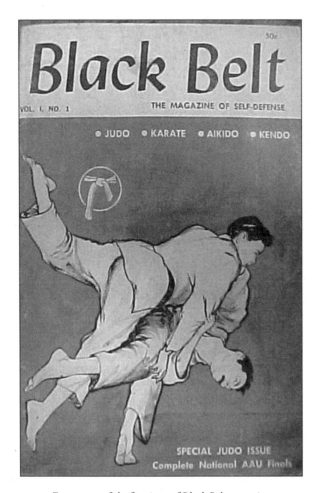

*Front cover of the first issue of Black Belt magazine.*

Chi Chuan and Shaolin. Woo was born in San Francisco, and his father was a Tong member; the family returned to China in 1928 where he began his training in martial arts. Years later Woo returned to northern California, where Parker found him. Parker recognized Woo's talent and invited him down to Los Angeles to work together. The two men had an ill-fated martial arts partnership; it was probably inevitable that Parker, the creative, innovative rebel and Woo, the traditional Chinese master, would have conflicting approaches. After about a year, they dissolved their partnership. Most of the advanced students (with the exception of Chuck Sullivan) went with Woo because they felt he had more to teach. Dave Hebler and Dan Inosanto also stayed with Parker. While this was a painful experience, Parker used it to motivate himself to further develop the depth and breadth of his Kenpo curriculum. This initiated a period of explosive creativity in the development of Parker's Kenpo system.

Parker had a better relationship with another northern California Kung Fu man, James Lee. Lee had a healthy skepticism regarding the mysticism prevalent in the Chinese arts. He began weight lifting in 1938 and developed a non-traditional approach to Kung Fu training. He published a book in 1957, *Modern Kung-Fu Karate*, detailing his basic training methods, emphasizing the development of "iron hand" breaking techniques. The 1963 edition has classic photos of Parker, referring to him as the "well known Black Belt Kenpo Karate instructor from Pasadena, California." Parker and Lee would frequently get together and compare notes. Parker describes these sessions: "James and I continuously discussed, compared, analyzed, and dissected the martial arts whenever we were together. He often asked me to interpret his Kung Fu sets and he was always excited when I would offer two or three interpretations to their meaning."

An excited James Lee called Parker one day and invited him to fly up to Oakland to meet a new Kung Fu acquaintance, saying, "This guy is fantastic! You've got to meet him."

Parker flew up and was introduced to Bruce Lee (no relation to James). Like everyone present, Bruce's demonstration of speed, power and exotic technique, as well as his intelligent command of Chinese philosophy impressed Parker. Moreover, Parker gained an appreciation for centerline theory, and Lee gained an appreciation of the limitations of his Wing Chun stance. The two men developed a mutual respect, and Bruce asked Parker to write an introduction to his 1963 book *Chinese Gung Fu, the Philosophical Art of Self Defense.* Even at that early date, Parker noted, "He is one of the very few that I have seen that is gifted with natural ability, a gift which he undoubtedly has put to work evidenced by his superb skill."

Parker collated the knowledge gained from the Chinese arts, filtered it through his creative and analytical approach, and integrated it into his Kenpo. His 1963 book, *Secrets of Chinese Karate*, (with an introduction by Joe Hyams) records this evolution. Kenpo gained long elaborate forms characteristic of Chinese systems. Parker also added the variety of detailed stances (bows, kneels, twists, etc.) utilized for power generation and as checks and attacks in themselves. The tiger and dragon symbolism (typical of Taoism) surfaces, and the Universal Pattern became part of Kenpo symbology. In addition, the relaxed explosive quality characteristic of some internal arts became an attribute of high level Kenpo.

While there is an undeniably strong Chinese influence in American Kenpo, Parker didn't limit himself to the realm of Chinese arts in his quest for knowledge. Parker made the acquaintance of another well-known martial arts maverick in Los Angeles, Gene LeBell. Parker rightly regarded "Judo" Gene as one of the most dangerous men around. It's noteworthy that Parker's first book contains, in addition to counters of typical jiu-jitsu holds like those addressed by Mitose (wrist grabs, chokes), counters to more typical wrestling holds like the hammerlock, headlock, and full nelson. In 1963, author Jim Beck wrote an article declaring "judo is a complete fraud" and asserted that "any boxer can beat a judo man," offering a thousand-dollar reward to any judo man who could successfully take up the challenge. Parker called LeBell, and the match was set up in Salt Lake City, Utah, on December 2, 1963. When LeBell arrived, he learned he was facing #5 ranked heavyweight, Milo Savage. Unscathed, Gene choked Savage out in the fourth round.

In 1964 Parker inaugurated his first International Karate Championships that were initially called the Long Beach Internationals. The tournament was open to all practitioners of any style, and ran continuously for more than three decades as arguably the most prestigious martial arts tournament in the world. Notably, Parker flew Bruce Lee to L.A. for the event and asked one of his black belts, Dan Inosanto, to show Lee around. The entire event, including Lee's electrifying demonstration, was captured on film. Famed Hollywood director and Kenpoist Blake Edwards helped Parker award the trophy to winner Mike Stone. Also demonstrating at the first

Internationals was another Islander, Ben Largusa. Largusa showed the techniques of Villabrille Kali, impressing even Bruce Lee. Parker admired the fundamental Kali strategy of "parry, check, strike" and asked Largusa to share his information. In early years, Largusa said Villabrille forbade him from showing Parker his techniques, but more recently he has admitted that they frequently worked out together.

When one of Parker's Hollywood contacts asked for recommendations for the role of Kato in an upcoming TV series, "The Green Hornet," Parker first called Ben Largusa. Largusa turned down the role, and then Parker called Bruce Lee. Though the series lasted only one season, Lee's dynamic presence launched his Hong Kong film career, and also the Kung Fu craze and martial arts boom of the late 1960s and early 1970s.

Any good teacher learns from his students, and Parker was no exception; during this period many of Parker's students would explore new strategies, combinations, or modifications to techniques and forms, and Parker would evaluate them. If the modification fit within the context of Parker's overall vision of Kenpo, it would be

*James Wing Woo*

incorporated into the art. A good example of this collaborative process is Chuck Sullivan's role in streamlining the classical Staff Set that he'd learned from Parker. Parker recognized the improvement and the modified set became part of the system. To further simulate the intellectual and technical creativity of his students, Parker required that candidates for black belt write a thesis pertaining to the art and create their own form. Brian Adam's book, *The Medical Implications of Karate Blows*, and Gil Hibben's Parker fighting knife are two well-known results of this long-standing requirement.

In addition to knowledge gained from others, intense study led Parker to many personal revelations. While looking for more creative ways to expose the art to a wider audience, Parker foreshadowed the current video boom by working with Chuck Sullivan to put a dozen Kenpo techniques on 8mm film. Watching the art on film gave Parker one of his basic analytical tools: evaluating techniques from the "three points of view" – attacker, defender, and bystander. One day, while running a film backwards to rewind it, Parker had an epiphany: he realized that the reverse motion that he'd previously overlooked as merely a rechambering could also be useful in self defense. This realization led him to even deeper personal explorations into theories of motion.

It is difficult to pinpoint the exact moment when all of these quantitative changes and refinements added up to create a qualitatively new and unique martial art. The essential theoretical structure, base techniques, training system, symbolism, and qualities of Parker Kenpo were well established by the mid-to-late 1960s. Years earlier, James Mitose had expressed the hope "that eventually Kenpo will be Americanized." William Chow had planted the seed, but it was Ed Parker who nurtured the vision to full fruition. The art had grown and blossomed to the point that less than 10% of the system could be attributed to Chow's instruction. Applying logic to traditional knowledge drawn from a mixture of cultures, Parker blended methods and techniques that could be tailored to the needs, goals and abilities of each practitioner. Edmund Kealoha Parker had created a martial art system shaped by the twin values of pragmatism and individuality. American Kenpo was born!

# *Our* *Founder*

## *Senior Grandmaster* *Edmund K. Parker*

### *An Interview with Ed Parker Jr.*

**M**y father was born and raised in Hawaii by devout Mormon parents. Throughout his life, he never actively tried to convert anyone to his faith, but felt that if he set an example that people liked, this might lead to a discussion of his religious principles.

The home was my father's sanctuary, his place of safety. This is where he stated to the world, "I'm done entertaining. I'm done working. I'm done teaching. This is where I'm going to relax."

Unfortunately he had five children who were always pretty wound up and excited to see him. There were times, however, that as a young boy I was very intimidated by him. He had one of the sternest looks on the planet, a voice, and a temper that would definitely put you in your place.

In the 1960s when we lived in the small house on State Street in

Pasadena we didn't have much interaction with our neighbors. Because my dad traveled extensively in the early years, he wasn't much of a socialite when he returned home. Even though our family was active with the Mormon Church, even at that level few had any idea what he was all about. There were many aspects of my father's life of which he did not volunteer information.

By the time our family moved into the house on South Los Robles, my dad had grown tired of traveling. Because the house was considerably bigger, he was able to entertain a lot more people, and the living room became the center of one business meeting after another. It was an interesting group in early years. There were a lot of Louie the Legbreakers in the group. These guys weren't poster boys for the Charles Atlas syndrome of "I'm a wimpy guy, so I need karate to help me out." These guys were already street tough and felt that what my father was doing would give them the extra edge.

My father had that same tough guy attitude and felt that karate could resolve everything. I remember one day I got my butt kicked in school by about five guys, and when I told him about it he said, "Well, if you took karate in the first place, this wouldn't have happened."

I fired back, "Karate doesn't work when they're more than two people. It's called tuck and roll and wait for them to stop."

My dad always viewed fighting as the way it was during his youth in the Hawaiian Islands where they had a different mentality. There, if a guy got beat up he told everybody, "Man, I got my dirty lickins" and he'd be okay with that. But when I was in junior high school what you would more likely hear was "I got my butt kicked and now I'm really pissed, so I'm going to come back with a gun and blow your head off." This was during the years of the Black Panther movement and considerable racial tension.

Looking back, I remember a lot of my friends equated my father and his art with assassination, and when I'd pass by they'd say, "Oh there's the neck breaker. Did you break any necks today?" It's just the stigma that martial arts had in an igno-

rant environment. Sometimes this would throw a real damper on my social life. I'd say to a girl I was interested in dating, "Hey, do you want to come to the house and meet my dad and all?" and she'd say, "No way! What if he doesn't like me? He'll kill me!" I usually made a joke and replied, "Oh yeah, we've got a whole backyard full of dead people, and there's another dozen stuffed in the trunk of that big Cadillac my dad drives."

The big highlight of our family life revolved around the Long Beach International Karate Championships. It wasn't just the weekend of the tournament. It was the big buildup that amounted to six months of preparation. It would start off with mailouts that consisted of piles of cover letters and entry forms that all had to be collated, stuffed into envelops, addressed and stamped. I believe back in the mid-1960s the Parker family members were pioneers in the art of envelop stuffing. The Internationals wasn't a tournament. It was our family reunion and our family project.

On the weekend of the tournament the whole family would go down to the Long Beach Sports Arena. The first couple of years my sisters and I wound up staying in the hotel room with a baby-sitter. After a couple of years we were allowed to go down to the arena and roam around. We didn't get to participate, and I ended up creating my own amusement. I was a pretty energetic kid, and I'd run up and down every set of stairs in the place, slide down banisters, and drive everyone crazy at the concession stands. It was during one of these whirlwind moments that the importance of what my father did really sunk in. I was a typical seven-year-old kid racing around the Sports Arena, and I ran into a cordoned off secure area where a half dozen karate guys with security badges were standing. The one closest to me reached out for my arm, but I managed to slip by him.

"Stop! No admittance in this area!" the guy yelled.

One of his cohorts suddenly appeared like a man facing a firing squad.

"Don't say that to him! That's Mr. Parker's son!"

One would have thought I was the child Messiah. This tough karate guy who had tried to grab me started apologizing profusely and finally asked, "What's it like living with the Ed Parker?"

To this day I can still recall staring back at him with a sense of total confusion and saying innocently, "Well, he's just dad." I just couldn't comprehend what had gone on.

The International Karate Championships helped immeasurably to promote my father and the art of Kenpo. But as the years went by, as with every other aspect of the martial arts empire he helped build over five decades, I don't feel that he ever really stood in a place of satisfaction over what he had accomplished. The reason was that he was always one or two steps behind where he felt that he needed to be. This problem was compounded by the fact that he was continually frustrated because he felt that he never had enough time to get his projects done. And to him, just about everything represented a roadblock. In the same way that JFK felt that eating was a waste of time (although with my father eating was a vacation) my dad felt that sleeping was a nuisance. He also felt that people with whining problems were a bigger nuisance. He did, however, have a balance to his life. To many that knew him he represented the true meaning of yin/yang. On the dark side of the symbol, he was mean and tough, stern, and all that, while on the light side he one of the most kind, loving, friendly, happy-go-lucky guys you'd ever want to meet. And when it came to amusing people, he was more than funny; he was downright hysterical. He loved to entertain people. He loved feeding off the positive energy he created. And it didn't matter if those around him were in awe of his Kenpo or his ukulele playing or his jokes. He just wanted people around him to feel comfortable and to have gained from the time they shared with him.

My father's perfectionism was the one aspect of his personality that got him into the most trouble. And there were times when his perfectionism went beyond belief. For example, he would sit and type up a manuscript, and the manuscript had to be right. So he would white-out every error with liquid paper and then retype the entire manuscript. Invariably at some point in his retyping, he'd discover another mistake and white it out, then type the whole thing over again so that the final manuscript didn't have any lumps on it.

When computers came on the scene, I went to my father with the good news, and told him, "Dad, there is this new thing called computers and word processing. It'll make your life so much easier." He got a computer and I taught him how to work it. But he treated it like a typewriter and would do a carriage return at the end of every line. As a result the tabs and everything else didn't line up right. So he'd spend days adding instant spaces instead of doing tabs, and I'd say, "Dad, don't do that. The word processing software will automatically do your carriage returns for you and then . . ."

And he'd scream, "I don't have time for this!" and that big fist would go crashing onto the table only inches from his tortured keyboard.

And I'd say, "Dad, you have time to add unnecessary spaces for three days, but you don't have five minutes to learn how not to do that?"

The huge drawback was that he would get so obsessed over doing something right, that he didn't realize how much of a time sponge it was. This was made far worse because he was an impatient man who always wanted everything done yesterday.

He was truly the most interesting character I've ever known. Ironically, the idiosyncrasies that bothered me when he was living were the first things I missed after he was gone. In his burning desire to get so much done, his biggest complaint was that he was always being interrupted by phone calls, but yet he was constantly asking people to call him. This was typical of the double-edged sword his life had become. In an effort to make life easier for him, we had an elaborate phone system installed in the house that allowed us to put callers on hold and then use an intercom system to let everyone know who was on the phone.

The problem, however, was my dad's insatiable curiosity, which was played out almost on an hourly basis. What would happen is that the phone would ring and I would answer it after a couple of rings.

"IKKA, can I help you?"

"Yeah, is Ed Parker there?"

"Can I ask who's calling, please?"

"Ben Johnson."

"Just a minute, sir."

This is where the problem would start. All of a sudden I'd hear a click from my father picking up one of the phones in the house. This was followed by the sound of his heavy breathing. As many times as I'd tell my dad that the caller could hear his heavy breathing, he never paid any attention to me. Suddenly my dad's voice would come booming over the intercom, "Who the hell is it!"

I'd quickly press the hold button, although still aware that my dad's line is open.

"Ben," I'd answer my dad over the intercom.

"Ben who!" followed by his heavy breathing.

"Ben Johnson."

"Tell that jackass I'm not in!"

Embarrassed beyond belief, I'd return to the caller.

"Uh, He's not available right now. Can I take a message?"

"Yeah, you can tell him to go chop himself in the nuts! I don't like the games he's playing!" and the caller would hang up abruptly.

As I said, this scenario wasn't played out once a month. This happened constantly because my father simply had to know firsthand who was calling, and then he would often go ballistic when you told him. As frustrating as that was back then, it was the first thing I missed after he died. Whenever the phone would ring and I'd pick it up, I missed his breathing. The silence killed me. Just picking up the phone and not hearing that heavy breathing. It was one of things that irritated me about him, but the first thing I missed.

My dad struggled with where and how he was raised, which led to him having insecurities about being a smart man. People would tell him he was smart, but I don't think he ever truly knew how truly intelligent he really was. Because of this he felt the need to use his art to project smartness.

For example, he used a lot of big words in the *Infinite Insight* series in order to add a degree of sophistication to American Kenpo. Earlier he had wanted to write a book called Advanced Kenpo, and right around that time J.T. Will came out with a book by the same title. My dad was furious. "That was my title!" That's when he started going in the direction of intellectual Kenpo and said to me, "I'm going to come up with something better" and came up with the *Infinite Insights* series. It wasn't that he felt he was more advanced but that within Kenpo there were infinite possibilities. To him the word advanced came to represent a level that the student could reach, and he felt the need to go beyond that definition. Ironically, he often used terminology to impute a greater importance to the art, not realizing that it could stand on its own basic merit.

Although my father created an entity separate from himself, everybody after the fact gives him sole credit by stating that American Kenpo is Ed Parker, even though he never looked at it that way. While he knew that he had been present at the birth of American Kenpo, he came to see very early in its evolutionary process that the art had taken on a life of its own. In many ways it was a bittersweet thing to him. I remember in the final year of his life he said, "What the hell did I create? What I wanted was to teach people to stand on their own two feet and what I've got is a lot of whining babies." If there was one negative aspect of his art that bothered him more than anything else it was the years of politics and petty bickering among many of his top students.

One of the major misconceptions people have about my father is that when he taught, his students assumed that, because he had this aura of being a Grandmaster, everything came out of his head. They had this vision of him going to the mountain where he would obtain all this deep knowledge and store it, and then at the right moment reveal it to some anointed individual or group of individuals. But my father's intelligence was not on that level. His true genius came from a completely different angle. Even though as he was conceptually highly intelligent, he often lacked a way to communicate his visions to his students. Because many of my father's ideas didn't have the terminology, or he didn't have the means to convey his knowledge from his head to the student's head, what he did was to throw out a concept or an idea in a teaching environment and ask his students to fill in the blanks. Inevitably some student would raise his hand and put meaningful words to my father's conceptual puzzle. If what the student said made sense, my father would often reply, "You're a smart guy." This would trigger in the student's mind, "Whoa! Mr. Parker was looking for somebody to give him the right answer and I gave him the right answer!" What the student didn't realize, however, is that my father wasn't looking for someone to give him the right answer, but was asking for someone to give him the terminology to explain the abstract concept that he had. Put another way, the student would walk away thinking that he gave Mr. Parker what he already had. But he didn't. Instead, what he gave him was the terminology that he never had.

Because my father was so terminology conscious and linguistically committed to the definition of words and their usage, he was very particular on how he, himself, used words and how he used scenarios. Nowhere is this more obvious than in his teaching method. My dad was just one person, and it was impossible for him to regularly visit his hundreds of affiliate schools. Because of this, he always maintained a small inner group that kept in contact with the network of Kenpo instructors and reported back to my father. As a result of this feedback, my father became increasingly concerned that Kenpo was becoming diluted and/or pared down, and as a result was in varying degrees (depending on the school) strayed from what he was currently working on. Given this, whenever he did teach a seminar at a particular school, he knew that it would be a political nightmare if he were to teach a technique that deviated from the long-standing prescribed standard. So when students would often ask, for example, "Mr. Parker, how do you do Thundering Hammers?" he would reply, "How do *you* do Thundering Hammers?" He'd always toss it back.

Sometimes when he would teach a technique outside the prescribed method, somebody in the back would whisper, "Do you know that Mr. Parker is doing that technique wrong?" As much as this would annoy my father, he inevitably came to accept the fact that this is the way most people think because we live in a society where people have this burning need to be right. But to my father Kenpo was never a matter of right or wrong, black or white. Rather he was so involved with trying to get the student to understand the principles of movement, that he would make a correction that would enhance the way the student did the technique. He'd leave believing that he had given that student something of value, only to later find out that the student was saying that "Mr. Parker *taught* me to do it this way" or "Mr. Parker *told* me to do it this way." And my dad never did because that's not the way he worded things.

Therefore, instead of performing like a puppet and having everyone mimic him, he would evoke thought. This should come as no surprise because he often said that Chinese Kenpo is how to fight, and if you add to the art of fighting the ability to think, the result is American Kenpo. So it's all about evoking thought. It's about programming the mind to think in such a way so that the student can always be problem solving.

My father was a dimensional thinker. There are few people who understand dimensional thinking. The movie "Searching for Bobby Fisher" does an excellent job of portraying the process of dimensional thinking, which is essentially the process of thinking many moves ahead. Most people in Kenpo are focused on the next move versus my father who was already thinking about moves eight, nine, and ten. Personally I feel this is partly why he often found life so frustrating, because he often was living simultaneously in both the present and the future.

My father called the places where Kenpo was taught Ed Parker Kenpo Karate Studios because they represented a chain of schools. But when he called the art Kenpo, he never called it Parker Kenpo, but instead called it American Kenpo because it was made up of the concepts and ideas of his many students as well.

I have often equated this to the brilliance of former President Ronald Reagan. When he was elected Governor of California, he took over a state that was on the verge of bankruptcy. Rather than attempt to tackle the potential catastrophe through his handful of personal advisors, he did something that no other governor had previously done – he took advantage of the vast pool of financial genius already in place throughout the state's college university campuses. These college professors, many of them tenured, who held degrees in finance and business management and had written books on the global economy, would offer their expertise at no cost to the taxpayer. By the time Ronald Reagan left office and headed for the White House, California's coffers were so full that tax rebate checks were sent out to it citizens. It was sheer genius, and not unlike what my father did for many years when he required those testing for black belt to write a thesis related to American Kenpo. The resultant continual influx of widely diversified knowledge is one of the main reasons my father always referred to Kenpo as "our" art, because through the decades it has grown from the minds of those that were, and still are, in the art. Kenpo never relied on my father's brain and his brain alone.

Whether it was intention or unintentional, my dad structured American Kenpo as a monarchy with him as undisputed ruler. Many feel this was the result of his legendary unpleasant parting with Jimmy Wing Woo back in the early 1960s, while others point to the fact over the years my father trusted a number of individuals whose greatest expertise turned out to be that of conning him out of considerable money. But perhaps the biggest issue had to do with the fact that every student my dad taught to become a qualified teacher of Kenpo was in reality a potential competitor in the karate business.

My father wasn't that concerned about a small number of his black belts going off on their own and opening schools in new locations. In fact, he felt this was good for Kenpo as a whole. What worried him was a group of his top black belts forming an association that might break the backbone of American Kenpo. I believe it is for this reason that he followed the wisdom of Julius Caesar and surrounded himself with alternating concentric circles of allies and enemies (at least those whose loyalty was in doubt). In this way his black belts kept a watch on each other and were quick to come to him with information they "felt the Old Man should know."

As many know, my dad used to like to stir up the coals now and then because it kept anyone, or any group, from getting too strongly rooted. In a practical sense, I guess it was simply a matter of survival. Many times I heard my dad say, "Keep your friends close and your enemies closer." He also was skilled at putting those who felt they were close to him in their place. Whenever one of his black belts who felt he was in the King Row would ask, "Mr. Parker, am I your right hand man?" my father would reply, "My wife is my left hand, my son is my right. Which foot would you like to be?"

On the other hand, my dad always placed high value on the positive attributes of his black belts and was quick to forgive them. I remember one time an incident that occurred with one of his black belts named Randy Streeter. To say that Randy was not one of the most refined Kenpo students would be a vast understatement, but he was awesome at sparring. Unfortunately, he had practically no control. It wasn't that he didn't try; he just didn't know how to pull punches. One evening he really got out of hand and ended up wailing on another black belt. My father intervened and broke it up. After class Randy felt terrible and sat in the waiting room, his head in his hands and apologizing profusely. My dad walked over to Randy, put his hand on his shoulder, and said compassionately, "Randy, you're a streetfighter Don't worry about it."

Throughout his lifetime my father often had premonitions of death. Usually he thought he was the one standing at Death's door, but then a relative or close friend would die. Just before my father died, he had another premonition of death, only this time he was worried that his mother was going to die, and he walked around saying, "Oh, I think Momma's going to die. I think Momma's going to die."

Because my dad was a devoutly religious man, he was not afraid of dying. And being baptized in the Mormon faith, he strongly believed that life is eternal, and that in the next life he will continue to be married to my mother and that his children and friends in this life will be his children and friends in eternity. And so it was not strange to anyone close to my dad that he sometimes actually looked forward to death. In addition, he was one of those X-files kind of guys that was intrigued by the supernatural. He was a "Star Trek" fan and a big storyteller of ghost stories and tales of the afterlife. As a result, he was very much looking forward to seeing what the experience of death was going to be like. He also felt that death would be a peaceful experience that would take him to a far better place than that which he left.

I am sometimes asked if my father died with any regrets. With one exception, I honestly feel that when he passed away he felt that he had accomplished all that he needed to do. The exception is that he really wanted to finish his videotape series. He had thirty-seven videotapes planned, and we had only filmed four and edited two. Apart from the videotapes, I think he was satisfied because he wanted to see Kenpo on the screen, not as a film with Kenpo in it, but a film having Kenpo as its theme. And even though he died before "The Perfect Weapon" came out, I know that he was very happy with the footage that he did see and was pleased that he had been a part of making that film.

The other question I am often asked is who of my father's many black belts do I feel he left as a successor. At the risk of sounding pompous and preachy, my sense is that those who ask that question are standing too close to the blackboard to see the entire picture. My point of view is that I look at Kenpo with a telescope versus a microscope. If one examines the progression of my father's training, he continuously analyzed Kenpo and said, "Wait a minute, there are things that

don't work traditionally that have been taught within the arts. They just don't work in our environment today." For example, he pointed out that there are low, squatty stances that were developed in the Chinese and Japanese-based arts that have an important history behind them. Those stances were used in rice paddies and mud fields to lower one's center of gravity in order to stabilize oneself in a battle situation. But because a century later we're walking in leather shoes on paved streets, this changes our footing. In essence, my father was quick to see that the radical changes in our environment call for radical changes in our martial arts. American Kenpo is the same way in that it was developed with a certain thought process that allows the student to adapt the material to today's environment.

Fifty years later we suddenly have a split in the way the members of the American Kenpo community view our art. There's progressive and there's traditionalist. The traditionalists say you can't reinvent Ed Parker, so leave Ed Parker and all his teachings alone. Alternatively, there are those who say take Ed Parker's teachings and perpetuate the art and let it evolve through a continuing thought process and with regard to environmental changes. With both sides of the issue adamant about their beliefs, how does the American Kenpo community go about choosing a successor? A successor to those who preserve or a successor to those who perpetuate? So in my opinion it is impossible to consider a successor until such time that everyone can agree on the mode of thought, which as we all know is not going to happen in our lifetimes. That aside, how does one become a successor of a thought process? You don't. You just contribute to it. You don't succeed it. Over the years my father was asked about a successor. Someone would say, "Mr. Parker, do you have any successors?"

"None," he would reply curtly.

"Who is the next Ed Parker?" the person would ask, taking a different approach.

"Put twenty of my students together and you'd have a good start," my father would answer with a grin.

I am not worried about the future of Kenpo because I believe in the people who are individually and collectively carrying the torch. What I do is follow my father's example of following the passions of one's soul. And I tell this to anyone who asks. I feel that if the people who have the talent and love for the art will invest their time and efforts toward giving the art to others, the future of American Kenpo is very promising. What I learned from my dad is that it's all about giving, not about taking. Those in Kenpo who take are the same ones who do all the complaining. Those who give, don't complain. This is why I spend my time with those kenpoists who give to the art, and together with them I watch the art grow exponentially upon what my father contributed in his lifetime.

As I reflect on the Honorees featured in this book, words cannot express how deeply proud I am of what they have done. It is because of this that I have spent hundreds of hours drawing their portraits, which collectively represent my heartfelt tribute to the living legacy of my dad. Many people give my father credit for the birth and development of American Kenpo, and I am truly happy about this. But he's been gone for over a decade, and it is the individuals featured in this book, and others, who have kept the Kenpo Flame burning brightly. Every one of these Honorees speak about my father in a voice of reverence, love, and respect, and so the portraits shown in this book are my way of thanking them for memorializing my father and the art that he loved so dearly and so passionately throughout his life-time.

I am proud to be a part of this community. If I could say one thing to my dad it would be "Thank you for giving me such a wonderful family of Kenpo brothers and sisters that have enriched my life beyond belief." They have added meaning and purpose to my life well beyond my wildest dreams, and I feel that I am the wealthiest man alive because of that.

In conclusion, I think that the thing my father would be most impressed with is his devoted Kenpo offspring who have taken responsibility for their vast contributions to the art. Over a decade after his death, Kenpo has taken on a tremendous positive momentum, and because of that there is absolutely no doubt in my mind, and speaking on every ounce of understanding that I have of my father, that he is enormously pleased.

# Dian Tanaka
## 6th Degree

*Born in Tokyo, Japan, Dian moved to the San Francisco Bay Area at the age of seven. After graduating from Woodside High School, she attended UCLA where she received a Bachelor's Degree. Dian is the owner of a highly successful electronic materials distribution business located in Silicon Valley since 1979, which requires her to travel extensively throughout the United States. After watching a karate class at Chuck Norris's Karate School in Los Angeles, she began her study of Kenpo in the late 1970s and went on to become a champion forms competitor. Because of her devotion and commitment to American Kenpo, Ed Parker Jr. recently stated that if he has a female counterpart to his title of the "Ambassador of American Kenpo," that person would be Dian Tanaka. What little spare time she has away from her company and the American Kenpo community is spent tasting and collecting wonderful wines. A strong believer in physical fitness, Dian is actively involved in Peter Johnson's "Total Impact Cardio-Karate" program that promotes strong martial arts basics with an intense cardiovascular workout. Her immediate-future goal is to play a decent round of golf! Dian is married to Calee Hoshiyama, a White Crane martial artist.*

**B**eing of Japanese ancestry, I knew about the martial arts from an early age but figured it was something that strong gnarly men did with huge fists and in an arena I wouldn't be privy to. My cousin Glen learned karate in Vietnam, and we used to listen to my uncle tell these great stories about how Glen used crawl through foxholes and tunnels and would wage war from the trenches like G.I. Joe. To me he was just the coolest cousin alive because he had a black belt, and it was something that I just held in awe.

*Dian at five years of age in Japan*

In elementary school I got interested in gymnastics. Although initially I took up gymnastics because my friends were doing it for fun, a year later I got hooked on the competitive aspect and began to figure out that some things I did brought on more crowd applause than did others.

Until recently it never occurred to me that being in the spotlight actually started much earlier Japan where I became involved in a classic Japanese dance studio at the age of five. It was here that I believe I first learned the fine points of performing.

When I reached high school, I was spending most of my free time training in gymnastics. After school I'd head straight for the gym where I prepared for competitions. My father was very demanding of me, particularly with regard to my grades and sports. He disapproved of the gymnastics because he felt there were only two sports worthy of my time – tennis and golf – because he felt they were the only sports with decent prize money. So he would rail on me sometimes, asking why I spent endless hours practicing gymnastics. But yet when I would bring home medals, he would be pleased.

When I began my first year at UCLA and lived in the campus housing, I was on a coed floor, and my next-door neighbor happened to be taking martial arts. He would have me stand on the bed and hold pillows and move them around while he kicked them. I just thought he was fabulous, and I remember thinking "Boy, this looks fun." Because I still had the flexibility from gymnastics, when I kicked the pillows, I was actually pretty good. At

*Dian performing classic Japanese dance at age six.*

that time, however, I still didn't feel karate was accessible to me because I was a woman and small in stature compared to a man.

Then one day I went with my college friend to a group class, which was at Chuck Norris's school on Wilshire Boulevard. This was around the spring of 1974, and I didn't know who Chuck Norris was, although my friend told me that Norris was a "famous guy" and had won a lot of tournaments.

I remember going down to Norris's school three or four times and suddenly coming to the realization that there were young kids there, and women. That's when the light turned on for me. It was going to those group classes and seeing ordinary people – not big old Japanese guys with gnarly hands who grunted and were beyond my aspirations. When I went home that summer from UCLA and came to northern California, I opened the yellow pages and said, "Hey, here's a karate school in Menlo Park, my hometown." And without any inkling that there were differences in styles, I went to the closest school to my house. It turned out to be an Ed Parker school run by Harvey Clary, a first generation black belt, and the setting was much like what I had encountered months earlier at Chuck Norris's school.

My first gymnastics coach was a real taskmaster. She was a Polish national, who came here after the war, so she had this Slavic accent that scared the heck out of me. I'd be upside down and she'd be holding my feet in a handstand, and she'd whack me into proper posture. "In, in, stretch, this, that, noooo, no good!"

*Dian with Sonny Allen (far left) and Harvey Clary (second from left).*

So I was used to being yelled at by a teacher. I guess it was for that reason that I found Harvey Clary so challenging. From the first night, I became profoundly aware of his plastic baseball bat that he carried with him as he prowled around the mat, swatting the legs of students who weren't low enough in their horse.

I progressed through the material quickly, and honestly it wasn't difficult for me because I could balance on one leg; I could walk and chew gum; I could bend low without my legs aching; and I could do something with my hands and something different with my feet, all without difficulty.

In the yellow belt classes when we were learning the techniques, I got to make light contract with Delayed Sword. I remember thinking, 'This is really fun to make contact,' and the male instructor said, "It's okay, hit me harder, c'mon, kick, chop, harder!"

I enjoyed the contact and started to like it, although I still didn't have a self-defense angle on it. I had never been given permission to hit someone. In the Asian culture it was improper for a woman to physically hit someone, and in a strange way making contact at the karate school enlivened me. I was treading on new territory. This was a notch or two above kicking the pillows at the college dorm. I was able to hit somebody

and with the instructor's permission.

Not all was smooth sailing, however. An incident occurred early on at that school that left an emotional scar on me for many years. Besides me, there was another woman in the beginning class training for yellow belt. Her name was Joanne, and she had joined shortly before me. The first time Joanne and I sparred, Harvey Clary kept saying, "Kick harder! Kick, kick, kick! Harder, harder, harder, punch kick!" No matter what I did, I felt like I kept turning the volume up a little. And he kept saying "Harder, harder, kick, punch!"

I knew that soon his plastic baseball bat might come out, so I felt I had to do something because his harping felt like the whole world was on my shoulders. I remember I did a front snap kick as hard as I could. The kick doubled poor Joanne over, broke her ribs, and she never came back. I can still see her agonized face. In retrospect, I think it might have affected me less had I kicked a man that hard instead of a woman, but I still didn't like the idea that I really hurt this person – not in a way that I messed them up in the back alley. This person was in pain and was suffering and was so traumatized that she quit class. In my mind she was there before me and had quit because of me. That was the first and only time I thought that maybe karate wasn't for me because I felt really bad. I still do. I can still smell and picture everything about that day.

When college classes resumed in the fall of 1974, I returned to UCLA and sought out the nearest Ed Parker Kenpo school. All I had was an address, and I really didn't believe they did the same stuff. I had the big red binder with the Kenpo crest on the cover that I carried around like a prized possession. When I went to that school and saw another red binder with the crest on it, I thought, 'Oh my god, it's true. I can do this here. This is great.'

I was just lucky enough to hit that school at the time Chuck Sullivan was teaching group classes on Tuesday and Thursday nights, and Sam Estrada was teaching Monday and Wednesday nights. It wasn't long before I was attending all four nights. While Sam Estrada was a perfectionist on forms and techniques, Chuck Sullivan would say to me, "This is not ballet! Power, more power! This is not ballet!" I still had this thing in my mind about kicking Joanne and breaking her ribs and having her quit, that something in me thought I can't really kick hard or this may happen again. But Chuck Sullivan would say, "This is not ballet, c'mon, kick, kick, kick!" And I can still recall Huk Planas that year teaching at the school. One in awhile he would give me a pointer on something, and I would think about it for the whole week. It was like a little treasure. The other thing that I thought was really neat was that Huk was teaching a girl who wore a green belt, and this really helped increase my incentive.

I left for that summer, and when I returned in the fall of 1975 the school was completely different. Chuck Sullivan and Huk Planas and all of the higher belts had left, and Larry Tatum was managing the school. Almost immediately I graduated into the intermediate and advanced classes, many of which were taught by Larry Tatum. The

*With Larry Tatum and Ed Parker on the night of my promotion to fourth-degree black belt.*

training was really tough. The WLA school was notoriously a very physical school, and for whatever reason it was okay with me to be bounced around and bruised, and I found it to be okay enough that I'd go back the next day, and I kept doing that month after month.

In August of 1975 I attended my first International Karate Championships that had been held annually in Long Beach since 1964. Prior to this I attended smaller, local competitions at high schools. I remember Beverly Hills High School with the floor that was the swimming pool, very impressive. That sparked the part of me that thought, "Hey, I'm not really finished with my competition days from the gymnastics." There was a routine, a sequence. You walked onto the floor and presented yourself. There was a beginning and end, and you had to be poised from the moment you stepped onto the floor to the time you closed and bowed out. In gymnastics I was told that the judges are judging you from the moment you step into the gym in the morning. Your hair has to be perfect. You just have to have the image. You have to start selling this thing from early in the morning to the point that you're on the floor. I have found over the years that karate competition is no different.

So here I was sitting at the Long Beach Internationals. Boy, that was a huge tournament! My goodness, my head spun! I remember resting my chin on the backs of my hands and watching

Rudy and Myron Tuiolosega, Steve Fisher, and the great fighter Ray Sua. There was a buzz running throughout this huge sports arena, and it was exhilarating. Best of all there was a division for me that I could do my little thing. Wow! That weekend marked the beginning of my return to competition (at least in my mind), but it wasn't until several years later that I won the kata competition at the International Karate Championships that I came to understand what had driven me to place myself in that arena.

An area of my Kenpo that I struggled with for some time was I often thought, 'Boy, it would be great if I could really use this. Won't someone just jump me in a parking lot so I can check this out?' Now and then, I still think even today, 'Gee, I just wish – if I could be guaranteed that I'd walk out alive, I don't mind taking a few bumps and bruises. I want to check this out.' The point is there has always been a part of me that has wanted to try this out in real time. But I also know that there are little tricks. As a female I have to be one step quicker in awareness. I can't wait until someone attempts a locking maneuver and actually locks in. It would put me at a great disadvantage. I would have to be faster, smarter, and use some of these tools to make up for my lack of height, weight, and strength. So even today I still have my doubts.

One of the things that was great about studying with Albert Cornejo twice a week for several years was he would say, "If the barstool is right next to you, don't punch 'em. Take that

barstool and whack him over his head. Take that scotch bottle and whack his knee with it." Until I was in his class, I never thought about it in this way. Instead, I thought, "Oh, I'll do Delayed Sword or whatever." And Albert would say, "Delayed Sword? Take this mug and smash it into his face!"

He really changed my outlook on these things. He'd blindfold us and say this is what happens if someone throws scotch in your eyes and you can't see. So let's pretend, and we'd have to grab onto something and he's say, "That's an arm, that's a hand, there's the elbow, there's a face." As martial artists we're not limited. We can use anything and everything in our environment to our advantage. That kind of training helped augment my unarmed self-defense techniques and was a welcome addition.

This brings me back to what truly motivated me to compete in tournaments. I've always wanted to test myself to see if Kenpo or the barstool techniques work in real time, and I thought that competition would be one possible way to see if I could perform under pressure. To get butterflies to the point that I'm almost sick, and to see if I choke. Scared. Nervous. Sweaty palms. My hearts starts to jump out of my mouth. To see if under those conditions I could go on and not blank out. I just wanted to test myself.

Obviously it's not the same as protecting myself on the street. It's not that kind of real situation, but it's an aspect of that, which is when the adrenaline is flowing, would I freeze? One valu-

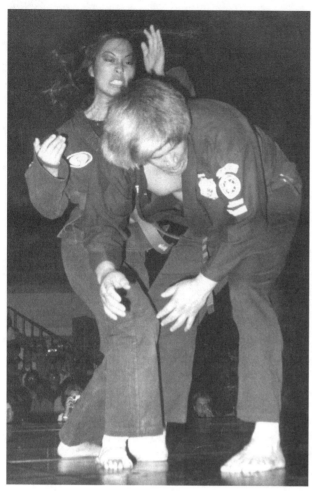
*Dian at 1977 IKC demo as a "nervous brown belt."*

of us our natural state is calm. But if you're suddenly accosted, you have to be able to turn on Niagara Falls instantly, and you have to be able to have that key or to have that switch or that faucet knob under your control, and you can turn it on or turn it off at will. You have to go from zero to one hundred miles an hour in an instant. Not warming up, revving up, but finally getting there is BAM! And you're on! That's what you have to do, and that's what competition does for me. It's an arena to practice going from zero to one hundred in an instant.

In thinking more about this over the years, I came to see there are a lot of people who are afraid to turn it on. Because they're afraid if they get to that point, that unresolved issues caused by their repressed anger and feelings they have locked up in a little box are going to come out. Essentially they are afraid of that person within. Maybe they have a tendency to want to beat up their kids or their wife, and there are a lot of unresolved issues that prevent them from turning on that faucet because they're afraid of what's going to come out.

So I believe for some there is considerable work to be done on many levels, otherwise one can never turn on that faucet because you're afraid to risk seeing this demon come out. And so forms competition is one small arena in which you can practice bringing this other you out of the bottle and then try to stuff him back in. It's a method of practice, but I think that for a martial artist this is the ultimate – to be able to have that alter ego available at your command. Not that it comes out when you get mad and angry and you go off – no, it's totally at your command and your control, and you can turn it off, and you can turn it on – at will. As a martial artist that is something I strive for, and I think it's one of the most important things. That's the lesson – when it's for real, you need to go for it, and if you rev up from zero to 20 to 30 to 40 miles an hour, you'll be dead. You'll be history out on the sidewalk, and someone else is going to walk away. So you've got to get to that Ferrari speed immediately, and we need ways to practice that because we can't go over to

able aspect that I think going to group classes or taking promotion tests is if you forget – you weren't supposed to stand there like a deer frozen in the headlights – you were supposed to do something and get out of there – and I always loved that element. To me, the worst thing that I could do in a test is forget and freeze. I wouldn't really beat myself up for forgetting something in a technique line and not being able to finish off the technique. I'd just revert to something else and cover out. That was my phobia because I always feared that was going to happen to me out in the street.

I guess what I'm saying is that competition is not the real world, but it's one aspect – really it's cross training for reality. It's a safe venue to get extremely stressed and nervous. To put yourself under the gun and try to perform. Every student needs to find a way to get to the realism. To most the shopping center and plaster everybody to the ground. We can't do that. But there are civilized ways to practice this, of which forms is just one.

Returning to competition after being injured in gymnastics helped put closure to that area of my life. Besides that, after awhile I realized I could take martial arts much further than the gymnastics because I was not born tall, long, and lanky, which you need to be in gymnastics to graduate to the elite levels. With martial arts, however, my stocky little legs just gave me a solid stance.

To elaborate on one more aspect of karate competition, there are instructors who when asked to bring their students to tournaments say "We don't do tournaments." That's typical of especially Kenpo schools. My take on that is tournaments represent a great opportunity for martial arts students to test themselves in a pressure situation. It's not a street situation, but it's a pressure situation. When I work with students, sometimes we just practice walking into the ring and introducing themselves. Believe it or not, most people cannot say their name straight the first time. "Judges, my name is – uh – uh – uh – uh," and they're blanking out on their own name! So to practice that, to me, is really valuable for so many things applicable in the real world where skill in public speaking is an enormous plus. It builds character by enabling the student to try and reach out to the judges and the audience. These are not just things one develops for the ring and keeps in the ring. They're very much applicable to many parts of your life.

I would also like to address the subject of the katas themselves. In the Parker system obviously the further one gets away from the original source – when one person passes it to another who passes it to another – and if it's the third incarnation or the fourth or the fifth, it can't help but to evolve away from the original. I've seen Form Four in a competition, and I think to myself "What's this form?" and then suddenly the light will turn on and I'll say, "I think this is four, but I'm not sure." And I watch and watch and watch and say, "Oh my god, it is four. Yikes!"

One reason I feel these changes occur is that today there are a lot of karate schools that aspire to do "some Kenpo." We're blah, blah, blah and we do Kenpo hands because, quote, Kenpo hands are – there's something to teach there. So a lot of people mistake flurrying hands for Kenpo hands, and as a result there are a lot of schools that don't know what Kenpo is. They just think that if they do a bunch of moves and do them real fast and slap themselves every once and awhile, that they're performing Kenpo hands. When it comes from a school like that, I can expect almost anything. What's more disconcerting is when I see this at a

*Dian (lower right) filming on the set of "Big Trouble in Little China."*

*West Los Angeles Thursday night advanced class.*

supposed Kenpo school. But again, it can't be helped if that instructor learned from his instructor who learned from another instructor. If this guy is the sixth guy in line to learn it, it's six degrees separation from Ed Parker, and we can naturally expect to see some changes.

I am often asked what advice I would give a student who desires to enter competition. First, you have to be able to work out some of the details with your instructor. If the school is not competition oriented; if your instructor is the type who says, "We don't do tournaments," and you're really interested in doing tournaments, I think it is important that you respectfully say to your instructor, "I am challenged by tournaments, and I would like to go to develop a certain aspect of myself and my art."

Another aspect is that you may have to change the form slightly in order to appear showier. As a judge, I don't like seeing competitors changing forms too much from the original intent, but I think a little is acceptable, depending on the venue, as long as you know, especially in Kenpo, what the original intention of the form is and know the standard version. If you want to

change something for a reason, know why you're changing it, but always know the standard version. And that way you don't practice something all the time that is wrong. Moreover, if you want to be successful in the competition arena, I feel that sometimes you have to put some accents into your presentation that may not be there in the form. If you're competing with a lot of Tae Kwon Do people and you don't do one kick, you'll probably have a good time competing but you probably will not win. So if you need to modify a form for competition sake, I think that's fine as long as you never forget the standard version of the form and be able to do that at any time in the dojo or when you're teaching.

When judging forms, to me the most important part of forms competition goes beyond the physical. By this I mean that the judges gravitate toward the person who performs the kata with such intensity that they stop seeing them as a competitor and can actually visualize the opponent getting hit. Moreover, they can personalize the experience, thinking, "Oh my god, if I was on the other end of that shot, that would hurt." And so when I work with people to ready them for a competition, I always say please do not forget this is not just a bunch of moves in the air. Think of the

32

shot. Visualize it. You have to feel this as if the opponent were right in front of your face. And you have to turn your head sharply because there is someone right on your back, and you just can't lollygag and turn slowly and make it unrealistic. It has to be real, and it has to be so real that the judges actually forget about seeing you. They're seeing the opponent be the recipient of all of your shots.

More than the sheer joy I have had competing, teaching Kenpo has given me abundant confidence that I know has enhanced my life. In addition, I feel I have a greater sense of awareness. When I'm walking down the sidewalk, I see men and women who are completely oblivious to danger. They're not looking over their shoulder; they're not perusing their environment; they're absolutely clueless. Being hit on the mat has taught me that it hurts to be hit. So I have a heightened awareness so that I can avoid being harmed. It's not overconfidence that I can handle every situation or I can kick butt anywhere I go. It's "be aware because the bigger guy can kick my butt," and it hurts, and I don't want to be there. Cross the street. Get out of there.

Now that Ed Parker is gone, I receive my continued instruction from a group of extremely gifted and knowledgeable kenpoists. Huk Planas is definitely one mentor and one of the few in Kenpo I feel is ego free in that he doesn't have to put his stamp on everything. I think that his fastidiousness to staying with the original Parker curriculum is marvelous. Frank Trejo is another kenpoist I greatly admire because his sense of sheer joy when he does Kenpo. Another is Bryan Hawkins who just quietly yet persistently stays on course and teaches by example. Bob Liles is a man who puts his money where his mouth is. He challenges himself every-

day, staying in top physical condition to take Kenpo into its extemporaneous and innovative state. Moreover, I have tremendous admiration for Larry Kongaika. He is awesome with raw talent rapped in a tremendous sense of humility, and he is really to me an emerging figure on the worldwide American Kenpo scene.

Like so many others in American Kenpo, I am often asked where I think our art is headed in the next decade now that our founder is no longer with us. Today there are many strong offshoots off the Parker IKKA main line, and each of these branches are predicated on the talent, personality and mission statement of their respective organization's leader. In essence, each of these new Kenpo leaders are doing their own thing, and each one of them attracts a certain kind of person. This is the logical progression because once in a millennium does a person like an Ed Parker come along who has the physical skills, the intellect, and the charisma to pull it all together and have an impact on other people's lives. There are a lot of Kenpo practitioners today who are awesome physical specimens and can control and completely dominate an opponent. Yet they are neither as charismatic as Mr. Parker, nor do they have his leadership quali-

*On the night of my promotion to fifth-degree black belt.*

ties, his degree of intellectual conceptualization, or his gift for writing. Ed Parker was special because he was one of those rare individuals who had the entire package. He was strong enough to be the father figure for so many people around the world, and because in his lifetime he was the baddest boy on the block, he could control all these black belts. I'm sure that all of us in the insular Kenpo world have not even a clue of how many people he positively effected outside the Kenpo community.

Now that he's gone, many

feel there should be a successor. But there is no one person in our generation that has the entire package to be the next Ed Parker, and therefore I think the logical progression is for all of these sons (and daughters) to leave home to plant their seeds in the world. And out of that, maybe in the next generation another Ed Parker will appear.

So I see the seeds of Kenpo and the variations being planted, and there are all these hybrids out there, and maybe it really isn't the logical conclusion that they result in the Ed Parker form of Kenpo being spread all over the world. It's such a monumental accomplishment that from the seeds of his Kenpo were created direct descendants and the hybrids. It's a mark of strength, not a mark of weakness. It's not dissolving. It's not diluting. It's flourishing. And really it's a mark of Mr. Parker's accomplishment that it takes on really a new persona with the new generation. It just shows how strong the system is to be able to accommodate these differences.

After I got over the initial shock of Mr. Parker's death, I began to wonder if there was anything I wish I had said but didn't while he was here with us. If there was any one thing, it would be, "Thank you." I don't think I truly thanked him enough. When he was alive, I would say, "Thanks for a great weekend," or "What a great seminar." I was lucky enough that he would say, "I'll stay at your house. I don't stay at everyone house, but I'll stay at your house." I think he only stayed at my house because I made him fish and rice for breakfast. Much to the chagrin of Bob Liles and some of the other people who would be almost ill thinking of having grilled fish and miso soup and rice for breakfast, but anyway, I was honored that Ed Parker felt comfortable staying at my home. And I would often say, thank you so much, that we had a great weekend, a great seminar, a great this or great that, but I don't think I ever said "Thank you. You've changed my life."

# Grandmaster
# Chuck Sullivan
## 10th Degree

*Chuck and his wife Florence celebrated fifty years of marriage on July 14, 2001, just prior to the publishing of this book. Retired since 1995, Chuck teaches Kenpo to a few select private students and a weekly class, along with doing his part in running the Karate Connection. Of all the Honorees featured in this book, he is the most senior, having received his black belt in September 1962. Chuck's hobby of sculpting in clay, from which he then makes molds for reproductions of his work, also takes up a good portion of his time. He is presently working on a five-piece set of twelve-inch figures depicting the Karate Connection Formal Salute, using his Karate Connection associates as models. Having been a performer since early childhood, Chuck is a gifted actor and in 1990 played the role of DEA Agent Jack Slade in the movie THE KILLING ZONE. Acting isn't a job to Chuck; it's a joy and a pleasure for which there wasn't enough time in the past. Now that working a full-time job is no longer a priority and living the good life is, Chuck and Flo are making the most of it. The journey just got real smooth.*

Growing up in Chicago during the Great Depression was not a lot of fun for most people, but I must admit that even though we didn't have much, our family always got along just fine. I never went to bed hungry, which is something a lot of folks couldn't say in those days.

There wasn't a lot for kids to do then, and whatever we did couldn't cost anything. I guess you would have to put fighting into the category of entertainment because I did a lot of it when I was a kid. No one ever really got hurt; it was just a kind of a one-up-manship sort of game we played on our way to and from school and on the playground during recess. The other kids would gather around yelling "Fight - fight - fight!" and you'd roll around in the dirt until someone either gave up or someone broke it up. The combatants would usually leave with their arms slung over each other's shoulders.

Then one day when I was about fourteen, I was slap fighting with a friend and without my realizing it, he got serious. We went to the ground, and I was still laughing when I went to help him up. As I reached for him, he attempted to kick me in the face, and his shoelace whipped across my eye. I really lost it, and I saw red. The next thing I remember was seeing my hands clutching his throat, his face gray and his tongue hanging out of his mouth. I panicked and started to shake him saying, "Are you all right?"

He finally stopped choking and started breathing. That was a real wake-up call for me. This was the first fight I ever had that was serious, and I almost killed someone. I could just see the headline in the *Tribune*. "Chicago Youth Kills Friend in Fit of Rage." I'd have been scarred for life. I vowed never to allow that to happen again.

The rest of my childhood was pretty calm, and I went from teenager to married man at nineteen. The Korean War came, and the United States Marine Corps grabbed two years of my life, from twenty to twenty-two. After that it was work and a family. At the age of twenty-seven, five years out of the Marines, I woke up one morning and realized I was in pretty lousy physical condition and had to do something. Back then there weren't a whole lot of options besides the standard gym, and I really hated pumping iron.

One day in February of 1959 my brother-in-law said to me, "Do you know there's a judo school up on Tweedy Boulevard?"

That sounded like something physical and at the same time a place I could pick up a little knowledge that might come in handy. I hadn't

*Chuck at age nine.*

had a fight in thirteen years, but that didn't mean I never would again, so this would be like buying insurance.

I drove over to the place a couple days later, but it was closed. I peeked in the windows and saw some strange mats on the floor, a little divider, a desk and chair, and a couple pictures on the wall. That was it. Two guys behind me were leaning up against a car talking.

"You interested in studying?" one of them asked.

"Yeah," I said. "How much are the judo lessons?"

"Well, we don't actually teach judo here," the fellow said.

I looked up on the roof at a big sign that said JUDO with a smaller sign on the window that read KARATE.

"What's karate?" I asked, making the word sound like "ka-rate."

"Ah - that's karate," the man said, rolling the r, then invited me to come back that evening.

That night I saw things I'd never seen before. A big Hawaiian was instructing, and when he moved, the whole damn building seemed to shake. His name was Ed Parker. Even though I'd been raised on the mean streets of Chicago and been through combat training in the Marine Corps, Ed Parker was in a league all his own, and I knew that right away. He could shake the building just with his movements. It seemed like his power transferred through his feet and into the walls. Besides Parker's moves, I was also intrigued by the gi. I'd only seen photos of people wearing them, and it was exotic. When I returned home, I said to my brother-in-law, "If they let me wear one of them white outfits, I'm going for it."

My first class was like love at first sight. I knew right off that this was for me. It was a marriage made in heaven. The next three-and-a-half years went along as smoothly as they could between Kenpo and me, and it was at about that time I saw the writing on the wall, and the writing said I was soon to be promoted to black belt. I was reluctant about receiving it because I thought it was a huge responsibility, and I didn't know if I was ready for it. I would like to have had another six months.

One evening after class when Ed and I were alone, I broached the subject in a roundabout manner telling him that I thought getting a black belt should be like earning a college degree, which typically takes four years. He gave me a look that clearly told me it wasn't my decision and said, "Chuck, a lot of people do it in less time." And I thought, 'He ain't going for it.' There had only been three black belts before me, and they were no longer around. My promotion to black belt took place on the 27th of September 1962. After I was promoted to black, Ed Parker began to really train me.

Another night after the others had left, I asked if he would spar with me. He didn't hesitate. I think he welcomed the opportunity. It wasn't something he got to do very often but probably would have, had others asked him to. To my knowledge Rich Montgomery and I were the only two students who ever sparred with Ed Parker. When he strode onto the mat, he became a changed man. He was scary, I mean really scary. His power was awesome, and I remember thinking if he hits me, I'm toast. But he had incredible control and exercised it because he knew the kind of damage he could inflict.

In 1963 he took a group of us to a big tournament in Chicago. There were all sorts of styles and systems there, and I got to see a lot of interesting things. I had never before seen a full-out spinning back kick as done by the Korean stylists, and I said to one of our guys, "I like that move. It's really good."

The guy said it wasn't good because you never turn your back on an opponent.

"Yeah," I said. "Then how come the guy who turned his back is up dancing around while

*A few months into my training. I'm wearing one brown tip on my white belt, which is the equivalent today to a yellow belt.*

the other guy is on the ground in a world of hurt? Get real. That's a good move, and if somebody pulled that on me right now, I don't know how I would react to it, so I think we better take that home with us and perfect it enough so that at least we know how to defend against it."

Ed was impressed with the move, too. When we got home, he taught us not only to defend against it but also to use it. Some of our guys like Steve (Sanders) Muhammad took that kick to a level of perfection that was just sensational. Soon he was beating the people who originated it with their own move.

One day in the early sixties Ed told a group of us that he had met an incredible young martial

*"The Promotion" - one of Chuck's first scuplture pieces.*

artist and had invited him to observe the class. He introduced a skinny Chinese kid to us named Bruce Lee, who sat in the waiting room watching us on the mats. After the class was over, Ed went into his office leaving us alone with Bruce. We were having a pleasant conversation until Bruce casually said, "I was watching you guys do something earlier, and I was wondering why you were doing it."

He then demonstrated what we had been practicing. Of course, the answer was obvious to all of us. We were doing it because that's the way

Ed Parker was teaching it. When no one spoke up Bruce dropped a bomb.

"Well, I just wondered because it's wrong," he said.

That was the first time I ever heard the words "Ed Parker" and "wrong" matched up, and I was stunned. I looked around at the other guys. A couple of them looked like they were going to grab Bruce by his skinny neck and shake him until his butt plate fell off.

Bruce quickly went on to explain that what we were doing violated a basic principle. Not a concept, but a principle. For example, the principle of gravity dictates that you can't stand on one leg unless that leg is directly under your center.

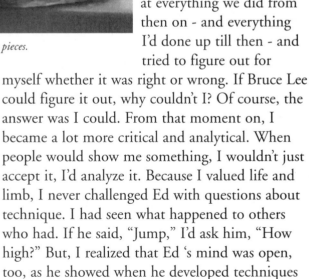

You can't do it any other way without falling down. Then he showed us why the move was wrong. It wasn't enough to destroy my faith in the system, but Bruce was right. I remember thinking how I never questioned Ed Parker. It never dawned on me to question what he was teaching. But if Bruce was right - and he was - then what else was wrong? I started taking a closer look at everything we did from then on - and everything I'd done up till then - and tried to figure out for myself whether it was right or wrong. If Bruce Lee could figure it out, why couldn't I? Of course, the answer was I could. From that moment on, I became a lot more critical and analytical. When people would show me something, I wouldn't just accept it, I'd analyze it. Because I valued life and limb, I never challenged Ed with questions about technique. I had seen what happened to others who had. If he said, "Jump," I'd ask him, "How high?" But, I realized that Ed 's mind was open, too, as he showed when he developed techniques like using and defending against the spinning back kick.

For example, when I was teaching at the Hawthorne school, I told him that I wanted to add some realism to the training.

"Fine," he said.

I started by having the advanced class spar and run the technique line without first warming up because that's how it happens on the street. There is no time to warm-up; you've got to be ready to go at the drop of a hat. Other times we used to spar in street clothes and tennis shoes. There was an asphalt driveway between the two buildings and a streetlight that threw a slash of light into the first quarter, and the rest of it went to almost total darkness. I'd tell the class, "We're going to free style in this driveway. You've got a wall in the back and a wall in front of you - nothing but asphalt and concrete and a couple of steel dumpsters. Get used to it because that's how it is. We don't walk around barefoot in a world of tatami mats." We would move furniture onto the mats to create a room in the corner. Then we would freestyle around and over the furniture.

As the years went by, and I reflected on the early days of my journey, I wondered how so many of Ed Parker's students got so good so fast. I think there were two reasons. First, he taught us impeccable basics that we practiced religiously to the point of exhaustion. Second, in the late fifties there were less than twenty-five techniques in the entire system. When he began to add to the system, everybody got real good quickly because we already had such strong basics. Unfortunately, when these people began teaching, they were so in love with the techniques that they started rushing through the basics or, worse yet, handing them over to an underling. Someone who in time handed them over to an even less experienced person. Before

you knew it, you have beginners teaching beginners, which gets more and more like the blind leading the blind.

The other problem was that the techniques were what sold the beginner on the art. Most beginners much preferred learning these deadly techniques to drilling basics, and the result was that students started exhibiting flashy moves with no base to make them effective. It is for this reason that I have for over four decades focused on

*Kicking at Ed Parker, circa 1962. Note the guns and clubs on the far wall.*

strong basics. To me, they are the foundation of every great martial artist.

Over the years, Kenpo has become very complex. In the beginning Ed Parker had no guidelines at all. None. He had to invent the ABCs of motion. During the years I was teaching at the Santa Monica school, I found people getting up to around blue belt and then they would drift. They would look behind them at what they had learned, and then they'd look ahead at what they hadn't learned and say, "I can't do this. It's just too much." The bulk of material was just too overwhelming.

It was during those years that I began asking myself if there was a way to get really good black belts within a reasonable period of time. There just had to be a way to get a student up to speed so that he could go to any school or any tournament and be able to hold his own.

The way was simple. Cut down the material and go back to our roots. Reformulating the long list of Kenpo techniques (and thus the forms) made sense to me because in meticulously examining them I felt that the techniques had far too many repetitions of the same thing. I thought that instead of spending all this time working on all these techniques and forms, why not put

*My sculpture piece of the Flying Kick.*

*My first 8mm Kenpo training film.*

more stress on the basics and emphasize the concepts and principles, then give the student enough techniques to make him effective.

Faced with a physical confrontation, my primary focus is not getting hit, then doing as much damage as possible as quickly as possible, and you don't need 300 techniques to do that. The guys in the old days did it with no more than a handful,

and they did it brilliantly. Once the student acquires a set of strong basics combined with accuracy, speed and power practiced to a degree of instantaneous reaction from all directions, they're set. From then on, it just takes enough practice to keep an edge. If they want to learn the rest of those great Kenpo techniques and lengthy forms as a hobby, fine. But a student shouldn't have to spend that kind of time in order to get good at karate. He'll be good once he's got his basics down cold and has enough techniques under his belt to be able to change anything at any time and switch from one thing to another, on demand.

In 1962 Ed Parker and I made a series of training films. This was long before video was available. They were sold on 8mm film without sound. What made this time special for me was that I got to work closely with him. When we started the project, I was under the impression that he was going to formulate what was going to be taught himself, but we soon began to share responsibility for the content. We spent long hours over a period of months putting together those films. There were many times when I didn't arrive home until after two in the morning and would surely have fallen asleep at the wheel had it not been for the energy he infused into those sessions. I was able to feed off that energy and the twenty-three miles I had to drive evaporated before my bloodshot eyes.

Our initial intent with those films was to allow people around the world to see Ed Parker move. Until then only a handful of people had known that privilege. The second was to teach Kenpo. Unfortunately, because the fims were silent we couldn't do much teaching, but a lot more people got to see him move than would have otherwise. Although one day he called me and said, "I just had two guys in from the East Coast, and they did the Black Belt Set for me. Except for a couple of minor corrections, they had it cold, and they learned it off our films."

One further note about those grainy black-and-white films - they are still around. In fact, portions of them were screened at the tribute held in Ed Parker's honor at the Los Angeles Bonaventure Hotel in February 1988.

The experience of making these 8mm films led to an epiphany that marked a third highlight in my journey - the birth of the Karate Connection with my partner Vic LeRoux.

Vic had been after me for years to make videos, and I'd say, "Vic, you can't teach through a video."

"Well everybody's making them," he'd remark almost monthly.

I've never much cared about what everybody else was doing, and I told Vic, "You can't teach by video, so what are you doing? You're going to be selling videos to people and taking their money, and for what? It's not even entertainment, so what good is it if you can't teach it?"

Teaching requires a two-way communication,

so even if you send someone a great video, there still is no way of knowing if they're getting the instruction.

Vic kept after me for three years about making videos, and I kept asking him what part of N-O didn't he understand? Then one night when we were talking about it for the millionth time, I had a flash of insight. Some years earlier a student told me that Chuck Norris sent an 8mm film to his instructors in Korea for some more rank and asked me what I thought about the idea.

"His instructors are professionals," I said. "If they told him what they want to see, and he shows it to them - what can be wrong with that?"

Then it occurred to me that practically everyone had a VCR, and camcorders were becoming commonplace. Anyone who really wanted to could get his or her hands on a camcorder, even a kid in a ghetto. Give him a few hours and he could score one. A kid on a ranch in Montana could find someone with a camcorder if he had to.

Once the initial concept was out, it was like the dam burst, the ideas came like a flood. "We can send the student an excellent instructional video, and control the content because we'll be doing the basics, not some purple belt," I told Vic. "When the student feels he has the basics down pat, he can get a camcorder. We'll tell him where to put the camera on a tripod, the distance he should be away from it when he does his movements and the field of view. There's no difference between our standing there watching him or watching him on the screen. Then we can critique him as we would if we were watching him on the

*Around 1964-5, a great way to break an ankle.*

*My promotion to tenth degree black on January 22, 2000.*

mat and do something Chuck Norris's instructors couldn't do. We can video a lesson specifically designed to that student right on his cassette at the end of his lesson, and he can study it until he's got it.

Our timing was right. Video was finally coming into its own. Most other sports had been using film and video to their advantage for many years. Many martial artists, however, still shun video and instead look in mirrors. As far as I'm concerned, mirrors are a distraction. Don't look in the mirror. If you really want to find out how you're doing, set up a camera and video yourself, and then take a look at it. I guarantee that, regardless of your degree of proficiency, you will look at that tape and say, "Oh, my god, I did that? That's terrible! I couldn't have done that! But I did."

Our tapes go through each belt level, starting with yellow (for children) orange, purple, blue, green, brown and black. We teach all the basics the way we learned them directly from Ed Parker and we break them down the way we had been for thirty years, using that experience as to how to best present it. Then we break down the breakdown. God, how I love the basics.

We've been successfully teaching on tape since we began in 1990. What's so great about it is that our videos offer a solution to anyone anywhere who wants to learn Kenpo but can't because they don't have access to a school.

People often ask me what I've gotten from over forty years of involvement in the art. For one thing, studying Kenpo has given me the ability to sense trouble. Besides giving me a strong sense of my environment, the martial arts has raised my level of confidence to where I truly feel I have nothing to prove. I know at a glance whether someone has the will and potential to be a real threat. In my opinion, street fighting is unnecessary. Most of the time people put themselves in dangerous places and situations. And I can still see that screaming headline, "Chicago Youth Kills Friend in Fit of Rage."

I always try to avoid physical confrontation, but if it seems imminent, I fall back on my training and my instincts. For example, in freestyle fighting I teach my students to be aware of the red, yellow, and green zones. The red zone is the attack zone, and you better not be there unless you plan to do the attacking. Action is faster than reaction, and you can be blasted while in the red zone before you can react. The yellow zone is where you set up your counter attack, that's where you nail your opponent coming in because you've given yourself the time to react. When I was younger I used to react faster, so now I stay back a little further, actually more toward the green or safe zone. Knowing how to cheat your way into the red zone and then immediately launch an attack is the real secret. Those zones work for freestyle and for life as well. When in the red zone remember those infamous words of Ed Parker, "He who hesitates, meditates in a horizontal position."

I have a simple philosophy about fighting. Don't do it because there's no effective halfway! If I were to blind or kill someone, later I would be able to say, "I didn't do that. You did that to yourself. You used my body to kill or maim yourself. It's like picking up my gun and killing yourself with it, I'll go home and sleep like a baby because

*My daughter Jeanine, Flo, my wife of 50 years. and my son Scott.*

I'll know I tried everything I could to make it not happen."

Every year in Seal Beach, California the Karate Connection hosts a tournament that I feel challenges each participant in a realistic setting. In lieu of point sparring, our tournament features three events. The first two are centered on the participant being attacked. We set up two scenarios, the first where the contestant turns his back to a group of attackers. Each comes up and applies a different hold or lock, six in all, to which the contestant must react immediately with a proper technique. He can't just "cut and shoot" meaning, do whatever he pleases. For our black belts, that would be effective but too easy. We want to see them use their art. The second event has the contestant facing five attackers in a semi-circle, with each attacking twice. The attackers are pointed to from behind the contestant so there is no verbal warning. He doesn't know which of them will be attacking or with which hand or if it will be a straight punch, hook, roundhouse or back fist. The techniques, of course, must be immediate, appropriate, accurate, fast and powerful. We nicknamed it "The Circle of Humiliation." Try it sometime and you'll understand why.

The final event has the participant doing the attacking. In this event the martial artist is required to deliver thirty-eight blows to a life-size dummy. These blows are delivered with full contact, at full speed and power, and include head butts, elbows, punches, knees, rakes, kicks, stomps and several others - a full arsenal.

When I first introduced the drill of striking the dummy, everyone's flow of motion stopped with the strikes. Their accuracy was off badly. Their power was poor and often they were striking with the wrong part of the weapon. With practice that all went away. You should see them now!

And so throughout my journey, these key aspects - striving for strong basics, continually questioning and analyzing, and realism - have been the pillars of my art.

This martial arts journey I've been on for over forty years has been fascinating. The things I've been able to do and watch other people do is nothing short of incredible.

What I cherish most of all about my journey is the camaraderie and the brotherhood I've discovered. From the first day I stepped on the mats on Tweedy Boulevard wearing a new white gi and white belt, I fell right in with the group. The martial arts brotherhood is great, and I've found most martial artists are exceptionally nice people. Every now and then I'll run across somebody and say to myself, 'I don't think he belongs here.' Before long he's not. It seems that the martial arts survives through natural selection.

Years ago my wife complained, "Chuck, you have no friends outside of karate. If a person doesn't wear a gi, you have nothing to say to them."

I disagreed.

She said, "Name one."

I did.

She said, "He doesn't now, but he did when you met him."

She was right, all of my friends are martial artists or were at one time. Thanks to the art, I've been blessed with so many truly close friends all along the way, I don't need any others. Less than a month after my first lesson I had people coming over to the house to work out on Sunday. And we used to have parties and barbecues at the house back in those days. Ed Parker threw a few, only he'd call it a luau, and I threw a few, and we'd invite all the students and their families.

But time marches on for all of us. Sometimes I reflect back with a degree of sadness to the old school Ed Parker and I ran on Crenshaw Blvd. Of the fifteen black belts that came out of that school between the years 1963 to 1972, only Vic LeRoux, Steve (Sanders) Muhammad, Bob Noe, and myself are still actively involved. Johnny Walker also was, up to the time of his passing. Inevitably the dropout rate is 100-percent, whether it's for health reasons and you can't do it anymore, or you just get too old, or life gets in the way. Or life just goes away.

It's been a truly fantastic journey. Until I die I will be grateful to Ed Parker for his friendship and guidance on the journey. I'll be seventy years old this year, and people often ask me how long I'm going to continue doing Kenpo? My answer is simple: until it's not fun anymore. Who do you suppose it was that got me to jump out of a perfectly good airplane at 12,000 feet? My Kenpo brothers, naturally.

# Professor
# Frank Trejo
## 9th Degree

*Frank's martial arts training began with Shotokan Karate in 1966. Three years later he enrolled in the Instructors Program that was held at Ed Parker's Kenpo Karate Studio in Pasadena and passed the course. Over the next three decades, Frank became a legend in Kenpo. Besides winning nineteen International Championships, he is the first and only American Kenpo practitioner to hold the distinction of placing first in both Kata and Kumite at the prestigious Long Beach International Championships in the same year, which he did in 1984. The following year he was made coach and captain of the Budweiser International Karate Team. Although retired from competition, Frank continues to offer his unique instructional techniques in seminars held in Ireland, Spain, Australia, Japan, South and North America, as well as continuing his work throughout the United States. In 1985 he founded a program called "Creative Physical Fitness," which has changed the lives of hundreds of physically, mentally, and socially challenged children through the remarkable benefits of the martial arts. Besides working as a bodyguard to many Hollywood celebrities, Frank has appeared in numerous motion pictures. His hobbies include singing and playing guitar and percussion in various Blues bands.*

M y first formal training in fighting was boxing through my grandfather. He and his two brothers were world champions back in the twenties and thirties. My grandpa Tony, his brother Ray, and his brother Joe. So growing up I remember my grandfather always talking about boxing. He gave me my first lesson when I was seven years old. He explained to me how to stand and how to hold my hands. He said to take my right hand and put it on the right side of my face. That way the other guy couldn't hit me on that side of my jaw. Then he showed me how to raise my left shoulder along the other side of my jaw, so that my opponent can't hit me on that side, and further illustrated how I should place my left arm across my stomach so as to protect against the body shot.

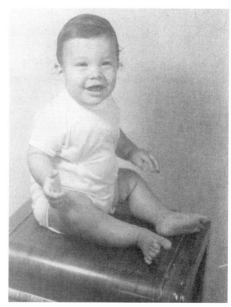

*My grandfather said my feet were blessed.
Count my toes.*

And finally he said to me, "Then once you're ready like that, then you say goodbye to your nose!"

At an early age I learned that knowing how to fight helped me out in the street with the older kids. I was raised in a tough neighborhood everywhere we lived. When I was twelve years old, my friend's cousin came over to stay at his house, and somehow we didn't hit it off and ended up getting into a fight. From my boxing, I knew if I hit a kid in the mouth that the fight would be over. But with this kid, every time I socked him, he socked me right back. Experience had taught me that when I hit a kid who's twelve, he's going to start crying, but this kid never did. We went back and forth, and I had a bloody nose, and he had a fat lip. Someone broke us up, and we ended up going our separate ways. After that I started thinking maybe I wasn't so good after all.

About a year later I was at a park when two guys got in a fight. One was considerably bigger than the other. They were fighting when suddenly the smaller guy threw a kick and nailed the big guy in the body and buckled him. The smaller guy followed this up with a sweep or takedown and totally disabled his opponent. The big guy tried to get up, and he started to come back with another attack when the smaller guy launched a spinning back kick that ended the fight. I was impressed, and thought to myself, 'Whoa! What was that?!' because I had never seen anybody kick before.

Months later I was standing with some friends outside a theater when a car pulled up to the curb. I recognized the driver and said to my friends, "Hey, you remember I told you about that guy who did karate on that guy? That's him,

*Remeber when*

right there!"

The guy pulled out his workout bag, and I spotted a gi with a black belt hanging out and a pair of nunchucks. I said, "Hey, those are those sticks!" The guy walked into a building. My friends and I stared at the sign displayed across the top.

"What is that place?" I asked.

"It's a karate school," someone said.

Soon we were climbing over each other trying to get in the door. The instructor (Tonny Tulleners, one of Tak Kobota's guys) came out and barked, "Hey, what're you guys doing?"

"Oh, we just came to watch," we said in unison.

"All right, you guys sit down there and be quiet," he growled.

We sat watching the guys working out doing forms. After awhile they began sparring. I turned to one of my friend and said in a hoarse whisper, "Whoa! See that move? That's the move the guy did on the other guy in the park!"

Just after I turned fourteen, I got a job at the Pasadena Car Wash. Back then you had to be sixteen to work there, and I told them I was sixteen and got in through a friend. Before long I was making a little money.

By that time, I already knew I wanted to be a coach. When I was in the third grade, the coach at Altadena Elementary School, Mr. Jackson, taught me how to play football, basketball, and baseball, and I used to see how the kids looked up to him. I also liked him a lot because he spent time with me. Wanting to emulate Coach Jackson, I used to help train my brothers and sisters in what I learned in sports, and would teach them how to bat, throw, and catch the ball.

When the time came that I wanted to start

taking karate, I didn't have the money to pay for all of us. So I took my nine-year-old brother, Mike, and enrolled him at Tak Kobota's karate school in the less expensive children's class. Then when my little brother would arrive home from class, I would drag him to the side of the house and say, "Okay, show me what you learned."

He would hem and haw, then mumble, "Ah, I don't remember."

I'd whack him on the shoulder and yell, "Man, pay attention! I'm not paying all this money for you not to remember!"

Later I started going down to the class with him, and I'd sit on the bench in a far corner of the room and give him the eye and mouth the words, "Pay attention!"

After awhile he got the hang of it and started teaching me. So my first karate teacher was my little brother Mike. That's how I got started.

A couple years later, my little brother was in junior high. He'd dropped out of karate and was hanging out with his buddies. One Sunday morning my mom was making breakfast, and she was looking through the papers for something, and all of a sudden she said, "Frankie, look. Here's an ad in the paper. It says karate instructors needed, no experience necessary. It says you can make up to seven hundred dollars a month."

"Let me see that," I said.

It was a one-inch ad and it had a phone number. I called the next day and the recorded message gave the address on Walnut Street in Pasadena. I drove over the next day and it was Ed Parker's Kenpo Karate Studio. Back then they were doing the instructors program for their fran-

*Early Kenpo years*

chise schools. I signed up for the eight week course that taught the basic blocks, punches, kicks, formalities, and some techniques, but mainly principles and terminology. The instructor who ran the course wanted to know how well I could explain the material, as well as demonstrate it.

At the end of the course, we had to qualify. Not everybody made it. We were all lined up. There was a group of guys in the office who suddenly walked out onto the mats. There were five chairs, and the guy in the middle was the big guy. At that time I didn't know who Ed Parker was, but I looked at the guy in the middle and thought this guy must be the boss. I'm going to align myself directly in front of him so he can see me. I'm going to qualify on this thing.

I stood in a horse stance with the others being tested, doing my blocks with as much power as I could muster up. When it came to demonstrating my teaching ability, the technique I was given was Five Swords. I broke it down and explained it to the panel utilizing the principles of the forward bow and weight distribution, then did the technique full blast on another student and crossed out. I looked at Ed Parker who had one eyebrow up like I had caught his attention. I was encouraged, so every time I crossed out, I glanced to see if he was watching me. He seemed to be nodding his head a little as if he were thinking, "This kid's all right."

At the end of the test, the panel went into the office and after about fifteen minutes came back out. We were all standing in a horse stance, and Ed Parker walked over to us with a frown on his face. Then all of a sudden he gave me this

mean stare. I thought, 'Oh, man, what did I do?' I mean he looked at me like I stole something. I could feel my feet sweating, and he's looking straight in my eyes. Again I'm thinking, 'Oh man, what did I do?' and I started to crumble. Then he got this little smirk on his face and he grinned, and I thought, 'Oh, he's a kidder! He's a kidder! I like that!' But right when he smiled, I thought, 'Yes! I made it! I know I made it!' This was a major turning point in my life. I knew I was in, and I knew that this was going to be the thing I was going to do for the rest of my life. From that day on, I've done karate my whole life.

After qualifying for the instructors program, it became necessary for me to continue my training at the Santa Monica school. Unfortunately, the school was thirty miles away, and I did not have a car. My girlfriend Rachel, who later became my wife, let me use her car, and had it not been for her kind generosity, I could not have continued with my training.

I was fortunate to have been surrounded by the best of everybody. I don't mean just in Kenpo, but in judo, wrestling, boxing, and kickboxing. Kickboxing was by far the most difficult because those of us who competed had to figure it out on

our own. There were no instructions, and it was anything but easy. At that time a lot of black belts who stepped in the ring got their whole face knocked off because they weren't ready for it.

I learned a lot from many of the fighters of that era, like Benny the Jet (everybody's hero), John Natividad, Steve (Sanders) Muhammad, Donnie Williams, and Byong Yu. All these guys were particularly good at one move. I would watch them and then try to perfect that move. The result was that I ended up with a fairly good arsenal of my own. In addition, I was always practicing and trying to come up with new moves. Of course, a lot of them weren't that good.

That's where Ed Parker was a huge influence. The first time I saw him move, he had Tom Kelly on his toes and was throwing him around like a rag doll. Back then Tom Kelly was trim at 300 lb. Mr. Parker would not break form. He worked his stances and his leverages and the principles that made his moves so devastating. That was when I began to realize there was more to Kenpo than met the eye, and I began to study how Ed Parker executed his moves and his angles, and I started to mimic him and adapt what he was doing to my own fighting style.

What impressed me most about Ed Parker's art was it was so beautiful while at the same time devastating. I'd never seen anybody move like Ed Parker. I'd seen big strong guys who could pound their opponent's head into the ground, but to see someone move without any wasted motion – that was perfection. Ed Parker was definitely a master, and I wanted to be like the master.

In August of 1970 I walked into the Long Beach Sports Arena carrying my white belt wrapped around my gi and looking to compete in my first tournament. I couldn't believe my eyes. In my entire life I had never seen a flying side kick. And here I was sitting down, and a purple belt flew what to me appeared to be ten feet over my head with his leg outstretched. He not only did this once; he did this four or five times. And I thought, 'Gee, what did I get myself into now? Man, look at that!' I was totally awestruck. I'd never seen so many karate people in my whole life. And with different colored uniforms. Up to this point I only saw white gis, and now I'm looking at red gis and black gis and all these patches with serpents and dragons!

An hour later I was called for my first match, and I'm looking at a guy in a black gi, and I thought, 'Ooohhh, man, this guy's got a black gi. He's going to kill me! Man, what do I do? I'm just going to fight him like I'd fight somebody in the street, because I've only known Shotokan sparring from Kobota's.'

I felt sorry for that guy after I beat the living daylights out of him. I grabbed him with both hands on his shoulders and planted a front kick right in the center of his stomach, and he flew out of the ring with me slugging him all over the place.

The referee said, "Hey, man, take it easy. Take it easy. You don't have to hit him that hard."

"Excuse me, man, I'm sorry, I'm sorry, man," I apologized profusely. "This is my first tournament. I'm kind of nervous."

"You'll be all right. Just calm down. Keep it to your basics," the ref said.

The referee was Ron Chap'el, and he didn't even wear a gi. He was in Levi's and a shirt, and he had a key ring hanging on his belt. I thought, 'What's this guy refereeing? He looks like the janitor.' Anyway, that day I ended up winning four matches.

Fourteen years later I had my best day as a tournament fighter. Ironically, the way things came together it was almost by accident. What led up to this "miracle day" occurred a year earlier in 1983 and threatened to bring an end to my fighting career.

I was at the Pasadena studio and was getting ready to spar Tatsumo Sakiyama, who later became one of Japan's world champions. We were getting ready to spar, only he didn't have a headgear. I had my headgear and another headgear that was small. I took the smaller one and tried to force it on my head. I thought if I could get it on my head, I knew it would fit him. I pulled on it hard when all of a sudden ZAP! and I thought, 'What the heck was that?' I had felt a tear or pull

*International Karate Championships 1972.*

and then a little squirt. I didn't know it at the time but I had ruptured a disc. It only hurt for about a minute, then it seemed okay. I gave Tatsuma the headgear and we went ten rounds.

After a couple days, I began noticing a weakness in my right arm and then numbness in my leg, but I kept training for the rest of that month. Then one morning I awoke to find that I was totally paralyzed on my right side.

I made an appointment to see the doctor, who ordered tests. Not only did I have a ruptured disc, but I had severed a nerve in my neck. After the surgeons repaired it, the doctor told me that I couldn't spar anymore, that it was too dangerous. That was all right with me. It was better than being paralyzed. I could still teach and practice karate. I just couldn't spar.

It wasn't long, however, before I started feeling sorry for myself. Here I was in the middle of my prime. I wanted to get out on the mat and put on the headgear and mix it up, but I couldn't. I was heartbroken. There were times I'd come home

*Posing for a picture with Ed Parker.*

*Another fight at the International Karate Championships.*

and I'd be so upset and mad, thinking, 'Why me? Why me? This is all I know.' My wife would catch me in the corner crying, and I couldn't take it. I was devastated.

The following year I took forty students to the Long Beach Internationals, and the parents started saying, "Hey, Mr. Trejo, are you going to compete?"

"Naw, I haven't even practiced in over a year," I said. The medications I had taken to help heal my neck had caused me to gain 100 pounds. Somehow I had managed to get in semi, half-assed shape, but I continued, "Naw, I'm not. I can't. I'm just getting over this broken neck. I can't take the chance." I was still scared.

An hour later another group of parents was on me. "Ah, Mr. Trejo, we came to see you."

I began thinking about all these parents and their kids, and soon rationalized that I couldn't get hurt doing forms. I filled out an entry form and headed for the arenas. There were about 100 people in the division, and when it came time for me, I opened and started Form Four. There's one part of the form where you go down on one knee in Bowing to Buddah. That's where I would usu-

ally gas out and where my second wind was supposed to kick in. As I approached that particular move, I was moving hard, really strong, and I dropped down to do Bowing to Buddah and it didn't even feel like I went down. I hit the floor like a springboard and was up and finished the form strong and took first place.

I felt a degree of closure. I had won for the parents and kids. I could quit. But the parents said, "C'mon, Mr. Trejo, you gotta fight. We came to see you fight."

"Naw, I can't. I just can't," I said, and the doubt returned. It wasn't long before I started doing a head trip on myself, thinking, 'You've been there, you've done that. You know how to block, you know how to punch. You know how to get out of the way. There's no way you're going to get hurt.'

I filled out another entry form and walked back to the arenas. The first guy I fought was nervous and lacked confidence. We started sparring and zap, zap, zap, I beat him. The next match was with this guy that I had it in for. I had beat him up once before in competition. This was my second shot at this guy, and this time I planned on really kicking his butt. We started fighting and he's running all over and I'm hitting him with everything I've got. The match was over practically before it even started.

My next match was with Ralph Allegria. This man is a legend in karate, and I'm thinking, 'Oh, man! I gotta fight this guy!' We step to the center of the ring. He's looking down at the ground, and out of the corner of his eye he looks at me, and I see a concerned look on his face, and I thought to myself, 'Oh, I got him. I already beat this guy. This isn't his day.'

We bowed and squared off. We fought hard, but I beat him. After it was over, I told him, "You don't understand what an honor this has been for me to step into the ring with you." And I still feel that way to this day.

*Frank Trejo with actress Lauren Cindy Tewes from the "Love Boat" series.*

Twenty minutes later I'm in the semifinals, and I'm thinking, 'Dang, one more and then there's the fight for first place. I can't back out now.' So I fought my next match and won.

Next came the final match. This was it. All right, cool. We squared off and I started doing all my best tricks. My drop kicks, my jump kicks, my hooking heels, when all of a sudden everybody in the Sport's Arena started coming down to that ring. Everybody crowded in, and I started hearing voices, "Get him, Frank! Frankie! Frank, Frank, Frank!" all over the place.

I thought, 'Wow! The last time I seen them do this was when Benny was fighting back in the Seventies.' And this is1984.

Finally it got so congested that a voice boomed over the public address to, "Stop all matches, stop all matches!" Manny Argrella was the referee that day.

Someone said, "All right, Manny, continue with your ring!"

We resumed slugging it out and I won. I

*Frank Trejo teaching handicapped children.*

said, "Man! Man! Two first places in forms and fighting!"

I wasn't even prepared. I'd been working to get half in shape but not for that. It was just one of those days, thank the Lord, He was shining down on me, and He said, "This is going to be your day, Frank."

Looking back, I guess that all those parents who were encouraging me were my angels. They were helping me that day and, although I didn't know it at the time, a sequence of events was about to take place that would give me the opportunity to help a group of kids who I feel those same angels watch over.

After I had won those two first place divisions, I was sitting in the audience, talking with actress Lauren Cindy Tewes of "The Love Boat" television series. She thought it was amazing how I had come back from my neck injury to win, and then went on to say that she was donating time to a program called "The Very Special Arts Festival," which is a program for children who are disabled physically, mentally, socially, kids with Down Syndrome and autism – it's a big festival of the arts, anything having to do with singing, painting, dancing, and music.

After Lauren explained the program, she asked, "Since karate is a martial art, is there any way you can do something with these kids?" She had plans to work with some of them at Pasadena High School, which was practically in my backyard.

I told her I'd be happy to help, and that

*Who wants to be the "Karate Kid"?*

I could do anything with karate. I really did have confidence in both my teaching ability, as well as my art.

The following week I met Lauren and her husband (who were going to act as my assistants) on the soccer field of Pasadena High School. Right before the kids were brought out, their P.E. teacher walked up to me and said, "Frank, what you're doing is very courageous, but if you're going to try to teach these kids something, forget about it. They're incapable of learning."

I was shocked by what he said, but at the same time had a sense that he was talking from experience. Before I could gather my thoughts, the kids, about two dozen, came running out, and were literally all over the place. They ran up and began hugging me, and half of them couldn't even speak.

My heart was pounding, and I thought to myself, 'Here I go again. Man, what did I get myself into this time?' I stood there looking around, and their staff psychologist walked up and asked me what had I planned to do?

"Well, line 'em up," I said. I watched her gather up the kids, and she seemed flustered.

"Guys, get over here and line up! Get your hands out of your pockets! Leave him alone! Quit messin' around! Pay attention and turn around!"

Two minutes later she had them in line, and all eyes were on me.

"Okay, my name is Mr. Trejo and I do karate!"

The kids looked curious and some peeked at me. This was around the time that the movie "Karate Kid" came out.

"Anybody here ever see the movie "The Karate Kid"?

Suddenly they all began yelling and cheering excitedly, "Yeeaahhh!"

I continued, "All right! Who wants to be the Karate Kid today?"

"Me-ee-eee!" they all yelled in unison.

"All right, the first move we do is this!" I brought my feet together and my hands overhead and slapped them down at my sides at attention.

Within a minute, the whole class had learned how to stand at attention. I said, "Good!" and now I knew I had them. "All right, the next stance we're going to do is called a horse stance. Everybody say horse!"

They all responded with a roar.

"All right, good! Attention – horse, attention – horse," the first two moves. Then we went into straight thrust punches. "Okay, everybody take one hand and punch just like this! All right, bring your hand back!"

A lot of kids left their hands outstretched, and I pulled a few back. That's when I recalled the time when my arm was paralyzed. I had to learn all over again everything from how to write to how to get a glass of water and drink it without spilling it all over me. What I applied to my paralysis was the knowledge that in Kenpo every action we make has a forward, opposite, and a reverse, and it occurred to me standing before these kids that if this had worked for me, it would work for them. Although they knew how to punch forward, they didn't know how to pull the punch back. So that's what we practiced – the reverse or return.

"This is your punch? Good. Now bring your hand back. Okay, punch again. Bring your hand back. No, no bring your hand like this. Okay, good. Put your left out. Okay, let me see you pull your hand back."

The kids began to pull back their punches, and soon we proceeded to the next part of the lesson. The P.E. teacher and staff psychologist just stood off to one side with their mouths open and with tears in their eyes. Maybe I was a little amazed myself, and I remember thinking, 'Yeah, I can do this!'

We had about three months to get the program together for the 1984 Special Arts Festival, and that was going to be it. One time for the kids. In those three months we learned all the basic blocks, punches, kicks, and Short Form One. We were a regular group class, and most people couldn't tell if these kids were disabled, except for those in wheelchairs or those who had a hard time walking. When festival day came we literally stole the show. Afterwards, many from the audience came up to us, including a host of celebrities who had volunteered their time.

Later that afternoon when things quieted down, a distinguished man dressed in a blue coat and sporting a shock of silver hair like Mr. Parker approached me and said, "Hello, Frank, my name is Mike Mertoff. I work for AT&T and I think there is a strong possibility that we can provide funding for your program."

I was stunned. In my mind I thought, 'My program? Oh, my god! My program? We were

*My sons Joseph and James.*

only going to do this one time.' Suddenly my mind shot straight into the future, and I replied, "Great. Here's my card. Let me have yours and we'll talk."

Later, after I arrived home, I said to myself, 'Oh, man, what am I going to do now?' I called the P.E. teacher at the Pasadena High School and asked, "Is there any way that I can continue to work with these kids on a volunteer basis? We've kind of tapped into something neat here and I want to see how far we can go with it."

That was the beginning of a wonderful new leg of my martial arts journey. I started back working with those kids, and then more kids starting coming. Soon I was introduced to the Lincoln School for Disabled Children and began working with them. I worked with 300 kids a week, ranging from the little ones to high school kids.

Ed Parker used to say that Kenpo is an art for everybody, and I have certainly proven that out with these kids. I've seen Kenpo change their lives – physically, mentally, emotionally, socially, and spiritually – Kenpo has made a difference.

Over the years the greatest gift I have received from the martial arts is that it has given me the opportunity to share with so many people my life and the knowledge that was unselfishly

*My kids Janine, Little Rachel, and David.*

given to me. When I look back at my beginnings, I can never forget that I grew up with a crowd of really tough characters. Many of them are dead and buried or in prison.

Our family has always been hard working, but we've been in the middle of all that stuff all our lives. We're still in the middle of it. As hard as I've fought to get out of the neighborhood, I'm finding myself fighting just as hard to stay in the neighborhood in order to make sure that these kids also have a chance to get out. That's why I spend time in my garage, working out with these guys. All the kids who came through the neighborhood made it. All the kids who came through me have made it.

The road is hard, and everybody who is on that road – if they can stay on it and get out of it on their own — are lucky, because there are so many paths that lead off. Every once and a while you'll find a little backyard dojo where somebody will help these kids, and every once and awhile we all get together. The kids who have come through me and learned the value of the martial arts or the value of life itself – those kids have gone off to college and many are raising their own families. I have two little boys now who I'm teaching whose father was one of the kids who came to me through my backyard dojo.

If it wasn't for martial arts I probably would be one of those tough guys, too, locked up or dead. But that didn't happen to me. I was one of the fortunate ones. At times when I reflect on a life that's been pretty good to me, I recall the day at the Pasadena school when I was giving it all I had, trying to qualify to be a karate instructor, and the grin on Ed Parker's face and my inner voice that said, 'Yes! I made it! I know I made it!'

# Associate Master
# John Sepulveda
## 8th Degree

*Senior Professor John Sepulveda has over thirty-two years experience in American Kenpo and for many years competed on the National and International tournament circuits. In addition to having appeared on television and in many popular martial arts magazines, he has written scores of articles on the art of American Kenpo. As one of the founding members of the "American Kenpo Senior Council," John joined forces with some of the best Kenpo practitioners worldwide in an effort to establish much-needed guidelines and standards in the American Kenpo community. Recognized for his tireless commitment to Kenpo, he is the proud recipient of the California Karate League's "Official of the Year Award" and the Associated Teachers Association of the Martial Artists (ATAMA) "Hall of Fame Award." Known for his precise detail in teaching Kenpo, John is in high demand on the tournament circuit. In addition to over twenty affiliate schools throughout the United States and Europe, Mr. Sepulveda owns and operates a long-standing American Kenpo school located in Santa Clara, California.*

I n the mid-eighties a housing construction crew working in San Jose unearthed a Native American burial ground. A headstone was discovered that read Sepulveda, and one of the workers at the site happened to be a former student of mine and called me, asking if I knew anything. Unfortunately, I told him I didn't, which was true. The reason was that as a child, although I knew I was Native American, I never knew specifically what tribe I was from because no one ever talked about it.

After getting off the phone with my former student, I researched the matter further and gave the information to my father, who said, "Oh yeah, my cousin is the chief spokesman for the Ohlone Indian."

This was the first time I ever heard the words Ohlone Indian. The man who my father referred to is Patrick Orozco,

*Around the age of eight*

*My early years in Kenpo at Jim Trevino's school*

and he teaches at UC Santa Cruz. Months later I participated in a three-day class at Mt. Madonna in the Gilroy area and learned more about my family heritage.

Back in the fifties and sixties when I was growing up, we never talked about this because to be Indian was frowned upon. As time went on and I got more into the teaching of the martial arts, my Native heritage would come up because I've always had a spiritual side and have a sixth sense about certain things.

I had a decent early childhood and played a lot of sports. Between the ages of ten and twelve I danced professionally with my sister. We performed ballroom dancing on television and at exhibitions, mainly to show the public that ballroom dancing wasn't restricted to adults. At the height of our popularity we were asked to audition for a popular television show featuring ballroom dancing. Up to that point our dancing had been fun but was now becoming work.

My parents divorced unexpectedly around the time I turned fourteen. Emotionally devastated, I became a loner and lost all direction. Worst of all I ended up being angry at the world. I developed a hot temper and would fight at the drop of a hat. It wouldn't take anything to get me into a fight, and it didn't matter to me if I won or

lost. I just seemed to like it. Soon, labeled a disciplinary problem, karate lessons were mentioned as a possible remedy.

I had no idea what karate was but somehow landed at a Kenpo school where I met Jim Trevino, who became my first instructor. Later along my journey, other influencial instructors were Stephen LaBounty, Tom Kelly, J.T. Will, and Bill Yazel.

From the moment I observed the karate class, I knew I would be doing martial arts for the rest of my life. What got my attention more than anything was the scientific approach to fighting. I thought I could handle myself until I saw that type of thing. Prior to karate, my only input of fighting was John Wayne westerns where fights started and ended with big haymakers. These karate guys were different. They moved swiftly and not just with one or two strikes, but with three and four and five that included kicks that appeared to come out of nowhere.

After three months of group lessons, karate was far more than I had initially thought, and I enjoyed the challenge. Not surprisingly, I loved the contact and didn't mind getting hit or hitting back. Best of all it felt good being around such positive people and hard workers. The karate school felt like family again and restored a sense of

*Brick breaking at a karate demonstration*

purpose to my life. It was something I thought I could do as an individual and do well.

Back then Kenpo didn't have a yellow belt, and so my first promotion was to the level of orange belt. It was a huge event for me, and I was hoping that some of my family members would come, but as things turned out I was by myself. That night I went home with my new belt and certificate and thought I was the greatest thing since sliced bread. To celebrate I bought a big Kenpo Karate bag. I was approaching my fifteenth birthday.

The few friends I had at school didn't know I was studying the martial arts. I was Clark Kent secretively hitching a ride or taking the bus to the karate school ten miles away. The first time anyone in school found out, I was a sophomore in high school. I was quite small – five-foot-three – and the one the big kids threw in the trash can.

In addition to studying karate, in my second year of high school I grew six inches and started getting even with these guys. I figured

which guy had hit me, which one had kicked me, and which one had stuffed me in the trash can. I would walk by these guys in the crowded hallways, chop them in the throat, and keep walking. Initially they didn't suspect me, but after three or four weeks they figured it out. One day they cornered me in the gym, and it was a standoff. Three of them approached me as I was doing pull-ups on a bar. I figured the biggest one gets it, and when they arrived, I kicked him in the gut and took off running. I guess that officially confirmed that I was a karate guy, and after that they left me alone.

About a year into my training I thought I'd enter my first major tournament. The year was 1966, and I can still remember being scared out of my wits. It was the year of the first California Karate Championships that culminated with Steve LaBounty fighting Ron Marchini for the Grand Championship. It was an awesome day, even though I didn't advance any further than a couple of fights. I hadn't known what to expect, and so I

*Tom Kelly bumping me to seventh-degree at Brian Duffy's Annual Karate Camp in Texas*

danced around and got hit a few times and finally thought, 'Oh, I get this.' The physical arena and mental mindset were entirely different from what I had been used to at the school. These guys were playing for keeps. While the rules disallowed con-

*Taken in Texas, from left to right, Gary Swan, myself, Tom Kelly, Huk Planas, Steve LaBounty, Frank Trejo and Bob Liles.*

tact, there was no guarantee with regard to control. I saw competitors in adjacent rings get knocked senseless and their opponent only got a perfunctory warning.

I finally loosened up and began applying some of the Kenpo theories and concepts of moving off-line or up the circle. When I finally realized that my opponents had no defense for what I was doing, I thought, 'Hey, I could have a good tournament year.' I was amazed by how many of the theories I was using in my Kenpo techniques actually worked the same in a sparring situation. Mr. Parker had been saying that for years, but it took awhile for it to register with me.

What was equally interesting was seeing many of the competitors picking up and trying to duplicate what I was doing. I thought that was a great compliment to Kenpo and its founder. The majority of martial artists in the San Jose area around that time weren't used to these principles because there were so few Parker kenpoists in the

area. It wasn't long before that began to change.

Following two years teaching Kenpo in Stockton, in 1970 I returned to San Jose and my study with Jim Trevino. I continued training and teaching until 1972 when I incurred a serious groin pull from overextending my kicks. Coupled with an emotionally painful divorce around that same time, my spirit all but broke and I stopped working out. For the first time in many years life became mundane, and I again became a loner. Gradually the anger I had experienced as a young child began to seep back into my gut.

Steve LaBounty once wisely said to me, "You will leave the art long before the art leaves you," and this was certainly true in my case. While I wasn't physically on the mat, my extended Kenpo family had not forgotten about me. Beginning just a couple months after I stopped training, Bill Yazel, Ray Arguilla, and Doug McLeod would call and leave messages or come by my work or home to tell me that so-and-so was asking about me, and "Why don't you stop in and say hello?" It worked. I eventually dropped by the school, and it was like homecoming. I was deeply touched.

Bill Yazel waited until he saw my eyes widening and sensed my fighting spirit returning and said, "Why don't you bring your gi in on Wednesday and teach the intermediate class, just to stay active." Had it not been for the concern and persistence of Bill Yazel, Ray Aguilla, and Doug McLeod, I may not have returned to my training, and for this I owe these gentleman my heartfelt gratitude.

I received my black belt in 1977 at the Kenpo school in Santa Clara. That night was a dream come true. All the years of training – the blood, sweat, and injuries – suddenly were a thing of the past. While I received my black belt through Jim Trevino and Bill Yazel, my promotion was under the auspices of Ed Parker.

Jim Trevino delivered the ceremonial kick with such force that the wax flew out of my ears. That evening, for the first time, I understood the root of the anger that had plagued my childhood, and in my understanding was able to see that all of us are doing the best we can with what we have at any given time, and that included my parents. That night I found closure to my early childhood of fighting. There was no more blame as I thought of the wise man that said, "Forgiveness is the scent the violet sheds on the boot that has crushed it." As a proud Kenpo black belt I chose to take full responsibility for my life – past, present, and future. And, after all, isn't that what the ceremonial kick is all about?

After obtaining my black belt, I took over the school from Bill Yazel and in 1979 decided to return to competition. I had been out tournament fighting for six years and felt that because I was now the head instructor of a school, I needed to be more visual. In the ensuing months I did well in local tournaments and tallied up a respectable fight record and filled my office at the school with trophies.

A short while after my return to competition, Mr. Parker accepted me as a full time student, and in addition to him coming here to my school to give seminars, I began traveling regularly to Los Angeles to study with him privately.

American Kenpo had for a decade undergone a major evolution and the changes Mr. Parker had made to the system were apparent to me from the first day I began to study directly under him. In contrast to what I had be previously taught, what initially impressed me the most was that Mr. Parker was employing more movement through the use of both hands. In the early years Kenpo was primarily executed through the use of one hand, mainly the right. This was, of course, before Mr. Parker had the revolutionary vision that resulted from when he inadvertently rewound a reel of 8mm film of him performing Kenpo. Upon seeing his own forward *and* reverse motion, he began to revamp the system so that it

incorporated forward and reverse motion through the use of both hands. As many in Kenpo know, this was a major milestone.

This concept clicked and made sense to me. Why was I just using one hand and switching stances in order to use the other hand? Until working directly with Mr. Parker, I didn't understand why I had to practice a technique on one side and then the other side when the "what ifs" were, according to him, already built in. So I began to stay on my strong side and employed two hands rather than switching sides and favoring the use of one hand. As a result I was compounding the action, which made absolute sense to me and improved my Kenpo tenfold.

Apart from learning the physical art of Kenpo, the martial arts instilled in me the self-esteem and self-confidence I lacked as a child. Looking back, I don't believe that many other endeavors could have accomplished in me what karate did. The reason I feel this way is because when I was initially brought to the karate school, I had become a loner and that is the isolated world in which I operated. It is for this same reason that my practice and eventual embodiment of the martial arts worked. I wasn't doing it for anybody else. Even though I worked out with scores of other students and instructors, my persistent effort and ultimate achievement was accomplished

*With Jeff Speakman on the set of "Hot Boyz"*

65

*In San Martin, California with my horses MV Madrigal (left) and Don Edmundo (right).*

*by* me and *for* me. While I have had my share of public and media recognition, this has never been a primary interest of mine. Rather, I have merely seen it as something that comes with the territory.

From the beginning of my journey, what I continued to pursue was the way success at martial arts made me feel inside. Ultimately this positive feeling of self-esteem and self-confidence moved from my internal being and began to be projected in my external world, and as a result I have over the years been able to be a positive influence in the lives and journeys of my students. This is perhaps the biggest Kenpo blessing of all.

Today I have far less fear in life because my training in the martial arts has bridged my physical and spiritual sides. Part of being a Native American, in addition to many other studies I have done, is that I am a strong believer in reincarnation. To this extent I believe we are all immortal. With this as a foundation, I have always been eager to try anything I feel will be beneficial, especially with regard to avenues of education. I have never feared venturing into uncharted waters, and I'm constantly seeking new

adventures because my own journey continues to present me with a new map. To me the excitement of life is to be found in the unknown, and more importantly having the ability to face the unknown with confidence and a positive attitude.

One of the most rewarding legs of my journey has been my experience with horses. Being a Native American I wasn't surprised to discover a spiritual connection to these magnificent animals. To the Indians, horses possess a profound connection to our Mother Earth through their feet or hooves. It is known that through its feet sensing the vibration of the ground a horse can detect the approach of another horse from miles off.

Not long after I started my Kenpo training I became interested in horses as a hobby. I wanted a release for myself outside karate and had dating back to childhood experienced a peacefulness whenever I was around horses. Over the years I've had other hobbies, but nothing so uniquely connected with my Kenpo as my love of horses.

Many years ago I had a conversation with Mr. Parker that touched on much of what I was feeling with regard to a silent communication that my horses and I seemed to share. The conversation was more one-sided, with Mr. Parker doing most of the talking.

The subject of kata led to the discussion of one's inner spirit, and he began to draw a parallel between an animal's natural instinct of self-preservation and that of Man, himself. Essentially, his feeling was that Man has lost his instinctual ability of fighting through centuries of becoming civilized. His point was that in the beginning no one had to teach Man how to defend himself any more than one had to teach a spider or an elephant. While Man has forgotten the instinctive knowledge of how to defend himself, the hard-wiring, although dormant, remains intact. And when we practice the martial arts, these instincts gradually become activated or awakened. He further went on to explain that this occurs because centuries ago the originators of the martial arts obtained the rudimentary movements from closely observing animals such as the tiger, crane, praying mantis, monkey, and so forth. And when we begin (most profoundly in our extended katas) to move like the animals, our instinctual self-preservation centers begin to awaken.

This was a fascinating conversation, and it helped me understand the heightened sense of awareness and communication I was beginning to experience not only with my horses but those of others. What had occurred over the years of studying the martial arts and mimicking the movement of the animal kingdom is that, unbeknownst to me, the breaker switches of my internal self-survival centers were switched on, so much so that the horses I was around sensed this through observing everything from my centered walk (with a tendency to toe-in) to my heightened peripheral vision. As a result my horses began to relate to me in accordance with their instinctual

*At the Monterey Fair Showgrounds in California*

herd protocol.

A major part of this has to do with my ability to anticipate the animal's movement. When the lines of communication were opened, I was able to connect with the unique personalities of each of my horses as I would a student of Kenpo. Because of both my internalized and externalized Kenpo, my horses understand me better. People at the ranch where I am now find it uncanny how I work with horses. To me this has become natural, but when I think back to my conversation with Mr. Parker, I realize this gift I have is a direct product of my martial arts training.

Eventually I became interested in showing horses and found that the relationship between teaching karate and teaching the horse is quite similar. With regard to communicating with the horse, it is both verbal and physical. For example, the horse naturally relates to a rider who sits in the saddle with his legs slightly bowed in and his body over his center (our horse stance). My Kenpo helped tremendously with my center with what professional riders and instructors call "your seat," which they more formally call equitation. I started taking lessons to not only learn how to teach horses, but to ride and compete. My instructor told me that I had excellent equitation on the very first lesson and asked where I learned to do that, and I told him I was in the martial arts. He shook his head with a grin as if this wasn't the first time someone had told him this.

I like to think of myself primarily as a coach rather than an instructor. When I look at all the things I learned from Mr. Parker, I am less concerned about whether I can ever look as good as he did and instead direct my efforts at bringing out the best in of my students. If I am true to my conviction and my art, my greatest hope is that my students will turn out to be ten times better than I was. And if I can speed up someone's growth in the art by showing him a shortcut I have learned from my own many years of experience, then I feel this is a major part of my responsibility. My main, if not only, task is to help my students realize their full human potential. This is what the martial arts is really about. I'm not here to be hurting people, or intimidating them, or beating them up. The martial arts is about the personal growth and development and helping the person next to you, if for no other reason than he is my heavenly brother.

Disraell once said, "The secret to success is constancy to purpose." The one thing that Kenpo has given me that I value above all else is the gift of patience. This is what my study of Kenpo has taught me. To patiently place one foot in front of the other and keep walking. There is no other path to achieving a black belt in this art other than persistence. When I first came to the martial arts I had little or no patience. As a result I was a disciplinary problem because no one could predict my behavior. I was a child without structure or boundaries. The martial arts changed all this. Today I am able to step back and patiently wait for the whole picture to come into focus before making a decision. Because of this, much of the guesswork is no longer a part of my life. Kenpo has given me confidence in my ability to make wise decisions. Before Kenpo, much of my life was a wild crapshoot. Today, in personal relationships and in business, the element of patience has made a profound difference. What a better world this would be for everyone if

somehow each individual and every country could find a way to simply double the amount of time they take before making what on the surface appears to be a rash decision.

The martial arts has given me confidence in myself and in so doing brought me to a better understanding of who I really am. I think this happened gradually as I began teaching others and saw what the martial arts was doing for them as a reflection of what it had already done for me. Eventually I began to see myself in them and recognized that the struggles they were going through were much the same struggles I had gone through years earlier. Guiding them through the process has made me aware that I had already traveled much farther along the same journey, and this gave me self-confidence.

To the new student coming into the martial arts today, my best advice is to shop around and do your homework before deciding on a particular school. The reason is simple. If you are intending to earn a black belt, you are talking about a substantial investment of your time and money. Ultimately the investment is in you. There are a lot of people out there who will sell a new student karate but are not professional teachers. Today prospective students have a great tool at their disposal in the Internet. Because of the worldwide web, it is much easier today to check into a school's credibility and an instructor's background and lineage. In addition, take the time to talk to the school's commercial neighbors and inquire as to how good a neighbor the school has been.

*In the early years with Huk Planas and Craig McCoy.*

Moreover, call the Better Business Bureau and run a simple public records check at the local courthouse. This doesn't take but a half hour and may save you months, if not years, of wasted time and money. Also, the prospective student should be clear about what exactly he or she wants to get out of the martial arts and then choose a school accordingly. Does the student want to study the martial arts for personal self-defense? If so, then he should

seek out a school known for its street and tournament fighting – a school that teaches the more practical aspect of the martial arts. If the student is more interested in an exotic or mystical martial art, then there are many such styles available. And finally, those interested in training should learn and observe the stark differences between the hard, linear styles of the Japanese and Koreans as compared to the softer, circular (but no less effective) styles of the Chinese. The point is, take at least as much time selecting a martial arts school as you would choosing a four year college university because achieving a black belt takes at least as much time as acquiring a college degree.

It is difficult to know with any certainty where American Kenpo is headed in the next generation. My main hope for the future is that Kenpo doesn't get anymore pared down than it already has been and that students and instructors alike will at least concentrate on the base moves of the 154 techniques, along with the underlying principles and concepts. When I watch many of the early kenpoists, their stances are picture perfect, and their movement is precise and clean. No matter what speed they're moving at, you can see

the incredible precision. I personally would like to see Kenpo return to this, and I feel the key is strong basics. The one thing that stands out in my mind over all else that Mr. Parker did is running basics drills.

Most important of all, I'd like to see a renewal to our Kenpo brotherhood. The following comes from a book called *Lessons from Geese*, which contains the basic facts about these wonderful birds. One fact about these animals is that when geese fly in formation and one of the geese gets sick, wounded or shot, two geese drop out of formation to help protect it. Even if the ailing bird falls to the ground, two others will stay with it until it either dies or is able to fly again, at which time they launch out into another formation to catch up with the flock.

The basic lesson is that if we were to have as much sense as these animals and stood with each other during the difficult or bad times, just think how much stronger we could be individually as kenpoists and collectively as a martial arts community. This is what I'd like to see more than anything, and I'm hoping this is what this book will help accomplish.

While there have been so many kenpoists who have helped me in as many different ways along my journey, I would like to particularly thank Stephen LaBounty (my mentor), Bob Liles (my long-standing workout partner), Dian Tanaka-Hoshiyama, Frank Trejo, Jeff Speakman, and Alan Myrtle.

In closing I'd like to end in the same manner as I do every Kenpo seminar where fellow kenpoists have gathered to learn from each other – I always like to thank the one person who brought us together Mr. Parker for had it not been for him we may have never met.

# Sean Kelley
## 6th Degree

*Sean Kelley is the poster boy for the classic wisdom, "It's not the size of the dog in the fight that matters, but the size of the fight in the dog." From early childhood, he became the protector of the downtrodden and disenfranchised, beginning with a small kid he saw stuffed into a locker in the eighth grade to the mean streets of the inner cities working alongside the infamous Guardian Angels. As the youngest Honoree featured in this book, Sean stands at the forefront of the new generation of American Kenpo leaders. For many years he has sponsored one of the most successful Kenpo seminar camps that is held annually in Florida and attracts many highly acclaimed martial artists from all systems and styles, including a substantial number of martial arts legends. A devoted family man and father, Sean Kelley is known for his sound and successful business practices in promoting the art of American Kenpo. A no-nonsense practitioner, he will go to any lengths to continue his study of the art and is often outspoken about ethics and the need for belt standardization. On the lighter side, Sean is best known for his infectious laugh and his overall optimistic nature.*

B ack when I was about five years old I lived in New Holland, Pennsylvania. One of my friends that I hung out with was a troublemaker. His name was John Dellinger. I'll never forget how he and this other kid held me down and literally tried to stuff a worm in my mouth. It really blew me away because not only did it gross me out, but also I felt like I was paralyzed because I wasn't capable of doing anything. At that age I had an older brother who came to my rescue, but I knew that with the passage of time he wasn't always going to be around to protect me. That was the first time I remember having this feeling of wanting to learn how to protect myself.

Six years passed, and then in 1973 the Bruce Lee craze took the country by storm. I was around the age of twelve when I first got started, and it was after seeing

*Sean Kelley with his prized Bruce Lee memorabilia collection.*

73

*Conde's Lightning Fighting Team, with coaches Francisco Conde (top row, third from left) and the PKA U.S. heavyweight champion Sam Shockley (top row, forth from left)*

"Enter the Dragon" that I was jazzed. Together with my best friend, I couldn't get enough of anything having to do with Bruce Lee. We actually got to the point that anything and everything from posters to magazines that had Bruce Lee either on the cover or a short paragraph about him, I had to have at any cost. So as a kid I became a huge collector of Bruce Lee memorabilia, including some of the first books written about him, 8 X 10 photos, and even those mock postage stamps that were actually glossy photos of him, all of which I still have, incidentally. So I have to credit Bruce Lee and his movie "Enter the Dragon" for sparking my initial interest in studying the martial arts.

Later I read about the mystical side of karate and began thinking that the people involved had superhuman powers. Although I had never witnessed any supernatural feats, I personally had a bizarre experience when I was in the fourth or fifth grade. Many have found it hard to believe,

but it's true. I hadn't yet started the martial arts and was living in Connecticut. One afternoon some friends and I were meandering through an old creek bed that had an adjacent 12-foot waterfall. As I walked through the water, which was up to my knees, I suddenly stepped on a snake. This snake was not only huge but I assumed it was deadly. It scared me so much that in a panic I actually ran up the waterfall to the top! Ask me how I did it, and I couldn't tell you to this day. Did I do it? Yes, I did. Over the years I've been told by other martial artists that this was an example of the incredible power of ch'i.

Apart from the existence, imagined or otherwise, of the mystical side of the martial arts, what intrigued me about karate was I felt it would help balance out my small stature. I was aware of the size difference and felt that having the upper hand of karate would put me on a level playing field in a physical confrontation and would make me feel more self confident, and it definitely did that.

*Sean and Papo Pagan in 1984*

Around that time, my father worked in Reading, Pennsylvania, selling life insurance. Up the street from his office was a karate school, and the person who owned the school was George Dillman, who taught Okinawan kempo. My father drove me up there, and I can still remember walking up these big stairs and seeing at the top of the staircase two huge posters of George Dillman with Muhammad Ali, and George Dillman with my hero Bruce Lee.

I was a student of that school for about a year and received a yellow belt. It was a hard style and most of my instruction came from one of the black belts named Jack McGuire, a former Marine.

I trained obsessively from the first day. I would get up early in the morning and train, then upon returning home from school, resume training, pausing only to do my homework and eat. Besides the official karate school up the street from my father's office, I had converted my family's basement into what felt to me like a Shaolin temple, and many of my friends who were also studying karate would come over and work out. At the age of thirteen I had become an official student of karate, which really excited me.

Eventually some of the kids at school became intrigued by my new image. When I was in the eighth grade, there was a mammoth kid named Theodore, who went by the nickname "Teddy." In sharp contrast, there was another classmate who had a bone disease that stunted his growth. As a result he stood less than four feet in height. Our school had lockers that lined the hallways, and Teddy used to literally put this kid inside a locker and shut the door. Everybody laughed, and it was funny for awhile, but to me the gag lost its humor when it became routine.

I knew the young kid who was being put in the locker. He was friendly and got along with everybody. At first he joined in the laughter, but then one day I could tell it wasn't funny to him anymore, and he was growing increasingly embarrassed and even verging tears. I walked up to Teddy and said, "You know, you're not funny anymore. Let's not do that anymore."

He glared at me and replied, "Who the hell do you think you are?"

And I said, "Well, today I'm going to be your worst enemy if you can't find a way to pick on somebody your own size." That's exactly what I said to him, as he stared down at me from his six-foot-three, 300-pound frame and then turned and walked off.

It wasn't long before word got around school that Teddy wanted to come after me and fight. Two days later I ended up telling him, "Ted, for whatever it's worth, if you're going to come after

*Ed Parker is given a Guardian Angels beret.*

me, I'm not that little kid you can keep putting in the locker. I hit back."

Minutes later I whipped his butt and threw him through a glass trophy display case. The incident landed me in the principal's office. Thankfully, the principal knew I was the type of person that didn't instigate things, although he also knew that no way was I going to be a welcome mat for somebody else.

From the first day I began to study the martial arts, I had the drive to become a black belt, because to me back in those days the black belt was the ultimate. I'd seen martial artists who were phenomenal athletes, and the things they were capable of doing with their bodies absolutely astounded me. I'd always been a tenacious person, and so from the get-go I just kept telling myself that if I stayed with it I could be a part of those people.

My first instructor, the former Marine, was every bit the drill instructor when he stepped on the mat. Often the lesson was short and sweet or, in the case of sparring, bittersweet! The first day the class was to learn how to spar, the instructor suited us up with all this protective gear and then proceeded to literally pound

the living daylights out of every one of us. He had a mindset of "I'm the instructor, and you're the student."

Like me, he was short in height, and I was amazed by his ability to generate the explosive power that he did. And that went far with me. I only attended one class a week, but I'd practice everything that was taught to me religiously. The instructor came to know my dedication, and he knew that when I returned the following week, I was going to show him that I wasn't wasting his time. I wanted him to know that throughout the rest of the week I was going to make the best lesson out of what he had just taught me. That's how much his teaching meant to me, and I felt empowered and enlivened every time I'd walk out of that school. I was a part of something special, and it felt like I was suddenly a foot taller.

My dad finally signed me up in a local karate school that was run by Francisco Conde. Compared to Dillman's school, it felt as if I had leapt from the frying pan into the fire. Two words summed up my new school - militant and rough!

Mr. Conde was Filipino, born in Manila. He had spent his life in the military and had been a POW for years. Because of this, he held loyalty in high regard, and to say his training was strenu-

*As a Guardian Angel, Sean teaches
self-defense to the elderly.*

*Sean Kelley with Billy Blanks.*

ous would be a vast understatement. He taught only one direction in fighting and that was straight forward. This school was definitely a fighting school. We had our shinai, one of those sticks, and you couldn't talk unless you were given the command. Looking back, I realize that the experience of Mr. Conde helped to instill a sense of formality and respect in the dojo setting.

Being five-foot-four and often training with martial artists who towered over me, I began to feel the need to see if what I was learning would really work in a more realistic, spontaneous setting, and so in 1976 I entered my first tournament that was sponsored by George Dillman. The division I entered was the junior-teen division. Back in those days tournaments didn't have the breakdown they have today for height, weight, and belt. Junior-teen was by age. It was a heck of an introduction to tournament fighting. Here I was a white belt teeing up with green, brown, and black belts. Although I received my share of black eyes and standing eight counts, after awhile I needed something more than what some referred to as karate tag, and soon sought out kickboxing. This was a different rodeo entirely, complete with a boxing ring and an opponent who had every intention of tearing my head off.

My first fight was in Easton Pennsylvania at a gym that was right down the street from Larry Holmes's main office. The kid I fought came from a school called the Red Dragon. Seconds after the first round bell sounded, I broke this guy's nose. There was blood all over the place, and the sight of it scared me and made me realize that I had no idea of my own strength. The referee instructed us to keep fighting, and my opponent's condition only worsened. Finally, I asked that the match be stopped, that this kid was finished. Awhile later, after my heart had stopped pounding, I sat in the bleachers and thought 'Wow!' It had its roller coaster effect  that continued for several years. I felt it was a good experience, and ultimately I did prove to myself that, as Dave Hebler says, I could deliver the weapons to the targets.

One of the greatest moments in my martial

*Sean teaches his children's class.*

arts journey occurred quite by surprise. I was teaching for Mr. Conde at the karate school and continuing to pound bags and sweep the mats when I learned that Ed Parker was coming to town to be a guest at Mr. Conde's 20th anniversary tournament in Baltimore. Around seven o'clock one evening the phone rang, and Mr. Conde was on the other end. "Sean, get your uniform and meet me at the school right away."

I grabbed my gi and headed out the door lickety-split, thinking that Mr. Conde needed me to fill in and teach a class. Upon my arrival, however, I found myself face-to-face with Ed Parker who was standing on the mats wearing his gi and tenth-degree black belt.

Come to find out, I was being tested along with a handful of other students for my black belt. It was the longest test I ever remember in my life. Nonstop. After it was over, Ed Parker laughed and said, "You guys need to be at the Internationals! You guys all should call yourselves the Tasmanian devils!"

To this day one of my most prized possessions is something Ed Parker later wrote to me about how he remembered my furiousness and

that he felt I had good speed. To him the elements of speed and fury, coupled with my small stature, would be highly deceiving to an opponent. I guess on a personal level those were my fifteen minutes of fame because Mr. Parker was, and always will be, a hero to me.

After I was awarded my black belt I remember wearing it and being overwhelmed. It amazed me how suddenly I was a black belt, and what came to mind was, 'You know something, now I've got to BE a black belt' knowing that everybody was now looking at me differently. They expected my Kenpo to have instantly jumped to a higher level. My kick just couldn't be a kick. It had to be sharp and practically flawless.

As my training progressed I began to notice a heightening of a particular element of my personality. Maybe it was related to the time when I was five years old and those older kids held me down and tried to stuff a worm in my mouth, or the memory of the kid with stunted growth who Teddy routinely placed in a locker. Whatever the cause, I began to take a personal interest in people I noticed being bullied and appointed myself as the one to tell the bully that his behavior was

*Sean Kelley with Master Larry Tatum and Grandmaster Dave Hebler.*

totally uncalled for, just to let him know that there are people in this world who will stick up for others.

On a physical level I feel that the martial arts have definitely sharpened my senses to the degree that I am able to quickly detect potential danger. In 1986 I became involved with the infamous Guardian Angels and began traveling with them around the country. It has been a valuable experience, and I have learned a lot from the organization's founder Curtis Sliwa.

This man is fearlessly tenacious and has cheated death dozens of times. What he has instilled in me over the past fifteen years is a belief in people's right to live in a safe and sane community, and that there are still more good people in this world than there are bad. As black belts we have a moral obligation to help the weak because as leaders we breed leaders.

There is much talk today about war in distant parts of the world, but the truth is we are at war in our own communities, particularly in our inner cities. As a martial artist I feel I have an advantage because the art allows me to reach out and change people who are on the verge of destroying their lives and the lives of others.

Over the years, Curtis Sliwa and I have gone into potentially explosive drug-infested, gang-oriented areas where life is cheap. I've been shot at and trapped in the middle of inner city riots. If it

were not for the physical skills and heightened perceptual awareness taught to me through the martial arts, I wouldn't be here today.

My work with the Guardian Angels has taken on a sense of civil and moral responsibility that goes beyond my immediate family. It's rewarding to know there are people in my neighborhood who know of my involvement with the Guardian Angels and see me as a community protector. I'm not saying I'm Superman, but I am one who will intervene if I encounter an ongoing crime. It's dangerous, but it's the life I've chosen. I guess I've felt this way since I was a child, and I've made a point to do all I can to help stop the rampant violence we have all around us. It's sort of like an old saying I have – Instead of pointing fingers, let's lend a hand.

On a social level, I feel that Kenpo and the martial arts have greatly improved my communication and confrontational skills. When I was in the tenth grade in high school, I still remember how I purposely chose to fail a course because the teacher asked me to stand in front of the class and give an oral report. The thought absolutely terrified me, and I refused the teacher's request. She told me if I didn't give the oral report that I'd fail the class, and I said, "So?" Over the years Kenpo has helped me confront other personal demons. Unquestionably Kenpo has been a formidable ally.

Once a black belt there is no turning back. The day I strapped that black around my waist, I took on a responsibility for the rest of my days. Most importantly I feel I need to continue to grow. I can't sit down on my journey. I have to keep moving. It's for that reason that I still have an instructor, and I think there's the problem with a lot of black belts today that once they become a black belt they no longer feel they need instruction. But it's like anything else - when you get a driver's license you go out of your way to prepare for it. You make sure both hands are on the wheel. Your seat belt is fastened and you make sure you don't forget to use the turn signals and set the emergency brake so that you don't fail the test.

But once you get your license, how many people forget to fasten their seat belt and use their turn signals and drive with one hand on the wheel and never set the parking brakes? To me having a driver's license is a privilege, and so is having a black belt. It's a privilege, and in order to maintain its integrity, I feel I have to maintain my training and continue to learn.

I still attend seminars and gladly travel long distances if I know there is someone teaching from whom I can learn. I think it's important to be well versed in other fighting disciplines and not blind myself in one area only. That would get quite stale, so in the spirit of keeping my interest high, I open myself up to learn anything I feel is useful. If nothing else, expanding my martial arts horizon enables me to learn about the weaknesses of other styles and systems. On a more local level, for several years I've sponsored a Kenpo camp in Florida that has become very popular and is attended by many prominent instructors of all systems and styles.

As to my own personal Kenpo, I feel fortunate to have found Richard "Huk" Planas, who has taken me under his guidance. Many in Kenpo today refer to Huk as the "encyclopedia of Kenpo," and I've greatly appreciated both his knowledge and the wisdom he imparts from years on the mats.

He has a saying that I, as an instructor, truly value. He told me once that "The way you got your rank is how you will give your rank.

*Master Richard "Huk" Planas and Sean Kelley.*

If you got it easy, you'll give it easy. And if you got it hard, you'll give it hard."

That has always stuck in my mind. As the owner and head instructor of a karate school, I often receive the stock phone call that asks two questions – (1) how much are karate lessons? and (2) how long does it take the average person to become a black belt? I'll never forget the answer to the second question that Huk Planas gave at a seminar. He said that *average* people don't get black belts. It's the other people who do. And it's true.

My personal journey would not be complete if I did not mention Lee Wedlake, who taught me how to communicate the art of Kenpo by using clear illustrations, choice vocabulary, and the mindset of an airline pilot who runs down his check list of details before takeoff. He has tutored me in understanding the symbolic meaning of the gestures done with the hands in the Kenpo salutation that show the theme of the Warrior and Scholar and how they unite in combat. From day one I've been a warrior, but to be a scholar one must be intelligent, critical to detail, and compassionate to those less fortunate. I am thankful to have trained under Lee Wedlake and truly feel he is a great carrier of the Kenpo Flame.

One aspect of being a black belt that I find surprising is that there is no differentiation between amateur and pro. What I mean by this is that once an individual receives his black belt he assumes three hats – one, he can own a karate school;

*Sean Kelley with karate champion Bill "Superfoot" Wallace.*

two, he becomes in the public eye a credible teacher; and three, he is a professional in his field. Whereas in football, basketball, and boxing, for example, one has to start out as an amateur before he can consider becoming a professional. But in the karate league of black belts everybody's a professional. There's no such thing as amateurs. And I think that if that was ever stated, boy, we'd have a whole lot of people changing their view toward being a black belt. Personally, I think we need to distinguish between amateurs and pros. I mean, in American Kenpo we do have ten degrees of black belt.

I am often asked what advice I would give the new student coming into the martial arts? The first advice I offer is don't get into the martial arts because you feel it will give you ammunition to go around and beat everybody up. Second, educate yourself because the technology that's out there today is quite extensive. Take the time to research the differences between all the martial arts styles and systems, as well as their curriculums. And three, when you go into a martial arts school ask lots of questions about

the instructor. Who is he associated with? What is his background and lineage? Then decide on what you are giving him and what you are getting in return. And it has nothing to do with price, because you make money, it doesn't make you. I feel that whatever someone charges for what they have to give you, it's only going to benefit you. To me it's an investment. That said, when you reach a decision to move forward, do it with dedication, and the end result is you'll be pleased with the turn of events.

I thoroughly enjoy teaching children, and I tell parents that any time they can get a child into the martial arts at an impressionable young age, do it. It will help with their learning and social skills that so many are losing to the computer and video industries. As a karate instructor who regularly deals with the public, what I have encountered is an increasing number of people becoming introverted. They hide behind screens and hardly ever leave their homes. And the health issues are phenomenally getting worse.

The greatest gift that I have received from

the martial arts is my beautiful wife Lesley, whom I met while she was training at another school. We have been married for four years and have three wonderful children – a son named Sean from her previous marriage, as well as a daughter Alex, also from her prior marriage. In addition, Lesley and I have a daughter together named Victoria. These children mean the world to me, and I honestly believe that my years in Kenpo have made me a better parent, mainly by helping me to develop patience and the ability to nurture.

Over the past decade I feel that Kenpo has gotten better because the teaching has greatly expanded. When Mr. Parker was alive, he was the only person teaching in-depth Kenpo seminars. Since his passing, however, a substantial number of students who were close to him have come out and are now doing seminars. As a result, I think there are more people studying American Kenpo today than when Mr. Parker was living. I see this as a positive note because all of these people have been an integral part of the American Kenpo system. Mr. Parker never said American Kenpo was *his* art. It is <u>our</u> art. And it has taken many people to help put the complete system together. I still have goals I want to reach, and my experience has shown me that the best guarantee to achieve that end is to continue to reach out to as many people as I can and share knowledge.

*Sean with his wife Lesley.*

*The Kelley children Alex, Victoria, and Sean.*

# Sigung
# Stephen LaBounty
## 9th Degree

*Arguably one of the most widely known kenpoists, there are many in American Kenpo who say that Steve LaBounty is the true definition of the "Warrior Spirit." Having initially come to Ed Parker with a background in judo and a black belt under the Tracy system, Steve went on to distinguish himself in American Kenpo. Both a national and international fighting champion, he is widely sought after on the seminar circuit where he is legendary for his "fighting drills." Mr. LaBounty has spent many years in police work and is active as a Law Enforcement Consultant and trainer. Having reached a level of excellence in the "yang" side of the martial arts, he spent years pursuing an education related to the opposite "yin" side, and today, as a practicing Acupressurist and Herbalist, teaches seminars in bodywork to martial artists. At times outspoken, he is always willing to support events and causes he feels will bring the brotherhood closer, such as the annual "Gathering of Eagles" held in Las Vegas. A friend to many in the Kenpo community, he is often sought after for his wisdom and experience and was one of the founding members of the American Kenpo Senior Council.*

I began my martial arts journey in Fort Worth, Texas in 1958. My father had died, and my mother was desperately looking for a way for our family to get out of the projects where we lived and were looked down on as trash.

My father had abandoned us before he died, and because of that I harbored a lot of anger toward him. Although I was known around the projects as being confrontational and was quick to challenge anyone who got in my face, I never liked the term tough.

I had thrown in with the wrong crowd, and my mother decided it would be a good idea to take me to the YMCA in Fort Worth and enroll me in a swim class. The swimming class was all right, but I soon gravitated to a judo class, which

I had always thought was interesting. Earlier I had taken boxing at the YMCA, but it seemed that everybody I worked out with had long, skinny arms and could beat the stuffing out of me from a distance.

My Japanese judo teacher was a black belt named Sam Namajura, and I instantly fell in love with his art. The way I perceived black belts in the late fifties was that they were something I could never be. Besides the mystery of being Asian, Mr. Namajura exuded this incredible power in his throws.

Judo was my first encounter with close-quarters battle, and I took to it naturally. I was large and could handle the inside exchanges.

Nevertheless, in my first few months I was

*Karl Maldern and Robert Wagner with students of the San Francisco school after shooting the pilot of "Streets of San Francisco." Steve LaBouty is on the far right.*

thrown all over the place. Everyday I went home sore and frustrated, but I loved it. After sixteen months, I tested for and was promoted to brown belt.

In 1961 I traveled to San Francisco to take a job as a fry cook and upon my arrival immediately began looking for a judo school. I checked the phone book and found three karate schools listed. Figuring that a karate school would be able to guide me to a judo school, the following afternoon I found my way to a Tracy Brothers Kenpo Karate dojo located on Ocean Avenue. I observed the class for awhile and was approached by a red-headed, bespectacled wiry man, who asked me what I wanted. I told him I was interested in studying judo, and he replied that they didn't teach judo but asked if I would be interested in taking karate. By this time I was pretty well enthralled by what I had been watching, although I didn't have a clue as to the meaning of Kenpo.

After recuperating from an injury, in early 1962 I began training in earnest with Al and Jim Tracy, although Steve Fox was my primary instructor in the beginning class. I became hooked on Kenpo from the very beginning. I didn't know exactly why, except that I knew it was important to me and that I was miserable when I couldn't practice.

I moved up the ranks fairly quickly. Back then there were no colored belts, but I did go from white belt to three brown tips (today the equivalent to blue belt) in about eight months. Soon thereafter Al Tracy asked me if I would teach some of the beginning classes, and I proudly accepted.

After studying karate for about a year, I noticed that my choice of friends began to change. In those days the drug of choice was alcohol. It was considered manly to drink, and my friends and I drank quite often. But as I trained more in Kenpo and began to experience the same soreness I had when studying judo, I curtailed my late night drinking. So I lost some friends, but I gained new ones, too.

*On the set of the pilot "Streets of San Francisco."*

street fighting. Eventually the tough karate guy image wore thin, and I did all that I could to discourage everyday people from viewing me in that light. Martial artists were another matter, however, particularly when it came to the tournament arena. Aside from this group, I personally prefer being a nonentity and let somebody else be top dog. This hasn't always worked. There are those who insist on pushing buttons, and over the years I had some confrontations that should have never happened and still haunt me to this day.

It wasn't long before Al and Jim Tracy were on the move again and opened a fourth school in Santa Rosa, California. By this time I had tested for my black belt in San Jose and passed. They asked me if I wanted to run the Santa Rosa school, and I accepted.

The Santa Rosa school was actually a health club that the Tracys rented to conduct karate classes. Not long after I began managing the place, one of the first students who walked through that door was a former Marine with a burr haircut and about 220 pounds of fire and brimstone. His name was Tom Kelly. Tom stayed with me, and probably is still with me to this day almost four decades later, although his black belt ranks after first-degree came from Ed Parker.

My life had become very hectic. I was commuting between the San Jose and Santa Rosa schools and also working as a fry cook. What I really wanted was to teach karate full time. As fate would have it, around the time the Santa Rosa school began to fail, an old classmate of mine named Paul Olivas called and said that he'd opened a school in Fresno and asked if I'd come help with the teaching. A week later I packed up my stuff, my wife and newborn and moved to Fresno.

Not long after I had been promoted to brown belt, Al and Jim Tracy opened a school in San Jose and took me down there to help with the teaching. In the ensuing years many kenpoists got their start at that school – Tom Connor, Ralph and Ben Castellanos, Jim Trevino, Harvey Clary, John Sepulveda, and others. The place was a hovel of a dojo without a back door or bathroom. But we were proud to be there, and I was proud to be their teacher.

It was around this time that I sensed that my image and reputation were growing faster than my skills. While I knew I could fight and could take and throw a good punch, I also knew, having been in karate and judo for some time, that there were some very lethal people out there walking the streets. And I also knew from being raised in Texas that there were people who were masters of

*International Karate Championships (year unknown) fighting the late Will Norris.*
*The man crouched on the right is the late J.T. Will.*

I always believed in the effectiveness of Kenpo, but in the street fights I got into, I abandoned the textbook Kenpo early in the fight. Everybody thinks that most fights last three to five minutes, but they don't. In reality most fights last less than forty seconds.

One thing that martial arts did for me – Kenpo in particular – is that they taught me continuity of motion and economy of motion. To round out the package, judo gave me balance. I never felt confident enough to do some of the kicks I had learned in a real confrontation, and later in my study tailored my Kenpo to foot sweeps and using a back leg thrusting front kick.

For awhile this bothered me, until one day I recalled the wise instruction of Ed Parker and, to their credit, Al and Jim Tracy, who often said that everybody will find his own niche and strength in the martial arts. Inevitably this proved to be true in my case. Over the years I often would start off primarily with a block, or might even take a punch, and then would reverse punch and go right for the takedown. I don't think in all the fights I had as a kid growing up and coming through my years of judo, Kenpo, and being a law enforcement officer for twenty years that I ever completed a self defense technique.

The Fresno school was without a doubt a rough-and-tumble, no-holds barred school. Long before the vast majority of the Kenpo world was doing it, we began fighting in every tournament we could get to.

I made most of my reputation in the arena of tournament fighting, which in the era of the six-

*Answering a question for a inquisitive black belt at Sierra Camp.*

ties and even the early seventies was very prestigious. Not only was the tournament circuit the place to be seen, but it was also an arena in which to hone one's skills.

Fighting was my forte. I loved to fight, and I always wanted people not to want to fight me. I wanted to be a thorn in their side, somebody they had to get by. The harder it was, the better it was. This was what I hung my reputation on, and I had a fair degree of success. I won three heavyweight championships and a couple of third places at the International Karate Championships; two third places, one second place, and one first place at the heavyweight California state championships. Moreover, I had victories in many smaller, out-of-state tournaments where I really made my bones, if you will.

Over the years I had gone to several Ed Parker schools and had met him through the state championships and the International Karate Championships. He was kind enough to give me some much needed business advice and, as a result, in 1966 I decided to bring my school

under the IKKA banner and asked Mr. Parker if I could be his student, and he accepted.

During the late sixties making a living running a karate studio was difficult at best, and the Fresno school began floundering. After handing the school over to my partner, I opted for teaching in judo clubs and my backyard and living room.

In April 1968 I was in San Francisco competing in the state championships when I received a call from Ed Parker. He had heard that I had lost my school in Fresno and suggested that I come see him in August at the Long Beach Internationals. His welcome and caring voice was music to my troubled ears.

That August I hitchhiked from San Francisco to Long Beach. It took fifteen hours to get there and I arrived hungry and with seven dollars in my pocket, and five of those dollars were earmarked for my tournament entry fee. I didn't have the guts to tell Mr. Parker I was broke and spent my first night sleeping under a hotel bench that overlooked the ocean.

The next day I went to Mr. Parker and asked if I could take a shower in one of the trophy rooms. He was always keen on reading people, and I decided to tell him of my sorry condition.

"You need to come to work for me, Steve," he said with a fatherly tone. "I'm opening a school in the Valley, and I'll need a manager."

That night he put me up in a room and made sure I had something to eat.

Six months later, after tidying up my affairs in San Francisco, I took a Greyhound bus to Pasadena, arriving with all my worldly possessions in a duffel bag and thirteen dollars in my pocket. I slept in the Pasadena dojo for a week, and washed all the towels and cleaned the place up to earn my keep.

Finally the day arrived that Ed Parker drove me out to the new school that was located in the Valley off Topanga Canyon. It was wonderful, a real dream come true. Not only was I now working directly for Mr. Parker, but I would no longer have to drive eight hours to get my lessons and could now be updated with all this new informa-

*Sigung LaBounty with Jui-Jitsu Professor Tyron Crimi, 9th degree.*

ization in order to scientifically attack the problems that arise with an ever-burgeoning art and society that require the individual to be far more accomplished and educated than he was four decades ago when I began my journey. The problem, as I see it, is that far too many kenpoists abandon the visceral – the gut or hand's on art – and in sharp contrast end up working out in sterile technique lines.

One aspect of fighting that helped me considerably was kickboxing, which arrived on the scene in the early seventies. Like many others, I donned the gloves and the primitive protective equipment and stepped into the ring. It was painful and often bloody, but I loved it because it was more authentic. And when the grappling craze came about it, I found that to be equally authentic, though I was too old to compete.

Tom Kelly and I were fortunate because around that time not only was Fresno a big judo area, but we had students from Cal Poly and Fresno State who were collegiate wrestlers. And if these guys got hold of you, they'd wrap you up in a Gene LeBell second. So we made a point of doing a lot of wrestling in our school, mostly to defend against the wrestlers, which wasn't always successful. Cross training is sorely needed in the martial arts, and the student who does not heed this advice stands a lesser chance of prevailing in a real confrontation.

The point is, this general curriculum led to the development of a strong visceral art – an art of understanding. And believe me, nothing beats physical contact in clearing away any doubt the student may have or for putting the student on a path to resolving that doubt. For better or for worst, over the years this approach has been my trademark.

Two decades ago, I began signing my name Stephen LaBounty, student of Kenpo. The reason

tion of 32-techniques per belt.

None of my students have ever been raised gently. I believe that the first thing a karataka (if one wants to use the classical Japanese term) or kenpoist must learn is how to be an ironworker, which is a term that is directly attributed to me.

An ironworker is one who has to learn the gross motor movements of strength, power, economy of motion, and continuity of motion. He has to meld the metal and stick it into the fire. He has to stand next to the fire and get burned. Sometimes he must risk being consumed by it. Ultimately his martial art will be made stronger with each blow until it has reached its zenith.

Having graduated the ironworker stage, the student progresses into the watchmaker, or intellectual, stage. Today there are many watchmakers in the Kenpo community. Many of them you wouldn't recognize their names. Others you would. Over the years, I've seen people change and become more of an intellectual practitioner and less of a visceral practitioner. As a result, they've lost some of their cognition as to what the martial art really is.

I'm not saying it's bad to be intellectual. Every practitioner needs to have a degree of intellectual-

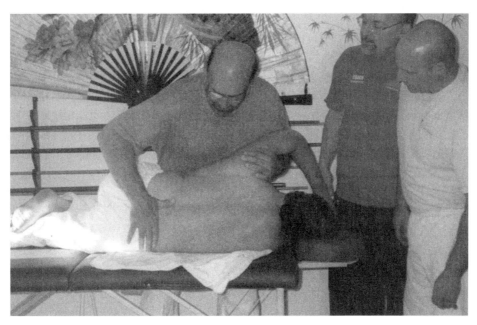

*Working the Healing Arts.*

for that is because I am a student of Kenpo, as well as the martial arts. I've returned to our jujitsu roots and worked out with a jujitsu master – a ninth-degree named Dr. Tyron Crimi. In my study I have seen some of our old time moves updated and are remarkably effective. So I always want to be a student who is eternally learning. I study Escrima and some of the blade arts. I'm a firearms instructor and have been in live combat. Over the years I've entered into these arenas to make me more of a consummate warrior. Those are the physical, yang aspects, or elements, of my art.

My art also has a yin side. Back in the early seventies when I had my school in San Francisco, I was fortunate to have my path cross that of a gifted Japanese woman named Helen Fujimori. Besides holding a black belt in judo, she was a skilled acupressurist and practitioner of shiatsu. Not long after being introduced to her, I took her six-week course in acupressure and shiatsu and soon began traveling upon yet another leg of my journey.

Acupressure opened up for me not only some of the Asian mysticism but also mysticism in the sense that it was a mystery to me at that time. Additionally, acupressure taught me how to recov-er from injuries and illness, how to relax the body, and how to focus. I had always been terrible at focusing because I always seem to have a thousand things on my mind.

After studying all I could about shiatsu and acupressure, I began looking into traditional Chinese medicine and Chinese herbs. I even began to make my own hand medicine – dit dat jow and yak jow, and a few others. Unfortunately, in those days I was still fighting in tournaments and still trying to get to one more tournament, and so I wasn't the most diligent student. This has changed dramatically over the past ten years, and I've made myself an acupressurist, a massage therapist, a body worker, a healer, and a western herbalist. The main reason I have done all this is because there is an inner (yin) warrior within me that I wanted to nurture as well.

I found that balancing the yin and yang sides of my martial art has taken me to a level I had never known before. Today I feel that this balance is so important that any student who studies with me to obtain a black belt is required to have a basic human anatomy course. In addition, the student must take a course in basic shiatsu and be certified in CPR. I think it is vitally important that my students understand how the heart works

*Team graduation from Hatian National Police Swat Team, Basic training, Port-au-Prince, Hati*

and how the body builds and repairs muscle tissue. This is basic first aid aimed at supporting and protecting the student's body, which is, after all, what transports and projects his Kenpo forward.

In 1996 I was part of a ten-man American police team that traveled to Haiti to develop a SWAT team for the Haitian National Police. Over a six-week period, this poor country that is heavily subsidized by the government had chosen 105 people to try out for this SWAT team. We graduated sixty, which is high. I taught Kenpo at that course, and these Haitians particularly enjoyed the techniques and kept asking for more. Many of them had seen some TKD because they had been with the U.S. Army and Marine Corps, but they liked the close hand combat and particularly loved the knives, which I demonstrated using Short Form Three. I'm very proud of those Haitians who under great adversity worked so hard to become skilled in high-risk police work. My fellow team members became as impressed as I did with the dedication of the Haitian students and their desire to do something positive for their impoverished country.

As I age and my body begins to betray me, I occasionally hit a stale part in my training. I know only one way to turn this around, and that is to walk away from it and do something completely different. There is an axiom in business. When business is bad and things are slow, go out and paint the front doors a different color. Put something new in the windows. Offer something different. It's the same way with my art. Change. I walk away from it temporarily. I give myself a chance to breathe, and then come back at it and hit it again. The thing is I have to go through it. I can't go around it. I can choose to avoid it, but there will always be that burr beneath the saddle that's going to bother me that I didn't accomplish this one part of my training.

I've had a lot of physical injuries over the years. I've had my nose broken four times in martial arts and twice in police work. I've had my hand busted twice, and my knees are very bad. I've had some health problems that have slowed me down, and I can't train like I used to. But I do train. I modify my art and my physical training. Instead of running, I walk as far as I can. I do a lot of Escrima work. I do a lot of bag work. I grapple with my jujitsu friends, although I am

*Kenpo principles in action, a crossover into law enforcement.*

very limited in what I can do. I practice my forms four days a week and try to go through the techniques twice a month. I shadow box; I work out with my students when I can and when my health permits it. I can't quit because there's no reason to quit. While I have to modify my art, I still have fire. I can still hit hard, and I can still keep going. The art has kept me young and mentally alert, and it has made me want to live at times when there was a possibility that I wouldn't. And that is how I have dealt with physical injury and depression.

I am often asked the meaning of my title Sigung, which was given to me by one of my advanced students Gary Swan of Universal City, Texas. Essentially, Gary did this in an effort to classify a stratum of seniority in the National Chinese Kenpo Karate Association, of which I was its first president. The word Sigung means "older/elder worker" and in the English language is most commonly referred to as the word "Grandfather." Apart from titles, a belt to me is recognition from a higher power, if you will, of an achievement that the practitioner has attained through meeting specified requirements. One's desire should speak of his innermost feelings, his wounds and his battles, as well as his victories and defeats. Unfortunately this is not always the case.

Moreover, a half-dozen times a year people ask me when am I going up to tenth-degree, probably because I am one of the most senior members in today's Kenpo community. I'll never be a tenth. I believe that tenth is a completely different rank than my ninth, and I don't think it is attainable by me. I realize we have about a dozen tenth degrees out there. I'm not besmirching them. To be a tenth an individual better have a lot more going for him than just time in the art or reputation or a bunch of clichés or a web site. I recognize one true tenth, and he passed away in 1990.

Lastly, I do have a LaBounty rule that says that once a student stops training in earnest, then he is no longer allowed to wear the rank that I gave him and must retire. This also applies to anyone who continues to train but can no longer, by choice or otherwise, perform all the material in American Kenpo that is the equivalent of his rank. This student is also asked to no longer wear that belt rank.

I think that had I not studied the martial arts and stuck with it, I'd be dead or ended up a drunk. I certainly would have been through several marriages and in all likelihood would have early on abandoned my faith, which, praise God, I haven't. Most importantly, I would have not met the incredible and highly valued friends I have today, nor would I have been able to sit at the foot of so many wonderful teachers, which again is why I continue to be a student. The martial arts have kept me from getting harmed while a police officer, many times. During serious illness the warrior spirit came up in me and would not let me succumb to the illness. Whenever my life has been in danger, the fire in my belly refused to allow me to be a victim without a fight. Moreover, the martial arts gave me the opportunity to look deep into the philosophy of humankind and ultimately come to the realization that there is a reality to the martial arts. One cannot just have an intellectual, posing system of movement and call it "martial" arts. This reality base is the lifeblood of my art. This is what the journey thus far has done for me.

I think my strength in Kenpo is my ability to

bring out the warrior spirit in people. Seminar and camp promoters often suggest that I be brought onboard to teach the history and my fighting drills. While I have substantial knowledge of the katas, sets, and techniques, I have never been one who has just been enamored with techniques and forms without the practical element of fighting. To me the student (and teacher) has to fight to make the material work.

So my strength is to be found in the warrior spirit. To stand before one's opponent with the confidence in knowing that the guy who is about to attack is going to be in for the fight of his life. Even if I was to lose the fight, my warrior spirit will survive.

I miss my teacher, Ed Parker, and often told him when he was alive that he was my surrogate dad. I told him not once but many times that I loved him and thanked him many times for taking such good care of me. He brought me in to run his school in Topanga Canyon, and even after it was failing miserably, he never gave up on me, like my real father had done so many years before.

In conclusion, my son once asked me how I'd like to be remembered in the karate community, and I told him that most of all I'd like to be remembered as a volatile warrior. Volatile in the sense that I believe that I went forth with the training. I never let the training come to me, but rather I attacked it. Sometimes the student has to find it. It may mean getting their head kicked in, and it may mean going out there and fighting a Tom Kelly, Bob White, Mike Pick or Scott Loring or someone of that caliber, and having them pound you for awhile, but the student will learn. Volatile in the sense that I was confrontational when it came to defending the art and those friends of mine who are in the art. I also want them to remember me as a warrior who not only sought the outer strength, but the inner strength as well because I strongly believe that rather than be an empty shell of a pretty uniform and pretty techniques and high kicks, we need an inner power to make this art viable.

*Taken after my elevation to Kudan (9th Degree) in 1994*

# Grandmaster
# Dave Hebler
## 10th Degree

*One of true "Old Timers," Dave Hebler was in 1962 the fifth student promoted to black belt by Senior Grandmaster Ed Parker, and was the first to be promoted to seventh-degree black. As one of the originators of the annual International Karate Championship held in Long Beach, California, Dave Hebler personally developed the set of rules for the first and many subsequent IKC competitions, and served as a Director of the IKC for twelve years. As President of Ed Parker's International Kenpo Karate Association for a number of years, Dave was instrumental in developing the basis of the ever-evolving curriculum of the Ed Parker American System of Kenpo. From 1972 to 1976 Dave was one of several personal bodyguards of Elvis Presley, and as a member of the "Memphis Mafia" his primary responsibility was the protection of Elvis and his family. Dave co-authored the best selling book Elvis, What Happened? and also Self-Defense for Women, which is a 350-page instruction manual on rape and assault prevention/protection techniques. Dave is the founder and executive director of the Original American Kenpo Karate Association with member-affiliated schools in seven states and Honduras.*

I was raised back East in Massachusetts. Along with my parents, my four brothers and I lived in an apartment in a tenement building without hot water. During the winter we would stuff rags under the windows and doors to keep the snow from coming in, and I had to go down to the cellar for heating oil. The cellar was a scary place with no lights and all sorts of things that went bump in the night. We didn't have a phone or television, and if we wanted to play, we invented the game. And if we wanted to go somewhere, we walked or hitched a ride because our parents didn't own a car. Despite being poor, we grew up happy, and that had a whole lot to do with our loving and stable parents.

After I reached adulthood, I served in the U.S. Air Force and was stationed at March Air Base in southern California. It was here that I first learned about the martial arts from a group of Hawaiian guys whom I met at the air base. They had a small group that worked out twice a week, and through a series of events and introductions I ended up training with them for a brief period. Upon my discharge from the Air Force, I planned to attend Pasadena City College, and one of my Hawaiian friends suggested that I look up a man named Ed Parker who had a Kenpo school not far from the college.

In the summer of 1958 I walked into Ed Parker's Kenpo Karate School in Pasadena. The

*In Kentucky with kenpoists (from left) Huk Planas, Lee Wedlake, Gil Hibben, Ed Parker Jr., Sean Kelley, myself, and David Stanley.*

only person there was Ed Parker, who within five minutes walked me onto the mats to show me a few moves. I never saw anyone move like that and was utterly awestruck. I mean the whole place shook. His combined power, grace and coordination was astounding, and I came to the conclusion right then and there that, whatever it took, I wanted to move with that kind of authority. Everything about it struck a chord in me. If I could put one word on the experience, it would be empowerment.

My first lesson was not with Ed Parker but with Jimmy Ibrao. Jimmy walked me onto the mat as he said, "Okay, come on out here and let's see what you've got."

I wasn't sure what he meant but soon got the point.

"You mean you want me to throw punches at you and stuff?" I asked.

"Yes. That's exactly what I want you to do," Jimmy said nonchalantly.

"You know, for real? You want me to try to hit you?" I replied.

"Just do your best," he said as he dropped into a casual stance. "Just come at me and mix it up."

The next thing I knew he was on me like white on rice with an endless barrage of strikes. Moments later I was up to my knees in floor looking up at Jimmy.

"I don't ever want that to happen to you again," he said with a smile as he helped me up.

I eagerly agreed, and by the grace of God and many years of Kenpo training that humiliating and horrifying experience never did happen again.

When I began my initial training, it was around the final days of the advanced class before Ed Parker split with Jimmy Woo. The ones I remember in that class were Rich Montgomery, Jimmy Ibrao, Rick Flores, Chuck Sullivan, and an individual named Bones.

After Ed Parker's split with Jimmy Woo, I was kept a step ahead of the students coming behind me. On Mondays and Wednesdays I would teach the beginning and intermediate classes, and then I would have a class from the Old Man that basically would feed me the material I would be teaching in the weeks to come. Along with Chuck Sullivan and Sterling Peacock (who later changed his name to Matt David), this is the way the teaching worked for some time. Later, Jim Grunwald and

Danny Inosanto began to help with the teaching, mainly taking over the Tuesdays and Thursdays classes.

Looking back, I think that after the split with Jimmy Woo the Old Man had to scramble because he didn't have any instructors and was forced to teach on a limited scale. Initially Chuck Sullivan was teaching more than I was, but it wasn't long before I was teaching all the adult evening classes on Mondays and Wednesdays in Pasadena, and that lasted for seven years.

The training was different back then. Today I conduct workshops all over the country, and a portion of the workshop I like to call a "return to the fifties," which is essentially fifteen minutes of a typical class. It doesn't take long before one by one and in groups they start to fall out, looking like they're verging a heart attack. One or two always remark, "I can't believe you really trained like this."

And I tell them, "Yeah, only back then I used to do it with you, and now I just yell. And the other difference is that forty years ago we'd do it for an hour-and-a-half, and it didn't stop. It was like this all the time."

"God, I wish we could train like that all the time," someone would invariably say.

I'd laugh and remark, "No, you don't. You only like it now because it's different. But if you had to do this every day, I guarantee you you wouldn't."

If a student gets nothing else from my workshops, I tell them what I have learned from experience, which is that they must reach and maintain a level of expertise with the basics, and if they don't do that, they won't be able to do anything. Period. Every quality instructor I know thinks the same way. While I can admire the athleticism of those people who do katas to music and all that, I am personally not deluded into thinking that such displays are the basic fundamental backbone of the art, regardless of style. Without having down solid the fundamental basics, the martial artist is going to be totally ineffective.

After Ed Parker's split from Jimmy Woo, I realized that to some I had practically overnight advanced several rungs on the Kenpo pecking order, although I wasn't focused on this. Instead, I thought of Kenpo in terms of us, collectively and individually, doing something pretty important.

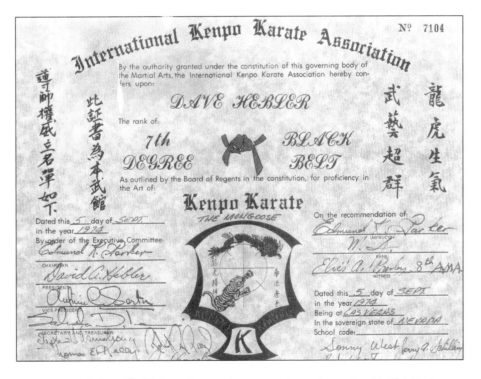

*My seventh-degree black belt certificate, unique to some because it was signed by Elvis Presley*

*Training with Elvis in Memphis, Tennessee, 1974*

Exactly what that was I didn't know, but it surely was something very powerful and seemed to have a life force of its own.

I never spent any time thinking about my "karate image" or lack thereof, although I do recall an incident in the early sixties that focused on this. I was working as a test engineer during the day and teaching karate classes at the Pasadena school at night. Four of my fellow engineers, who knew nothing about the martial arts, had taken to teasing me about my Kenpo training and teaching – often disrespectfully. In those days I weighed all of 155 lb. and didn't scare anyone.

One day I told these guys that I had heard enough and invited them to come and watch our advanced class. They accepted and a few days later came to the studio just as the advanced students were walking onto the mats. My coworkers' first surprise was when I casually walked to the front door and locked it. An hour-and-a-half later the four of them sat in the waiting room as white as sheets and speechless.

The next day at work the kidding and dissing stopped completely and never resumed. Although I wasn't looking for personal respect from these coworkers, they certainly treated me with a large measure of respect from that point on. And I have to admit – I liked it.

It is true that back in the late fifties and up until the mid-sixties, the advanced class was not open to viewing by the general public and the door was locked.

In light of the fact that today the lion's share of the knowledge contained in the American Kenpo system can be bought by anyone in video tape series, it seems strange to some that back in our beginning we did not allow the public to view any of the advanced material. One of the reasons we did this is because some of the beginning students who had early on watched the advanced class found the intensity troubling and had remarked, "Those guys aren't doing that to me! No way anyone's getting me in that class!" and then quit. The other reason the door was locked was because back then knowledge was guarded, and it was not unusual for a brown or black belt to stop working out if a lower belt wandered into the school, and he wouldn't resume until the student had left. Back then we were pretty sensitive about giving out material to students before their

*2001 with Bill "Superfoot" Wallace*

time. The main reason was we wanted to make it a privilege in the sense that the student must earn the right to learn brown belt material. And the way they earned it was they busted their butts through the ranks to get up to brown belt material, and later black belt material. None of the instructors ever wanted to make it easy. I know I didn't. I wanted my students to earn every inch of their belt just the way I had. Anything less would rob them of the pride they deserved on the day they strapped on that brown or black.

I still remember with clarity the day I made first-degree black. It came from out of the blue, although I later realized that both Ed Parker and Chuck Sullivan were actually testing me for about a month prior to the actual promotion.

When Ed had me kneel to receive my black belt, I didn't want to take it because it was the same color as the belt around his waist, and I didn't feel that I was worthy to wear a belt that was the same color as Ed Parker's. What is important to note is that back then black belts did not wear red stripes (or tips) on their black belts. I'll never forget Ed Parker's response, which was that as my instructor, it was his place to decide when I was worthy of a black belt, not mine.

I remember thinking that now I had to live up to the honor and challenge of being a black belt, and my dedication was cranked up a notch or two. I was absolutely determined not to dishonor that black belt and all it stood for.

I have had several hurdles to get over in Kenpo and as many valleys and speed bumps. The biggest, however, has been the fact I have no visual depth perception because I am blind in one eye. When I was a kid, I owned a BB gun and so did my close friend. One day we had a war, and the last bit of vision I had in my right eye was that little glimpse of copper just before it struck.

I tell this story today not because I'm looking for sympathy, but because of the horror of not being able to see. When I'm talking about self-defense tactics, one of the things I say to people is that if I cause you not to be able to see, I promise you that my battle with you is over.

The other reason I tell this story is that I can

*Florida Kenpo camp 2000. Back row from left to right: Lamar Fike, David Stanley, Richard Planas, Karl Lindroos, Curtis Sliwa, Gil Hibben, Dave Hebler, Al McLuckie. Front row: Lee Wedlake Jr., Sean Kelley and Martin Wheeler.*

punch at someone's face full power and full speed and miss them within a fraction of an inch. The point I want to make is not that I'm that good, but that I overcame a debilitating handicap, and through my training in Kenpo I feel that I've accomplished this in an exemplary fashion. Ironically, through years of practicing Kenpo, I react faster to things coming at me from my blind side than I do on my sighted side.

One particular arena where my handicapped vision was put to the test was when I worked as a personal bodyguard to Elvis Presley. If there was a group of people that wanted to talk to him at an airport or standing outside a hotel, and the atmosphere was casual, he would talk to them. In this regard he was much like John F. Kennedy, who used to frustrate the Secret Service agents by wandering into crowds. Like JFK, Elvis loved his admirers and didn't mind walking right into the midst of them. This made watching his personal safety all the more difficult because it meant that I had to watch all these strangers at extremely close quarters and with a heightened peripheral

*"The Elvis Experience" show that I produced in 1999*

vision. Everything was a potential red flag from the sudden shifting of one's weight to someone sliding his hand into a coat pocket.

The problem was further compounded because the crowds would increase exponentially every twenty seconds. I mean it was amazing to me how quickly a dozen adoring fans could suddenly turn into a hundred! These people would literally come out of the woodwork.

Another aspect of Elvis was that many of his fans gave new meaning to the word fanatic. Out of love and worship for Elvis, things would happen like we'd be moving along, and Elvis would have a scarf around his neck and someone in the crowd would suddenly attempt to grab it and nearly rip his head off. Besides wanting a piece of his clothing, many just wanted to touch him, and that could snowball into a major problem when the herd stampede mentality took over, often without warning. Most important of all, along with Elvis's other bodyguards, I had to protect him without hurting anyone because rarely did anyone ever truly want to harm Elvis. As a result, not only was my handicapped vision constantly honed, but also my work as a bodyguard for Elvis called for a highly versatile Kenpo.

If I could offer one piece of advice to new students it would be that whether or not you know it, you are absolutely unique in the entire universe. I came to that realization one day when I was looking at my sleeping three-year old daughter when it suddenly occurred to me that out of all the three-year-old girls who resided on the face of the planet, I could single her out from a crowd of ten or ten million as being the only one I call my daughter. Equally amazing is that out of all the adult men walking around the planet, I was (and still am) the only one this little girl would point to and say, "That's my dad." It was at that moment that I realized how unique we are ourselves, to each other, and outside ourselves. And everyone who breathes life shares this same uniqueness, which includes his or her special experience with Kenpo. To this end you are highly valued in this art, and you have every right, if not duty, to persevere to become the best martial

artist you can possibly be. Establish worthy principles and be a credit to you and to the art. Above all else, do not ever give up. You are worth it.

Probably the single most controversial and contentious subject in the American Kenpo community today is rank. Maybe this is because there is no single authority to certify and authenticate rank in the Kenpo world and, for what it's worth, I don't think that there ever will be. Besides, who would run such an organization if there were one? Even our great founder, Ed Parker, couldn't bring all of Kenpo under one roof, and frankly I don't think that he ever wanted to.

If someone started training with me with the primary interest of attaining high rank, I would attempt to redirect this person's goal to the attainment of all of the personal benefits that the conscientious student can acquire from the study of Kenpo.

Rank is certainly an indication that some of these skills and personal benefits have been attained, but the lessons to be learned and the benefits to be gained never stop and, viewed from this perspective, the journey never ends.

In 2000 I spent a terrific ten days doing workshops in Pennsylvania with Sean Kelley and Bill Wallace. Bill and I had a brief conversation about rank, and he said something that I believe is truly profound. He said, "I have no quarrel with those who carry high rank around on their belt – they're the ones who have to wear it." Truer words were never spoken.

Since the passing of Ed Parker, I've gone on to establish my own organization through which I teach primarily what I refer to as Original Kenpo. Many people ask why I focus on the original Kenpo of the fifties and sixties rather than the new Kenpo of the seventies to the present. It is because there's a part of me that thinks a fifteen-move technique is really a mini-form. When I see the original material with extensions tacked on the end of it ad infinitum, some of which is pretty good incidentally, I am inclined to look at it from the perspective of its street realism. And I understand the fascination with developing a series of movements and continually hungering for more

*David Stanley (Elvis's step-brother) and myself.*

material. After all, that's why the original kenpoists broke away from Ed Parker and trained with Jimmy Woo. They wanted more material, at least that's what they said. Unfortunately, the hunger for more material has grown into a hunger for more spectacular material. It's not that I'm against more spectacular material, it's just that I'm from an era where students paid far more attention to the timing and power aspects of simple combinations of movements.

The other area in our Kenpo community that I feel needs to be revitalized is the sense of honor and commitment that I and many of us experienced in the fifties and sixties and that a person's word was his bond. My first studio was with Jim Thompson, and we were partners on a handshake for eleven years. I don't know that one could do that nowadays. While in my travels in and around the Kenpo community I am gratified by the degree of respect and commitment that I see, I wonder if it's really an ingrained part of the Kenpo world like it was back in the early days.

Back then we were tight, and we knew we could count on each other. And it didn't matter what part of the country I was in or what time of the day or night. If I had a problem, all I had to do was call the nearest Kenpo school and say, "Hello, my name's Dave Hebler, and I'm a Kenpo black belt who needs some help." And invariably the first words I would hear on the other end of the phone were, "Where are you?" and ten minutes later a carload of help would arrive to help with everything from a flat tire to a barroom brawl. I'd like to think that things haven't changed over time, but sometimes I do wonder.

A couple years ago I quit my casino job as a 21-dealer so that I could return to teaching martial arts on a full-time basis. I had worked at the casino for six years as a dealer. It was a good casino with good customers and everyone liked me. I could have stayed there forever. When my coworkers learned that I was quitting, they were astounded. Many of them asked why, to which I replied, "You know it sounds kind of arrogant, but one of the reasons why I want to get back into the martial arts world on a full-time basis is that in that career I sign autographs." My coworkers looked at me, and I looked back and continued, "Now let me explain that so I don't sound like a jerk. I literally do sign autographs, but the underlying reason is that that's the kind of respect I get for the effort I produce in that world, which begs the question when was the last time any of these card players asked for your autograph when you dealt them a blackjack? You never got that kind of respect. So can you blame me for choosing the martial arts world over this one?"

Looking back over the past forty-four years, I know that in some primal way that from the first day Kenpo was important in my life, and I knew that I was going to be a better man if I would just commit and train as hard as I could for as long as I could. And as things turned out, I was right. The best thing that has happened to me is that I gained a sense of self-confidence. I put myself on the line, and I think I was tested and I for the most part received passing grades. And because I was successful at something on a personal basis

*Gregg Townsley and I opening day (June 2001) at our new studio American Family Karate in Hillsboro, Oregon.*

that was pretty darn difficult to do, I ended up with a sense of realistic self-confidence about me. I knew I could function against heavy odds. I knew I was competent. I knew I was able to move with authority and some skill. And the only way I came to know this is I learned how and I was tested, and I think that translated over into the rest of my life into mostly positive terms. Not long ago an old friend observed in me what he called peacefulness. I'd like to think that what he sees is a man who today is comfortable in his own skin and doesn't have to prove anything anymore. Kenpo has given me this.

What do I wish for the future of American Kenpo? Most of all I'd like to see us all work on bringing back a sense of unity. When I speak of unity, I'm talking about unity of purpose. I am not advocating that all American Kenpo stylists should join together under one giant organization. To the contrary, it is my strong belief that all Kenpo stylists should remain loyal to and support their own schools and associations to the best of their abilities. I believe that the real strength, and indeed the very foundation of American Kenpo, is at the local school level and through the dedicated people who work and train there. Like America, our strength and our

greatness comes from our rich diversity. We just need to channel all of our great talent and our energies toward projects of mutual interest and mutual benefit.

Over the many decades under the leadership of our great founder Ed Parker, we created one of the finest martial arts systems ever created by anyone. Sadly, Ed Parker is no longer with us, but his legacy lives on in every Kenpo student who continues to travel along the journey. In the spirit of betterment of our collective body, I feel it is our responsibility to see that our local schools, our associations, and American Kenpo in general grow and prosper to the mutual benefit of all of us. Beyond that, we also need to reach out to all of our martial arts brothers and sisters, regardless of style or system, in the true spirit of friendship and co-operation.

In closing I'd like to share what may well be my most special moment in my Kenpo journey. It occurred one day when I realized that I had made a positive change in someone else's life.

Many years ago in the days when we were still teaching in degrees of pain, it was standard operating procedure to physically crank on every student in the school. The thinking was that if you could survive the training, you'd have no problem coping with a street situation. Good, bad or indifferent, that's the way it was back then.

There was this one student that I taught in those days who was the single most uncoordinated klutz that I have ever seen. He literally could not walk and chew gum at the same time. He had a problem tying his own shoelaces. For almost two years this guy trained with me and apparently the only thing he could do was take a lot of punishment. And boy did he take punishment. It seemed he was everyone's punching bag. But he never missed a class. Finally the day came when I decided to promote him to orange belt in spite of the fact that he could barely get through Short Form One. When I promoted him to orange belt, he was so shocked he couldn't speak.

I didn't see him again for a few weeks when he showed up at my office door one day to ask if he could talk to me. I said, "Sure. What's on your mind?"

"I wanted you to know that I know that you just gave me this orange belt," he replied, then held up his hand to keep me from speaking and continued. "Dave, you know that I try to do the best that I can. I never miss a class and I also train and practice at home. I work hard at this, but in spite of everything I just can't get it. There is something about me that for some reason keeps me from being able to get it. Anyway, I wanted to tell you that I'm moving back east and won't be able to train here anymore. I also wanted to tell you that I will treasure this orange belt the rest of my life, and because you believed in me enough to give it to me, I have found that now for the first time in my life I can look people in the eye."

WOW!

Well, we said our farewells with tears in our eyes, and I never saw him again. Maybe he'll read this book and recognize this story and get in touch with me again. I sure hope so. If not, God speed, my friend. You gave me so much more than I ever gave to you.

# Bryan Hawkins
## 6th Degree

*After having spent time in wrestling, boxing, and gymnastics, Bryan Hawkins began his martial arts training in 1976 in Shotokan karate. He studied Sho Shu and then began his Kenpo training in 1980 at Ed Parker's West Los Angeles studio. In December 1987, as a third-degree black belt, he became manager and head instructor of the West L.A. school where he remained until 1991. He was a Kenpo technical advisor working with Ed Parker for the film "The Perfect Weapon" and has since worked as an advisor on numerous television projects and theatrical releases. Mr. Hawkins owns and operates Bryan Hawkins Kenpo Karate Studio in West Los Angeles and heads up the martial arts program at various private and public schools in southern California. He is President of the United Kenpo Systems, a martial arts organization with affiliates throughout the United States and Europe. He is also co-founder of M.A.P. (Martial Arts for Peace), a non-profit organization whose goal is to help teenagers at risk, and runs a summer Kenpo Camp for kids from all styles and systems. Bryan is an avid hiker who lives with his wife Melissa and their two young sons in Granada Hills, California.*

I grew up with nine brothers and sisters in Paradise, California, a small gold rush town near Modesto on the banks of the Tuolumne River. My parents had their hands full with ten kids to feed, clothe, and send to private schools. My mother worked sixty hours a week as a nurse. My dad worked even longer hours as a federal meat packing inspector in the stockyards. With little parental supervision, my brothers rode herd on me and had no hesitation about giving me an occasional whupping.

My two role models at the time were my dad and grandfather. In addition to being in tremendous physical condition, my dad was wise, scholarly, and devoted to his family. My grandfa-

*Gene Autry had nothing over young Bryan.*

*My family, from top left: sister Rebecca, sister Kathleen, sister Julieanne, brother Scott, my mother, me, my father, brother Mark, sister Lorraine. Front from left: sister Margaret, youngest brother David, and brother Jimmy.*

ther was a warrior. He'd served eighteen months in WWII as a gunner on a battleship. After his tour ended, he worked Shore Patrol and used to regale us kids with stories of his fights and exploits.

By the time I was fourteen I was an angry kid with a horrible temper and got into fights all the time. After a fight one day in school I sat on the bank of the canal wondering why I kept getting into brawls. After much thought I realized that I never mixed it up with smaller or younger kids. My opponent always had to be a challenge. It was almost as though I thought of myself as a dragon slayer. Or maybe there was a demon inside of me that had to be controlled before I did some real damage.

I skimmed a few stones into the canal and thought, 'If I could beat anybody on the planet, I'd feel confident enough so that I wouldn't have

anything to prove by fighting. I'd be able to walk away from a fight and not feel like a coward.' The solution to my problem dawned on me. What I needed to do was get the best training in fighting and then no one would mess with me and I'd have no reason to mess with them.

I'd started acrobatics when I was ten and joined a wrestling class when I got into high school. By the time I graduated I was one of the best on the team. But I still had a temper and anger burning inside.

One day a wrestling buddy and I got into a fight with five adult cowboys. We did what we'd been taught to do: shot in, picked two of the guys up and slammed them to the ground. We mounted them and were getting ready to throw a few punches when their three buddies attacked us. I was beat up pretty bad and my buddy landed in the hospital. I learned from that experience that

*1983 at the West Los Angeles school.*

desk and karate pictures on the walls. A big man, half-Caucasian and half-Japanese, and about my size, 6'3", came in and introduced himself as Dana Carter. My first impression was that he was a hard guy, like my wrestling coaches. He told me to come back at six that evening, but I just sat down on a couch until a few instructors showed up. After that first lesson with one of his black belts I was hooked because the moves felt so natural to me.

Later I learned that Carter had been trying to get into the *Guinness Book of World Records* by jumping over cars that were speeding at him. The last time he tried that stunt he clipped the top of a little MG sport car and messed up his feet.

Carter taught hard-style Shotokan using a very aggressive straight-line attack and some kicks that nicely filled in some of the gaps in my wrestling and boxing. Unfortunately, he closed the school about a year or so after I started studying.

A few months later one of my sisters told me about a karate school across town called Moore's ShoShu Karate where she'd been taking lessons for about a year. I went in and learned that ShoShu meant "The Way of the Animal" and was really a combination of Kenpo and White Crane Kung fu.

Al and Ralph Moore, operators of a chain of karate schools in northern California, owned the studio. Steve LaBounty, one of Ed Parker's first black belts, had been their instructor. Jim Peterson ran the dojo for them.

ShoShu employed circular motion with parries, blocks, trapping and some weapons techniques. In a sense it was very much like the Kung Fu I had seen David Carradine do on his television series and I liked it.

I trained there until I was seventeen and earned a blue belt with a green stripe. I loved the workouts, but I was tired of living in small towns that were like dust bowls. I had relatives in Los Angeles and decided to visit them. When I told Mr. Peterson I was planning to go to LA he said the next best karate system on the planet was Ed Parker's Kenpo Karate with schools in the LA

wrestling was ineffective when it came to a real fight so I began taking boxing lessons in a local gym. Six months later I decided that although boxing covered some of the gaps in my fighting arsenal, it still left a lot to be desired.

Like most young guys at the time I was a big fan of the TV series "Kung Fu." I'd watch David Carradine as an itinerant Buddhist monk in the Old West defeat multiple attackers with all sorts of strange mystical moves. No matter what the odds were he always prevailed. Many times I thought, 'If that's martial arts, that's for me.'

One day as I was riding my bike to boxing practice I noticed a karate school had opened up in the neighborhood. I went in and looked around. There were a lot of trophies on the office

for awhile and thought, 'This is what I've been looking for, something that will fill in all the gaps.' I signed up for lessons.

I worked out in the morning classes and all day Saturdays. In between workouts I took business classes at WLA City College. But, I was always focused on trying to get back to the studio in time to get into a class.

I began to bond with the other students at the studio and found I had another family, my Kenpo brothers and sisters. Some of them were actors and stuntmen and they wanted me to get into their business, but I had to earn a living. To make ends meet I got a job driving limousines. That gave me time off to study Kenpo six or seven times a week with some of the senior black belts. I lived for those workouts, even had restless nights dreaming about Kenpo and waking up with it still on my mind.

In the spring of 1983 the school's head instructor told me to prepare to test for my brown belt. I'd never met the legendary Ed Parker before the day of the test. When I learned he would be one of the judges I was a nervous wreck. Even the black belts were nervous. Someone shouted, "He's here!"

I ran into the bathroom and had the dry heaves. When I came out, Ed Parker was standing in the hallway tying his belt and just looking around. He wasn't trying to look mean or impressive, but he was awesome. I swear to this day that I've never been that scared or nervous because he was like a super hero to me. I was finally in the presence of the man who gave Bruce Lee his start and I was thinking, 'This guy came before everybody else.'

I was so nervous that I got on the mat and started doing Long Form Three and damn near ended up out on the street. When it came time for me to fight and Mr. Parker said, "Move," I hit my opponent with a back knuckle and knocked him down. When he tried to get up he couldn't get his feet under him and had to be literally dragged off the mat. My next opponent was an ex-police officer who had hurt his back in a motorcycle accident and was working as Hugh

area. He mentioned Ed Parker's name with reverence.

One of my uncles in LA got me a job driving trucks while I looked for a junior college I could afford. I'd been in LA about eight months when one Saturday afternoon in 1980 I stopped at a red light on the corner of Santa Monica and Sepulveda Boulevards. I saw an enormous mural of two karate men in fighting stances painted on the side of a commercial building with a large pagoda sign that read, "Ed Parker's Kenpo Karate."

I parked the truck and went into the studio. No one greeted me, so I walked down the hall to the mat area and looked in. I saw a student fighting two opponents and thought, 'Now, that's real.' Another student was practicing staff techniques and another whirled nunchuckas. Others on the mat were doing katas. Everyone was doing things I'd never seen or imagined before. I watched them

*Early 1988 as the manager of the WLA school.*

Hefner's bodyguard. When I heard "Move" I did a full spinning leg sweep and took both his feet out from under him. He landed flat on his back groaning in pain. He had to be dragged off the mat, too.

My final bout was to be with John Corrigan who was testing for his fourth-degree black. I was certain he would kill me. The head instructor was about to call him up when Mr. Parker said, "No that's enough."

Apart from the injuries I'd inflicted, it was a wonderful evening ending when Mr. Parker kicked me. A solid kick. I had a bruise from his toes on my stomach for a couple of weeks.

But I still hadn't decided what I wanted to do with my life. I'd hit a speed bump in my training. In the summer of 1983 I went home and worked at landscaping. It was great being with my parents and siblings still at home. After about three months, however, I realized I missed my Kenpo family. I returned to LA and got a job driving limousines. I'd been sleeping in my car until the school's head instructor slipped me a key so I could have a place to shower and change clothes. I was twenty-three years old and at a crossroads in my life. All that was really working for me was my Kenpo training. Then on June 21, 1984 a major step in my Kenpo journey happened when Mr. Parker awarded me my first-degree black belt, which marked a major turning point in my life.

One of my buddies at the studio was Jeff Speakman who I'd met in the fall of 1983. Jeff had studied a Goju style. After class we'd hang out and have some beers. One day he asked me about the limos I always had parked in front of the studio. I told him I was a driver and he said he was looking for a job.

I introduced him to the company I was working for and they hired him. About a month later I quit the company. I borrowed and scraped together enough money to get my hands on two used limos. I put my own company together with Jeff and me as the primary drivers which gave me some income and time to train.

In 1986 the Bel Air Hotel offered to take over my limos. I was more than happy to give them the keys, but as part of the agreement I drove for them part time. One day the hotel manager who knew I had been studying karate told me that some of their high profile guests asked for occasional light bodyguard service.

A few days later I was summoned to one of the exclusive bungalows and knocked on the door. When I was shown into the living room I recognized actor Don Johnson, not from his hit television series "Miami Vice," but from years earlier when he played an Indian boy on the old "Kung-Fu" series. Don Johnson couldn't believe that I remembered him wearing that awful jet-black wig.

We sat down and started talking. He said he'd already interviewed twenty other guys with impressive resumes.

"I understand that you do martial arts," he said.

"I've studied several hard and soft styles but mainly I do Kenpo."

"Kenpo?" Johnson said, and suddenly lit up. "Ed Parker?"

"Yeah," I answered, not knowing if that was good or bad.

"He was Elvis's instructor, right?"

Johnson slid forward to the edge of his seat and like a little kid and starting asking questions about Mr. Parker and Elvis. Half an hour later he

*My sister Lorraine, who became one of my black belts.*

stood up and shook my hand like he was pumping water from a well. "Can you start tonight?"

For the next year I continued driving limousines for the hotel and working as Don Johnson's West Coast bodyguard. His business manager later told me that the second Don heard the names Ed Parker and Elvis Presley, I had the job.

Those were pretty heady times for a sod kicker from the farm country. Driving limousines for the rich and famous exposed me to a lifestyle that soon began to affect my timing and speed on the mat, and as a result I eventually adjusted my work so that it was more in line with my Kenpo training.

*With Jeff Speakman and our students on the set of "The Perfect Weapon."*

*1992 seminar at John Sepulveda's school. From left, John Sepulveda, Bob Liles, Dian Tanaka, Vintin Koklich, and myslef.*

The first major turning point in my life occurred in September 1987 when the head instructor and manager of the WLA school went off on his own, and Mr. Parker offered me the job. By then I was a third-degree black belt. Ironically, that was the same time that Don Johnson offered me a full time job as his body-guard for more money per day than Mr. Parker paid for an entire month. I thanked Don and told him that I wanted to do karate for the rest of my life.

"I understand," he said and hung up the phone.

We haven't spoken since.

I went to Mr. Parker's home in Pasadena every week for three years beginning in 1987. Every time I walked up his driveway I'd have butterflies fluttering in my stomach. I was even nervous when I knocked at the door.

For the first half-hour we'd discuss business related to the school. During the next half-hour I could ask him anything I wanted to.

"It doesn't matter if it's martial arts related, business, whatever – you ask and I'll answer," he said.

Thinking back on it I realize that one of the reasons I so much loved and respected Mr. Parker was because he combined all the elements of my father and grandfather: He was physical and scholarly.

The way Mr. Parker approached and resolved problems always inspired me. Even now when I am faced with difficult situations, I try to imagine what he would do.

Thursdays I joined a mini-group class, really a semi-private lesson at Mr. Parker's home. The day I went in for my first lesson, Mr. Parker had Pat Salantri spread-eagled against the fireplace. He was demonstrating the technique called "Taming the Mace" and was whipping Pat with a barrage of blows to his back like a whirling dervish. I was speechless as I watched. After Mr. Parker finished the lesson he was called away to the telephone.

Pat came over to me and said, "Did you notice anything about that demo?"

"You mean about Mr. Parker whacking you?" I asked.

"Yeah. He never hurt me," Pat said.

I knew what he was referring to. His former instructor sometimes beat on him pretty hard.

115

Like Mr. Parker, Pat believed that you don't have to hurt someone to teach them. As Mr. Parker often said, "If you can hit, you can miss."

When Mr. Parker died just before Christmas 1990 I felt desolated. Soon after his funeral I told one of my students, Jay Hill, that I was thinking of giving up karate and going back to full time bodyguard work or opening up a dojo of my own.

Jay sat down in my office with me. "I've taken karate classes for the last ten years in a dozen karate schools and studios around the world," he said. "When I came here and took your class, it was the best. Kenpo is your passion. You were born for this. Follow your dreams."

The second turning point in my life came when, with Jay's business plan and some loans from students, I opened up a studio over a chiropractor's office in Cheviot Hills.

It was slow going at first until word got out that I was back in business. Many students and instructors from the WLA studio joined me, and from Sacramento Bob Liles, my senior, came onboard.

In May 1995 a young couple came into the studio and signed up for classes. The woman's name was Melissa Swiderski. She was blond and everything I had ever envisioned as the perfect woman for me. The man she was with soon quit studying, but Melissa kept coming to classes. One night she broke her hand while working out. I called her at home to console her and found out that, much to my delight, she was available for dating.

The third turning point in my life was our marriage eighteen months from the day we first met. Although I loved teaching and was enjoying life, I'd gotten complacent and had settled into a routine. After Mr. Parker's death, my passion for the art of Kenpo dwindled. I was only paying lip service to the things I had always lived by and taught my students: "To be the best you possibly can be," "Learn new things every day," and "Continually strive for excellence."

Melissa inspired me to rekindle the fire and helped me grow emotionally and spiritually. She gave my life the directional harmony it needed. That is to say all my energies focused in one direction with very specific goals.

We now have two young sons, and I awaken each morning eager to go to work. The demon, or whatever it was inside me when I was younger, has been under control for a very long time. As Mr. Parker told me years ago, "Mastery of Kenpo

*With my sons Jonathan, age two, and Frank, four months.*

*Group class with Ed Parker. There are six Honorees present (Dian Tanaka, Skip Hancock, Mike Pick, Jeff Speakman, Frank Trejo, and myself.) Can you find them?*

can only be achieved by self-mastery," and he quoted a samurai maxim that states, "A man who attained mastery of a art reveals it in his every action."

There are many golden keys to success in the martial arts. One of the things I try to drill into my students is another thing Mr. Parker once said. "I learn something new from my art every day of my life. Almost everyone you meet has something to teach you. Hang on to what you know and don't be embarrassed by what you don't know. Rather than fight or argue, learn."

I tell my young students, particularly on their belt tests, that they're on a journey to develop their mind, body, and spirit. The main reason they are studying Kenpo is to learn self-defense and self-discipline. If they can properly combine those two things, everything else in their lives will fall into place and they will conduct themselves with honor and integrity both on and off the mat.

The concentration required to study Kenpo carries over to every aspect of my life. Kenpo compels me to constantly attempt new and difficult things so it is also a source of learning. The studio is a place where we can learn a great deal in

a short time about who we are and how we react in the world. For that reason anyplace where martial arts are studied is traditionally known as, "the place of enlightenment."

Kenpo can't truly be learned without having a profound effect on the student because Kenpo requires as much use of the brain as physical ability. Every principle touches on two relationships that are paramount in my life: how I relate to others and how I relate to myself.

Like anything else in life that one endeavors to achieve or excel at, whether it is basketball, mathematics, Kenpo, or linguistics, one must practice! As the philosopher Aristotle said centuries ago, "Our habits make all the difference!"

Ed Parker left his students a legacy. It is important for us to remember his enormous contribution to the martial arts, both technically and spiritually. Those of us who were lucky enough to study under him must remain united as a group and bring Ed Parker's Kenpo System into the 21st Century with honor and accountability.

My own journey was not easy, but it was always fun. I thank God every day of my life for allowing me to take it with Ed Parker as my guide and mentor. I'd like to thank the following martial artists, without whom my own journey would not have been possible: John Corrigan, Barbara Hale, Tony Martin, Mike Pick, Lex Sensenbrenner, Jeff Speakman, Mohamed Tabatabai, Larry Tatum, Frank Trejo, and George Waite. I am especially thankful to my Kenpo Dad, Howard Silva, for being the guide and mentor along my journey, and to Bob Liles for being the friend I so much needed, especially after Mr. Parker's death.

# Professor
# Bob White
## 9th Degree

*Passing up a professional baseball career at a young age, Professor Bob White has contributed to the art of American Kenpo for over thirty-years. On the tournament circuit, he won numerous state, national, and international fighting championships. Besides fighting on the first International Kenpo Karate Association's team that defeated the Chuck Norris team for 1st Place at the International Karate Championships, Bob White fought on the National All Star Black Belt Team, which went undefeated in 1973 and 1974. As a teacher and coach, he has consistently turned out some of the world's finest Kenpo fighters. Over the past twenty-five years, Bob White's karate school has won more than 1200 trophies at the International Karate Championships, and each year throughout the 1990s his students accounted for at least one of the Black Belt Grand Champions at the International Karate Championships. Professor White provides seminars on a wide range of Kenpo-related subjects that include sparring and special self-defense presentation. With headquarters in Costa Mesa, California, he has affiliate schools throughout the U.S. and teaches Kenpo worldwide. Besides the martial arts, Bob enjoys game fishing, running, and is an avid tennis player. He and his family live in Costa Mesa, California.*

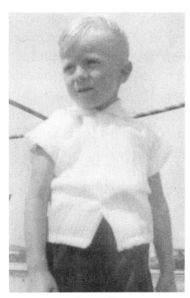

*Future karate champion.*

Since my early childhood, I was athletic and sports came easy to me. In high school I was captain and most valuable player of the baseball team, all league, and also played football. In 1967 I could have signed a minor league contract right out of high school, but I would have gone right to Vietnam. Instead, I wound up playing baseball at Golden West College and was granted a student deferment from the war. The late sixties were hectic times. The hippie and peace movements were radically opposed to the Vietnam war, and as a young man of twenty I was really weighing things out.

A few years earlier I had a high school teacher who was teaching karate at a local health spa, and my dad took me down to join. That

*High school baseball.*

Tuesday and Thursday nights, mostly technique and basics classes, and Fred Brewster would come in and teach the fighting classes. I became immersed. How little did I know at the time that over the long haul karate would turn out to be a humbling experience.

Years of winning at competitive sports had taught me the importance of spontaneity. In all the years I played baseball, I never once played a scripted game. Winning teams often won off the surprise bunt, and the player who stole the most bases was the one who best understood how to read the pitcher's timing. Equally important was playing the spectator crowd that both applauded my efforts and enlivened my competitive spirit. It was for these reasons that I feel initially I had little interest in the softer (yin) side of karate and spent considerably less time learning the forms and the

was in 1964, and in 1966 Ed Parker opened a school around the corner from where I lived. I'd like to say I'd heard of him back then, but I really hadn't. I just went down to his school because it was so convenient.

Not long after I enrolled in the school, I became really impressed with the sparring. I watched the upper students fight, and they didn't move like the traditional stylists I had studied with before at the health spa. These guys were fluid and had a quickness and spontaneity that looked really effective. The fact that they were going to tournaments made my blood surge. Back then I lived for competition. It was my passion and what drove me. So I already had the competitive spirit in spades, and I felt I could be good at karate.

I started spending more and more time at the school. Bob Perry, who was for years the voice of the Long Beach Internationals, taught

*Bob White fighting as Steve (Sanders) Muhammad referees.*

*One of my fights at the International Karate Championships.*

interrelationships between the techniques. In sharp contrast it was the explosive yang side of karate that appealed to my burning competitive spirit. I loved the sparring, and I started fighting in tournaments immediately and getting some success. The fighting came a lot easier for me than the forms and the techniques. I guess it had a lot to do with my basic competitive nature, but what I really wanted to do was fight in tournaments and win trophies. That competitive arena was more real to me. It wasn't scripted. I had won baseball games out-foxing my opponents. Unless the game was tied and went into extra innings, at the end of nine innings one team was crowned the victor and the other ate crow. That scenario worked for me. It was short and sweet. And so with all my guns loaded up, I went to Ralph Castro's CKC and lost my first fight!

Boy, my ego was really effected, and I know that I was really down because I was so accustomed to winning. I had this big ego that just wouldn't give me or those around me much rest. In the early part of my martial arts journey, my ego was the fuel that kept the coals of my fighting spirit red hot, but as I came to find out this enormous ego was the same fuel that was indirectly responsible for inflicting the worst possible burn.

Up to this point in my life I had never been a quitter, although around this time I found myself oscillating between karate and baseball. If I were to achieve perfection in either endeavor, it would require my complete focus and commitment. Something had to give, and in fact it did.

I continued to divide my time between the karate studio and playing baseball for Golden West College. I still had aspirations about being a

*Bob White receives the ceremonial kick on his promotion to 7th Degree.*

major league baseball player and even had a tryout scheduled with the Los Angeles Angels, but it was rained out. I took that as an act of providence, or something, and turned my attention to karate.

The following week our school entered a karate tournament. This was it. The big drum roll. Not long after I swaggered into the tournament, I broke my leg in the first fight. I didn't know it was broken and kept fighting and somehow managed to take first place. But the fact that my leg ended up in a cast for two months pretty much dealt a deathblow to my baseball career. This would end up being one of several major turning points in my life. I decided I wanted to make karate my life's work.

My first major promotion was brown belt.

Mr. Parker came to the Garden Grove school, where I was training, and tested us. I remember feeling very proud that I got to test in front of him. I recall that when he kicked me for my belt, I had decided I'd roll with the kick, and just sort of absorb it through distance. This may have been a good theory on paper, but by the time I started to tuck into my roll, I had already hit the back wall with such impact that it felt like I'd been shot out of a cannon! I'll tell you it made a tremendous impression on me – just how much power that man could generate. Like so many others, I wanted to be just like him.

Not long after I received my brown belt, I had an opportunity to start working out at the Pasadena studio directly with Mr. Parker. This was

*Long Beach International Karate Champioinships winners.*

great because this not only afforded me the chance to be taught directly by Mr. Parker but also gave me exposure to a number of his black belts like Tom Kelly, Dave Hebler, and John Henderson who were fighting pretty regularly both in the school and in tournaments.

Over the years of tournament fighting I incurred broken legs, broken ribs, broken noses, broken hands and toes, but never a broken fighting spirit. The types of sports I've always liked are ones that are physically demanding. Michael Jordon says that when the game is on the line, he wants the ball. I understand that feeling. When I fought team fights, I liked to fight last because I felt that if we were behind I could bring us back. As time passed I won more than I lost, as did many of my students. So impressive was our fight record that by the early seventies our school was arguably a force to reckon with on the tournament circuit. If I sound like I'm bragging, it's not my intention. It's just the truth. Back then we'd have team competitions, and maybe there would be, for example, thirteen team divisions at the Long Beach Internationals and our school would win ten of them.

This turned out to be a double-edged sword, however, and eventually led to the second major turning point in my life. What had happened over time was that the tournament notoriety had really gone to my head, and I had become increasingly arrogant. Gradually this arrogance began to infiltrate into many aspects of my living.

This had a great deal to do with acquired image. I don't believe that many competitive athletes, especially those that are physically confrontational like fighters and football players, want their soft side exposed. And this does have a negative aspect because you put forth this confrontational attitude. Whether it is real or put on, a lot of fighters have it. I can give you a good example. Back in the late sixties some Samoan friends of mine wanted to go down and see Mike Stone. Mike had just won his second Long Beach Internationals Grand Championship, and his school was located in Orange County. As we drove up, some of his students who saw us went in and got him. As we started to get out of the car, Mike came out looking like he was ready to start tearing telephones poles out of the ground and hitting us over the head with them. He

*My last fight.*

loomed over the car and told us that he had seen us at several tournaments and that he did not like spies coming around his school. Then he made a strong suggestion that we leave or that we would find out why he was so well known. It is funny now because Mike and I are good friends, but at the time I thought it would be a great idea for my friends and I to leave. Believe me, back then Mike Stone was not known for his congeniality. When you talk to him today he says that anyone who claims he was his friend during his fighting days is not telling the truth.

Ed Parker said that half of knowing what you want is knowing what you have to give up to keep it. If I had the early part of my martial arts journey to live over again, I hope I could be more of a humble person. I think I would have liked to have been friendlier in the earlier years of my school. But as I said, for many of us the double-edged sword I carried was the armor one takes into the fighting arena. Put simply, the confrontational attitude and aura of arrogance come with the turf.

Around the close of the seventies I started feeling burned out. In a strange way I had begun to think like a victim, and the result was I didn't

like myself. I took a couple weeks and did some deep soul searching. Then one day something that had happened years ago flashed into my mind. It was the day I lost my first tournament, and Fred Brewster came up to me and told me that one day I'd come back and win first place in the black belt division. I relived the tremendous feeling of gratitude I had for Fred that day for picking me up when I might have quit. Tears came to my eyes, and then it suddenly occurred to me that with the passage of time I was now in Fred's shoes. As an accomplished black belt, I was in the position to help and encourage new students coming into the martial arts in the way Fred Brewster once helped me. Best of all, if I focused on being a teacher, it was no longer necessary for me to see everyone as a potential opponent. For me this was a moment of clarity and another major turning point in my journey.

Over the next ten years I focused on looking at the martial art entirely from the perspective of a teacher building strong students rather than a competitor destroying weaker opponents. Today my primary job is to empower my students and peers so that they can accomplish the things they never felt they were capable of doing. This is the

126

*Our daughter's yellow belt test.*

gift that Fred Brewster, by example, gave me seemingly a lifetime ago. And I'd carried this gift with me for many years. It just took a long time for me to unwrap it.

What has happened at our school as a direct result of the changes I have made in my personal journey is a much more balanced and harmonious atmosphere. From a business standpoint this change in focus has been equally astounding. When I placed myself at the center and focused on making money, my school maintained a level of paying bills and with little joy. But when I made my students my top priority and was motivated simply by seeing what I could do to be of service to them, my school has never had it so good, and there is almost an overabundance of joy and fulfillment in my life. It was all about priorities.

Looking back, I realize this was a great lesson that has since helped me become a better instructor. Somehow I have managed to place the sword back into its scabbard. The result is that

I've amassed tremendous compassion for my students and intuitively seem to have an inner sense of what they may be feeling or what they might be experiencing. If I can remain open and sensitive to the subjective, or emotional, side of my students, as well as continue to instruct them objectively, I have a better chance of living up to the high standard I have placed on myself as a teacher.

Today my strength is coaching, and I'm trying to educate myself on various methods of communication and motivation. I feel that an instructor has to be well rounded in order to appeal to different students with varying interests.

Almost from the beginning of my karate training the fighting came easy for me and was my passion. But eventually I came to see that in order to get to the higher levels I had to focus equally on my forms and techniques. And as is often the case with head instructors, my school roster for years was a reflection of my own personal emphasis of the art, and as a result was com-

*Retired from tournament fighting, Bob White now battles game fish.*

prised mainly of tournament fighters. Because of my decision to realign the central point and focus of my own Kenpo, I feel that over the last ten years the overall curriculum and focus of the school has changed accordingly. As a result, we have students and instructors who excel in all aspects of the art, including self-defense, forms, physical conditioning, and sparring. I'd like to think that the time I have spent developing the softer side of my own personal art has enabled me to help balance the curriculum and student base of our school.

I am constantly amazed at how much there is to learn about Kenpo. Things that I thought I had created are constantly being re-discovered as something that were there all the time and I had taken credit for it. Simple moves like Leaping Crane and Circling the Horizon in which we step out to a 45-degree angle and come back at our opponent at a 45-degree angle is something we have done at our school for years in sparring, and I thought I had created this fantastic method of attack, but it was there all the time. I have even done magazine articles that were written about these angles, and I have taken credit for "innovative concepts," only to find out later that Ed

*The White family.*

*Bob and Lupe White*

Parker had been showing us such things for years. The old saying about when the student is ready the teacher will appear certainly has applied to me.

I find equally fulfilling learning new things about old material. The orange belt technique Calming the Storm is a sparring technique that we use often at our school, and it is part of our beginning curriculum. It amazes me that no matter how many years we do this, the answers lie in the basics. I guess that is why I will always be a student of Kenpo. I personally will never wear a tenth degree. This is American Kenpo, and I am a student of Ed Parker's American Kenpo. We have had our Grand Master.

Since my retirement in 1986 from tournament competition, many people have asked me how I have redirected my passion for fighting. The answer is that I handle competition differently today. The Chinese have a term that is called Wu Wei. It is a frame of mind that allows me to practice my art from a more peaceful energy center that is very gratifying, so much so that I no longer feel I have to perform. I only have a need and desire to demonstrate my skills. This is something I try to instill in my students for their tournament preparation. Putting so much pres-

*One of my greatest passions.*

sure on oneself to win at all costs takes the sheer joy out of competing. Rather, let your goal be simply to put forth your best effort. John Wooden, the greatest NCAA basketball coach of all time, never talked about winning. He only talked about being ready.

Another important discipline I used in the years I was fighting was the Floyd Patterson method of preparing for big events. I would train hard and deprive myself of the things I liked to do because I felt that sacrifice was necessary to help develop my mindset. I felt the more I gave up (or as some might say, empty my cup), the more I deserved to win (or fill my cup). I try also to instill this in my students today. It is not the will to win as much as the will to prepare to win that is important. A wise man once said that failure to prepare is preparing to fail. Muhammad Ali used to talk about all his victories taking place in the gym long before he entered the boxing ring.

Mr. Parker's death had a major effect on me. He was larger than life, and his untimely and tragic death made me realize the importance of bal-

ance. Since Mr. Parker's passing, I've redoubled my efforts to stay in the best possible shape that I can. I cross train with running and weightlifting and also play tennis and work out in Kenpo daily. Recently I did a video on American Kenpo fighting, and I was watching myself fight during the seventies and eighties. The last time I fought was in 1986, and I weighed about 210 lb., and now I weigh about 180 lb. I'm actually in better shape than I was fifteen years ago. I certainly know I'm training harder, and I think probably because I have to train twice as hard to get in half the shape. Physical condition is such an integral part of the martial arts. I tell my kids, every time you play basketball, every time you run, every time you ski, anytime you do any other athletics you're bettering your karate.

Through the process of my own living, I have come to see that Kenpo is more than just a system of self-defense. Within the art Mr. Parker gave us are the tools, the Golden Keys if you will, to help the practitioner along life's journey. I owe a tremendous gratitude to Mr. Parker for sharing

*My father.*

his invaluable knowledge with me. The lessons I have learned walking the path (at times perilous) of the martial artist for nearly four decades have ultimately given me a deeper understanding of myself and the world in which I reside. Coupled with my religious commitment, I feel the martial arts have made me a better person. I believe as we get older and have more time in the art, our definition of manhood changes. I used to think that being a man was how much money a guy had in the bank, how much he could drink, how many fights he could get into, and how many women he could surround himself with. Today I have a different definition, one that begins with giving up control of my own life as well as giving up on trying to control the lives of others. In an ironic sense, the journey of the martial artist has a great deal to do with control and release, yin and yang.

Another incredible gift I've received from the martial arts is that I have been blessed with a vast brotherhood that I consider family. The best friends I have in life are fellow martial artists, and this includes my wife Lupe. She and I have an interesting history together in that I have known her since she was five years old when she was brought to me as a student. Later in her adult years she became a fighting champion in her own right. Professionally Lupe is an airline transport pilot with a degree in aviation science. Like myself, she is a born again Christian and has been an important part of my spiritual path. Together with our four children, I feel deeply blessed.

I also owe tremendous gratitude to my father. He was an athlete and kept himself in great shape. We didn't have a lot of money in our family, but I know that every time I needed something from an athletic standpoint, my father made sure I had the best equipment. I'll always be grateful to him for the unselfish love and attention he gave to me. Earlier this year I watched Tiger Woods win his fourth consecutive championship, and the camera panned over to his father standing on the sidelines. You could see the pride and dedication in his eyes, and I could really relate to that. My father passed away about five years ago, and still every time something good happens that has to do with athletics, I feel like picking up the phone and calling him. He was such a major influence in my life, and I truly feel very fortunate.

Looking back over the past forty years, I've seen that people are seeking different things in the art. Some come for self-defense, some for getting in better shape, some for sports, some for friendship. But no matter what initially brings an individual to the martial art, what I have witnessed time and time again is that if you stick around long enough you can have it all. It's just something that if you get out of your own way and suit up and show up on a regular basis, then chances are that you have rewards ahead of you.

The greatest lesson I've learned in the martial art is the same lesson I've learned throughout life, and that is in order to keep something, you must give it away. I thank God each day that I've been able to share my knowledge and in return get so much back. An endless flowing circle of knowledge and growth – the endless journey of Kenpo.

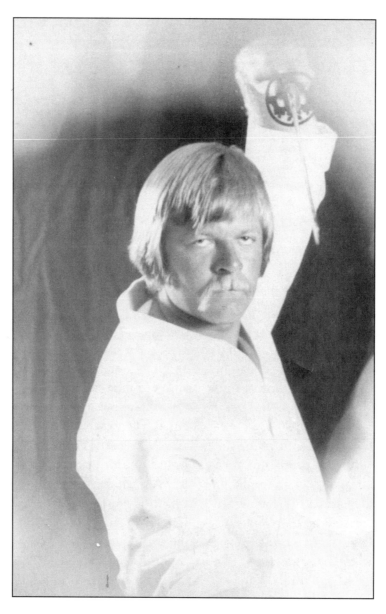

# Richard "Huk" Planas
## 9th Degree

*Considered by many as the consummate "unmoved mover" of American Kenpo, in the early 1970s "Huk" Planas was instrumental in helping write the original teaching manuals that collectively became known as "Big Red." While initially these manuals were meant to be a major part of the proposed franchising of the Parker Schools, when the franchise venture folded, the manuals survived amid a stormy sea and shaky future of Kenpo. Overwhelmed, Huk packed his bags, fishing poles, and guitar and sought the sanctuary of Alaska, retired from teaching Kenpo. It didn't last. Hounded by a loyal following, he returned to teaching and is today consistently booked months in advance on the seminar circuit. Frequently referred to as a walking encyclopedia of American Kenpo, he is well known as a man who cuts straight to the chase, often answering the questions of students with the same tried and true responses that worked decades earlier. An admitted loner by nature and by choice, he has been described as a rare Kenpoist without an ego, as well as a wandering monk. Besides his martial art expertise, Huk is an equally talented archer and also uniquely skilled with a bullwhip.*

**A**s a kid I was interested in taking up the martial arts. My brother and I really didn't know much about it, except what we saw in the movies, but we used to drop into our stances and yell as we'd break dried out boards.

As I grew older, my father, being Filipino, used to teach me the Filipino martial arts such as Kali. I traveled around the Filipino labor camps with him and often ended up learning a particular move from one of my many "uncles." In the Filipino tradition, the father usually does not teach the children, probably because early on the parents discovered that kids don't listen to daddy. As a result, Filipino chil-

*Richard "Huk" Planas at ten years old.*

*1968 playing back-up for Neil Diamond.*

dren inherit a long list of non-blood related uncles. Along with my father, these were the men who collectively and individually planted in me the seeds of the martial arts that would in later years establish roots in every aspect of my life

I was a brave kid from the beginning and would jump on any kid who gave me a problem. I can still remember my first fight in grade school. The kid started the fight by hitting me with a baseball bat. I got him down and started beating him over the head with my yo-yo. Eventually the teacher broke it up and dragged us both to the principal's office.

My adolescent years were relatively smooth sailing. I was raised in the county and felt comfortable in that setting. My entire family used to listen to country music and watched all the popular country music television programs. As was the case with many of my friends, as I approached my teen years I developed an interest in the guitar and in 1957 began taking lessons. I played that guitar all the time and in high school joined a band. We played together from 1960–1969 and eventually ended up playing in nightclubs and bars. Later in my adult life, I played professionally with many

well-known recording stars, including Neil Diamond.

Even though I had begun a lifelong passion for the guitar, I had not lost my early interest in the martial arts. Not long after graduating from high school, I was playing at a dance when an old friend stopped by. During a break, we got to talking, and he mentioned that he had been taking karate lessons. I told him I thought that was great, but that I was a musician and needed my hands to play the guitar. I didn't want to beat them up and turn them into useless meat hooks.

My friend tried to convince me that wasn't the case and invited me to drive over to the school with him that evening after the dance. He wanted to stop by to check the bulletin board to see if he had passed his blue belt test. Back in those days, a student didn't know if he passed until about a week later when the list was posted.

That evening I accompanied my friend to his school that was run by Steve LaBounty and Tom Kelly. Anyway, no sooner had I entered the school than I recognized several other friends of mine, who were also musicians, wearing karate uniforms. I launched into the same spiel about not wanting to turn my hands into useless meat hooks and got the same reply. After talking further with them and their instructors, I signed up that evening and, my childhood interest rekindled, have been studying karate ever since.

From my very first lesson, I took to karate like a fish to water. I drove sixty miles to Fresno in order to take lessons. Often I'd be so exhausted after class that I'd stay overnight at the school. I loved every aspect of the art and couldn't get enough of it. It was both interesting and captivating, and the instructors were friendly off the mat and dead serious on the mat. I remember Tom Kelly was a first-degree black belt, and Steve LaBounty had just been awarded his second-degree. I thought they were both unbelievable. Back then a black belt was god. Fast, powerful, mysterious, knowledgeable. As far as I was concerned these guys could walk on water. Since then, the image of a black belt has changed considerably. Nowadays every ten-year-old kid on the block is a black belt, and the main question has become, "What degree are you?" Back in the old days I never thought about rank. Today rank is a necessary evil. I often wonder how many people would study karate if it weren't for belts and karate uniforms?

When I began training under Steve LaBounty and Tom Kelly, their school had just become a Parker affiliate, although they were still teaching the Tracy material. Their system didn't have a yellow belt, and so my first promotion was to orange belt. About a week before I received my first rank, Tom Kelly approached me on the mat and told me that Steve LaBounty wanted to see me in the office. I thought I was in trouble. When I walked into the office, Steve looked at me and threw a set of keys my way.

"I want you to go to work teaching for us," he said with a stern look. "I'll give you ten seconds to make up your mind."

A week after I got my orange belt I taught my first class. It would be the first of many thousands to follow.

I continued my training religiously over the next two years, making it through the ranks to

green belt. Then in 1969 I won the Sam Allred's First Southwest Black Belt Championships in Albuquerque, New Mexico, and that evening returned to the school to find everyone celebrating. The following week I was awarded my brown belt. Not long thereafter, Tom Kelly, who was then running a school in El Paso, ended his business relationship with his partner and left the school.

As has been the case with so many of the kenpoists featured in this book, Tom Kelly soon made a pilgrimage to Ed Parker's Pasadena Studio, and I soon followed. I drove from Texas to California and sat in the office with Tom, who had been hired as manager. A half-hour later, Mr. Parker walked in through the back entrance, and after talking with me for five minutes, said, "You've got a job here if you want it."

*With Mike Pick at the Pasadena school in 1971.*

*1981 doing a classic wheelie on my dirt bike.*

*My former girlfriend and first woman Kenpo black belt, Lorna Kee.*

"Great," I said, relieved.

"You can start by teaching this evening's beginner's class," Parker said.

This caught me by surprise because I had been trained in the Tracy system and had not yet gone over the material contained in Ed Parker's American Kenpo. He thanked me for my concern and over the next several weeks made a point of coming in every day to personally take me through the transition.

It was around this time that Ed Parker was approached with the business proposition of franchising his schools throughout the United States and Canada. He had observed several other noteworthy heads of karate organizations accomplish this with lukewarm success, and the notion appealed to him. The problem that soon surfaced was that he did not have anything tangible to offer the potential buyers of these franchises. In addition to a physical school and an instructor, these franchise holders insisted, and correctly so, on having a set of guidelines in the form of teaching manuals, as well as managerial material on how to successfully run a karate school.

The issue of teaching manuals had never been an obstacle. I mean, if one thinks about it, Ed Parker was an ass-kicker long before he put

anything down on paper. If somebody saw him in the islands kick the stuffing out of some guy and asked him how he had done that, Ed Parker would probably have said, "I don't know. Let me think about it" and would start writing things down. But the point is he was an ass-kicker long before he was a master of the martial arts. Much of what he knew was in his head. It is just that no one had yet suggested that he write any of it down.

In any event, a millionaire financier based in Canada wanted to franchise Ed Parker schools into what was to be called Can-Am Karate Schools. Under the guidance of Ed Parker, Tom Kelly and I were handed the job of putting together these teaching manuals, and the three of us often worked together on Friday and Saturday nights at the Pasadena school. At the time, I held the rank of first-degree brown, and one night we were all talking about what technique should go where and laying out the requirements for each belt when Tom Kelly said to the Old Man, "Huk certainly knows all this material. He talks like a black belt, and we both know he can move."

The Old Man looked at Tom and said, "You're right," then turned to me and added, "You're testing for black next week."

*The Old Man kicking me for my 7th degree Black Belt.*

Two days later they threw me into the test, and I passed. That is how I got my black belt. I never chased that rank, or any rank for that matter. I didn't even think about it.

It wasn't long before I was embroiled in this Can-Am project, and as everyone knows who was around at that time, the whole thing blew up in everyone's face. No sooner had the dust settled than a second proposal hit the table. This one from a man who was attempting to resurrect the franchise project. Within two months this second brilliant scheme turned into a debacle. As well intentioned as these outside people may have been, there just seemed to be a cardinal rule of thumb that the martial arts don't gel with a lust for the almighty dollar. In any event, my bills were stacking up, and my landlady was pounding the paint off my front door. I stayed on as long as I could and then was forced to quit in order to keep my own ship afloat.

Although both franchise projects failed, the teaching manuals survived. Ironically, over the years they became a double-edged sword. The problem is they were never meant to be a substitute for a knowledgeable instructor.

Unfortunately, there are Kenpo students today who are for the most part self-taught from those manuals. Mr. Parker used to say that we could give ten students that red binder and ask them to teach themselves a particular technique, and a half hour later we'd have ten students doing ten different techniques. And the real enigma would be that every one of them would be convinced beyond any doubt that they were doing the technique exactly by the book.

The point that needs to be stressed is that those teaching manuals were to be used only as a reference. That's how we structured them originally. The student was to be taught on the mat, and then when he or she later read the book as a reference, it would remind them of how the technique was performed.

*Gil Hibben and I fishing in Alaska.*

Over the years, many students, particularly at seminars, have asked me about the importance of all the intricacies in Kenpo and whether all the seemingly endless extensions to the techniques are functional in the street. My answer to that is no. It's not all functional in the street nor was it ever meant to be. When we put those manuals together, we did so based on a foundation of category completion. This is so critical to understanding Kenpo that the number of students, old and new, who do not know that term, constantly amazes me.

The Old Man used to say that everything in Kenpo has a reverse and an opposite, and it's all in category completion. The student can use a particular series of moves in specific situations and under specific circumstances. Some of the moves we do are uniquely designed to work from a right or left side. I tell people all the time that their brain instinctively will not allow them to react from their weak side when confronted with a life or death situation. Rather, you're going to react favoring your strong side. If you're left, it'll be left. If you're right, it'll be right. But there is a substantial amount of material in the teaching manuals that was included to satisfy category completion

and, again, to complete the franchise package. But was it all necessary? No. The Old Man often said that if a guy only knew Form Four, and he knew everything in it and could do it and understood it, that man was a black belt, and he would hang a black on that guy any day.

So in a pure, practical sense all the intricacies and convolutions of the system have little or no value unless the student fully understands the underlying principles. I often explain this by relating a man who walks into a gun store, carrying a gun bag. He places the gun on the counter and says to the dealer, "What is this? How does it work? What caliber is it? Give me some shells. Show me how to work it."

The gun dealer sells the man a box of bullets and spends a half-hour explaining how to load the gun and pull the trigger. The result is a man with a gun who is now fully capable of killing somebody. He knows how to load and fire, but that's all he knows. Just the motion.

He takes the gun to the gun range and fires it at a paper target when suddenly the gun stops working. Packing it back in the bag, he returns to the gun shop and places it back on the counter. The dealer examines the gun, identifies the prob-

*With a baby bear cub.*

lem and fixes it. He then hands the gun back to the man and says, "Here, you're back in business."

You see, the dealer knows that gun inside and out. I tell people that the martial artist is much like the gunsmith. The more the student knows why Kenpo works in addition to the rudimentary moves themselves, the better that student will be able to comprehend the art and teach it to others. That said, one doesn't have to understand Kenpo inside and out to be a good kenpoist. I've known people who are good martial artists, but they couldn't tell you why.

I personally feel that Kenpo, because of its complexity and scientific principles, is difficult to teach to children. Kenpo is not like the traditional hard styles in which the beginning and advanced students are doing the same thing, and the main difference is that the advanced student looks a little better. When all a child has to do is move up and down the floor doing kicks and punches and the basic blocks, his task is relatively simple. But when the Kenpo instructor attempts to explain marriage of gravity, or back up mass, or the interrelationship between a complimentary angle and an angle of incidence, or torque, and what makes it work and how it all gets put together, children often become confused. I've had that experience many times, and the kids will say they don't understand, and all I can tell them is, "I know you don't. You will when you get older."

I travel the world over, and unfortunately many of the Kenpo schools that cater to children have turned into Kenpo daycare centers. The instructors teach these kids other things and play games with them. We've all had those horrible, chilling dreams where we find ourselves pitted against an opponent who simply will not go down no matter how hard we hit them. My sense is that this is related to the early stages of our Kenpo training where the student often feels overwhelmed. So it came as no surprise that in my experience children have these dreams at a much higher incidence than adults.

Returning to the franchising deals, after they both fell through, things got really bad. There were hard feelings and threats and nowhere near enough money to pay the outstanding bills. I was so disgusted I left Los Angeles and moved up to Alaska with Gil Hibben and resumed teaching karate and making knives. At that point, I had no intention of staying in karate as a lifetime career, but the students wouldn't let me alone. As soon as I moved to Alaska, I started getting phone calls. "When can I come up?" or "When can you come down and teach us or do a seminar?" So I tried to quit that one time, and the students just wouldn't let me. Looking back, I'm glad they kept after me.

In 1985 I was in Sacramento, California with Steve LaBounty participating in Gary Garrett's seminar when Ed Parker arrived and promoted both Steve and me to seventh-degree black. Following the passing of Mr. Parker, my promotion to eighth-degree was sanctioned through the Worldwide Kenpo Karate Association that was formed by Joe Palanzo, with me holding the office of Vice President.

Several years later, after I ended my affiliation with the Worldwide Kenpo Karate Association, I started being approached by people and Kenpo organizations that wanted to promote me to ninth-degree. I was uncomfortable with this because far too many black belts were promoting

*1993 Chico seminar working with Bill Sheehan.*

*1997 training in the Guatamala Jungle at "Tikak," the oldest Myan ruins.*

themselves to high rank, and I didn't want to become a part of that. So I respectfully declined, but they kept hounding me.

Finally I agreed, but only under the condition that my promotion to ninth be sanctioned by a substantial number of signed petitions. And these people did that and actually sent stacks of petitions signed by instructors and school owners and students from all over the world. I still have those petitions and keep them in my file cabinet.

A short while later we had a big ceremony in Louisville, Kentucky on my and Gil Hibben's annual birthday bash that we throw every September. Gil Hibben's birthday and mine are a week apart, and we've been putting on this combination seminar camp and birthday bash for many years. Anyway, my promotion to ninth-degree was held during that seminar/birthday weekend. A lot of people came and stood up and made speeches about me and got me crying. At the conclusion of the ceremony, Bill Wallace came up and delivered the customary promotional kick. It was a very special day for me, and one that I shall never forget. It was something else.

I am often asked what advice I would give to the new student coming into the martial arts. If

I could put all my thoughts into one phrase, it would be "Stick to it." There are no crash courses. You can't learn this overnight. The Old Man used to say, "You want to be good, just keep working out, and years down the road you're going to be good." He also used to say this stuff is so simple that it's hard. Or people make it hard. I often say that a black belt is just a white belt who never quit.

But it all comes down to the continual practice of the physical moves. Yes, there is a mental aspect to the martial arts because there is knowledge the student must learn. But the lion's share is physical. You can't crack a bullwhip or shoot a bow or ride a bicycle with your mind. At its root level all these endeavors are physical.

I often tell students I encounter in seminars that I can teach them a technique in five minutes that will take them five years to perfect. And the key to this scenario is that I, as his or her instructor, accomplish my part in five minutes.

What made me think of that was swimming school. I can't swim, but I wanted to learn how to swim, so years ago I went to swim school. The instructor walked me out to the pool and laid me on a bench and demonstrated how I should kick my hands and feet and then said, "Okay, now get in the water."

The point is it took that swimming instructor five minutes to do his part, and the rest was up to me. I never returned to that swim school because I thought there must be more to swimming than a five minute crash course, and I certainly didn't want to end up at the bottom of the deep end floundering around by the drain. So I left and went to another swim school to find out what else they could show me. As it turned out there wasn't anything else. So I tell people that the process of becoming good at Kenpo is much the same. As an instructor it only takes me a few minutes to show the student a technique, and all I'm going to do after that for the next few years is keep going over that same thing until the student practices it to perfection. It really is just that simple –

142

*September 5, 1995 Bill Wallace delivering the ceremonial kick for my 9th Degree Black Belt.*

and yet at the same time, hard.

Another thing I like to tell students is that you will fight like you train. If you don't train hard and realistically, you won't fight that way either. I also tell students, "There are two kinds of black belts – good ones and bad ones. Which kind do you want to be?"

In this regard the art is like buying a gun. You can buy a Smith and Wesson 44-magnum with an engraved ivory grip and polished barrel and take it home. And when you hear a prowler lurking around in the dark, you have a choice of loading that gun with real bullets or putting blanks in it. The gun works and goes bang regardless of whether you load live rounds or blanks.

*Jamming with my close friend and Kenpo brother Frank Trejo.*

The difference is that one hurts somebody and the other doesn't. You don't want to be one of these people out there shooting blanks. You have to remember that it takes good, solid hits to put somebody down who is trying to inflict injury to you. Train hard and realistically, and then you'll fight that way – maybe.

Another aspect of the art that I strongly suggest to students who have been studying for awhile is the importance of cross training. In my personal art, especially now that Mr. Parker is no longer with us, I look at other systems and styles and incorporate what works for me into my own personal expression of Kenpo. The number of people who are doing this now is dramatically on the rise. Back when I was coming up in Kenpo, Mr. Parker was opposed to other arts being introduced to his students. I remember I used to try to convince him to allow other instructors to come into our schools and share their art with us, especially masters of the Filipino martial arts, but he wouldn't allow it. I learned the wise lesson of cross training early on from Dan Inosanto, who over the years has trained in a variety of styles and systems. I personally am proud to be his Kenpo brother, as well as his Filipino brother.

Throughout the years I am often asked my thoughts with regard to the present state of

American Kenpo. Personally, I feel that it has done a ten year backslide. The untimely death of our founder has inadvertently thrust a substantial number of individuals into a teaching position that I feel are not as qualified as they should be, especially those who are teaching on the national and international seminar circuit. Too many of these individuals were taught Kenpo by a student of a student many generations over. And the quality of their teaching clearly shows their lack of understanding. I am hopeful that in time these individuals will either take the time to thoroughly learn the system or perhaps find a less substantial position in the Kenpo community.

In sharp contrast there are new generations of highly qualified kenpoists who are also of high character and possess a great love and respect for the art. The best example who comes to mind is Sean Kelley, who is one of the Honorees featured in this book. I have personally known Sean for many years and have had the pleasure of working closely with him in Kenpo. In my opinion there is no one who loves the art more than he does, nor is more loyal. If the art had more Sean Kelleys, we'd all have far less worry.

In conclusion, I got into the martial arts right out of high school and somehow just became an instructor. There was nothing planned. I just awoke one day to discover that I was a karate instructor. Mine has been a wonderful and exhilarating journey. Today I travel the world, teaching what I love to do – American Kenpo. Everything else – the close friends and new ones still to come, the camaraderie and caring of our brotherhood – are all extras. If it were not for Mr. Parker, it is unlikely that any of what I truly cherish today would have become a reality.

When I think back to our times together, I often reflect on a great wisdom told by a fisherman who said, "Give a man a fish, and I feed him for a day. Teach him how to fish, and I feed him for life." Thank you, Mr. Parker, for teaching me the tools that will feed me for a lifetime.

# Skip Hancock
## A Journey to Excellence

*Having taught linguistics at the college level, Skip Hancock is a well-seasoned perfectionist and organizer who worked closely with Ed Parker on revising the Kenpo teaching manuals. It is perhaps for this reason that when Ed Parker was asked who was he wanted to do the Kenpo demonstration at the 1988 Tribute held in his honor, he replied without hesitation, "Skip Hancock and his demonstration team The Flames." Those who were present at the Tribute will long remember the onstage, beautifully choreographed demonstration performed to "Princes of the Universe" by Queen. Today Skip is active on the seminar circuit and heads up Kenpo 2000, based in Montana. He has also made considerable renovations to Kenpo through his formal education in linguistics. Skip's mother always said that Skip had the two worst kinds of blood – "Gypsy Blood" and "Fishing Blood." His fishing blood has led him all over Montana, Idaho, Oregon, Alaska, Canada, and the South Pacific. Skip likes the freedom to go to the mountains, hike through the wilderness, fish great streams and lakes, gather wild mushrooms, wild berries, interact with the great animals of nature, and have solitary moments with his God.*

I grew up in an athletic family and practically all I ever did was play sports. My father was a professional football player and coach, and a true perfectionist. I played on my high school's first unbeaten football team and won every game by a large margin. After the games were over and everyone else was off to the dance, I went home. My father and I would convene in the living room where he would spend two hours analyzing the game and correcting everything I had done wrong. This is the way it was every Friday night for two years. Although it was harsh and had a negative effect on me, I learned that it doesn't matter what standards others set for me. Knowing my own truth, I will set my own standards of excellence.

Upon graduating high school at the age of sixteen, I attended college on a scholarship and was a straight-A student who rarely studied. I had gone to the university looking for a challenge that

*Skip with his first judo instructor Bob Harder.*

would link up the physical and mental and allow me to test myself to the fullest, but I never found it.

A year later I became the youth director at a YMCA in Spokane, Washington. A guy who worked there was a black belt and had arranged to have his teacher give a demonstration, which I attended. I was amazed. This man was the epitome of the traditional image of a martial artist at that time – a short little guy who moved like a cat, fast and strong, and with a foreboding air about him. I likened his honor and physical prowess to that of the ancient samurai and kung-fu masters.

Bob Harder was a sergeant in the police department and taught judo at the YMCA. I heard about his class and went down one evening to see if I might like it. It looked great, and I joined.

My first lesson was about learning how to fall to the rear. I was required to lay on my back and slap the ground hard, which I did for the entire hour – not just that night but every night for the next two weeks. I was such a fanatic that I probably was the only guy in the world who went home and practiced that. Because the instructor could see that I was intelligent and eager, in retrospect I think that perhaps he was testing my

patience or, better still, my desire to learn. Bob Harder was one of my first martial arts models, and we have remained good friends for thirty-five years.

I studied judo for a few months and then took off traveling around the world, returning at the end of each semester to take college finals. Two years later, I happened to notice while driving through town that a kenpo karate school had opened. I walked in and for twenty bucks purchased five introductory lessons that would soon dramatically alter the course of my life.

My first Kenpo instructor was Jack Oyler, and he and his art instantly intrigued me. For years I had been paying attention to myself, and I knew that I was looking for a different mode of expression. I wasn't looking for a team sport. Whatever anyone else did in class was of no concern to me. Karate was personal, even intimate. What attracted me were the kinesiology of the body moving through space and the application of realistic self-defense. Mixing it up with other students in a graceful but potentially deadly exchange served as a proving ground where I could test myself to the fullest.

I was a fanatic from the beginning. When, as a white belt, I was first introduced to freestyle, I would go home every night and write up a hundred ideas about what I was going to try in freestyle the next day. Almost immediately, I discovered that ninety-nine of them didn't work. Undaunted, I continued making my lists for a month. At the end, I realized that I found only two or three moves that worked, but I also knew thousands of moves that didn't work. That was a lot of useful knowledge. Perhaps the most important lesson I learned in that month is that the martial artist can learn as much from discovering what doesn't work as he can through discovering what does work.

At the time I received my yellow belt I was teaching foreign languages at the university and having difficulty devoting as much time to karate as I wanted to. The way I got over that hurdle was I quit the university. It was just that simple. Soon I was practicing sixteen hours a day every week

*With my first Kenpo instructor Jack Oyler.*

and resting only on Sunday. During the first two years I did that, I only made five dollars income the whole time. I lived on my mom's farm, surviving on the acres of fruits and vegetables. I needed no alarm clock. My burning desire to train in karate was all that I needed to get out of bed in the morning before the sun rose.

I never thought of myself as being the toughest martial artist or greatest martial artist because I've never been in competition with anyone but myself. All that really mattered – the only question I ever posed to myself – was how does my Kenpo stack up today compared to yesterday? When viewed from this perspective, I was always the very best martial artist working out at my mom's farm at five in the morning.

After finishing my morning workout, I'd drive to the Kenpo school and open up at nine in the morning and then train and teach until nine at night. One of the greatest personal motivators, Anthony Robbins, once said that if you want to know what someone truly values, watch where they spend their time.

My dedication was intense and this gave me a sense of true inner worth. I always loved doing physical things, and Kenpo became my passion. I belonged to a group that sparred every Friday night for five hours, often turning off the lights after midnight. I liked hitting and getting hit. Like many martial artists, I was and still am a bit of a masochist.

I continued walking the path one stance, one punch, and one technique at a time. Upon making purple belt I began competing in tournaments, often having to travel long distances because there was only one tournament a year in Spokane. Then one day I awoke to learn that Jack Oyler had to close the school. (As a footnote, the incredible humility of this man is that years later he became my student and has been training with me for the past fifteen years).

With the school closed and Jack Oyler having left Spokane, I was without a teacher. I did, however, have four or five guys who were training with me, and we truly valued our time together. One day we were sitting around together, and I said, "Look, guys, we love what we're doing, but we're kind of playing around in the dark here."

They agreed. The following day I obtained the phone number of the Kenpo school in

*Ed Parker demonstrating a technique.*

Pasadena. I called several times and finally got Mr. Parker on the phone. I took a deep breath and got to the point.

"Mr. Parker, I know that you model your life after Jesus Christ. And Jesus told his disciples – You guys are really lucky. I'm right here for you to touch and to talk to. But the people who really need faith are the ones who are a thousand years away and a thousand miles away. They're the ones who can't see me or touch me, but they will have to have faith." And remembering that, I said, "Mr. Parker you've got myself and four other guys here who have faith in your ideas. We can see your ideas, but we don't understand them fully."

"Come on down," he said.

I didn't have two nickels to rub together, so I packed up a bag of fruits and vegetables from my mom's farm and hitchhiked to Pasadena. Two days later I found myself sitting in Mr. Parker's living room in the company of several other black belts. I remember feeling awkward in my bib overalls as I glanced over at Mr. Parker wearing his bright Hawaiian shirt. The night before, I had a ton of questions I was going to ask him, but I had to pare them down to just two because I didn't want to waste this man's time. My eyes bounced from one black belt to another as they shared in the conversation when suddenly Mr. Parker said

"Skip, do you have a question you wanted to ask?"

I had my first question formulated in a sort of inverted pyramid so that when I asked Mr. Parker the question, whatever answer he gave would lead to a list of another ten questions, and then I would just keep repeating the process, ad infinitum, or until I began to sense I was wearing out my welcome. While this approach sounded good on paper, it worked even better in reality because the answer he gave to my first question made it unnecessary for me to ask 90 percent of my remaining questions! Within two minutes he took me through the entire spectrum of ideas that I had, eliminating everything except the direct path. I mean, literally in two minutes he saved me twenty years of study. I then moved to my second major question, which had much the same result. It was a pretty amazing experience.

One of the earliest and most valuable lessons I have learned on my journey came from my first judo instructor Bob Harder, who one day put his arm around me and said, "Skip, it is no disgrace to be thrown."

When I began fighting in tournaments, I observed that I was like the majority of other martial artists in that I was primarily concerned with hitting and not getting hit, or winning and losing. I came to defeat my opponent, to cause him to make mistakes and lose. While the practice of karate has never been a team sport, I did come to realize that without other participants, karate is of little use, at least from a self-defense perspective.

A wise man once said, "One chimpanzee is no chimpanzee." This simply means that we need otherness in order to define ourselves. So it is with my martial art. Without others, the aspect of self-defense is lost. This is different than progress as it relates to competition. Tournament fighting embraces the element of mutual participation. And in this regard, two separate expressions of martial art, for a short time, become enmeshed into one. This reminded me of an old Chinese saying, "He who seeks revenge should dig two graves," and I began to change my motivation for entering tournaments to that of participating in a mutual dance with my opponent, oblivious of

*In competition.*

winning and losing and which of us was going to come out "looking good." When I began coming from a place where I applauded my opponent's excellent move and either silently or vocally commended him for his performance – because it was one we shared together – the joy of tournament competition rose to new heights. The lesson was really about motivation and values. When I came to defeat all opponents in my path, the going was rough; but when I came to participate in the joy of sharing my martial arts with another human being without regard to winning and losing, I often could beat anyone in the house. This is similar to a wise track coach who often told his runners, "If you can't win, make the one ahead of you break the record."

With the onset of the new millennium, I am enthusiastic that Kenpo offers an alternative to mediocrity, self-indulgence, senseless violence, irresponsibility, and negative attitude. To me, this alternative rests on the element of kindness, and I often remind my students to be kind. Yes, it is that simple. Be kind, but remember that every good kenpoist has a back-up. Kindness comes from an inner strength. I don't want to be nice out of fear. I choose to be kind because I want to, knowing that if violence comes my way, I will be aware and ready to take appropriate action.

I have been fortunate throughout my journey in that from the time I became an orange belt, I was never again shown another technique, form, or set. Rather, I was required to think for myself and figure things out.

Early on I discovered that self-defense is not about doing what others tell me to do. Rather, self-defense is about making decisions. For example, one of the highest principles in Kenpo is Economy of Motion. Economy of Motion - means to choose the best Target, choose the best Weapon, and choose the best Angle in the least amount of time and get the desired effect. This definition has become misconstrued to mean "doing techniques faster." As I now understand it more clearly, Economy of Motion is about being extemporaneous. It is about choosing! Choose the best Target, choose the best Weapon, and choose the best Angle.

Along my journey, guides helped me in making enlightened decisions, but as a student I came to realize that I had to accept responsibility for each lesson. Once I understood the lesson and could demonstrate that I could do it, I had reduced my options to two possibilities: (1) I could choose to pay attention to myself, or (2) I could choose to be lazy. This is the crux of self-discipline.

If I could offer a single piece of advice to the new student coming into the martial arts, as well as those who have been walking the path for awhile, it would be this: keep your passion and desire in direct proportion to your perseverance. Throughout the years the one common ingredient that I have found in all black belts is willpower. Yep – plain old stick-to-itiveness is what we need along the journey, or often best said, "If at first you don't succeed, try, try again."

*The Flames Kenpo demonstration team on the night of the Tribute.*

There are so many obstacles. Ask any Kenpo black belt if he or she ever had to survive instructors not showing up for class, rain leaking through the ceiling, the electricity being shut off, their school being closed down, the instructor running off with the money. All the banging, injury after injury, failed tests, bullies, emotional stress, strain on personal relationships and finances, hurt feelings, disappointments and discouragement. The key is the willpower to persevere (note the word actually means "with severity"). Mr. Parker often reminded us that attitude is always first: First we need to accept, then we need the desire, then the conviction, and finally the willpower to follow each task through to its conclusion. The Key to Success is Never Give Up! I have a favorite motto that all my students and schools hold, which is:

---

**TRAIN HARD**
**TRAIN REGULARLY**
**TRAIN INTELLIGENTLY**
**AND**
**MAKE NO EXCUSES**

---

When I was eight years old my father taught me a valuable lesson. While watching me practice baseball one day, he took me aside and said, "Skip, whatever you do in practice is what you will do in the game."

Over the years I have discovered the truth of these words. When I first began learning karate, I trained my basics fanatically. Later I began to wonder for what purpose because it seemed that the goal had changed. Suddenly the prevailing idea was to learn more and more techniques and a new form or set. This fit nicely into my basic nature, although I was unsure as to what avail.

I became the ultimate memorizer. I was trying to understand Mr. Parker's art, and I wanted to have all of it at the tip of my fingers and the tip of my tongue. Even later as I helped write the extended manuals with Mr. Parker, I memorized every term, every form or set, and every technique in order. The result of my vast and complex memorization was that I had hard-wired thousands of choices in my brain. This meant that when faced with a real confrontation, what else could I do but "choose" from what I know? The problem with this is that when I memorize, I can only remember about 10 percent of what I've studied, but when I experience something, I can remember 85 percent.

What is critical is that the process of memorization does not match the reality of the street. If a student memorizes his art, he will seek the memorization side of his brain in a real confrontation, and could in all likelihood be doomed. "Whatever you do in practice, you'll do in the game." Thus began a new leg of my journey. I let

152

go of learning the art on the memorization side of my brain and began to relearn the art on the doing side of my brain.

Initially my focus of collecting Kenpo basics, techniques, forms and sets led to the "magic pill" syndrome. "Hey! It's America! I paid my $60.00 last month to learn Five Swords, and Five Swords will protect me! I have no responsibility to actually learn self-defense. I simply pay more money to learn more self-defense techniques. If I get beat up on the street, I can say that the technique didn't work, the system didn't work, and I have no personal responsibility."

The point is, in my opinion, learning self-defense techniques is not the same as learning how to defend myself. Today I like to apply the following saying to my own personal Kenpo: One piece of logic will replace a thousand basics.

I am a human being, and solving problems is what human beings do best. Therefore, today I attach no names to any of the basics. Only action is action. I hammer, thrust, whip, launch, step, drag, pivot, crossover, kick, lock, choke, and so forth. I feel I have touched the essence of my art and found simplicity, and with it the growth of an art so sophisticated that I can truly say, "One answer for a thousand problems."

I think the future of American Kenpo is toward the creation of a totally extemporaneous art. One that is not a memorized art, but an art that works on a larger generalized principle whether we're on the ground, or standing, or facing multiple opponents, rooted in simplicity or non-simplicity, doing, doing, doing – and not memorizing.

To my way of thinking, it doesn't matter what we call our art, whether it's Ed Parker's Kenpo or Hideka Nishiyama's Shotokan. There are only so many lessons in the martial arts. So for example, let's say everyone was to agree that there are 150 lessons to be learned about kicking. Aren't those lessons going to be true no matter what style we call them? If those are the lessons we know about how to kick, when to kick, where to kick, why to kick, and who to kick – those are the lessons, and they're the same for everyone. It doesn't matter what style it is. And when all the lessons have been identified and listed – whether it's kicking, or punching, or stances, or attitude, or any spiritual fitness exercise – the ultimate result is a universal martial art. The lessons will be the same. Regardless of system or style, the lessons are the same and so is the demonstration of those lessons.

Traditionally my achieving a black belt has meant that I made it to the beginning - not the end – of my journey. Along this next part of the

*With Mr. Parker doing a demo in Mexico.*

*With my student Lawrence Robinson training in Sedona, Arizona.*

journey I feel that I especially need awareness. Awareness must supersede willpower in order to reach the next levels of proficiency and maturity. I must have greater awareness of my own attitude and the attitudes of others. I must have greater awareness of my environment. I must learn more about who I am inside, while at the same time becoming sensitive to all that is around me. I must reach higher levels of kinesthetic and spiritual awareness. This journey that I am on is so much about awareness. Becoming aware of how I learn something is just as important as what I learn. The process of how I learn something is the real journey.

It has taken me many years to recognize that in the martial arts there are really two points of reference, an object point of reference and a spiritual point of reference. To me an object point of reference is when I refer to things outside myself, while a spiritual point of reference is when I look inward and value those things that go on the inside of me.

When I first entered into the world of the martial arts, I was confident that I would ultimately experience all the benefits embraced by the ancient samurai and kung-fu masters – honor, fearlessness, physical and mental prowess, wisdom, charity, kindness, and especially profound awareness of all that surrounds me.

As I continued with my training and teach-

ing, I began to see that it would be easy to get caught up in living and training with an object point of reference that focused on trophies, belt rank, applause, titles, fame, fortune, mass number of student-slaves, how many books I had written, how many videotapes I had made, and how I had done this or that. Ultimately I came to believe that for me to structure my Kenpo from this object point of reference would result in giving me a false sense of power that emanated from outside of me.

But occasionally, I would meet and spend quality time with someone on the journey toward a spiritual point of reference, and they would help guide me through unknown territory. One of those guides who led me through the darkest corridors and into the light was my teacher, Mr. Parker.

Ultimately, when all is said and done, I can

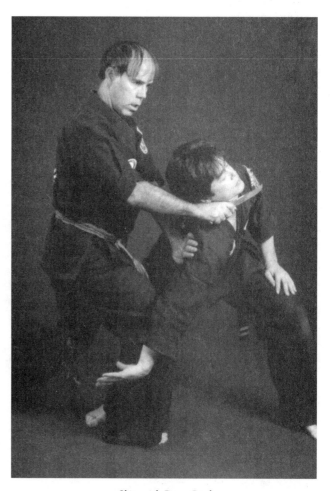

*Skip with Barry Paul.*

154

*Skip and his student Dennis Lawson in Germany.*

sum up what I learned from him: The value of Kenpo is not whether you know more of certain things than the other fellow, but what intelligence, wisdom, and character you develop by its means. This is similar to the wisdom stated by the father of Japanese karate, Ginchin Funakoshi, who years earlier said, "The ultimate aim in the art of karate lies not in victory but in the perfection of the characters of its participants."

Since Mr. Parker's passing, I am sincerely hopeful that I have taken revolutions that he had done in the martial art to the next level. I am confident that he would be extremely happy to see where I am going with his art in terms of using every single part of Kenpo that I learned. I am no longer collecting individual pieces of it, but instead am working diligently with the larger generalized principles with the goal of understanding Kenpo to its fullest.

While the art is a gift, it is not a free gift. I often share with my students a conversation I had with Mr. Parker years ago. One day we were eating in a restaurant, and I said, "Mr. Parker, I just want to thank you for all the things you've given

me over the years."

I didn't get any further. He became mad in a way that only Mr. Parker could become mad, and he said, "Skip, I have never given you anything. You have earned every single bit of it."

I have never forgotten those words. And so while Kenpo can in the broad sense be viewed as a gift, it is not a gift in the sense that it is free. We all work hard to embrace it, and I have always been appreciative of Mr. Parker for sharing that with me. As a result, none of my students have ever received a free gift from me. Every single ounce of Kenpo that they have, they have earned the same way I earned it with Mr. Parker.

Lastly, I would like to address the subject of rank for those who may have wondered why I chose not to include rank as part of the banner head of my profile.

In simple terms, I claim no rank at all. That is a paradigm that doesn't work for me. My students simply see me as their teacher, and all the rank and promotions are for them.

My personal philosophy on this is simple. Mr. Parker was my teacher. He promoted me. The rank was an indication of a personal relationship in the art between Mr. Parker and me. He is no longer with us, and I will never be promoted again, which is why I have not taken any rank from anyone else, or promoted myself, or had my students promote me. This has simply been the way I intuitively feel things should be in my heart and is not in any way a judgment or criticism of others, who must follow the dictates of their own hearts.

Thanks to the thousands of people who have thus far traveled the journey with me; here is only a small portion of them:
Agee Family, Al Covey, Andy Nauman, Annie Olson, Arlene Schmidt, Arnold Lee, Art Copple, Barry Paul, Bill Haney, Bob Harder, Bob Veith, Burt Schwab, Church Family, Chris and Pattie Crews, Chris Martin, Chris Springer, Clint Carlson, Dale Swedberg, Damon Tong, Dan Kaufman, Dan Morlock, Danny Van Vlaslaer, Daryl Little, Dave Burchett, Dave Swingley, Dennis Lawson, Drew Ota, Enrique Flores, Frank

and Lynne Owens, Frank and the Pollara Family, Frank Trejo, Geert Vleugels, Gerard Kropholler, Gilbert Claes, Hernan Carrasco, Jack Morris, Jack Oyler, James Harr, Jeff Williams, Jesse Ballou, Jim Crabtree, Jim Rice, Jimmy and the Gronenthal Family, Joe Jones, John Fitzgerald, John Monserrat, Jonathan Sisemore, Jorg Wasser, Jorge Gris, Justin Olson, Ken Martin, Kosy Phibulphanuvat, Krissy Shull, Kurt Booth, Langs, Larry Carmichael, Lawrence Robinson, Leach Family, Leo Felice, Leo Lacerte, Loren Broyles, Louie Cornay, Louie Morbacher, Mario Gaxiola, Mark Ireland, Marvin Weber, Matthew Moncreaff, Miriam Ascher, Mike Doe, Mike Pick, Moriarty Family, O'Bryan Family, Parker Family, Paul & Arienne Christ, Paul Mills, Paul Quick, Peter Rezey, Phil Bertholf, Rainer Schulte, Randy Easley, Rene Jones, Rich Burkhardt, Rick Macdonald, Rich Peterson, Rick Scoggan, Ron Bearry, Ron Cowan, R.S. & Melody Mitchell, Rulon Day, Ryan and the Bunker Family, Sam Griffel, Sandy Sandoval, Scott Gordon, Scott Marker, Sean Wold, Shayne Simpson, Shawn Gants, Steve Hawk, Storer Family, Tattersall Family, Tom Rondeau, Tony George, Tyler Hawk, Uale Family, Vaughn Range, Wade Henry, Wayne and the Missamore Family, Wim Sterckx, Yves Beukenhout, and the two great joys of my life, my mother, Marguerite, and my wife, Shirley.

*My wife Shirley and son Drew.*

# Grandmaster
# Steve Muhammad
## 10th Degree

*Born Steve Sanders in Topeka, Kansas, Steve Muhammad was one of fourteen children. He was raised in an athletic family: his father was a well-known baseball player and his older brothers were boxers and weightlifters. He received an athletic scholarship to parochial school and upon graduation was offered a football scholarship to Kansas University. In the early 1960s he enlisted in the Marine Corps, becoming a Pathfinder, and first learned the fighting aspect of the martial arts. In Vietnam he was exposed to the brutal realities of combat. After returning home, he began his Kenpo journey to become one of the most respected and successful martial arts competitors of all time. During his fighting career, he won the prestigious International Karate Championships lightweight division on numerous occasions, and accumulated countless trophies on the tournament circuit. In 1970, at the pinnacle of his competitive career, he joined with Donnie Williams, Jerry Smith, and Cliff Stewart to form the Black Karate Federation (BKF) to address issues of racial discrimination on the tournament circuit. Steve Muhammad changed his name after embracing his chosen spiritual path of Islam. Mr. Muhammad remains active and eager to share the gifts he has received from the art of Kenpo.*

M y first recollection of the martial arts was when I was in middle school back in Topeka, Kansas, although at the time I didn't have the faintest idea of what I was looking at. It was summertime, and I asked my mom if I could get a job and she said yes. So I went downtown looking for employment and was having a real tough time finding anything. After spending most of the day being turned down I got lucky and landed a job washing dishes in a Chinese restaurant. When summer was over, I told my boss that school was starting and that I couldn't come back anymore. I must have been doing a pretty decent job because he said why don't you ask your parents if you can come early in the morning and wash the dishes from the night before and then you can go to school. So I asked my mom and she

*Steve Muhammad in 1975*

said that was fine. I had to get up around three-thirty in the morning to get there around four in order to get the job done before heading off to school.

Early one morning, I tried a shortcut and as I was getting ready to jump the fence, and I saw the guys who worked there doing something in the way of a physical exercise in the yard behind the restaurant. I didn't know then what it was, but I found it fascinating and I watched them every morning before I started work. One day I asked if I could join them and they allowed me to. I didn't realize what I was doing, but I did this all the way through middle school and the first two years of high school. What they were doing was the art called Tai Chi.

I didn't realize I had taken any type of martial arts until I got in the Marine Corps and went to Okinawa, and that's when I saw that what I had done as a kid were the root elements for a martial art. It was in Okinawa that I was really introduced to fighting side. It was a style called Goju-ryu. I didn't really learn that much Goju-ryu. I never got any rank or even learned all the basics, but I learned enough to know that I wanted a lot more. Unfortunately, when you are in the service of your Uncle Sam your time isn't exactly your own so it had to wait until I returned to the states to continue my search.

It was then that I found out about Kenpo. I started at Ed Parker's WLA school. I was there for about two years, but my training was interrupted by a tour in Vietnam. I think I was a two-tipper when I left, which is the equivalent of purple belt. I remember I was gone for a good eighteen months. That Vietnam thing was so bad we were afraid that when we came back that people would really - well, let's just say, they weren't very nice. So I kept the fact that I was still in the military to myself.

When I came back I didn't have a gi and I didn't have money to actually purchase one, so the guys at the WLA studio scrounged around, finding a piece here and a piece there, and they eventually put a uniform together for me. It consisted of a little thin belt, an ill-fitting jacket and pants that hit me somewhere between my ankle and my knee. But Vietnam was behind me and I was back. The instructor was Danny Inosanto.

When I was going to the WLA school, it was tough because I had a part-time day job as well as my duty at the El Toro Marine Corps Air Station in Santa Anna, hooking up forklifts all night. I also had a daughter I had to take care of, so time and money were both tight for me during that period.

One evening Chuck Sullivan came from the Crenshaw school to WLA. He brought a film of him and Mr. Parker putting on a demonstration that was fantastic. That's when I first saw Mr. Sullivan, and I was impressed by his form, skill, and physical appearance. I thought, looking at him, 'He's my size; if he can do it, I can do it.' I had been trying to thunder like Mr. Parker and it just wasn't working for me. So I started going down to the Crenshaw school. When I first got there I explained to Mr. Sullivan that I might not be able to make it on a regular basis because of finances and family obligations.

"Steve, don't ever let money stop you from being here, we'll figure something out," he said.

*1968 Long Beach Internationals winner*

160

He helped me a lot because he said I could come for free if I would help to teach and help with whatever he needed. So I was able to continue without interruption.

There's no way I could have gotten as good in another style as I did in Kenpo. When I came to the Crenshaw school I was freer there than I was at the WLA school. One day when we were putting on a demonstration, Mr. Sullivan surprised me when he said, "Steve is going to come up and do variations of the techniques that we have just done."

I had not practiced on the variations of those techniques! When you try to do something exactly like another person - some things you can, and others you cannot. When I tried to do the techniques exactly like Mr. Sullivan did them, I found that I could do them, but I had to do them very slow. But if I rearranged them in some way, more in line with my own body structure, I could do them much faster and stronger. So my way of doing it was already a variation. I realized that when he said, "Steve will do a variation of these techniques," and I found that sometimes I could flow with the variation better than I could with the actual technique that was given to me.

Until I got to the Crenshaw school I didn't

really know how to start making the Kenpo system work for me. Once Mr. Sullivan allowed me my own expression of the techniques, I became a much better fighter. He used the example of being able to move catlike. He spoke one time about how the movements in martial arts came from the animals and to study the animals to see the way they fight. They have a delivery system for their weapons. You look at different animals and study how they strike and how they rake and I've seen different animals that actually kick. By watching and studying animals you get a better understanding how to deliver certain things.

Another thing about Mr. Sullivan was that, even though he didn't care about fighting in tournaments, I could see that he could really actualize the Kenpo system. To be able to watch a master put these things together was really illuminating. He would do things with such a natural ease that I'd say, "Does he really realize he's doing it?" and that's what made me say, "Well, if he can be smooth like that, then I can do it too. Because he had to learn it, so I can learn it, too."

Fighting Mr. Sullivan was like trying to fight a Tasmanian devil. He never hurt me (much), but I always felt that I was fighting for my life! The way he brought his techniques at me, it was relentless. I remember one day I got my teeth knocked back in my mouth by him. He pulled my teeth back in place, tapped me on the head and said, "You'll be fine." The reason he tagged me was, I was such a runner, my reflexes were pretty fast, and he had to come out as hard as he could to catch me. So he lunged and accidentally trapped my foot, and I got hit! Hard! But it was an accident and he felt worse about it than I did. At least that's what he said.I

In order to fight Mr. Sullivan you had to be either with him or ahead of him. Body language was one of the things I had to learn. It's not an easy thing to learn and even harder to teach. Once you've learned it, you'd use it with everyone, but particularly with him, in learning and watching how he'd deliver things. Then again, being in front of him was a whole different game. I would much rather be standing on the sidelines when he delivered. I'd have to say it was actually magnificent because I learned so much about delivering those movements by watching him move against me. Also how to change them around; he was never the same. Every time I fought him, he was different. I asked myself, what am I going to have to do? Corral this guy? So I'd say, heck, if he's never the same, why should I be the same? I tried to emulate and change up, too, so that if you fight me, I'll be a different fighter every time.

I used to ask, "How can I get into the head of Mr. Sullivan?" I had to figure out what he's thinking and which direction he is going. I didn't realize it at the time but he was actually giving it to me every time we fought. I was trying to figure out a whole different way to get it out of him, and all the time he was handing it to me, but I just didn't understand. It was when his students start-

ed to fight each other; we began to say, "Hey, we can make this stuff work too." We got better and better.

The first time I realized I wanted to get good at Kenpo was the first tournament I went to. I tried to do techniques like Five Swords against an opponent coming at me. I was thinking, 'I can make those techniques work pretty good on the street, so how come I can't do it against these guys?' I couldn't figure it out that day, so I only lasted one fight. It was an entirely different thing fighting a trained karate fighter who knew all the things I knew. That's when I set out to learn how to beat those guys.

It was during a match with Scott Loring at

*Steve Muhammad competing in 1979*

162

*With Ed Parker, Danny Guzman, Ralph Castro, and Moroni Mederos in Hawaii*

the WLA school that made me begin to see the light. Whenever I had to freestyle Scotty I was constantly praying because he always made me fight hard. He always drove me into the floor or into the wall. One evening at an interschool tournament I was praying not to get matched up with Scott. And suddenly I heard "Scotty Loring!" I was sitting there with my fingers, my toes, my legs crossed, everything crossed and they said, "Steve Sanders" and I said, "Ah, hell."

I got in front of him and we bowed. This is the first time I realized that I could actually see him when he moved and understand what he was all about. He moved and I shifted back. And that's when I started making flinching type movements. I flinched at him, and he didn't move. That's when I said to myself, if he didn't move for the flinch maybe he won't move for the real thing, so instead of flinching I just went for it and I hit him in the face. Which is something you didn't do with Scott Loring. Coming close was bad enough but hitting him, forget about it. He came after me and ran me around the mats two complete laps,

until they finally grabbed him. In this case I literally turned my back on him and ran; later on I got good at running backwards and striking while I'm moving. With practice you would be surprised at how much power you can develop even though you're moving away. Most people don't think of that as a viable technique until they get nailed. When you learn how, you can hit really hard

I got my black belt around July 1966. It took me six years. It was because of the military; going away and coming back. Start and stop. It was really a blessing because it gave me an opportunity to be in a position to really learn how to make this system work.

I never experienced racism in the Parker WLA or Crenshaw schools. But I did in tournament competition, oh yes. I can remember some of the early tournaments I entered as a new black belt. To get into the finals, to fight for first place, I fought as many as eight times! When I would ask other black belts who were fighting, "How many times have you fought?" They'd say, "Well, I fought twice." I would be around seven or eight

during the fight they'd be yelling for me to do this or that, but not this time. They were strangely silent. It wasn't something I spent a lot of time thinking about at the time, it was only afterwards they let me know why. The match was over almost before it began. I got two quick points and everyone ran into the ring to congratulate me. It seems I had just beaten the Lightweight International Champion, Carlos Bunda. They didn't want to tell me before the match who I was fighting for fear I'd get nervous or something. I didn't know who he was and I don't know if it would have made any difference if I had. I've had a lot of interesting matches but that one, and doing two laps around the WLA school with Scott Loring on my tail, stand out most in my memory.

I also competed abroad. Mr. Parker took me to Spain, and I went to Hawaii a couple times, and Jamaica once. I also went to the Philippines. I went over there for a full contact match. Even though I won the match I never wanted to fight full contact again because it didn't really prove anything to me. It verified that I could go full contact and take a shot without going down, but between the rules that they had and the actual punishment to the body, it wasn't worth it. Nobody could fight full contact for more than three years without getting really damaged. I realized in that one fight that if I continued, I would probably suffer serious damage to my body, or possibly to my brain, that I would never recover from. If you look at those full contact fighters of that era, all of them are living with pain today because of it.

A friend invited me down to the boxing gym where he trained. He said boxing was fun and I'd probably get a kick out of it. I got in the ring with this boxer and they told me we were going to go easy. So I'm tapping around and I'm connecting because I'm not bad with my hands. I'm mixing it up pretty good, and all of a sudden this guy starts hitting me pretty hard. I pushed him back and I said, "Hey, I thought we were supposed to take it easy." So we start to peck a little bit again. Then he gets me in the corner and starts pounding the hell out of me! I pushed him back and blasted him up along the side of his head with a roundhouse kick. Everybody in the place jumped in the ring and they pulled the

ahead of them because they would move me from one ring to another, "Mr. Sanders, Ring Two." I would step out for about a minute and then, "Steve Sanders, Ring Eight." I'd go to ring eight and be out for a minute, and "Steve Sanders, Ring Ten." I'd go to ring ten. But what they didn't realize is that I was getting better and better from all that fighting experience. I was in good shape, so I never got tired. I'd like to thank them for giving me a lot more than my money's worth.

Of all the matches I've had one stands out in my mind because of the strangeness that surrounded it. It was at Ed Parker's International's in Long Beach. When it was time for the match everybody from our school gathered around the ring but they were real quiet. Usually before the match they would be patting me on the back and

*Steve Muhammad today*

gloves off my hands. My opponent was stumbling and staggering around the ring. Anyway, they grabbed me and pushed me out the door and I'm yelling, "I was just trying to get him off me!" They told me to hit the bricks and not to come back.

Things started to change as my reputation grew. I had won the lightweight divisions of so many tournaments they always used to put me in the lightweight division without even weighing me in. I was putting on some pounds but I never really showed it. Then one day they made me weigh in! Ron Marccini jumped up behind me, grabbed me by the back of my gi pants, and lifted me. He said to the official, "Steve Sanders, a hundred and forty five pounds, thank you Steve." He let me go, and that was that.

As the championships began go pile up, people started to treat me differently. They started treating me like a champion, as one who could actualize the Kenpo system. It also made it easier to meet young ladies. They somehow found it easier to approach me. That was a fun time. I was

young and a champion and for some reason that was a big draw for young women to come up and talk with me.

In 1969 I opened my first school on Western Avenue. Mr. Sullivan helped me open that school. He gave me all the things I needed to open up, tatami mats to go on the floor and all kinds of business information because I didn't know much about the business end of the art. And that was when a group of us decided to form the Black Karate Federation. We really wanted to come under the IKKA, but when I inquired about it, the answer came back, "not at this time." So that's when Mr. Sullivan said, "Steve, why don't you do your thing?" So I did.

One of the things that Chuck Sullivan actually taught me was there was a time to fight and a time not to. We were in a club one night and this guy said something derogatory toward me. I stood up, and I remember Mr. Sullivan putting his hand on my arm and saying, "Steve, you know you can destroy him, don't you?"

"Yes, and that's what I'm getting ready to do," I said.

"If you already know you can do it, then there's no need for you to," Mr. Sullivan said with a smile. I never forgot that. If you can destroy something, there is no need to destroy it unless it becomes absolutely necessary.

I was with the Los Angeles County Sheriff's Department for twenty years. Kenpo helped me get that job and Kenpo helped me keep it, in good health. My first assignment was working undercover. I worked undercover dope dealers, and there were times that I had to wreak havoc on some of those guys. I lasted two years, and they had to pull me out because the word was out that they planned to kill me. Undercover, I got into a lot of fights and I never lost one. Kenpo becomes so devastating once you build the power to do damage every time you hit. If you can hit with all your weapons and generate damage with all your weapons, nobody can withstand that. Also, what I had learned over a period of time was how to actually break when I hit. There were a lot of broken bones during that time on the job and fortunately none of them were mine. I was glad to leave that aspect of the occupation.

I started doing outside security work while I

was still a police officer. In 1989 I set up a company and we started doing security for things like fur shows, art shows, and jewelry shows. Most of these were out in Beverly Hills. We got paid well for doing that. I've worked with several recognizable names, including Wesley Snipes and Mr. Louis Farakan. Oh yes, I've done security for him for the last nineteen years and traveled extensively with him.

On rare occasions I've had to tell a client, "This is not a place that we should be. We've got to leave now."

And he'd disagree, "No I want to stay."

And we'd have to grab him and carry him out. That's not a good thing to have to do. One of my clients let me go because we had to physically remove him. He found out later that we had done the right thing. I accepted his apology but refused to take him back as a client.

With Wesley I've always had an agreement. He said, "If I do something that is unruly or we need to go, grab me and take me," and when he'd wake up the next morning he'd ask, "Did you guys beat me last night?"

We'd laugh and say, "No, we didn't beat you." He'd be sore from dancing and whatever he was doing. We'd move him when things got out of hand, but we never had a problem with him.

When I was younger, I was less comfortable giving advice and answering questions. But now, because I live a much more righteous life, I'm really at ease with people coming to me for advice or council because I can answer in a much better way than when I was thirty years of age, in the street doing things that maybe weren't proper.

There are nine young men in particular who told everybody that I was their father, so I said they were my sons. Some of them lived with me for years. I bought them clothes, fed them and everything. I did it for years and I didn't mind doing it. Even though we didn't have a lot, we had enough to get by. And I treated them like my very own kids, I whipped them when they needed whipping, but I also went to bat for them and stood up for them when they deserved it. I tried to lead by example and when that failed I tried to put the fear of a father figure into them. There was a whole group that I did that for, but there are nine in particular that stand out and whom I consider my sons.

The martial arts and Kenpo in particular has given me so much I would love to be able to give something back. I would like to open a martial arts studio here in Georgia that would have everything in it, including child-care and a library, a place where we can bring the family in the evening and teach them martial arts. I'd like to have tutors for the children to help them with their homework while their parents are doing martial arts. I want to have refreshments and a state of the art kitchen, where everything prepared will be healthy. I'd also like to have sleeping quar-

ters for about seventy or eighty people so that when we have seminars they don't have to stay in a hotel. We're looking for land now to set that up on. I'm going to try to do it by myself because I would like to say that this is my legacy.

I have some books coming out, a total of three, along with some films. One of the books is *The God Side of a Warrior* or *The God Side of Kenpo*. It has to do with what I call "brain sight," which is actually subconscious fighting.

Subconscious fighting is magnificent because the subconscious only takes the good. It does not accept bad. It only deals with the good side of a person. Even in fighting, the subconscious will take that and actually help in creating the movement. The subconscious has no delay, you can't trick it, and you can't fool it. You actually have to train the subconscious to do this for you; the mind can actually learn to use the subconscious in fighting.

You also have the potential for superhuman strength. There are times when you are in desperate need and you pick up something that you wouldn't normally be able to lift. You wonder where you got the strength to do that. What I've been trying to do is learn how I can call on that when I want it. This is where brain sight or subconscious fighting comes into play. I'm working on that now, working with the senses that God has given to us. We use them everyday but we don't realize it.

I found in Vietnam that the enemy could sense us and we could also sense him. There were times you couldn't see him or hear him or even smell him but you knew he was there. We could go for the longest time without contact and then someone in the group would say, "He's here, I can feel him" and he would be.

I would say that when you start out in the martial arts, in order to learn you have to be totally in tune with your instructor. I found that when I was in Mr. Sullivan's school I seldom asked questions that weren't relevant. I would suggest to always watch and listen no matter what the instructor says; you kind of key off of everything he does because he is the one you are going to have to emulate, until you can come into your own. So shut up, look, and listen. Don't just look, but see. Don't just listen, but hear what your instructor has to say. This is a starting point for you. To be able to emulate your instructor because he is the best example for you to follow at the time. You need a starting place, but as you get to a certain point, you become freer in your movements and in your thinking. Then you can start doing it the way your body and your personality will tell you to do it. You have to start thinking for yourself because your instructor can't think for you.

I will always love Kenpo because it has given me the freedom to be me.

# Gilbert Velez
## 9th Degree

*Gilbert Velez is the highest-ranking black belt promoted under the IKKA and since 1992 has traveled over a half-million miles on behalf of the IKKA while actively promoting American Kenpo throughout Europe. Besides being a professional musician whose award-winning Mariachi band has appeared at the White House and performed with an impressive list of entertainment celebrities, Gilbert has been a restaurateur for nearly three decades, and his Mexican cuisine specialty dishes have received awards internationally. Since 1973 he has owned and operated a Kenpo school in Tucson, Arizona and is a strong advocate of combining a cardiovascular workout with martial arts training. Over many years Gilbert developed a highly successful Pre-K Kenpo program for children ranging between the ages of four to twelve years. Some of the kids that started at three-and-a-half years old are still training at Gilbert's school fifteen years later! For many decades a successful businessman on multiple-levels, he is a strong advocate of NAPMA (National Association of Professional Martial Artists) and other similar programs that offer business consultation to professional martial artists. Today Gilbert's primary focus in American Kenpo is helping to standardize the teaching curriculum.*

I was born and raised in South Tucson, Arizona along with my two brothers and one sister, all older. South Tucson was a rough Hispanic and Native American town surrounded by the city of Tucson. My father died when I was five years old, and my mother, Julia Velez, worked hard bringing us up in tough neighborhoods. I attended catholic schools throughout my education and, all things considered, had a relatively happy and secure childhood.

My first recollection of the martial arts was around the age of ten. My brothers were studying judo at one of the original judo schools located in Tucson. It was, and still is, called the RendoKan

*Gilbert Velez and his International Mariachi America. Courtesy of the Los Angeles Times.*

Dojo. I believe it was founded in 1948. A cousin, Dr. Carlos Velez, also joined the school, and later went on to obtain a black belt in Shotokan. So my first recollection of the martial arts is watching my family members working out, primarily in judo. All my life the martial arts was something I wanted to study. It wasn't so much the fighting part. I was attracted to the mystique that surrounded it.

I took up wrestling while attending high school in the sixties, and so I had a grappling background when I joined the Air Force in 1968. It was during basic training that I was first introduced to Kenpo by a group of airmen who were working out together. While I don't recall their names, I do remember that they kept crediting Ed Parker for the moves and forms they were practicing.

I was first introduced to Ed Parker in 1968 at a social function unrelated to the martial arts. Back then I had formed a world-class mariachi

group and was heavily involved in the music industry. In addition to playing the top casinos in Las Vegas and Lake Tahoe, we played at Disney World, Universal Studios, and even at Presidential inaugurations. So when I first met Ed Parker, it was as a musician and not a martial artist. Many know that Ed Parker was, himself, a gifted musician. For years I have played music all over the world, and he is the only one I've ever heard play Malaguena and Granada on a six-string ukulele!

Five years later I officially began my training in Kenpo in Tucson. Just after Bruce Lee's "Enter the Dragon" was released in 1973, several chains of martial arts schools opened across the country, and I joined one of them that was an offshoot of Ed Parker's American Kenpo. I trained there for about a year and a half and acquired a strong regimen of basics and much of the Parker forms and techniques. By the end of 1974 my training in the martial arts had become of such great importance in my life that I bought the school and immedi-

*Singing with Linda Ronstadt.*

ately switched it over to a full IKKA affiliate.

Although I had acquired a solid foundation of American Kenpo, I truly felt a strong need to train directly under the master himself. At that time I was performing at a restaurant in Tucson that was doing very well, and so I arranged my schedule so that I could begin traveling to California for private lessons with Ed Parker on a weekly basis. Beginning in late 1974, I would leave Tucson every Sunday night and drive 500 miles to Pasadena where I would get in as much Kenpo training as I could until late the following Thursday afternoon. Then I would drive the 500 miles back to Tucson in time for the long weekend at the restaurant and my three Kenpo schools.

When I first began taking lessons from Mr. Parker, I was totally petrified and in complete awe of the man. I think just about everyone I've talked with over the years has had that same reaction to their first meeting with him. In fact, I was so

overwhelmed that I don't believe I understood much of the first few lessons and had to try to piece them together on my long drives back to Tucson. Reflecting back on those days, I remember how he would demonstrate a move where his huge hammerfist would sail past the bridge of my nose, followed by an elbow and heal of the palm crashing together a hairline in front of my quivering jaw. I would stand there frozen for a few seconds thinking to myself, 'Thank God he didn't hit me!' I mean, I could clearly see where he could easily break an opponent in half. The sheer power he could generate was at times horrifying.

Because of the distance factor, part of my learning process included printed material that was given to me by Ed Parker and would serve as a preview of our next set of lessons. I would take this material back with me to Tucson and figure all the techniques out in advance so as not to waste Mr. Parker's time. In addition, upon my

*Playing for Beatle Paul McCartney*

I have a certain theory about all art forms. I see the art of the eyes expressed through paintings, drawings, and sculptures. The art of the ears I hear through music. And the art of motion is expressed through dance and, for many of us, the martial arts. Regardless of the art being expressed, they all have form and intensity, while at the same time are entertaining and educational.

Much of my innate understanding of Kenpo has to do with its rhythm patterns and syncopation, which to me is enmeshed with my understanding of music. Like playing the piano, my fingers can play in different octaves and keys. It's the same with Kenpo. It wasn't hard for me. A knee here, a hand there – it was no problem because adding weapons and power in Kenpo were like adding notes and musical instruments in music. The two are intimately similar in structure and are expressed in volume, mass, and line. In its total expression, Ed Parker would move and BAM! – suddenly color would explode off the page. Looking at the total picture, I can syncopate it all to 1/64th of a second. That's just from hearing music. Ed Parker understood all that because he was a talented musician himself. People sometimes ask how fast can a skilled Kenpo black belt hit? I tell them, for example, that there is this technique where we hit our opponent nine times from head to toe and everywhere in between with six different weapons. Then I'll demonstrate the technique and afterwards ask, "How fast was that? That was instantly. Do you know how fast instant is? Hitting you five to seven times instantly?" And they can't comprehend instant. Not within a second. It's instant. Kenpoists can comprehend things like that because we deal in instantaneous movement, and as a musician I also deal with an explosion of instantaneous sounds.

To this end I personally feel that natural musicians and other artists seem to pick up the martial arts faster because they have a certain talent for innately understanding the inner structure. Besides music, in college I was drawn to the form and structure of all the liberal arts. This has proved to be invaluable in my teaching of Kenpo. When I teach an accountant, I relate to his num-

return to my school in Tucson, my teaching staff and I would teach the previously learned material from ten in the morning until ten at night.

I grew up as a musician. At ten years old I played piano and guitar, and was particularly drawn to just about all the stringed instruments. Being a musician, I have an intimate understanding of rhythm patterns, which I believe is why much of the timing of Kenpo came easily to me. Besides being a musician, I have a degree in art, which gave me knowledge of form, color, and explosion of lines. As my training in the martial arts progressed, I found that I readily identified with Kenpo's explosion of power, speed, and syncopated rhythms.

*Ed Parker applying his own culinary skills.*

bers; or when I teach an architect or engineer, I instruct them through body mechanics. This general theory I have about art also extends to cooking. I've owned a world-class restaurant in Tucson for the past sixteen years. It's called El Mariachi Super Club. Initially I bought the restaurant in order to feature my mariachi group, but over the years ended up putting together dishes that have won international awards. My shrimp flambed in tequila is my favorite, and believe it or not I owe much of its artistic creation to my understandings of music and Kenpo.

Over the past twenty-five years, I have probably taught close to 30,000 first lessons, which to me is the best way to learn Kenpo. I've never been bored with teaching because students are different, and I view each one of them as a new challenge. Coming to an understanding of each unique student through teaching is one of the greatest gifts I've received from the martial arts. What I have learned to be of great importance is not to put myself on a level above my student. In my early

stages of teaching, I thought it would be helpful in getting their attention if I impressed them with my speed and power. But I found in many cases that this proved to be counterproductive, and so I've long since changed the perspective from which I teach, and I find the result to be far more rewarding to my students and myself.

Since 1974 my schools have undergone many changes in their overall teaching curriculum. One that I feel is long overdue and highly valuable is a pre-kindergarten class that teaches three to five year olds. We teach these children discipline, confidence, respect, and hand-eye coordination – and the parents love it. This Pre-K program has been tremendously successful. These kids pay attention. We have a follow-up course for six to nine year olds, and another one for nine to twelve year olds. The youngest ones we don't teach to fight but rather how not to beat up on their siblings and peers. Some of the kids started at three-and-a-half years old and they're still here fifteen years later!

Like many others who have opened schools, I've learned a lot about business. Before I began running my first school, I thought that the restaurant business was hard, but there is nothing harder than running a karate school, especially in the

*Gilbert Velez with the Pre-K three and four year olds.*

175

early days of the seventies. For me what made it so hard was that nothing runs like a karate school – not a health club, not a restaurant, nothing – and initially I tried to run it like a standard business and came up against many a brick wall.

Today instructors opening schools and forming associations have a tremendous advantage in that over the last eight years several new previously unavailable marketing programs like NAPMA (National Association of Professional Martial Artists), and others, are being offered to school owners. These programs are spearheaded and staffed by professional business consultants who are very good at what they do. If Mr. Parker were alive today, I personally feel he would be strongly attracted to and supportive of these programs. Looking back, I feel that what programs like NAPMA are offering is what Mr. Parker was trying to put together for his franchise schools back in the early 1970s. These marketing professionals show the karate school owner business practices without telling him what to do. These programs don't care about what system or style is being promoted, and they don't certify individuals or put their stamp of approval on anyone's organization. Instead they talk about how to keep students, how to treat them, how to market them, how to handle insurance, how to advertise, how to close. And it's all done under the umbrella of sound ethical principles. In addition, they have a general program that addresses how to handle children, how to teach them with the aid of a child psychologist, and a philosophy about how to teach women. Best of all, anybody can join because they are nondenominational and nonpolitical.

Another incredible milestone to the martial arts community has been Billy Blanks's Tai-Bo, which has created a surge in interest in the martial arts reminiscent of Bruce Lee's "Enter the Dragon" or David Carradine's "Kung-Fu" television series. As far as I'm concerned the martial arts community should give Billy Blanks a medal.

I have found that if used correctly, kickboxing is a great supplement to Kenpo. Kickboxing is another way that I can easily and successfully demonstrate to my students how to execute a jab, rotational torque, a snapping punch, and how to properly launch a roundhouse, uppercut, and hooking punch in Kenpo. I teach body mass and all the concepts and principles. Two and a half years ago I instituted kickboxing into my school

*1997 near Aztec pyramid of the Moon with representatives from states of Sonara, Veracruz, Puebla, and Mexico D.F., Mexico City.*

and within two years signed up 250 kickboxers, of which a substantial number were women. The best thing is, I'm actually teaching something to my students. They're not dancing out on the mats. What I'm teaching is Ken-Bo, for lack of a better word. I teach them Kenpo's power sources and concepts. I've known for years that it's difficult getting a good cardiovascular workout in that standard Kenpo class because Kenpo is so technical. So I had to find a way to augment my classes with a strong physical fitness program, and Tai-Bo set a good example. As far as getting in shape, Tai-Bo opened my eyes. And again, I don't do TaiBo; I do American Kenpo kickboxing. The way I teach it is unbelievable because my students really learn how to throw a punch. In a month these guys can fight better than a student who only practices Kenpo for a year. In a single kickboxing class they throw 1,000 punches and 500 kicks. Add those numbers up over a period of three months, and you will readily see the value.

Today my school curriculum has what I feel Kenpo was missing. So now in addition to getting their Kenpo lessons, my students get a solid cardiovascular workout that includes stretching, calisthenics, kickboxing, bag work, obstacle courses, and jumping kicks. It's fantastic, and the results are impressive. As an aside, in my travels throughout Europe I haven't seen people out of shape. You just don't see this in Europe. These students are all in shape, regardless of age.

If I were to offer advice to the new student, it would be to listen and keep an open mind. This is not only with regard to learning Kenpo but applies to all art forms. Over the years I've been a student of many masters of painting, drawing, and music. And sometimes I have seen a master of music tell a student to do something in a particular way, only to have the student reply, "Yes, but I prefer to do it another way."

Then the master says to the student, "Fine, then do it your way." And the student misses the whole point of the lesson. I've seen students of art make the same mistake. They'll ask a great painter how he painted such an incredible and astonishing work of art, and the painter will give the wis-

dom behind how he created his masterpiece. But the student wasn't listening and has some cocky response about how he or she feels they may have a better way. The master looks at them and says with a smile, "Fine. Then you keep doing it that way. That's very well." Like I'm sure is the case with other kenpoists, I saw Mr. Parker respond this way on many occasions.

The greatest gift I have received from Kenpo is the worldwide travel and meeting all the people. This was not always the case. In my beginning years in Kenpo, and with the exception of my travels to Pasadena to work with Mr. Parker and the twenty martial arts tournaments that I sponsored for Mr. Parker in Tucson, I stayed pretty much to myself. Besides my restaurant and my mariachi group, I had three Kenpo schools in Tucson. As a result, I did not associate much with the Kenpo communities on the east and west coasts. Since the passing of Mr. Parker, however,

*Mike Pick, Ed Parker, Susan Broussard, Huk Planas, and myself.*

Dian Tanaka, Bob Liles, and Sasha Williams. Nearly five hundred IKKA members attended our seminars. It was a moving display of our overseas support of the brotherhood.

What is particularly meaningful to me is how Kenpo is rapidly spreading throughout the Spanish speaking countries, resulting in enormous followings in Spain, Chile, Mexico and Argentina. In response to this, I have translated much of Mr. Parker's curriculum – particularly the theories, concepts, and terminology – into Spanish. So when I travel to these countries, I don't teach these students in English, but in Castillian, which is Spanish. These people knew the English terms when I first arrived nine years ago, but they were astounded when I started explaining Kenpo to them in Spanish. They respected that.

this has substantially changed and I have become extremely active in the Kenpo community, particularly out of the country.

Since 1992 I have traveled over a half-million miles on behalf of the IKKA, conducting seminars throughout the United States, as well as in Greece, New Zealand, England, Ireland, Sweden, Germany, Mexico, Holland, Spain, Portugal, and the Channel Islands. This has turned out to be a major leg of my Kenpo journey in that my primary focus is, in addition to teaching Kenpo to new students, improving and standardizing the Kenpo that had been previously taught in these countries.

These Europeans have a great degree of honor – the Spanish, English, Dutch, Irish, etc. – they have virtue and truly want to do Kenpo correctly. These people are tremendously noble, and the martial arts gives them a further sense of old honor. This has nothing to do with the samurai. We're talking about people who still are both highly respectful of kings and queens. These people respect authority and hierarchy. They care

While initially I traveled to these countries by myself, over the past couple of years I've had a substantial number of esteemed kenpoists lend their help. I am truly impressed with our IKKA affiliate schools, as well as other martial arts associations in Europe. In May 2001 a group of us traveled to Portugal, including Doreen Cogliandro, Mrs. Ed Parker, Dennis Lawson, Larry Kongaika,

*Jersey 2000. After the tournament, the brotherhood dance and dinner celebrated by all the countries.*

*Program from the 5th Tucson International
Tournament started in 1976.*

*With Doreen Cogliandro.*

*Seminar in Plymouth, England, 1993.*

about rank and honor a man's belt because they know that the person earned it honorably. As a result, they thrive on the discipline, honor and structure of the martial arts. They expect the martial arts to have integrity, and they bring integrity to the martial arts.

As martial artists the Europeans are good and constantly improving. To me what stands out about them is that they have a natural fighting and competitive spirit. And when the seminar or tournament comes to an end, they come together that evening in joyous celebration, and eat and dance into the wee hours of the morning. It is a true festival that pays tribute to our Kenpo brotherhood. Even for those who have traveled with me who don't know the foreign languages, it doesn't matter. The language of the brotherhood and family spirit of Kenpo is spoken by all present.

For those who are interested in the history, the European IKKA was started in Ireland thirty-eight years ago by John McSweeny. Back then there was one, maybe two, Kenpo associations in Ireland. Today there are twenty-six. Not just Ed Parker's American Kenpo, but twenty-six different Kenpo associations. John McSweeney's dates back to 1962, and they still teach the old style Kenpo and wear the old patch displaying the single fist. From one or two Kenpo associations to twenty-six – it's unbelievable! What incredible growth in a country thousands of miles away from the Kenpo epicenter in Pasadena.

As to the future of American Kenpo, I envision everybody coming back together. Not under one association. They all have their own banners, and they're not going to give them up. And so once you make that realization, you accept that. You have to. But I do see everyone coming back together in a different way that as yet I haven't really crystallized in my mind. I can't tell you how I came to this, except to say that in my years of walking around this planet, I've learned that life's too short. As individuals and as a community, we've all been carrying around substantial baggage for far too long. Maybe it's time we as a brotherhood just forgot about all that and started over.

Meanwhile, I continue on my journey that for now, anyway, is focused on helping to standardize and spread the IKKA both nationally and internationally. If I could say something to Ed Parker today it would be that I kept my promise to him that I would remain loyal to his family and to the IKKA.

# Dennis Conatser
## 5th Degree

*Always a kid at heart, Dennis Conatser has been involved with the Boy Scouts of America for over ten years, both as a Leader and a Committee Chairman. He has two boys, Dennis II, age twelve, and Stephen, age eleven. Together they enjoy traveling, drag races, professional sporting games (Diamondbacks, Cardinals, and Suns), as well as collecting rare coins, Beanie Babies, and Pokemon cards. Besides looking after his elderly mother, Dennis is an active member in his church and is a 4th Degree member of the Knights of Columbus, which is a catholic men's fraternity. Being very civic minded, Dennis is actively involved with many community functions throughout the year, including pancake breakfasts, blood drives, youth projects, and the Annual Law and Order Dinner that honors local fire departments and law enforcement agencies throughout the state of Arizona. As a successful fund-raiser, Dennis recently chaired a committee that raised $150,000 for scholarships to catholic high schools and colleges. He enjoys the Internet where, in addition to being a regular poster on message boards and a participant in chat rooms, he is the webmaster of one of the most popular Kenpo websites on the Worldwide Web.*

I grew up in Denver in the small suburb of Arvata. I was an only child, who was somewhat isolated by my parents. They had lost two daughters prior to my birth and, as a result, were overprotective of me. I spent most of my time in the house and acted out a lot of role-play in my room. Separated from the other kids, my self-confidence began to wane, and I often became the target of the local bully.

Like many adolescent boys, I became fixated on the male attributes and one of the tens of thousands who ordered the Charles Atlas body building program. I wanted to learn how to tear telephone books and develop bulging muscles. I did Atlas's dynamic tension exercises for about a month and got a certificate that I still have in a drawer somewhere.

My first recollection of the martial arts was in the movie "Roustabout" with Elvis Presley. There was a scene in a pub where Elvis sang a harassing song to a couple of Ivy League college guys. When he walked out of the place and went to climb on his motorcycle, the two guys started giving him a hard time and tried to put their

*My early martial arts years, posing with a staff.*

of my stay I had lost considerable weight and looked and felt frail. The doctors told my parents that if I stayed in Denver's wet winter climate, there was a possibility that I would become ill again and this time might die.

Two months later, in 1963, my parents relocated to northern Arizona and opened a motel and restaurant along a quiet stretch of the infamous Route 66. For me this was a dramatic change in my environment, having gone from a big city to an isolated cowboy town of 1,000 residents. So small was the community that the fifth and sixth grades were combined in one classroom. Unfortunately I arrived as a fifth grader.

The pecking order was alive and well in my new digs, and in the first week of school a strapping kid named Billy challenged me to a fight. Courageously I told him to meet me after school. This was my first fight, and the truth was I was scared to death. The fight lasted all of fifteen seconds and ended with the two of us on the ground with this kid's legs crushing my kidneys in a scissors hold. I gave up, and everyone left.

My feeling of defeat at the hands of this tough ranch kid began to fester, and I finally concluded that I needed to find a way to defend myself or face a thousand real and imagined defeats throughout the rest of my days. But in this small cattle town there wasn't much to do and no visible means through which I could be taught self-defense.

Over the next two years I continued to be harassed by Billy and was often the brunt of his jokes and snide remarks. Then one day in wood shop, a kid whose older brother had learned karate in Vietnam gave an impromptu demonstration of board breaking. He stacked three pine boards between a couple of chairs and busted them. I was amazed and thought it was the coolest thing I had ever seen. What I found more impressive was that after giving this demonstration, nobody in school wanted to mess with the kid, who up to this time was looked upon as a nerd. I was so fascinated by the experience that I became obsessed with brick breaking, all the while continuing to watch those movies that fea-

hands on his bike. Elvis dropped into some weird stance and dropped one of the guys with a chop to the neck. The other guy gasped, "No, no, man – that's karate!" Everybody backed off, and Elvis grabbed his leather jacket and raced off on his motorcycle into the sunset. I thought, 'Wow! Was that cool or what?' I was eleven years old.

Around that same time, there was a sugar-coated cereal advertised on television called Rice Crinkles. There was a little Chinese guy on the box by the name of SoHi, and he would appear on screen with, "SoHi say, eat the Rice Crinkle!" There was a little dragon in the background with an oriental setting. I made my mom buy the cereal because of SoHi. The cereal tasted all right, but there was a magic lure to this dragon pictured on the box. In the commercial he would do karate moves and yell, "Hiya!"

When I was twelve, I caught a virus that within days caused my kidneys to shut down, and I was hospitalized for six weeks. Although I entered the hospital as a chubby kid, by the end tured the puny guy triumphing over the town bully.

In junior high I enrolled in Little League and became active in basketball. It was a pleasant and rewarding experience. Then in my freshman year I went out for football and endured a season of utter torture. Besides being beaten up on the football field, this kid Billy continued to dog me. Once again my self-confidence began to crumble, and I confided in my dad that some of the kids at school were bugging me.

"Why don't you haul off and knock the hell out of them?" he said.

"It's not that easy, dad. I mean they can hit back. And I don't want to get hit in the face. It kind of scares me."

"Ah, hell, you're as big as those guys," he replied in a gruff voice. "Just knock off and bust 'em one. You watch what will happen. They'll probably leave you alone and never talk to you again."

I didn't believe him and knew I had to take action, so I went out and bought a book on judo written by Bruce Tegner. By the end of the week I was doing back falls in my room and talking big to inanimate objects like my desk, which I felt I could bust in half with a single chop. Within a month my confidence was restored, and I placed the book on the bookshelf in our family den.

Finishing out my senior year at high school, I lettered in football, basketball, baseball, and track. I even set the school record in the discus, which still stands to this day. One day before graduation, my archenemy Billy and I were doing pull-ups in gym class, and for the first time I actually matched him. He was so furious and humiliated that Friday at the school dance he egged me into a fight. He should have stayed home that night because I busted him up pretty

bad. The incident finally put closure to nearly six years of his mean spirited and continual harassment. After word spread that I had beat up the town bully, my self-confidence soared to its highest level.

Upon graduation, I passed on an appointment to Annapolis in lieu of playing football in Phoenix and in 1971 enrolled in Mesa Community College. One day I was driving home from football practice when I spotted a sign mounted over a storefront that read "Karate." I pulled to the curb and glanced at the small school. In my mind I conjured up images of mist emanating from the place, bamboo walls and a little Chinese instructor like SoHi from the Rice Crinkle commercial.

I thought back to the kid in my junior high school wood shop and his impromptu board breaking demonstration. I remembered he had told me that I would have to break the bones in my hands in order to be able to break boards. Over the next couple of weeks I thought about joining the karate school every time I drove by the place, but kept driving nonetheless. Finally it occurred to me that if I could play football and beat up the town bully, maybe I could handle this karate stuff as well.

Days later I walked into the school and was greeted by a little chubby guy. I told him I was interested in breaking bricks and that I felt that if I could break a brick, then I could break anybody's head. He didn't have much to say about the bricks, but he did offer me an introductory course amounting to five lessons for the price of fifteen dollars. We set an appointment, and I went home clutching my receipt. The place wasn't quite what I had envisioned because there was this white guy with a beard who looked like a miniature Viking instead of SoHi and his dragon, but I was jazzed.

The afternoon of my first lesson, I arrived to find no one in the place except that same guy. After I'd been on the mats for a few minutes, I knew that the physical aspect would be a breeze. I still remember thinking, 'What is this? This is absolutely nothing. We do this at football practice just to limber up.' After the warm-up and stretching, I learned the training horse, the basic punch, the inward block, and the neutral bow. Topping off the lesson, I hurled a few kicks at the bag, and I was hooked.

*From left: Skip Hancock, Lee Wedlake, Ed Parker, and Dennis Conatser in Europe.*

From the beginning I could see the light at the end of the tunnel and honestly felt that becoming proficient at karate was within my reach. Most important was that I believed I had finally found the easy solution to conquering my low self-confidence and the undercurrent of fear that had pervaded my life up to that point. No longer would it be necessary to pump iron for hours or run miles on the track.

After completing the introductory course, I signed up for group class and purchased a gi. It was official now. I was a dues paying member of a real karate school, and I felt fantastic. Upon arriving home, I couldn't wait to get my gi on and start looking like karate. I ripped open the cellophane wrapper and smelled the cloth. I washed and ironed it, and then turned my attention to trying to figure out how to tie the belt so that the ends fell evenly. I fumbled around for what seemed an eternity, but by midnight I was suited up and standing before my bedroom mirror. It was a supreme honor to be a white belt. I was ready to have my official instructor bring on the stuff. I was eager to become a fighting machine like SoHi and Elvis.

From the outset I was obsessed with karate and attended class six days a week. My room was filled with charts and diagrams, all related to Kenpo, and every night I would sit in bed and pretend I was a fly in the corner of the ceiling and would watch myself in the middle of the room practicing my techniques.

Not long after I was awarded my orange belt, I told my instructor, Lonny Coots, that I wanted to start learning to become an instructor. He told me he'd let me know when he felt I was ready, which went in one ear and out the other. I really wanted to become an instructor, and I kept ragging on him. Finally he had heard enough and called me into his office one evening just before the beginner's class.

"Okay, you've got about a half-dozen guys out there. Go run them through class."

"What do I do?" I asked with an air of confidence.

"You know how to go through class. Go out there and warm them up."

I retied my belt into my most professional knot and headed onto the mats. It was an hour-long class, and so I bowed them in and started counting jumping jacks, then swung into all our routine calisthenics. Upon completing the warm up, I grew concerned upon noting from the wall clock that only five minutes had elapsed. I excused myself and walked back into Coots's office.

"Okay, what now? What do I do?"

Mr. Coots looked up from his paperwork, surprised to see me.

"Well, look, did you stretch?"

"Uh, no, no, I didn't," I said in a strained whisper. I hustled back out and led the class through some stretches and a few sets of sit-ups. It felt like another eternity had passed, yet I had only managed to knock another five minutes off the one hour class. Jesus! I hustled back into the office for the third time.

"What do you want now?" Mr. Coots said, annoyed.

"Well I did the stretches and – "

"Did you do some techniques? Did you show them a new technique?"

"Oh, yeah, that's what I should do," I said with renewed confidence.

I sailed back on to the mats and showed the class a new technique, knocking another whole ten minutes off the clock. This was the longest hour in history. It felt like I had fallen into a time warp. I returned to Coots's office. He spoke before I did.

*The early 1970s seeking the connection between mind and body.*

"Don't you walk through that door. You get out there and you teach a good class."

I stared back at him with an utterly deflated expression, then walked back out for the last time. I was embarrassed because I was sure that everyone in the class had heard Mr. Coots chewing me out, and I was certain everyone thought I was a real numskull. I sucked it in and got through the class, hardly knowing what I was doing.

Years later, I accompanied Mr. Parker on his international seminar tour and, along with a group of assistant instructors, worked with as many as 1,000 students. During those seminars there were times when Ed Parker was called away for something, and he would turn to me and say, "Take over." I never batted an eye. I just slipped right into gear and carried on with the seminar. I'd come a long way since that night in Mr. Coots's office. For all of us, progress is part and parcel of the journey. All that was required of me is that I stay on the path and keep walking.

Admittedly, I began my martial arts training fueled by obsession, a major part of which was my need for immediate validation. The problem was I wanted more recognition than what is normally extended to a beginning white belt, and so I made up for this by devoting more hours to the school than did any of the other students. Over the years I've talked with many martial artists who have fallen into this trap. Although I was neither the owner nor the head instructor, I opened and closed the school, swept the mats and cleaned the showers, windows, and mirrors. My title was that of the dojo janitor, who often worked for lessons through an array of activities that included everything from answering the phones to building weapons racks and doing demonstrations. Out of love for the school and a passion for the art, I had become consumed in an unhealthy way.

After six months of wearing all these hats, I came to feel that I was doing more and more work in what was increasingly becoming a thankless job. Worse still, I sensed that every time something went wrong, I was the one who received the lion's share of blame. Not only did I begin to feel that my instructor expected more of me with regard to my daily chores, but in my eyes he began raising his expectations of me on the mats. If the class was doing fifty pushups, how come I wasn't doing fifty-one? In my gut I eventually began to feel I'd never be good enough for my instructor, and I developed a resentment that almost resulted in quitting karate.

Today looking back with considerably more experience, I realize that the issue had to do with my own unrealistic expectations. Driven by an

*With Steve LaBounty at the Long Beach Internationals.*

obsession for advancement, I had raised my level of expectations and in so doing put pressure on my instructor. In order to counterbalance the pressure he was feeling, he began raising his expectations of me. In the ensuing months, this seesaw effect began to grind on both of us. If there is a lesson here to be learned, it is that it is all right to have one's head in the clouds, so long as one keeps his feet on the ground.

I was able to open my own studio a couple of months after I received my third-degree brown belt, with Mr. Coots acting as my head instructor. Then nineteen months later, I received my black belt and began working with one of Steve LaBounty's black belts, Gary Swan, through camps and seminars.

As is the case with everyone chronicled in this book, my journey eventually took me to the International Karate Championships in Long Beach. I wasn't in the Sports Arena for long before I spotted Ed Parker. After following him around for a half-hour, he finally took a breather, and I walked up to him.

"Hello, Mr. Parker," I began somewhat nervously. "My name is Dennis Conatser, and I study Kenpo."

"Who's your instructor?" he replied with a raised brow.

"I study in Tempe, Arizona, originally under Lonny Coots. For the past year I've been working with Gary Swan and Steve LaBounty."

He suddenly lit up like a Christmas tree.

"Ah! Steve LaBounty – good man! Good to meet you. Keep studying hard."

He slapped me on the back and disappeared into the crowd, leaving me momentarily speechless. I took a deep breath and thought to myself, 'Whoa! Ed Parker!' He was nicer than I had expected.

As time passed, I did not forget my first meeting with Mr. Parker, and eventually I was given the opportunity to train directly under him through the recommendation of Steve LaBounty. I think I broke the speed limits all the way from Scottsdale to Pasadena, California. I walked into the Pasadena school and stood in the waiting

area, my gi and black belt tucked under my arm. Frank Trejo walked up to me. I immediately recognized him from the Internationals.

"What're you here for?" he asked with a stern look.

"I'm here to take a lesson from Mr. Parker. I'm studying with him now."

"Really?" he said with a half-smile. "Hey, welcome aboard, brother."

He told me that Ed Parker wouldn't be arriving for an hour and, in what I later came to know as typical Trejo camaraderie, invited me to join him for a margarita down the street at the Acapulco Restaurant. I thanked him but said I was about to have a lesson.

An hour later I stood on the mat in my horse, my eyes glued on Ed Parker, who was barefoot and dressed in one of his colorful Hawaiian shirts. I was totally enamored just being in the great Pasadena school. All these legends were walking in and out as Frank lounged in the office, strumming his guitar. Everyone was having a good old time, and while it was probably quite normal to them, the atmosphere made me feel uncomfortable. I felt there were a hundred magnifying glasses all around watching me, and whenever I heard laughter, I thought it was about me.

After awhile, my stomach stopped churning, and I began to focus on the lesson. Ed Parker asked me what I wanted, and I told him that because I was just beginning my study with him,

I wanted to start at the bottom and go through all the basics and all the yellow belt techniques and the first couple of forms. The reason this was important to me was that I had a school back in Tempe that I was switching over to the IKKA, and I felt a great sense of pride and responsibility about that. American Kenpo was Ed Parker's creation and his passion, and I wanted to make sure that I was teaching it correctly. And, of course, pride breeds loyalty. That he was agreeing to share his system with me, I felt I owed him my full loyalty in return.

Not surprisingly, I found Mr. Parker to be the ultimate "complete" instructor with his own unique way of teaching that wasn't necessarily the same for every student. When I first said to him, "Look at my Kenpo, and if there's something you can expand, then expand me," for some reason he hated that. Later I found out that his approach to teaching was like that of a college professor. From my perspective, he much preferred teaching Kenpo in terms of specifics and principles. He didn't care so much about orders and standardizing everything because he was adamantly opposed to getting locked into one way of doing things and losing the ability to creatively teach each individual.

One major aspect of my journey has centered on my love for teaching, which is why in college I majored in physical education. The reason I related so well to athletics was because there was always a lesson plan. The lack of standardized lesson plans in Kenpo proved to be a stumbling block in my early years as an instructor because I was better able to teach if I had an ordered, graduated system of lesson plans in front of me. By the same token, I feel I might have progressed more quickly as a student had there been more structure.

Encouraged by my instructor Lonny Coots, who was a state champion, I entered my first tournament around the middle of 1972 as an orange belt and thought it was the biggest tournament on the face of the globe. I mean there must have been sixty people there.

*Self defense competition*

Unbeknownst to me I lined up next to a purple belt that in the previous year was the state champion. Seconds after the match started, I swept him and got a point. His eyes flared up and he responded with a backknuckle that sent me backpedaling out of the arena. My momentum was such that I went through a nearby open door and practically made it to the street. He won the match, and later I found out that he thought I was arrogant for sweeping him and lining up next to him in the first place.

In the ensuing months I began scourging through *Karate Illustrated* and *Black Belt* magazines for upcoming tournaments around Arizona, Colorado, New Mexico, Texas, Nevada, Utah, and up and down California. I was convinced that nothing would beat experience, and from 1972 through 1978 I traveled to a tournament two to three weekends every month. I experienced a lot of highs and lows, although the best part was that I got to meet most all of the Who's Who on the tournament circuit at that time.

My most memorable moment was at the 1977 International Karate Championships in Long Beach. I was fighting as a relatively new black belt. I won my first two matches against nobodies, and then went over to the eye chart to see whom I was fighting next. All of a sudden I see the name Ray Sua and I said in a loud voice, "Ah, Sh . . ! Not Sua!"

Ray Sua was a champion fighter and one of my idols. As we stepped into the ring I suddenly noticed this large crowd developing all around ringside. We bowed and squared off, and I was so nervous that all I could think of was attack. But before I could launch anything, he scored a point. Whatever he hit me with, I never saw it. I came back and attacked him and I got a point. I was amazed. We went back and forth to a four /four tie, and then he beat me with the last encounter. It was an action fight and the crowd really got into it. I felt so good to have actually done that well against a fighter of Ray Sua's prominence. Ray went on to win the

him, I had an arsenal of strong basics that I knew I could always retreat to if I got in trouble. I had earlier proved this to myself at the Internationals the year I had fought through the ranks.

Having brought to Ed Parker this arsenal of strong basics, he then became a catalyst in helping me fit together the remaining pieces of the puzzle, which in its entirety represented my own personal, and tailored, Kenpo.

This stage is what Ed Parker often referred to as the Engineer Phase. I like to refer to it as the Architectural Stage. For me, this was the level of Kenpo where I felt I had a solid understanding of all the principles and reinforcing material that explained why I do things in Kenpo the way I do them. It is one thing to look at an architect's set of blueprints and another to understand how everything fits together in the finished house – to see beyond the blueprints and be able to visualize the walls, framing, and the plumbing. For example, to know that the visible electrical outlets that are affixed to the wall have invisible wiring that is interconnected behind the sheetrock.

Mr. Parker once asked me what kind of Kenpo stylist I intended to be? Without thinking, I said, "I want to be the best."

"Well, what is the best one?" he asked.

"I don't know. What are you talking about?"

He could sense my confusion, and answered, "Well, there are practitioners of Kenpo, and you're certainly that. And then there are the mechanics of Kenpo. A good mechanic fixes a car. And then there is the engineer who designs the car."

Today I know that ultimately I want my Kenpo to be centered and have a foundation from the perspective of what Ed Parker called the Engineer, which to me is synonymous with the Architect.

While I cannot recall where it began, for many years I have Kenpoized everything to the degree that my life and my Kenpo have become so intertwined that I can no longer tell whether Kenpo is mimicking life or life is mimicking Kenpo.

Internationals that year, and I walked away reassessing my ability and progress. I had come to the martial arts and the tournament circuit hoping to build up my confidence, and the next thing I knew I was in the ring with one of the best fighters in the world and doing halfway as well.

My first school under the instructorship of Lonny Coots was according to Steve LaBounty an Iron Worker School, which he defined in one word — GRUNT. I spent most of my early training pounding out set after set of hard basics. If one viewed Kenpo as a puzzle, then the perimeter pieces of the puzzle were the primary focus of the Iron Worker school. This was the realistic, bread and butter aspect of Kenpo. Hard strong stances and blocks coupled with hard kicks and punches. All the other, more advanced stages of Kenpo are attributed to the Watchmaker School, of which Ed Parker was unquestionably the most skilled watchmaker. Thankfully, when I finally got to

I discovered that there is no easy road to attaining a black belt and that the main, and perhaps only, requirement was my willingness to do a lot of hard work over a long period of time. The same principle applies to the various expressions of the martial arts. Because I wanted to learn how to be a good fighter, I had to place my art and myself into that arena. I cannot learn fighting by reading a manual or hypothesizing the fight by explaining, "Well, if he did this, I'd do that."

Steve LaBounty once said me, "You'll leave the art long before the art will leave you." In my experience I have found that to be true. A day has not gone by that I have not thought about Kenpo in some way, shape or form. There were times when I tried to divorce myself from the art but failed. Somehow, some way, Kenpo always found a path back to my very core. I have gone beyond the fail-safe point. Kenpo is an integral part of all my perceptions, my actions and reactions, and the general flow of my life. My Kenpo has become internalized. It is the blueprint that runs the software of my being.

Perhaps my greatest realization about the martial arts is that there is so much more to the art than self-defense. True, the lure of self-defense was initially what attracted me to Lonny Coots's Kenpo school when I was in college. However, many years have passed since I acquired the knowledge to physically inflict serious harm to another human being. Along with that acquisition, I bid farewell to the fear that had walked beside me since childhood. The point is, over the past three decades I have not been placed in enough physical confrontations to justify the hundreds of thousands of hours I have spent acquiring the expert ability to adequately defend myself. One can become a world class champion, and even a world class instructor, but what he has become for the great majority of his life is a world class paper tiger because, thankfully, there is rarely an arena in today's society for the true warrior to enter. As a result, fighting long ago ceased to be the nucleus of my art. Today I am interested in information. Friends often tell me I'm an infomaniac, and it's true. The philosophical and spiritual sides of the martial arts intrigue me. A sort of Kenpo-aikido, if you will. Is there such a system? Perhaps I'll find it further up the road apiece as my journey continues.

# Doreen Cogliandro
## 8th Degree

*Doreen Cogliandro has often said that, ultimately, her Kenpo journey has been one of discovering her sexual identity. Clearly, since beginning her study of the martial arts while attending high school, she has walked in many of the deepest valleys and climbed many of the tallest mountains. In addition to students of American Kenpo, on an informative and inspirational level hers is a profile that should be read by every female student entering into the martial arts in general, regardless of age. In 1987 Doreen was selected to fight on the Atlantic World Karate Team along with Christine Bannon Rodriques, Billy Blanks, Steve "Nasty"Anderson, Jean Fernette, Richard Plowden, and Linda Denley. Since retiring from her stellar tournament career as one of the all-time winning fighters, she continues to teach Kenpo at her school, which she first opened in Revere, Massachusetts 21 years ago. As a staunch supporter of Ed Parker and the surviving IKKA, Doreen is also a regular participant at many of the popular camps and seminars held annually throughout the U.S. and abroad. In addition to operating her school, she is a full-time mother of two sons, Anthony and Joseph, who are both active in American Kenpo.*

Every year on my birthday my dad reminds me that I was a breached baby born feet first. When my mom was about to deliver me, the entire maternity staff came to witness my birth because breach births were uncommon in the fifties. My take on this has been that even at birth people were lining up to watch me kick my way into the world.

I was raised in a strict Italian family. My father was very protective of my sisters and me. He never wanted us to struggle the way he did growing up on the streets of East Boston. Although his protective nature gave me a feeling of security, it did little to prepare me for the real

*My father holds me up for my first kick*

*Far right, Doreen playing on high school basketball team*

world I later encountered as an adult.

While my father focused on my outer world, my mother doted on me and made sure my bedroom of pink and lace was filled with all the things she felt that little girls were supposed to have.

At age seven I learned the difference between what girls should do and what boys should do. Many of the girls in the neighborhood were taking dance lessons, and one of my cousins was in a dance recital. I wanted desperately to join because I loved to dance and everyone looked like they were having so much fun. But when I asked if I could dance with them, their response was "You're too fat to dance." I was so embarrassed and humiliated. Nobody had ever called me that before. Besides what did being fat have to do with dancing? I was so confused.

When I was eleven, the neighborhood boys were playing baseball and needed one more player to even out the teams, so they asked me. Much to their amazement, if not embarrassment, I could hit the ball farther than all of them.

Soon thereafter I began playing softball and basketball on teams sponsored by the local parks and youth organizations. I absolutely loved athletics and was always the first to arrive at practice and the last to leave.

It wasn't long before a group of boys became intimidated by my athletic ability and began dogging me and calling me a tomboy. Their taunting served only to further inflame my competitive spirit, and I began swinging the bat harder and jumping higher for rebounds, all the while stuffing my emotions.

It wasn't just the boys who laughed at me. Much of the taunting came from girls. With them it wasn't so much that I intimidated them but that I was a girl and an accomplished athlete. I think this was the root of much of my childhood anger. I was too fat to dance, and a girl wasn't supposed to play baseball.

My problem was that I had this deep need to express myself physically, and so eventually the drive to play sports became so overwhelming that I did it anyway, no matter how much ridicule and resistance I got. It's not that I wanted to be a boy; I just loved to play.

Five years later at the age of sixteen, I was play fighting with one of the neighborhood boys. He kept trying to punch me in the head, and I kept blocking his punches. Suddenly he stopped and lowered his hands to his sides.

"Do you take karate?"

"No," I answered simply.

"It sure looks like you do," he replied and walked away.

His comment prompted me to watch a karate class that was held at the local elementary school. What I saw looked challenging, and I was especially drawn to the intensity of the training.

The label of tomboy had stuck with me, as well as the taunting, and I had grown into an angry teenager who kept to myself. Since I was just finishing softball season and had to wait until November for basketball to begin, I decided to join. I figured that at least karate would help keep me in good physical condition through the summer.

During this time there was a big woman's rights movement emerging, and female athletes like Billy Jean King were viewed by both the public and the media with skepticism. I feel that the message that many women gave was that they could outdo men or they were better than men were. I never felt that way. I wasn't trying to overshadow the boys or be better than they were. I just wanted to be my own best.

Not surprisingly, my parents weren't keen on the idea of my taking karate, but they didn't stop me. By now it was part and parcel of my competitive, aggressive nature, which they were hopeful I would eventually outgrow. Apart from their feelings and occasional side comments, I was becoming increasingly aware of others who subtly were beginning to question my femininity.

I can still vividly recall my first karate lesson. I arrived at the school early so I could register and try on my uniform, which felt to me like I was wearing pajamas. It was so hot that sweat was pouring down my face before the class even began. I watched my fellow classmates enter the gym. Each one looked meaner than the next. What soon became obvious to everyone was that not only was I the youngest student, I was the only female.

When we lined up, I was motioned to the back of the class. The teacher stood before us, holding a broomstick that had a boxing glove taped to the end. We were ordered to begin running around the room as the teacher yelled, "Arms up!"

Each student let out an ungodly yell as they were hit in the stomach with the boxing glove. Utterly terrified, I approached the teacher, who hit me squarely in the gut.

"Meet the magic wand!" he roared angrily.

The broomstick was so labeled because the instructor felt that the fear of being hit by it made his students magically learn their lessons.

The next day I could barely move, but the crazy thing was I couldn't wait to return to class. Over the ensuing months, my training was tough, and I was taught to take a punch and give a beating. This turned out to be a basic strategy that I later used in tournament fighting. Without exception, all my training partners were men. In the early seventies I was a young blonde-hair-blue-eyed girl with a ponytail on each side of my head, sparring with men who were much older.

Martial arts soon became my passion. I had finally found a way to vent my hostility and, of course, the sparring was ideal because I could hit someone and not get in trouble. The karate workouts made me tough and confident.

Having been involved in competitive sports

since childhood, I couldn't wait to fight in my first tournament. In 1973 karate tournaments were considerably different than they are today. Competitors wore either a black or white gi, and we fought without protective gear, including a mouthpiece. One could denote someone's style by their school patch or the forms they would demonstrate. Women of all belt rank, ages fourteen and older, were placed in the same division. Thirty years ago there were not many women wearing brown or black belts.

*At a seminar from left, Sita Van, me, Jeff Nelson, and Sarko Gergerian*

I entered my first tournament as a white belt and in my first fight squared off against a woman brown belt who punched me solidly in the nose. With blood dripping down my face, I thought, 'At least I got a point for contact!' Instead, my opponent was awarded the point, and I eventually lost the match. I wasn't discouraged. In fact, I couldn't wait to return to do it all again.

Looking back, I know that what I was feeling was something awakening inside of me. When I practiced karate it was as if something became alive in my mind, my heart, my body, but mostly my soul. When I fought in tournaments and in the school, it was a release of all the anger and hate I had inside me. Throughout my competitive career, anger was the fuel that kept my training alive. I couldn't fight enough, and no matter how many tournaments I won, and no matter how many times I fought, the anger never subsided. Although I noticed I began speaking up more, the only emotion I still felt comfortable expressing was anger.

My first teacher was really old school hard core, and our classes were extremely intense. Just the command "Line Up!" would make me start sweating. While all of the name-calling and

pounding toughed me for the street, it also bred resentment and confusion. If I brought friends to watch my class in the hopes of having them join the school, the only comment I ever got was that I was crazy and, of course, they never joined.

Being female in an all-male dojo presented other challenges. Women who worked out with guys were labeled as either being butch or more interested in the men than the training. I didn't fit into either category. I just wanted to learn. Many times there were inappropriate innuendoes made and boundaries crossed. But despite all the obstacles, I think subconsciously my soul had a mission, so I kept quiet and kept training.

I always hid the bruises from my parents. If they ever saw them, I know they would have forbid me to continue training. No matter how tough things got, I refused to give up. I saw many students leave because of the way my instructor made them feel.

Once when I was a green belt, he was teaching the class a throw technique that I couldn't get. I began to show my frustration, which he mistook as a sign of disrespect toward him. He walked over to me and picked me up and dumped me flat on my head, then began to yell and swear at me. I started crying, which was an uncommon response for me. I went into the locker room and decided I had had enough. Minutes later I stood outside the gym with my green belt in my hand and handed it to him and said, "I quit." "Why?" he replied in shock.

I told him I was trying my best and I couldn't take the way he treated me. I asked him if I ever did anything right. He said sure, but even if I did 999 things right, he would address the one

*Fellow teammember Christine Bannon Rodriquez*

*Warming up with another member of the Atlantic World Karate Team*

thing I had done wrong. Positive reinforcement was not part of the teaching strategy. Somehow he convinced me to stay. I was a naive seventeen-year-old at the time. In retrospect, I feel I stayed because it was my destiny. It took many years for me to realize what I had experienced.

I entered my adulthood feeling that people were beginning to wonder about me. Closer to home, my parents began to subtly question when I was going to get a boyfriend and start making plans to get married. Back when I was a teenager, boys were taught to find themselves and become a man, while girls were taught to become a woman and find a man.

At the age of eighteen, everyone was greatly relieved when I began dating a young man who eventually became my husband. I was a brown belt at the time, and my boyfriend decided to join my karate school. Although this made me feel safer, his presence did not stop the classroom beatings and the verbal abuse. I kept going, but as time passed it became more difficult. Outside the school we encountered other harassment, and there would be comments directed at him from other guys such as "I bet you have to let your

brown belt girlfriend fight your battles."

Due to my father's job being relocated, my parents moved to Washington DC, and I stayed with them during one of my coop terms in school. It was during that stay that I decided I would not be returning to the karate school. I just couldn't take it anymore.

When I returned to Boston for my next school semester, my boyfriend, who had continued with his training, begged me to come and visit our karate teacher. He promised me that my former teacher had changed and was no longer abusive. With reservations, I drove to the school, where my teacher called me into his office and closed the door. I didn't know what to expect, and my heart started racing. He pulled a black belt out of his desk and handed it to me. I refused it because I felt I hadn't earned it.

"Yes, you did, for everything that you've been through in the past five years."

In November 1979 my boyfriend and I were married. We took all the money from our wedding and three months later opened the Revere Karate Academy. I had my reservations. We were both in our early twenties and fresh out of college

with no experience in business. After opening the school, all that remained was $15.00 in the bank. Although my husband promised me everything would be all right, I was scared.

The studio did well. We made a lot of money, and we spent a lot of money. Based on our initial success, we took a huge risk and, with the help of his parents, purchased the building that housed our school.

It wasn't long before our good fortune soured. Because of our inexperience, we did not know that karate schools are seasonal and trendy and are greatly effected by children's school vacations. Soon our cash flow slowed and the well went dry. In order to pay bills I sold my wedding ring. In an effort to stay afloat, we decided to put on a tournament and managed to pay our bills from the revenue we were able to generate. One week after the tournament I gave birth to the first of our two children.

Being a female black belt has definitely presented many challenges. For years my family thought I was crazy, and hardly anyone understood why my school was so important to me. In public people would make a mock karate yell and raise their hands in two karate chop positions.

Men would ask, "Aren't you that karate chick?"

"Do you really think you could take me?"

"Do you think you could beat up Mike Tyson?"

"I better not fool around with you."

"How do you teach men?"

"I bet your husband doesn't give you a hard time?"

"Can women really learn karate?"

My favorite was a woman who said, "Just think people would really think you're just a woman." I never knew what she meant, although her husband looked at me apologetically.

My training in martial arts was not as difficult as running a karate studio. Being a female martial artist was hard, but being a head instructor of a martial arts school a stone's

*My sons Anthony and Joseph meet Grandmaster Parker*

throw from Boston was harder. Although I had the respect of my old students, many of the new male students tended not to take me seriously. In my early years of teaching, I thought of myself as "good for a woman" and it took a long time for me to drop the gender qualifier.

I remember the day it all changed for me. I was about to close the class when a group of guys in the back row started horsing around, which was something they often did. I tried to get them to stop, but they kept it up. I stood in silence and waited for them to stop, and when they finally did, I said, "Sometimes I get the feeling that you are just trying to patronize me and that you don't take me seriously. Let me just say this – I have a lot of knowledge and a lot more experience than anyone else in this room. It's your choice whether or not you want to learn what I have to share."

Almost immediately the atmosphere in the school began to change. I think the person who was most convinced with what I said was me! From that moment, I began to see myself as a karate instructor, not a female instructor or a male instructor, just an instructor. I postured my atti-tude in this way – when looking up teacher or student in the dictionary, gender was not in the definition. When I came to that realization, nothing of a negative nature that anyone said after that had an effect on me.

Twenty-two years later, the Revere Karate School is going strong. It hasn't been easy. Running the studio, raising my children and taking care of a home has often felt like three full-time jobs. The key has been that I was committed, and I kept going.

In September of 1982 my first karate teacher retired from karate, and five months later the most important experience in my martial arts career happened – I met Mr. Parker. The timing was right because I would have never left my first teacher for another, which is a very traditional belief. I almost didn't attend the seminar where Mr. Parker was scheduled to appear because I had just found out I was pregnant with my second child. It was not a planned pregnancy, and the news put me in a horrible mood. Plus, who was this master anyway? It seemed to me that everyone was claiming to be a master around that time.

*Teaching in Madrid*

I went to the seminar kicking and screaming the whole way. Dressed in my karate pants and maternity shirt, I was standing by the main door when I spotted Mr. Parker making his way down the hallway. As he drew nearer, I couldn't help notice that he was a big, strong man with incredible eyes. He stopped and looked at me and said simply, "Hello. I'm Ed Parker."

I was impressed. He never said, "I am Master Parker" or even called himself mister. He just said Ed. All I could think about was how nice he was. As he taught the white to green belt seminar, I watched from nearby. He had the most incredible presence, and I was totally mesmerized.

Becoming a student of Ed Parker's has changed my life. Mr. Parker has a system that combines scientific principles and fighting strategies, and it is organized in such a way to be easily conveyed to students.

In March of 1987 my husband and I became separated, and soon thereafter I was faced with a major crossroads in my martial arts journey. We had been in business together for several years, and under the circumstances felt it unwise for us to continue operating the karate school together. Ultimately, he sold the building that his

parents had helped finance, and I received half of the proceeds. It would have been easy for me to take the money and start a new life, but that would have meant leaving my students without an instructor. After considerable thought, and realizing I now was a single parent with two small children to support, I decided to take the money I made from the sale of the building and relocate the school.

In April 1987 I was selected to be on the Atlantic World Karate Team, which was the first professional karate team for both men and women. It was a dream come true because I had always wanted to compete on a national level. When I asked the coach why I was selected, he said he'd seen me fight for many years and felt I was as good as any woman he had seen on the national circuit.

Fighting on the Atlantic World Karate Team was an awesome experience. Some of my teammates were Christine Bannon Rodriques, Billy Blanks, Steve "Nasty" Anderson, Jean Fernette, Richard Plowden, and Linda Denley. What I loved most about being on the team were the training camps that were held in Connecticut. Not only was I training with some of the best fighters in the country, but also the way the camp was designed each team member participated in the coaching. Nasty talked about ring strategy; Chip Wright talked about being prepared mentally; Billy Blanks taught conditioning; Anthony Price had the corner on ax kicks; Kevin Thompson had the best reverse punch; and Terry Creamer was better at reading an opponent than most.

Running into my former husband at karate tournaments was at times overwhelming, but I always behaved professionally. I may have held my head up high when in public, but there were times I cried the whole way home. My emotions were really out of focus and my performance suffered as a competitor. Although my life was starting to come back together, my anger had not subsided. I was angry at life. I was angry with my parents. I was angry with my ex-husband for leaving me. Then I remembered a conversation that I had with Mr. Parker just before he died. I was at a seminar, and my ex-husband was there. I always felt uncomfortable, and this time tears rolled down my eyes. After the seminar ended, I started to leave when Mr. Parker stopped me and asked what was wrong. I told him how I was feeling and he gave me a hug and some words of encouragement. It was at this moment my martial arts training took a turn. As I left the seminar and reflected on the conversation I had just had with Mr. Parker, I realized that of all the things he had shared with me, the greatest gift he had given me was love. It was his belief in me that had kept me training; it was his confidence in me that had uplifted my soul; it was his example as a teacher that had inspired me to want to become a better person. Kenpo is an exceptional art that has concepts and scientific principles that surpass any other I have seen. But most of all we had Ed Parker. What I remember most of him was the way he unselfishly gave to all, many times at the expense of his own family's well-being.

Up until this time it was hate and anger that motivated my art, but it was here that I learned that if my motivation was love, I could rise to a new level. This is what I do today. Following Mr. Parker's example, I use Kenpo as a vehicle to give encouragement, support, guidance, and most of all love to everyone I teach.

After Mr. Parker died, I made a commitment to myself that I would keep the promise I made to him, which was to study and teach his art. I began to travel worldwide and meet other high-ranking Kenpo black belts. This presented another challenge. Receiving recognition in my own school had become standard, but now that I was on the open seminar circuit, I felt like I was starting over again.

Once, while in Europe, a male instructor who I outranked, said to me, "I think it is wonderful for the Europeans to see such a strong female martial artist."

I looked at him and said, "Drop the female. I have earned it."

I remember something that Dian Tanaka once said to me.

"Wouldn't you rather be considered the 99th best black belt on the mat than have someone say you're the best female out there?"

I had finally found another woman who understood what I was feeling, and at that moment Dian and I became kindred spirits. I had seen so many women who were willing to remain in the shadow of men and revel in the title "The Best Women." Over time I grew to hate it.

The proudest teaching experience I had was while I was in Madrid. The first time I traveled to Spain was for the IKKA European Championships. I visited one of the schools with a fellow black belt, and as we entered the school, he was introduced to the class and I was not acknowledged. This didn't upset me because I was aware that the students didn't know me, even though I outranked everyone in the room.

I suited up and walked onto the mats to join the class. Even though I could not speak Spanish, I could speak the language of Kenpo. After an exchange of techniques with another black belt, they began to look at me differently.

A few years later I was invited back to teach several training seminars with a particular emphasis on sparring, of all things. What made me proud of this experience was that I didn't force my rank on anyone but waited for them to see me for my own ability and invite me to teach. I had broken through not only a language barrier, but a gender barrier as well.

I turned forty-five this year, and the injuries resulting from this high-impact, high-collision sport have taken their toll. I no longer can do the things I did two decades ago, but I am grateful that my injuries are the battle scars that reflect a stellar fighting career.

I pushed myself to a level of skill that I always felt I could one day attain, always striving to be better than I was the day before. I never tried to be the best, just my own best. As I grew older, I realized that the best things the martial arts have to teach I hadn't even begun to learn. Sometimes I feel that Kenpo is the vehicle we use to touch the lives of many. It is like leaving your thumbprint on someone's soul.

I never set out to become a black belt, let alone an eighth-degree black belt. I never tried to outdo men. It sometimes seems as if I blinked my eyes and twenty-eight years went by.

I have always had training goals, teaching goals, and learning goals, but I have never set a rank goal. To me, rank is someone else's recognition of what I have accomplished. Once I was supposed to test for a higher rank, and I declined for personal reasons. One of my students was upset over my decision because he felt that I deserved the recognition. He asked why I decided not to test.

"I already have the accomplishment," I replied.

"What do you mean?" he said.

"I trained and I improved. I studied and I gained more knowledge. I set goals and I achieved them. The rank only means someone else thinks I did, too."

Today I am seen as a strong and confident woman. I hold a eighth-degree black belt, I have owned a karate studio for twenty-one years, I have a college degree, I am an accomplished fighter who has won scores of championships, and I teach seminars worldwide. This is the way the world sees me, and these are titles that I have been given along my journey, but not one of these was ever my goal.

Looking back, it seems that I just wanted the pain to stop. It wasn't easy. In fact, sometimes the emotional and physical pain I endured was so overwhelming that had it not been for my love of and faith in Kenpo, I feel I would not have made it. Truly, the battles I fought, over which I ultimately proved victorious, were not just in the tournament arena. Once I learned to control my anger and tame my fears, I grew tremendously and began studying from a different perspective. I will always be a student who is looking forward to traveling her Kenpo journey for the rest of her life.

*My family. Back row: brother-in-law Tom Batchelor, son Anthony, sister Donna Batchelor, father Alfred DiRienzo, sister Christine Klopher, me, and son Joseph. Front row: Niece Valerie Batchelor, nephew Mathew Klopher, niece Elizabeth Klopher, brother-in-law Stephen Klopher Sr., and nephew Stephen Klopher Jr.*

# Grandmaster
# Michael Robert Pick
## 10th Degree

*Referred to by Ed Parker as Kenpo's premiere knife-fighter, Mike Pick may well be the strongest man in American Kenpo. Standing 5'8" and weighing 250 pounds, he wears a size 52 coat and in one week wields more raw iron than most men do in a lifetime. As a former Marine, he fought in Vietnam where he was awarded the Purple Heart, Combat Action Ribbon, Vietnamese Service Medal with two Bronze Stars, and several Presidential and Naval Citations. Besides defending our Flag, Mike was a member of the Jewish Defense League and spent considerable time hunting Nazi war criminals. An accomplished blacksmith, he collects miniature anvils and cast iron cookware that he uses to cook over his open Dutch oven, and also collects Damascus 10-gauge shotguns and makes his own black powder shotgun shells. Mike and his family live in a sprawling ranch house nestled on ten acres in the Colorado mountains where he enjoys collecting natural bonsai trees in the nearby million-acre national forest. When not practicing and teaching Kenpo, he enjoys fly-fishing, hunting deer and elk, and driving his classic 1947 Ford one-ton panel truck that he restored and converted to 4-wheel drive with a 460 V-8*

My journey in Kenpo began when I was about ten years old. One day I was beat up by five older punks while on my way to school in Pasadena. They wanted my lunch. I refused to give it to them so we fought. They kicked my ass, but I kept my lunch.

That sandwich was important to me. Food was scarce in our house. My parents were divorced. My mother, who had some serious psychological problems and chemical imbalances, had custody of me and my two brothers and two sisters. We lived in a small shack in Pasadena overrun with cockroaches. As the oldest, I was the man of the house and supported the family. There was only one thought in my mind then: to survive every day and keep the family together.

*At three years old imitating my grandpa.*

*At around fifteen years of age at a park in Pasadena*

*Locust Street, a garage full of beer cans*
*Brother, thirteen, shooting jays in the*
*backyard*
*Brother, fifteen, back in the swamps of*
*Florida*
*Drinking, thinking in his Studebaker*
*chariot, looking for our father*
*I missed my brother*
*Mother in a mental hospital*
*Sisters, seven and ten, no one to teach them*
*how to sew but me, sixteen.*

<u>*Childhood, Namhood, Manhood*</u>
*A book by Mike Pick*

I'm not proud of it, but I was an independent hoodlum. Beginning at the age of eleven I did some strong-arm robberies and stealing and worked at odd jobs such as gardening. I was a tough kid and grew up in the streets during tough times.

On the day I got beat up I went home from school on another route. I passed by Ed Parker's Kenpo Karate School on Walnut Street and saw some men fighting. I walked inside. There I was, a little kid with a fat lip and dried blood under my nose, when a big man with a lot of black hair and wearing what I thought were pajamas greeted me and said he was Ed Parker. I told him my name and said I didn't have any money but I'd like to take lessons.

In retrospect I think Mr. Parker was probably amused that a little kid from the wrong side of the tracks wanted to study Kenpo. He smiled and said he needed someone to clean up the school, not an easy task because the workout area had heavy thick tatami mats. If I took the job he would give me lessons. We struck a deal.

Since there weren't any children's classes at the time and minors weren't allowed in the adult classes, Mr. Parker gave me private lessons in the basics almost every day. For the first six months I did nothing more than stand in a horse stance for hours. Then he taught me inward and outward blocks, crossovers, and covering, which is learning how to fight in one direction and then turning to and fight in another direction without opening my position.

There were railroad tracks behind the studio. On my way to and from the school I walked down the tracks practicing crossovers and covering. By the time I was fifteen years old I was doing 1,000 kicks, 1,000 strikes, and 1,000 blocks every day.

To celebrate my sixteenth birthday I stood in a horse stance in a corner of the school for sixteen hours. I'd read in an issue of *Black Belt* magazine about a Chinese woman martial artist who celebrated each of her birthdays that way until she was seventy-two years old.

I found my whole body resonating and

expanding and contracting with each breath. My whole body glowed from energy, and I recalled from reading the book *The Secret of the Golden Flower* how light and energy would circulate through the body and through the organs and empower the organs to grow and expand. Soon my legs began to shake uncontrollably. My back ached and I had to go to the bathroom. I remembered reading about a spiritual leader in India who had learned to internalize his biological processes, so I concentrated on internalizing my urine into my body.

Although many people came in and out of the school, I wasn't aware of them. Maybe it was a hallucination, but I went through many physical, mental and spiritual changes including a metamorphosis in which I felt myself growing to ten feet tall.

There were a lot of negative forces in my life at the time stemming from living with a totally dysfunctional family that relied on me for support. I'd probably put my mother in a mental institution at least twenty-five times. Although I did my best to keep the family together it was beginning to deteriorate. I was arrested once for strong-arm robbery, but a sympathetic juvenile court judge let me off with a lecture. The only thing keeping me from exploding with anger and frustration was Kenpo.

My Kenpo family became my real family, and Mr. Parker my surrogate father. I never told him how I had been stealing to support my family because I knew that he would have thrown me out of the school.

At one point I became emotionally overwhelmed, and so I took some time off and went to San Francisco where I hung around the Haight Ashbury district. In the early sixties Ravi Shankar, Alan Watts, and Timothy Leary perpetuated many of the philosophies that were part of my lifestyle. For awhile I had a good time. I met some girls, smoked some marijuana, got into some fights, and drank too much alcohol. But after a few weeks I decided that dissolute life wasn't for me so I returned home to Pasadena to again face life's realities.

I got a job as a caretaker for Paul Fussil, who at that time was the President of the California Bar Association. He gave me a place to live on his property that was near the famous Huntington Library. When I had free time I went to the library and began to read books about Oriental philosophy: *Bushido, Go Rin No Sho* by Miyamoto Musashi, *The Art of War* by Sun Tzu, and *The Way of Zen* by Alan Watts who I'd met in San Francisco.

From time to time Bruce Lee would come to the school to work out with Mr. Parker and exchange ideas and techniques. Bruce would spar with the black belts and occasionally I went on the mat to spar with him.

Mr. Parker learned Bruce's Wing Chun technique of chi-sao, or sticky hands, and made some changes in the basic methods of entering and attacking. In turn, Bruce learned how to handle the nunchucks from Mr. Parker.

There was an old orange tree on the other side of the railroad tracks where we used hit the oranges. I still remember the day one of the sticks bounced off a branch and inflicted a cut over Bruce's eye. He ignored the pain and blood and went right back at the target.

Mr. Parker was gaining an international reputation for his Kenpo. Even Shotokan masters like Hidetaka Nishyama were frequent guests. Among the many Samoans and Hawaiians I met at the school was "Tino" Tuiolosega, who later created the Limalama art of self-defense and is today its Grandmaser. Tino soon became my big brother. It was from him that I began to learn Lua, an ancient Hawaiian martial art that strongly relied on knowledge of anatomy and nerve and muscle centers. Most important to me, Lua also had a core of spirituality leading to enlightenment very much like that found in Judaism.

The war in Vietnam was then raging. My life at home and on the street was becoming even more complicated what with dealing with two teenage sisters and a mother who could not cope with the pressures of life. I enlisted in the United States Marine Corps and after several months of training was sent to Vietnam as a Rifleman in the

*Vietnam with an M-60*

3rd Marine Division.

I'm not much for war stories but Kenpo saved my life once when our patrol was overrun by NVA with me in the middle of the perimeter. A NVA bayoneted me in the back. The moment I felt the point of his blade I covered and turned. The bayonet slipped off my shoulder and through my skin, enabling me to close with him. At that point I realized how important Kenpo was to me because it saved my life. Ed Parker taught me how to cover. So far it's the best lesson I've ever had. Earlier I had written a thesis about the peripheral vision of the predatory tiger. I explained how the eyes of the tiger absorb motion and light, and how the tiger can maneuver into a position that allows him to scan 360 degrees. I am still proud of what I wrote then and teach it to my students as a double cover-out.

*Haggard, torn and beat*
*We moved on through the brush*
*Hot, musty air choked our lives*
*We were all there*
*wishing we weren't*
*A man falls, your gut tears*
*He dies, you cry*
*You bury him in a bag*
*put him on a chopper*
*He's gone.*

In 1969 I returned home from Vietnam with a chest full of medals. The day that I arrived at Los Angeles International Airport a dozen hippies pelted me with tomatoes and eggs while shouting humiliating insults. I quickly did enough damage to them so that the police were called. Luckily, an airport security guard sympathetic to returning vets allowed me to slip out a side entrance before the police arrived.

I was confused, angry and in a daze when I got on a bus to Pasadena. Within a few days I was in bed with recurring malaria and jungle rot and weighed only 127 pounds.

It was months before I was physically able to

*And a lonely lost boy returns for a parade*
*of rotten tomatoes and eggs*
*So proud to be home from hell*
*Stars and stripes killing glances from*
*mothers whose sons never came home*
*But good old guys pat your back*
*buy you a beer, talk about the real war*
*in '42 in the Pacific*
*Where was the time when a walk for a*
*lonely boy was so lonely*
*God, I am not a barbaric conqueror*
*I am a human being*
*I know, I know*
*So was he and he and he and they*

*Today in my traditional ironwork shop with 120 tons of equipment.*

go back to the karate school and find work. I did some roofing, painting, bar tending, even some bouncing at a Pasadena bar. When the future began to look better I got married and bought a house in Monrovia. A son Michael was born in 1973 when I was twenty-four.

The marriage dissolved and I moved to a forty-acre ranch in Yucca Valley deep in the desert where I worked as a painter and got married again.

Back when I was a kid I loved horses. Dressed in my cowboy hat, cowboy boots, and Levi's, I used to go down to the stables in Flintridge and watch the horses. So when I moved to Yucca Valley, I bought a wild mustang stallion from the government for $150.00. I had him gelded, and that was my main horse for riding in the desert. Life was good.

As a hobby I had started collecting Japanese swords and had about twenty-five of them. One huge sword used for fighting on horseback didn't have a hand guard, and I couldn't afford to buy one. I read some old books on iron working and bought a barbecue, some charcoal, and an old vacuum cleaner. Then I made a forge and taught myself how to be a blacksmith.

I began to designed knives, and to test the blades I went into meat lockers owned by another kenpoist and practiced cutting animal carcasses.

Then I began training myself in knife fighting using Kenpo principles. It is a source of pride to me that Mr. Parker always referred to me as his "top knife-fighting student."

I consider the knife to be one of the most important weapons in my self-defense arsenal, and I believe it important that kenpoists be properly trained in use of the weapon. According to the Torah, "To live by the sword is to die by the sword."

Despite my quest for some sort of spirituality, I still had difficulty adjusting to society after Nam. I was also beginning to have marital problems. I knew that I needed to get away from the mounting pressures for awhile and start cleansing my inner self.

I bought a used Datsun 4x4 truck, loaded it full of sugar, flour, salt and pepper, a 100-pound sack of potatoes, and headed for the Bitteroot Mountains in Montana. I filled the gas tank and drove into the mountains until there was just a half tank of gas left so I would have enough to get back when I was ready to leave.

I'd brought along some books on mystical Judaism, Zen, and enlightenment. I had visions of Oyama doing ascetic exercises and Zen meditation beneath waterfalls. I built a lean-to next to my truck and spent the days reading and working out even in the harsh winter weather.

There was a big fir tree nearby and I developed an exercise I call "chunking." I'd go around the tree hitting it hard enough to break off a piece of bark. When one hand got bloody, I'd use the other. As each hand healed I'd start the process all over again.

During my ten-month stay in the mountains I wrote an autobiographical book of poetry about my early life and Vietnam experience called *Childhood/Namhood/Manhood*. Another form of soul cleansing, probably better for me than psychoanalysis because it helped me come to grips with myself and start to bury the past. A reviewer later said that I was "a powerful writer" and my book was "a visual, sensitive mind travel into and out of the past and present after Vietnam."

When I came down from the mountains I was strong and healthy in body and mind. But the inner peace I sought still continued to elude me until I realized it was in Judaism principles and ethics.

I began traveling around the country taking whatever jobs I could find in Texas and Arizona. I graduated from Oklahoma Farrier's College with a degree as a horseshoer and followed the rodeo circuit for awhile as a farrier. In Arizona I taught Kenpo at Gilbert Velez's school in Tucson and got married again.

My wife and I moved to Washington where I opened a Kenpo school at our home in Steptoe and worked as a horse shoer and blacksmith. While living in Washington, I spent five years as a member of the Whitman County Mounted Posse, which was a quasi-law enforcement agency that helped the sheriff and police departments with special or anomalous situations. It was quite an honor to be part of that group.

Our next move was to Colfax where I opened a Kenpo studio. Although I had 150 students, the school didn't make much money. Times were tough and the marriage was dissolved, but I had two wonderful sons born of that marriage, Zachary Kealoha and Zephaniah David.

One day Mr. Parker called and asked me to go with him to a tournament. It was there that I met Mary Susan Fitzgerald. She was six foot tall and strikingly beautiful. I came on to her with a line that still embarrasses me. I told her that she had good teeth, great legs and hips, and a strong back. She asked me what planet I came from? We were married within a few months. It was my fifth marriage and has lasted for fourteen years. Mary Susan brought her oldest daughter, Nicole, into our family and we were soon blessed with two daughters, Micah and Hannah.

In 1982 I began to study ornamental black-

*Branding cows in Texas.*

212

*With the Whitman County Mounted Posse in Washington. Mike Pick is seen in the top row, second from the right. Below with Francis Whitaker.*

smithing from Francis Whitaker, who had been a blacksmith since he was fifteen, and is the most knowledgeable man in the field. He considered his craft to be a spiritual journey. He also taught me to complete a job to the highest standards I could achieve and told me that his craft was also a vehicle through which one could attain enlightenment.

During the next few years I immersed myself in time tested ancient methods of joinery. In 1985 while I was living in northern California I made a Chanukia – a Menorah for Chanukah – to commemorate the Maccabean revolt in 162BCE. It's six feet high, six feet wide, and weighs 300 pounds. I hammered the entire piece out by hand and made it historically accurate in strength and concept. I had turned my physical craft into a spiritual one that united me with the four basic elements of the universe: fire, water, minerals, and air.

I traveled with Mr. Parker to many parts of the globe and on one particular occasion accompanied him to the funeral of his teacher, Professor William K.S. Chow. Mr. Parker was always the most important and consistent force for good in my life and I saw him often. He kept me out of trouble and straightened me out. "Only the pure of heart can succeed in Kenpo," he once told me. Mr. Parker purified me with the white-hot iron of

work and responsibility. When Mr. Parker died in December 1990, I not only mourned my teacher but a good and cherished friend. I was honored to be a pallbearer at his funeral.

After Mr. Parker's death, his organization, the International Kenpo Karate Association (IKKA), became divided by political rivalry and a struggle for control. In an attempt to continue Mr. Parker's high standards I founded the Universal Kenpo Federation seven years after his death, the traditional mourning period prescribed by my religious beliefs.

I am now fifty-three years old and have been on a Kenpo journey for more than four decades. I've designed a combative program for the military that encapsulates empty hands as well as knives. I am currently teaching hand-to-hand combat to

*With Ed Parker at my school in Colfax, Washington.*

tough. "To be bad is to be a punk," he said. "To be tough is to face the challenges of life and overcome them."

Mr. Parker taught me to never compromise my integrity, dignity and humility. He believed that a man should fight only when necessary.

In every class I always stress the need for each individual to create his personal ethic and the Special Forces at Ft. Carson, Colorado and will be going to Kosovo this summer to continue their training. I was recently honored as the 22nd member of the International Close Combat Instructors Association. In addition to the military groups, I've taught knife techniques to dozens of police organizations, and thousands of students.

Regularly I am asked to attend Kenpo seminars and speak to young students. It has never mattered to me whether the audience consists of youngsters just starting their journey or old-timers like myself who have been on the path for decades. As the great Chinese sage Jo-Shu once said, "If I see an old man on his path that needs my teaching, I will run him down and teach him. But, if I also see a young boy that could teach me, I will also run him down and let him teach me also."

One of the main things Mr. Parker taught me was the difference between being bad and

*With Ed Parker a month before his passing*

214

*Mike Pick designed and forged these door hinges of his balcksmith shop. ©Copyright Don Murray.*

I teach my students to be like a raging river as it races through a canyon. An observer might believe the river is out of control, but the river is really in perfect harmony as it flows around obstacles that it will wear down in time.

To me Kenpo is a way of life to protect my peace. When I teach children Kenpo I always tell them that to hurt someone is not to hurt just to hurt, but to hurt to stop your enemy from hurting you. With the passage of time I have learned not to fight with weapons and my skill, but instead to project my spirit of peace. That spirit penetrates all negativity and dishonesty, and cannot be stopped even in death.

I am often asked what I think is the status of American Kenpo today now that our leader has passed. I believe Kenpo is still alive and well. Ed Parker's greatest lesson was to teach his disciples to evolve as human beings as well as kenpoists into

*Mike Pick standing before the Chunukia that he designed and forged.*

moral code and be willing to kill for it if necessary. There must be no confusion or hesitation because, as Mr. Parker once said, "He who hesitates meditates in a horizontal position."

As a warrior in many arenas I have learned that a true warrior must have a code of ethics that will enable him to determine what he is willing to fight for and, ultimately, what he is willing to kill for.

One thing I learned on the mats and in actual combat was to always attack the attack. Relentlessly. When I was in Nam and my squad was ambushed while on patrol, we didn't fall back hoping to gain a tactical position. Instead, we attacked the attackers, gained fire superiority, and destroyed the enemy. This has always been my fighting style and the one I recommend. Ed Parker taught me that Kenpo is when "pure knuckles hit pure flesh" the engagement is in control.

the next generation and into the next dimension. Although there are many offshoots of Kenpo today, I feel certain Mr. Parker would approve and applaud them. He designed Kenpo to evolve as an art and to help its students evolve into better human beings.

Today my family lives on a secluded twenty-acre spread behind Pike's Peak in Colorado backed up against a national forest where I enjoy hunting deer and elk for food. I also collect native trees that I prune and train for bonsai. Our family is members of a local temple and we are involved each day with our spiritual beliefs.

Outside my open living room window I can see deer in the forest and hear the wind whispering across the fields. It's peaceful outside just as I am at peace with myself. My anchor in life is Mary Susan, my soul mate and best friend. Without her I would never have discovered what love is and how to live a life of peace and joy.

The fire in my forge is down to embers, like the fire that was once in my soul. My journey will continue tomorrow.

*Mike's sons: from left Michael Jr., Mike Pick, Zachary, Grandmaster Tino Tuiolosega, Zephaniah*

*Mike's daughters from left to right: Hannah, Nicole, and Micah.*

# Paul Mills
## 9th Degree

*In 1966 Paul Mills began his Kenpo journey in Ogden, Utah and has been consistently training in the art of American Kenpo since that time. He is currently the President and founder of the American Kenpo Karate International (AKKI) association, serves as the Chief Examiner at all international tests, and is the Chairman of the AKKI's Board of Directors. During the 1980s, Paul often accompanied Mr. Parker in his travels to various Kenpo schools. It was during these trips that Paul Mills earned the name and reputation as the "Smiling Guillotine." During this time, he also served as a member of the IKKA Systems Council, the National Testing Director, and was the Regional Representative for a ten-state region. Having held world records as a quick draw artist, Paul Mills is internationally known for his speed, which he has integrated into his Kenpo. As to hands-on experience, he spent two decades working security in the rough nightclubs in the cowboy town of Evanston, Wyoming during the "Boom Town Years." Shortly after Mr. Parker passed away, Paul was one of a handful of black belts to teach at the 1991 IKKA Ed Parker Memorial Camp that was held at the Pasadena studio.*

I was raised in Cedar City, Utah in the late forties and fifties era. My father was an FBI agent who oversaw the Agency's operations in Southern Utah and Nevada during the Bugsy Segal days. As a child I wanted to be like my father and even had my own plastic gun, badge, and set of handcuffs. I was fascinated watching him practice the self-defense movements he learned at the FBI academy and was particularly intrigued by the way he would speed draw his service revolver. Because of the admiration I felt for my father and the influence of the

*With my brother John, holding my first bullwhip.*

TV westerns of the fifties, I became obsessed with learning to use a firearm (especially how to fast draw a western style single-action gun), shoot a bow-and-arrow, crack a bullwhip, and throw knives and tomahawks.

My first experience with the martial arts was in 1955 when I was eight years old. My father taught me how to frisk suspects, and I used to enjoy playacting on his friends who would stop by occasionally. One evening I had my plastic gun aimed and ready as I held one of my father's friends spread-eagled with his hands high against the wall. My father taught me to place my right foot inside that of the suspect, and I had this guy really stretched out. All of a sudden my play-suspect decided he didn't want to do this anymore

*My first karate gi and proudly wearing the rank of white belt.*

and started to push his hands away from the wall. I immediately gave him the command to stop, as my father had instructed me, and when he didn't, I swept his leg backwards. I didn't even know if the move would work because I'd had never practiced it for real. Because of the degree this guy was stretched out, it only took an ounce of pressure for this move to be effective. The side of his head hit the wall, and he was like a cat with his fingernails clawing down the wall as he tried to regain his balance and crashed to the floor in a heap. Needless to say, I was in trouble with my father, but at the same time I could see this proud look coming across his face, pleased with the performance of his junior FBI agent with the plastic badge and gun.

When I was in the sixth grade I was in a snowball fight with a dozen other kids that had chosen up sides. One of my snowballs hit one of the other team players in the head, and after school this kid and four of his friends confronted me. They threw me to the ground, and the kid who I had hit earlier towered over me while his friends pinned all four of my limbs.

"We're going to show you how it feels to have a snowball thrown in your face," the leader roared as he crunched a snowball and packed the snow as tight as he could, making an iceball out of it.

I'll never forget how utterly helpless I felt. There was nothing I could do but watch this kid throw this iceball squarely into my face. It was a terrifying experience for a kid my age, and I remember thinking that if this could be prevented, I was never going to let that happen again.

Throughout my high school years I continued to be intrigued with my father's FBI work. Besides excelling in school athletics, I took up the sport of fast draw and began studying what little martial arts I could from a book that I discovered somewhere written by Bruce Tegner.

In 1966 I was attending Weber State College in Ogden, Utah and was driving down the main boulevard one afternoon when I spotted a storefront sign advertising "Ed Parker's Kenpo Karate Studio." At the time I didn't know the differences

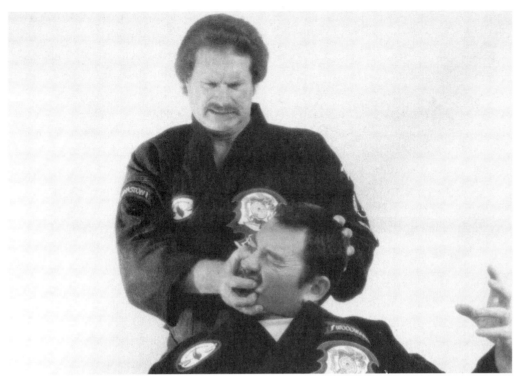

between Tae Kwon Do, karate, judo, Shotokan, Kenpo, and all the other martial arts. To me karate was karate, and my image of a black belt was that of a mystical man who could crush boards and bricks with his bare hands.

I walked into the school and was approached by the head instructor and owner, Terry Arnell, one of Ed Parker's first generation black belts. Terry stood five-feet-two inches in height and weighed around 120 pounds. With a friendly, unassuming twinkle in his eyes, he invited me to sign up for classes and become part of the first group of students that he had at that studio.

While being instructed on the mat, I couldn't believe what I saw. This little guy with a black belt and callused knuckles started executing techniques with incredible speed and power. I couldn't believe how deadly this guy was and realized that had I gotten into it with him in the street, I would have had my hands full, even though I had boxing experience. I mean this little guy could rap out combinations with the speed of lightning and the power of thunder. This was a whole new world to me, and I remember thinking, 'Wow, if he can do this, this is a tangible thing. I should be able to do this if I work hard at it and put my mind to it.'

I signed up that night, and over the ensuing months I could not persuade my instructor to teach me fast enough. I was hungry as a lion with an insatiable appetite to learn everything about this awe-inspiring martial art. I couldn't stop thinking about Kenpo, which had truly become an obsession.

Back in my early years of training, which I remember as the blood and guts era of the sixties, we didn't have all the protective gear that is available today. I can still remember as if it were yesterday the excruciating pain of crashing the shin of my lead kicking leg with the lead shin of my opponent. Invariably, while kicking with our front legs, our shins would collide in the exact same spot they had two nights previously. The sight of that golf ball sized contusion jutting from my shin became commonplace. The mass attacks in the school were unquestionably the most unpredictable, and getting out from the middle of that deadly whirlwind reminds me today of the six o'clock news that shows these gang members "jumping in." Because ours was such a small school, most every test I ever took was a solo test. At the end, invariably I came away bruised and bleeding. I have mixed feelings about whether

*Receiving the ceremonial kick from Grandmaster Parker*

today's students new to the martial arts are actually missing anything from this bygone era. Surely with the increase of lawsuits and the restrictions placed on karate school owners by liability insurance carriers, the risk and occurrence of physical injury has been dramatically reduced. Whether the actual training is weakened as a result is perhaps debatable. It just occurs to me that students today might be missing something by not having to go through the rigorous training that was prevalent in the sixties.

In the late sixties while attending college, I continued my ongoing training with Terry Arnell and would often come home to work and visit my parents on the weekends in Evanston, Wyoming where they owned and operated a family motel business. My confidence and sense of security had grown tremendously, and I was aware that my family and friends were looking at me differently. When I'd come back and mention to people that I was studying the martial arts, they didn't know how to react because their image of a black belt was that of a mystical, almost supernatural person with unbelievable powers. I'm relating this to a small town, but I think it was the same everywhere.

I can still recall the first weeks of my training and how I felt when I would put on my karate uniform. It was almost magical how simply putting on two pieces of cloth and a belt could be so empowering. Even today, my wife jokes with me. I'm fifty-four years of age, and she'll say, "I've seen

you on the morning before a seminar when your lower back is hurting, then you put on your gi and tie that belt and suddenly you're a new man again. It's really wonderful to see. It's almost miraculous."

When I began my training in 1966 under Terry Arnell, the school was an Ed Parker school and taught the standard Parker material of the time. In the early 1970s, with the Bruce Lee craze and the accompanying popularity of Kung Fu, Terry changed the name of his school to "White Dragon Gung-fu Karate." Terry claimed to still be teaching me 90 percent of the Ed Parker material with some slight adjustments, and the rest of his curriculum was from a Kung-fu system, which he learned from another black belt who gathered his knowledge in China.

By this time, I had permanently moved back to Evanston where throughout most of the seventies I trained and taught, although to continue my ongoing training with Terry, I had to drive a long distance to Ogden, Utah. I had been a black belt of Terry's for several years and had as many years of teaching experience under my belt. On certain occasions I would assist my brother with security at his country entertainment dance hall and saloon where some of the top country singers would perform.

One day during this period I called Mr. Parker and asked if he would teach me if I came to California. While on the phone, Mr. Parker said to me, "Paul, you must first empty your cup and set some of your previously learned knowledge aside. In this way I can teach you the way that I would like to teach you. If you do this, then you will not be wasting my time or yours." This was one of the finest lessons I ever learned from Mr. Parker and one that I highly value to this day.

A month later I stood on the mats of the Pasadena school, suited up in my gi. Like many in the martial arts, I've had my share of low points along my journey. Besides the usual physical injuries, feelings of not getting anywhere, life's trials and overwhelming family obligations, this particular day in Pasadena left me in a state of despair.

As I started to get ready to execute my movements for Mr. Parker, I looked up at him and saw that focused and intense look in his eyes, as he seemed to penetrate right through my soul. Needless to say, my hands and feet were having a hard time coordinating with my mind and body. I went through a substantial number of moves and then performed Long Form Four. I could tell by the look on his face that there was a problem, and he soon told me that what I was doing, while generally based in Kenpo principles, was not entirely his Kenpo. I was devastated and felt utterly despondent. Nevertheless, Mr. Parker renewed my hope, and we started going over the entire Kenpo system the way he wanted to teach me. It wasn't easy but I never gave up.

There was a period of Evanston's history that became known as the "Boom Town Years." As a result of huge reservoirs of oil and natural gas being discovered in that area, the landscape became filled with oil rigs that started hammering and drilling the ground. While the gas refineries were being built, thousands of workers flooded into a town that had limited housing. Literally overnight tents began appearing along the hillsides, and two enormous man-camps, each holding over 500 workers, were hastily thrown together.

Within six months what used to be the quiet town of Evanston became home to a lot of rough and tough characters. Between the cowboys who lived here and the oil field roughnecks that moved in, Saturday nights began to resemble the days of the Wild West.

It was during the ten year Boom Town era that I worked security and as a bouncer in my brother's country western dance hall as well as in my father's lounge and nightclub. Much of my practical experience in American Kenpo came from the street during these years. Besides outright barroom brawls, knifings and shootings were not uncommon, and many times I had to disarm these people of knives and environmental weapons such as bottles and glasses. Thankfully, since the gas and oil field boom backed off, Evanston has returned to normalcy and is one of

*Above, my childhood dream to one day learn how to handle tomahawks. Below, with Ed Parker.*

the most beautiful and peaceful places to live or visit in all of Wyoming.

Because of Mr. Parker's keen interest in the practical aspect of Kenpo, he often would ask me about my confrontations I encountered while working security during the boom town years. I'd say, "Boy, this worked good or this particular lock worked good." Or I'd say, "Mr. Parker, I did this move and this technique, and I just didn't get the results that I wanted."

He would listen intently and then tell me what I might want to try if the situation arose again. But whenever I'd come to Pasadena or he'd come up to Evanston, he'd always ask. He really did like hearing about the real time application of Kenpo. This made sense to me because his fighting days on the beaches of Honolulu were a thing of the past. He had nothing more to prove, not to mention the legal nightmare he'd be up against had he injured someone. But he did have people in Kenpo who were known streetfighters or worked as bodyguards or in law enforcement that he could talk with about the effectiveness of Kenpo. In a way, I guess we represented a form of

*The AKKI Camp in Las Vegas*

quality control.

I still remember one particular incident that I related to Mr. Parker. It happened on a Saturday night when two roughnecks were slugging it out in the street and one of them unconsciously went to the ground with blood streaming from his face. This leather faced guy with working calluses all over his hands continued kicking the man in the face. Nobody wanted to interfere, since this brawler carried with him a horrific street fighting reputation. He was strong, and with his adrenaline pumping he became ten times stronger. At first, I didn't want to get involved, but my intuition told me that I had to try to stop this guy from killing this man, even if it meant that I was going to get my clock cleaned, which I felt was a good possibility. Anyway, I was lucky and was able to stop this mauling with some physical Kenpo on my part. When I later told this story to Mr. Parker he said, "Paul, there are big guys, strong guys, rough guys, and tough guys, but we in American Kenpo can be vicious if need be." I've never forgotten that because it is so true.

If there is one area of my particular journey that stands out in my mind, it is my lifelong quest to acquire a deep understanding of speed as it pertains to human performance.

In the early seventies I was much thinner than I am today and weighed approximately 165 pounds. After studying Kenpo for a few years I realized that I needed to find a way to substantially increase my power. Eventually I found that I could accomplish this by focusing on and harnessing the velocity contained within my movements, which is something I had learned from the sport of fast draw.

During the early seventies when I was shooting, I twice tied the current world record of twenty-hundredths of a second for the fastest recorded shot in a potluck shoot held after the tournament. I also set a number of state and one world record, which have since been shattered because there are so many great shooters with new techniques and styles. But what I found when I watched and competed against the fastest shooters in the world was they all shared a common denominator – they

*On the main floor of the Las Vegas AKKI Camp*

were using the same patterns of motions that enhanced the speed mechanics. After I observed and studied these patterns for some time and applied them to my shooting, a physical therapist said to me, "Paul, you are one of the few people that I've seen that can consistently stay in the D1 and D2 motion patterns." When I use these patterns correctly, they greatly enhance my speed and power. Not surprisingly, it is clear to me from the way Mr. Parker structured his techniques that he thoroughly understood those patterns. Where he learned them, I have no idea.

When drawing a gun, it's not just grabbing the gun with the hand. It's the snap of the shooter's hip, trunk, knee, and shoulder coupled with the opposing motion of his hands and body; how his head snaps; how he pulls–it's the total synergistically synchronized body mechanics that when done correctly result in optimum speed.

When Mr. Parker would come to Evanston, I would strap on my fast draw rig, and he would watch and analyze my shooting. I was amazed how he would break everything down to the Kenpo concepts and principles of torque, opposing forces, contouring, body mechanics, and so forth.

Stimulus and reflex is a major part of the art of fast draw. We don't shoot when we feel like it.

We react when a light goes on. Essentially the shooter walks up to the line and takes his stance in preparation to drawing. He then says "ready or set" and waits for the light to come on, which happens randomly at anytime between two to five seconds. When it comes on, the shooter draws and fires and must hit the target for the clock to stop.

In Kenpo there are three categories of speed – perceptual, mental, and physical. What I found from watching hundreds of shooters over the years was that some of them had devastatingly fast hands, but their eyes weren't picking up the light as fast, while others could pick up the light but weren't as quick with their hands. This meant that I was dealing with essentially two aspects of speed in fast draw: 1) quick hands (physical), and 2) reaction to the light (perceptual). It occurred to me that if I could perfect the principles of the fast draw and apply them to my Kenpo, I might really have something.

After considerable study, not surprisingly I concluded that practically all Kenpo black belts have remarkably fast kicks and punches. What differentiates the fast from the super-fast is their relative reaction time to stimulus. In other words, the light.

Years ago I was told that some of the greatest fast draw champions trained themselves by watching the light over and over. They'd flip it on, flip it off, flip it on, flip it off. And the day that they knew they had become a potential world class shooter was when they had perfected a flawless draw, developed excellent body mechanics, practiced their fast draw thousands of times and could catch the light coming on instead of seeing the light on. It doesn't sound like much until one realizes that world records are measured in hundredths and thousandths of a second. Often a shooter doesn't fire only one shot, but draws, fires, hits the target, and holsters several times at different targets, in different events, to become the overall state or world champion. Also, most professional world-class shooters can draw their gun, cock the hammer, and squeeze the trigger before you can pull the trigger and fire your gun that is already in your hand.

Very few shooters can actually catch the light coming on. Mr. Parker had mastered all three of the categories of speed, but I personally believe the reaction to the light (perceptual speed) is what made Mr. Parker so fast. He was one who saw the light coming on. According to Mr. Parker, those who do have mastered the internal energy of ch'i. It is the ultimate of extreme concentration

and focus when one is physically, mentally, and spiritually synchronized. In the A.K.K.I. this is part of our definition of ch'i, which we refer to as "Martial Synergy." It is this tripartite relationship between the physical, mental, and spiritual master keys.

When I first began to watch Mr. Parker move, I thought, 'Man, how does he do this? I do the same techniques and it doesn't sound or look the same.' But being a shooter and understanding the micro precision timing, focus and rhythm that shooters must use, I started to incorporate these speed elements into how I performed my techniques. Ultimately I found that what I learned in fast draw greatly helped my Kenpo, and what I learned in Kenpo greatly helped my fast draw. When I would be on the mats and see a guy stepping through with a punch, I'd think, 'Wow, that seems so slow to step through with that punch.' I'm used to drawing in hundredths of seconds — drawing, cocking and firing a gun within hundredths of seconds. This step through punch looks like it's in slow motion coming at me. I've got to get these guys to learn to punch quicker and to teach them like they're drawing a gun when they do an inward block. I've got to teach them how to

explode into it a little bit more. This became a teaching tool that helped me cross reference these two arts or sports – the fast draw and Kenpo – to try to enable me to have better analogies to teach my students.

What I have learned from my comparisons of Kenpo and speed draw is to understand how to integrate the D1 and D2 patterns into my motion and then to apply what I call my master key rhythmic timing patterns. Both the D1 and D2 motion patterns along with the A.K.K.I. rhythmic timing patterns can be learned through practice and is what I try to teach my students. By doing these patterns they stay in the optimal line or path of movement, which is referred to as the "groove." I'm positive that Mr. Parker used them in some fashion. He always seemed to have that X factor that no one could explain. As with the art of speed draw, these tangible timing patterns that I created help the kenpoist to whip the shoulders, trunk, and hips simultaneously with the arms and feet to generate incredible speed and power. This synchronized with accuracy; elastic recoil, penetration and breath control creates tremendous energetic conversions in one's actions; generating spiraling and diagonal movements with a tornado like force. I honestly don't know of a better way to hit more powerfully or more quickly in combinations. I believe that they are what made Ed Parker

move with such speed and power.

Like Mr. Parker, some have labeled me as a rebel. Perhaps this is a fair assessment and the result of having been taught by Mr. Parker to think, dissect, question, innovate, and create so that I can continue to move forward and not become stagnant and traditionalized in my way of thinking. I believe that change and progress are directly proportional. I was always willing to accept new paradigms and open my heart and mind to a new way of thinking. For those that do challenge change, they might consider that it takes hundreds of hours of dedicated devotion and an intense desire to learn more about a subject. It takes time and is the road less traveled. I never wanted to fall into a comfort zone but preferred to travel new streams, rugged terrain, or unexplored mountain passes. It is far easier to stay with the accepted ways of doing things. It takes less time and effort to stay with the natural current of the stream. But, fishing new streams and lakes is refreshing and exciting and adds much more insight to my already existing base. What I will become depends upon what I will explore.

I look at the Honorees featured in this book, as well as the other well-deserving American Kenpo black belts who are not in this book, that have, and have not, directly trained under Mr. Parker, as a unique instrument in a

*IKKA black belts promotional line.*

227

huge symphony orchestra that we call American Kenpo – an orchestra conducted by Senior Grandmaster Edmund K. Parker. We can each experience the joy and satisfaction of playing our unique part that individually and collectively can be heard and appreciated by all martial artists of all styles and systems throughout the world.

I believe that my physical, mental, and spiritual qualities have grown throughout my journey in Kenpo. I feel I have always been a caring person with a strong devout faith. Moreover, I believe that having a loving and close family helps balance out my life and my chosen life's work teaching Kenpo, and I feel blessed by all of my family members who have given me such overwhelming and continuous support throughout my lifetime.

I could not begin to direct and operate the American Kenpo Karate International association (A.K.K.I.) or my International Las Vegas Kenpo Camps without the assistance of my kind, patient, and charming wife "De." Her wonderful spirited personality and positive attitude contribute immensely to the success of the A.K.K.I. She is truly the "Wind Beneath My Wings." Together we have five wonderful children: Tabitha 28, Ryan 27, Jesse 23, Wesley 21, McKayla 6, and my grandson Randy 10. My mother (Zina "Tanny") and brother John recently passed away. My father is eighty years old and is still a great influence in my life.

My proudest moment throughout my Kenpo journey has been watching my students progress and execute their movements with tremendous power, speed, and rhythmic timing similar to what I saw in Mr. Parker. I cannot help but believe that Mr. Parker is smiling down upon us with joy and satisfaction in his heart. I feel content in my mind that I have contributed my little part in Mr. Parker's overall plan to help perpetuate the art of American Kenpo into the future.

I miss Mr. Parker and the time we shared together. He taught me many things and for that I will be eternally grateful. I could never thank him enough for sharing his inspired and embodied wisdom that brought forward the genius in him. There are many lessons we can learn from his lifetime of achievement.

*The Mills family. Top, left to right: sons Ryan, Wes and Jess. Below, left to right: Randy (grandson), daughter Tabitha, my father (Jack "Dub"), daughter McKayla, Paul, and De.*

# Master
# Larry Tatum
## 10th Degree

*Larry Tatum took his first lesson in Kenpo from Ed Parker in 1966. Following two years away from the mat during his army service in Vietnam, in 1975 at the age of twenty-six Larry became the head instructor at Ed Parker's legendary school in West Los Angeles. Now a tenth-degree black belt, Larry has a studio in Pasadena and is recognized worldwide as one of the foremost authorities on Kenpo. In 1988 he established his Kenpo Karate Association and began to create twenty-three videotapes on the art of Kenpo, which encompass all the basics, freestyle methods, techniques, katas, concepts and principles of the Kenpo system. He has recently completed another comprehensive series of twenty-one videotapes representing a virtual technical encyclopedia of the entire system from yellow belt through third-degree black, and has also written three books on self-defense, including Confidence, a Child's First Weapon, as well as other works on Kenpo such as The Art of Kata. When he is not busy teaching Kenpo, giving seminars and demonstrations throughout the world, Larry continues his journey to enlightenment through his own continuing study.*

When I was a fifteen-year-old growing up in Pasadena in the sixties, I tried to wear my hair long, as did many teenage boys at the time. My father ordered me to get the hair cut around my ears and took me to his barber, Dan Eddy.

Dan could tell I was in a foul mood. "I'll take your mind off the haircut," he said. "Show me your best punch."

I was happy to oblige with a roundhouse. Dan blocked it easily and hard enough that he practically snapped my elbow.

"What in the world did you do?" I asked him as I rubbed my elbow.

"What I did was Kenpo. I'm studying it with a guy named Ed Parker who has a school in the neighborhood."

*Playing guitar at age fourteen.*

I'd seen some television shows like "The Wild, Wild, West" in which the hero, Robert Conrad, always did some spectacular kicks or takedowns. I'd been intrigued by what I'd heard about karate, which was that it gave a small man the ability to scientifically outmaneuver a larger opponent.

When I got home I told my older brother, Bob, what happened. "Let's go to that karate studio Dan told me about," I suggested.

Bob said he'd like to check it out first, and two weeks later told me that he'd met Ed Parker and taken a few lessons. "It's great," he said. "Next time I go, you come along with me and we'll sign up."

I still remember the first time I saw Ed Parker's karate school. It was about the size of a volleyball court with mirrors on the walls. The first thing that struck me was the pungent smell in the air, probably a combination of the tatami straw mats on the floor and the body odor of the dozen students on the mats. Their teacher was a big man who wore what looked like white pajamas, and he moved with blinding speed and controlled power.

"That's Ed Parker," Bob said.

What followed was monkey-see-monkey-do time on the mat. One of the students accidentally hit another, and Parker threw up his hands in disgust.

"If you can hit, you can miss," he shouted.

Bob led me into a small office. Moments later Ed Parker came storming in, sweating, and plopped himself behind a battered desk. Without even a glance at us he started doing some paperwork. My first impression of him was that he was intense. He finally finished what he was doing and looked me over.

"Why do you want to study Kenpo?" he asked.

I told him that I was a sophomore in high school and hated class instruction because all I did was memorize what I read or was told in order to pass a test. Although I was good student and excelled in sports, school was punishment for me because I never had a sense of empowerment. Mr.

Parker nodded as though he understood and signed me up as a student.

Ed, as he preferred to be called at that time, taught some of the classes himself. At my first lesson he taught me a side kick. When I came home that night I proudly demonstrated it for my mother who snapped a picture. My father was impressed. He had been a tough street fighter in his day and approved of having his sons learn to handle themselves.

During another early lesson Ed told me to "Open your horse."

He didn't say a horse or the horse, but *your* horse. I realized he was empowering me. This basic stance was mine and mine alone. For the first time I was learning something new. I left each session excited by my discovery of something new about my potential and myself.

Ed taught my mind, not just my body. I felt that his true gift was his ability to instill in me the passion he felt for his art. He also taught me not to take things at face value but to look at my environment as a place that was going to control me

*The night of my first karate lesson*

unless I controlled it first.

I remember the day that our class was sitting on the mat after a workout, and Ed Parker said, "The only reason a man is a doctor or lawyer or a man of some importance in his community is because he's been in his field for some time. He wasn't born with prestige. It was bestowed upon him. When I first came to the mainland from Hawaii, I realized that I was just as important as these men were because I had something they didn't have. I could teach any one of them how to defend himself and his family."

I realized he was saying that I was learning a rare art form that was just as important as getting a college degree. Ed Parker was a profound teacher because after every lesson I truly believed I had learned something special and useful. Every time I went to the studio and put on my gi it was like being reunited with an old friend. When I wore my gi, I felt special even when I went crawling home after class all battered and bruised.

Our class worked out hard three times a week. Ed believed that in order to deliver a kick or punch with effectiveness you had to be able to take a kick or punch. I wanted to improve, not for Ed or for a belt, but for my sense of self worth. Sparring with adults gave me self-confidence, and I soon realized that the so-called tough kids in my high school weren't really all that tough.

I adapted to Kenpo instantly because the moves seemed to come naturally to me, and I became passionate about attending classes and learning more every day. Kenpo soon became not just a fighting art but a way of life. After eighteen months of training, I had risen to the rank of four brown tips on my white belt, which was equal to green belt today.

Around that time I used Kenpo on the street for the first time. I was at a restaurant with a couple of friends when an argument started between two big guys who were ragging on two hippies about their long hair. One of the hippies was getting pounded to a pulp against a concrete wall, and the other was thrown to the ground where his assailant began kicking him in the head.

A crowd of about thirty people had gathered, but no one tried to break up the fracas. The hippie on the ground was unconscious.

*Filming self-defense tapes for Panther Productions*

233

Something possessed me, and I jumped in and tried to pull off the big guy, who shoved me back and said he was going to kick my ass, too. When I continued trying to pull him off, he swung at me. I dropped into a stance and thrust punched him in the side the way I had practiced on the mat. He dropped with a broken rib.

I looked over my shoulder and saw the guy's buddy behind me throwing a punch at my head. I blocked it, put him in an arm-lock, threw him down to the ground, and held him there with a knee in his back. I remember how calm I was all the way through and how at the end of the fight the rain felt cool on my face.

When I arrived at the studio the next day, Ed was sitting alone in the office. I told him about the fight that had taken place the night before. He looked at me and said, "You should have kicked the first guy, not punched him," then stood up and walked out of the office without another word.

I'd expected praise but soon realized that Ed was teaching me a lesson. If he had praised me, there was a chance I'd mix it up again with someone and this time get into real trouble.

Also, I'd made a wrong opening move, which got me to thinking about the art I had learned and reminded me not to be impressed with myself.

In May of 1968 I had held the rank of four brown tips when I joined the army. The first thing I did after my tour ended three years later was to return to the karate studio in Pasadena where I found a large group gathered in the waiting room. Ed had advertised in the newspaper announcing his karate instructors course, and a lot of people

had responded. I went to Ed, who tested me to see if I was still sharp. I told him I'd like to work for him as an instructor, and he said, "Welcome back. I can use some good instructors."

I began teaching at the Pasadena school and two years later in 1972 tested for brown belt at the Santa Monica studio. A group of twenty students seeking to improve their ranks was on the mat, never stopping, moving for four hours with only a five-minute break. One student threw up, another passed out, and one quit. It was the most grueling test I had faced to date, but I passed.

A few weeks after my promotion to brown belt I arrived early at the Pasadena dojo and waited outside smoking a cigarette. I was smoking two packs a day in those days, a habit I had picked up in the service. Ed Parker arrived in his Cadillac Eldorado, got out and came over to me.

"You know that smoking is going to restrict your growth in the art," he said and went inside. I threw the cigarette down and never smoked again.

Mr. Parker had gotten involved in some business deals that had gone sour, and as a result the Pasadena and West Los Angeles schools were in danger of closing. I met with Ed and agreed to manage the Santa Monica school. When I arrived, the place resembled a ghost town. I looked around and viewed it as a proving ground for my martial arts teaching ability. I wanted to start with a clean slate and went to work. Over the next two weeks I swept the floors, scrubbed the showers, cleaned the windows and painted the walls. After that I redecorated the office and placed fresh flowers on my desk. I tightened my belt, ready to teach.

When I first arrived at the WLA school there were only a handful of students who had continued with their training on raw faith and a passion for the art. They were hungry. It didn't take long before word spread that the school was back in business.

The first student to knock on my office door was Bernie Bernheim, a sixty-one-year-old with the body of a muscle builder. Bernie had been a bomber pilot during WWII and had escaped from a German POW camp. He stood in my office holding his orange belt and told me that there had been no one to promote him in over a year and asked how he could go about getting a new rank. I had watched Bernie move during the past two weeks of classes, and he was as strong as a bull and knew the material.

"Get in your horse," I said, and I kicked him. "You're now a purple belt."

Then Ron Leff appeared and said that he had also been an orange belt for many months and asked if I would promote him.

"Show me how you move," I said.

After Ron performed a couple of katas and techniques, I kicked him.

"You're now a purple belt," I said. I need some help."

I was beginning to feel like Yul Brenner in "The Magnificent Seven," and over the next two months a substantial number of students with raw talent were brought back into the fold.

In the spring of 1975 I told Ed that I felt ready to test for black. The test was intense, and amid the sheer pain and toil of that day I remember Frank Trejo the best. He was one of my closest friends and had for months been working with me on side kicks. When he got into the technique line behind me and stepped forward with a punch, I executed the technique Leaping Crane and inadvertently nailed him in the back of his knee and hyper-extended the joint. Frank suffered extreme pain, and the immediate atmosphere that followed was tense, to say the least. But we both had learned self-restraint, and the fact that we reacted to the moment in a mature manner I believe spoke highly for both of us in the minds of the judges, and we were both awarded out black belts.

*With my wife Jill*

Several months later I was in Long Beach helping Ed Parker with the International Karate Championships when a beautiful blonde woman approached me and introduced herself as Jill. She further explained that she had come from Mexico with two black belts in Lima Lama, which is a Polynesian offshoot of Kenpo. The men didn't speak English, so she translated. I got them into the tournament and soon forgot about her. Six months later she walked into the WLA school. In the quieter, more private setting she shared with me that she was a dancer and a model who had studied Lima Lama in Mexico and was now living in Los Angeles.

"The only thing that really makes me feel at home is martial arts," she confided.

If God had given me a lump of clay and told me to sculpt my ideal woman, it would have been Jill. She turned out to be a natural at Kenpo, and we were married a year later. Jill is now a sixth-degree black belt in Kenpo and has never relented in her studies.

*At one of my seminars in the Channel Islands*

As I look back on my Kenpo journey, I remember how each belt was a moment in time when I could stop and reflect on where I'd been, where I was, and where I needed to go next. At tenth-degree, this has not changed, but only shows me that these truths are constant. There are three phases in life that allows change to occur, and perfection is not some final completion but continual change. With regard to rank, my advice to students is to set their sights realistically, never too far out of reach. Once the goal is achieved, savor it for awhile and be proud, and when the novelty begins to wear off, then begin a new leg of the journey.

If there is one accomplishment in my Kenpo career of which I can be truly proud, it is the fourteen years I spent building up the Santa Monica school. Over the years I have heard this period referred to as the Golden Era of the WLA school. While I stood at the helm, I had an abundance of raw talent, dedication, and a passionate desire to learn the art of Kenpo for scores of students I shall never forget. There were eighteen black belts listed on Ed Parker's Family Tree that came out of those years (sixty-four when I left the school in Dec. 1987), many of which are still training and teaching the Kenpo that I taught them.

Being the head instructor of a karate school in a big city is not without its problems, and often I felt like a sitting duck.

The WLA school was only a few blocks away from the Veterans Administration Hospital. During the day the VA would let some of the patients who were in for drug abuse out for the day on medication. Over time, the school became a magnet for some of these outpatients, and on occasion they would stop in to wander around the school or watch students working out.

One day I was sitting in my office when in walked a young man in his early twenties. His eyes were glassy and sunk back into his head, and he walked stiffly with unmoving arms. With a look of a possessed man and without warning, he sat down and glared across my desk at me. My senses immediately went on alert, and I decided to test the waters.

"My friend, when you come into someone house, you ask to sit down."

He gave me no regard and said, "I'm on a

> *Zen in Kenpo: You are never going to live any longer than you know right now.*
> *–Larry Tatum*

236

mission, but I'm not able to handle people." With that he began to reach inside his tattered coat as he said, "Before I kill someone, I . . ."

Suspecting the man had a gun, I leapt out of my chair and flew around my desk toward him. My thoughts went to my wife and my newborn daughter. My primary, if only, task was to stay alive for my family. My mind and body were on high alert as I moved to chop his neck in order to counter any action from his arm that had moved inside his coat. With only a fraction of a second from committing to maiming or killing this man, I suddenly noticed him bring a black object from beneath his coat. Instantly I identified the object as a bible and stopped my action just in the nick of time.

The man looked up at me in bewilderment, seemingly confused as to why I was hovering over him. I took a deep breath and told him he did the right thing about going to the bible but that now I wanted him to leave. Without a word he did so, his head hanging down as he quietly walked out of the school. It took two hours for me to come down from the adrenaline rush and the high level of conviction I had gone to. For the rest of the day and evening my senses were so acute that normal life seemed mundane.

My best-loved story of triumph through the art is that of a young boy named Billy who wanted so much to learn Kenpo and become good at it. His mother told me while she was signing him up that her son had a coordination problem but had a big heart.

Months into his training I realized that this was going to be a long journey for him. As much as he tired, he could not balance himself and coordinate his moves. In sparring, he was trounced again and again. His mother suggested that we should let him go, but I disagreed with her and suggested that we give him more time. While this was easy for me to say, watching him fall over and over hurt me as much as his mother.

Around Christmas time, his mother told me that they would soon be taking a vacation and wanted her son to test for his first belt before they left. I was honest with her and told her that he

would not pass the test but that I could promote him in the hope that he would grow into it. I knew he would never accept his belt as a gift, and his mother agreed.

After Christmas, I was opening up the school one morning when the boy's mother arrived. With tears in her eyes, she said, "Mr. Tatum, I bought Billy a new bike for Christmas. He was so proud of that bike and couldn't wait to take it to school to show it off."

She told me that he'd never before been late, but that day he didn't come home on time. "I waited until I couldn't wait anymore," she said. "I went to look for him, and when I pulled up in front of the school, everyone was gone except for my son who was tangled up in his bicycle. I ran over to help him, and when I got to him he was a bloody mess and the bike was bent and scratched up."

"Mom, it's okay. They didn't get my bike," the boy told his mother. Four boys had tried to steal his bike. "I tried to fight back, but I had to hold onto the bike," Billy continued. "I guess they got tired of trying to beat me off my new bike and left. Please tell Mr. Tatum I'm not the best

*Taken at my children's class at the WLA school in 1987*

*Teaching a seminar in Venezuela*

fighter, but they didn't get my bike."

The next day Billy came into the studio and I promoted him to yellow belt. While he hadn't developed his offense, he'd developed enough heart to take a stand for what he believed in. It is priceless stories such as this that encourage me to continue with my teaching.

Over the years I was managing the WLA school, Ed Parker often worked with me between classes. His speed and power were awesome, and at times it was hard to even stand in front of him

> *As a fighter you stand over your opponent victorious, as a teacher you stand alongside him victorious.*
> *–Larry Tatum*

because when he punched I could feel a static wave emanating from his hands, even though he didn't touch me. While to some this may sound incredible, it is true.

I once mentioned that feeling to Ed and he laughed.

"You have it now, but just wait until you're in your early fifties and your ch'i will develop

until you have that ability, too. It's there, I know it and can feel it. It will happen, and when it does, have fun with it but be careful."

On my own I began to study some of the classic documentary films made by the legendary martial art masters, films of seemingly frail old men surrounded by a dozen men who suddenly charged him. The masters didn't appear to strike their attackers but sent them sprawling to the ground with ease. I read these books and became intrigued by the power of ch'i. This was a major turning point in my life as a martial artist.

Not surprisingly, it turned out that Ed Parker was right when he told me that my ch'i would develop after I turned fifty. About six months ago I gave a Kenpo seminar before 100 black belts on the East Coast. My dummy for a demo was a man who stood well over six feet and weighed 250 pounds. As I moved on him I felt the ch'i coming out of my body, and my hand stopped just short of hitting him. There was a loud crackling sound as he dropped. Everyone was astounded.

"You never touched him," one of his friends said.

It was true. I had not made contact, but my force field did.

*My black belt class at my school in Pasadena.
Below, teaching Sidney Poitier, one of the many Hollywood
celebrities I've taught over the years.*

***As a teacher, educate,
cultivate, then celebrate
–Larry Tatum***

I discovered that there's a time when the mind, body and breath are synchronized, and the resultant power is awesome. I began meditation and breathing practice in an attempt to develop

my mind-body connection and soon found that the conscious mind cannot harness or redirect ch'i. Put another way, the conscious mind only allows one to function normally in daily life. I walk into a dark room and turn on the light switch, and I apply the brakes when a child runs into the road. It's the unconscious mind that combines all my energy and spirit and that then explodes into action.

I realized that when I wanted to move my body quickly, I didn't want any lag time between what I wanted to do and my action. To be faster and more powerful I had to rid myself of that separation, so I began to experiment with quickness through mind games I made up. Soon I learned that the key to speed was action without thought, which is what the Japanese call mushin.

I continued to study ways to increase my power and speed. One way to accomplish my goal was to use what I call controlled rage. When I was acting from my subconscious mind there was no break between what I thought and what I did. They happened together. It just happened.

When I began my study with Ed Parker in the mid-60s there were fewer than 300 kenpoists in the United States. Today, largely as a result of our founder, there are nearly 1,000 Kenpo schools worldwide, many of them run by his several generations of black belts. As a result of this vast networking, the dynamics of Kenpo are set up so that the art adjusts itself easily.

That said, I feel that if there is anything that tends to impede the positive advancement of Kenpo, it is the politics of Kenpo. My experience is that the small politics start from the fact that anything that helps a person gain a better understanding of themselves also tends – too often – to inflate the self. The important politics, those of a positive nature, are rooted in the desire to teach, and to teach the art well. At the moment we become committed teachers, we open ourselves to worrying from time to time about whether our efforts to help students are being substantiated everywhere else. As a result, jealousy often raises its head in a vain attempt to be seen. None of us are immune to these processes, and so from time to time we must put ourselves in check.

When I see politics starting to creep in, I walk the other way. My primary involvement in the Kenpo community is that of a teacher, and if my teaching helps in a positive fashion, then it has fallen in the right place. Alternatively, the day I awake to find that my teaching is being wrongly used to manipulate and control others, then my teaching days are over.

In 1989 I opened a studio on my own in Pasadena. Even though I've been in Kenpo for thirty-six years, I still try to teach the way Ed Parker taught me. The first thing I do is to instill a student with confidence in me as his teacher. The next stage is to teach the student to have confidence in himself.

Even during a short lesson I want the student to feel that he has been on a journey, and the day's lesson was a stepping stone along the path. I want him to realize that it's the journey that's important and not just a belt. My hope is that at the end of each lesson, the student will know a little more about himself than he did at the beginning of the lesson.

Although I have a willingness to teach my students how to garner knowledge, I know that I do not give them something they do not earn. It is like my father often told me – to pay attention to my own work, and don't worry about what others do. If my work is honest, everything else will fall into place and the world will open up to me. I try to pass this wisdom on to my students.

I was deeply saddened on the day I learned of Ed Parker's passing. I had been one of many Kenpo companions on his journey and the thought of a future with him depressed me. But I knew that the time had come for me to continue the journey on my own without my leader, following my own compass.

As he had often told me, "Life goes on, Larry."

I felt also that it was my responsibility to carry on for him and to help fulfill his dreams for the future of Kenpo as the leading martial art in the world. My journey continues.

# Lee Wedlake
## 8th Degree

*Lee Wedlake is an accomplished author, having written nearly two dozen featured magazine articles for Inside Kung-Fu, Black Belt, Karate Illustrated, Martial Arts Professional, and Karate International, as well as two books, Kenpo Karate 101, What the Beginner and the Black Belt Should Know and his newest, Further Insights into Kenpo. He was inducted into the "World Martial Arts Hall of Fame" in May 1993, and his school was named "School of the Month" by Black Belt a year later in May 1994. Widely sought after on both the national and international seminar circuits, Lee has taught throughout the US and in Australia, England, Ireland, Sweden and Denmark. In addition, he has served as either a state, regional or national rep for the American Karate Association (AKA), IKKA, WKKA, AKKS, and was a founder of the Chinese Karate Federation in the 1990s and co-founder of the North American Kenpo Kai in the 1970s. Besides being an accomplished combat shooter (IPSC style) and aerobatic pilot (flying routines in the Pitts S2B), in December 2000 he flew a P51 Mustang at Wanaka, New Zealand and a SAAB fighter-trainer in Sweden. For relaxation, Lee rides a Harley.*

I was born in 1954 on the south side of Chicago where I grew up with three younger sisters and hard working parents. My mother was a nurse, and my father was a microbiologist who worked for one of the biggest companies that made industrial detergents.

Because my mother was primarily focused on a career in the medical profession, she was forever looking for ways for my sisters and me to occupy our time doing things like ballroom dancing, swimming, fencing and the like. This is how I ended up at the age of eleven taking judo lessons at the local YMCA.

*1967. Being carried by my judo teacher's son as my sister looks on.*

My judo instructor was not all that great. Either he didn't want to teach kids or just wasn't a good teacher – or both. I remember coming out of each class with a pounding headache that resulted from me whacking my head on the mat and slamming my body to the floor while attempting to execute break falls. Not long into my judo lessons, my mother asked me if I liked the class, and I told her I did because I didn't want her to go looking for another place to enroll

*Above, as a brown belt at a tournament with my dad in July 1974. Below, Ed Parker signs a portrait for my mom.*

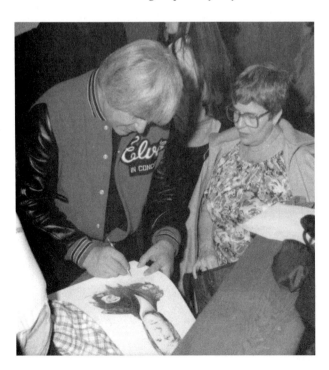

me that might be worse. This turned out to be a bad move on my part. Ironically, a few nights later she was up watching one of those first televised auctions for the public broadcasting station when the owner of a judo school called in and put a month of judo lessons up for auction. My mother was the highest bidder, and when I awoke the following morning, she said, "Well, guess what I've got for you? I have real judo lessons in a real judo school."

This new school was called Shindo-Kan, and I began my first lesson with more of the same disastrous break falls and began to feel the first stages of a headache. Then about five minutes into the lesson an event occurred that dramatically changed the course of my life. A woman instructor walked up to me, and after watching me do a couple of break falls said, "No, you really don't want to do it like that." She wasn't curt or condescending, but spent the next ten minutes carefully demonstrating the correct method of executing a break fall and stayed with me until she was convinced that I had it right. At the end of the class when I was leaving, she took the time to tell me that I had done a good job that day and that she was looking forward to working with me on my next lesson. That night I didn't have my usual headache and my body wasn't aching. I remember thinking that judo had become fun. That day probably marked the first true step in my martial art journey, and if that kind woman instructor just happens to read this book, I'd like to thank her indelibly in print for setting me on a path that I have continued walking for nearly four decades.

Now that I no longer had an aversion to attending judo classes, I looked forward to each new lesson. The school was a classical school in the traditional kodokan judo. The instructors were skilled black belts who threw their students hard and fast, and because judo is a hands-on system I saw immediate results. We spent the first hour doing calisthenics and stretching, and then we got into the actual techniques. I learned a lot of positive technique in that school and more importantly the teachers developed in me a positive attitude. It felt great to work hard at learning a technique and to be told that I had done a good job and receive a pat on the back. I eagerly attended classes at that school every day after school and on weekends until our family moved away in 1969. Unfortunately that began a two-year stretch where I didn't do any martial arts because there was nothing offered in the area where I lived out in the suburbs of Chicago.

The late-1960s was a real hotbed in Chicago, which was the site of mass rioting at the Democratic Convention. I was in high school during the 1968 civil rights riots that swept throughout our country. Incidents of rioting were not uncommon at my school, even to the degree of students pulling shotguns inside the lunch-room. To make matters worse, I was a minority and the school was overcrowded. With high enrollments of blacks and Hispanics, the local high school designed for 2500-3000 kids had 5500 students when I was there. I think that, at best, it was an uncomfortable situation for the majority of students. I remember one day we were let out of school early, and I was making my way home and just barely escaped getting run over by four black guys in a car.

In late 1972 while living in Palos Heights, Illinois, I met two guys who were training at a Kenpo school that was an offshoot of Kenpo. One evening I watched a class and was impressed by what I saw. Although I had seen karate previously, it looked to me like nothing more than punching and kicking at the air. This school was different because the instructors and students were the first ones I'd seen who actually put their hands on each other. The self-defense combinations looked inter-esting, and I had never before seen forms, which really grabbed me. In a strange way I found myself mesmerized by the fluid movement of the forms and instantly felt there was far more to them than their obvious outward appearance. It almost felt as if there was something deeper to their meaning, and that the experience of per-forming kata could be deeply internalized and at its height of perfection become even spiritual.

My initial exhilaration soon soured and I gradually became increasingly disenchanted.

*Mike Sanders, like a brother to me. Killed on a Harley in 1979.*

Although I remained drawn to Kenpo, the school lacked the positive attitude that was so prevalent at my previous judo school. Part of the problem was that mostly teenagers ran the dojo, and there seemed to be an absentee boss. Several of the instructors liked to go out on the street and antagonize people into a fight just to see if the moves would work. Their attitude was unruly and they regularly prided themselves on getting disqualified at tournaments. Not surpris-ingly I didn't learn much at that school other than physical movement. There was nothing else there. At times the atmosphere became so negative that I considered quitting, but my drive and my ability kept me going for nearly two years. I took my brown belt test at that school and flunked the first time around but passed several months later on my second test.

On perhaps the only positive note, the owner of this school did have two other schools in the Chicago and often held interschool tournaments. I entered my first one as an orange belt and several more until earning the rank of blue belt. It was at that time that I had enough confidence to venture outside the school and entered my first medium-sized martial arts tournament in the Chicago area and was quickly eliminated. Later, after obtaining my brown belt I began to realize a degree of success. In the latter part of 1974, having previously flunked my brown belt test, I proceeded to flunk my black belt test. Looking back, I know that failing these major promotions taught me the value of perseverance, which years later proved to be a formidable ally on the highly competitive national tournament circuit.

By late 1974 I had come to realize that the instructors at my first Kenpo school were not giving me the keys to unlock all the doors. And at night I would fall off to sleep knowing in my deepest place that there was someone somewhere who could tell me why I was being taught to do the things in a specific way and not just teach me the physical moves.

Shortly thereafter in early 1975 I met my second Kenpo instructor. His name was Michael John Sanders, and I credit his diligence and expertise in helping me restructure my Kenpo so that it was more in line with the Parker material. Mike had studied with Mills Crenshaw, who is one of Mr. Parker's earliest black belts. Because Mike held black belts in Tae Kwon Do, Shito-Ryu, and Kajukenbo, he taught what he called a more hard-style system called Bujin Kenpo. My training under Mike Sanders was during the period often referred to as the "Dungeon Dojo" years when instructors taught with a stick in one

hand, and broken ribs and knocked out teeth were common.

For some time, Ed Parker's Kenpo system was truly what I wanted to learn, so much so that I was willing to drive 120 each way to train with Mike Sanders. The initial training I had acquired at the first Kenpo school was not good and had resulted in my developing many bad habits that needed to be unlearned. More important, because I had not received the proper instruction in the basic principles and concepts of Kenpo, my basic foundation was weak. The only thing that kept my head above water was the solid training I had received in judo.

What made Mike special was that he encouraged his students to ask questions. This is one of the greatest lessons I have learned both as a student and a teacher, and it is a lesson that was four years later echoed by Mr. Parker. In all the years that I have been studying the martial arts, I do not know of another way to learn. If I don't understand something, I can't integrate it into myself and make it mine. This is one of the beautiful things about Ed Parker's system and what was missing at the first Kenpo school where I trained.

After receiving my black belt from Mike in 1975, I opened a school the following year in

*My first meeting with Ed Parker August 1977 at the IKC.*

Palos Hills, Illinois.

Although I had started entering local tournaments around the time I received my brown belt, after I received my black belt I redoubled my efforts and began taking the national tournament circuit by storm. Over the next several years I entered the American Karate Association Grand Nationals in Chicago, the USKA Grand Nationals in Milwaukee, Roy Kurban's Fort Worth Pro-Am, the Diamond Nationals in Minnesota, Ted Kresge's U.S. Open, Joe Corley's Battle of Atlanta, and Ed Parker's International Karate Championships in Long Beach. My basic strategy was simple. I just kept hitting them all until I started to win.

An old Zen saying says that when the student is ready, the teacher will appear. This was surely the case with my finding Mike Sanders. This burning need to know the why is what motivated me into seeking out Mike and then eventually working my way up to Ed Parker so that I would understand as much as possible about the system.

Over the years I had seen Ed Parker in magazines and on a talk show where he beat up Larry Tatum when Larry was a second-degree black. That was the first time I saw Ed Parker move, and

*With Frank Trejo, a Kenpo brother I treasure.*

I was really impressed. Although I would occasionally cross paths with him on the national tournament circuit, I formally met him in 1977 at the International Karate Championships in Long Beach. The Sports Arena was buzzing with activity, and I spotted him sitting near the stage talking to someone. He saw me and waved me over because he probably had the sense that I'd like to meet him. I walked up, introduced myself, and

*Barefoot in the Chicago snow. Note the license plate on my Vette.*

told him who had taught me. He was very cordial and made me feel comfortable. Two years later we met again at a tournament in Cleveland when all of a sudden during out conversation he said, "So when can you come to California to train?"

It took me a second to catch my breath, then I said, "Man, you tell me when to be there and I'll be there."

Over the next several years I commuted from Chicago to Los Angeles to train with Ed Parker. I'd stay in a Pasadena hotel for a week and train at the Pasadena school and take lessons at Mr. Parker's house. During those years Frank Trejo managed the Pasadena school and was like a brother to me. To this day I truly value his friendship. After a week of training, I'd return to Chicago and work on the material Ed Parker had taught me until it was as near to perfection as I could get it. A couple months later I'd return to Pasadena for more of the same training, then back to Chicago. I kept this up for a number of years. It was a workable and successful teacher /student arrangement for me and for Mr. Parker.

In 1981 I received my third-degree black belt along with my first ceremonial kick from Grandmaster Ed Parker. Having been accepted as one of his students was the biggest moment in my martial arts journey. As a young man I had dreamed of studying with a true master of his cal-

iber, and a chain of events had occurred in my life to bring this to reality.

Since the beginning of my adult martial arts career I always took the position that the art would take precedence over all else in my life. From a business standpoint, running a full-time karate school is just that – it's a full-time business. The hours are often long and include weekends. Coupled with the tournament and seminar circuit that required extensive travel, both nationally and internationally, this left little time for a social life, particularly a committed personal relationship. The girlfriends I did have over the years had a tough time with my work and competitive demands and often viewed me as someone who was always off on a mission to spread this thing I called Kenpo. During those years I felt this attitude I had was a martial arts sort of thing that everyone in the art possessed to one degree or another. My journey seemed to be that of the warrior that by definition included a lifestyle of solitude and contemplation.

This mindset of contemplative solitude worked ideally with my passion for performing kata. As early back as my first Kenpo school I liked doing those forms. Initially I wondered what they were good for because I was wrongly led to believe that they had no practical value. It wasn't until I began training with Mike Sanders and then later Ed Parker that I discovered the profound depth of their application. There is a blend of spirituality and physical movement in the martial arts that I am able to tap into when I perform kata or forms. This connection between my inner and outer worlds is spiritual in nature. Ultimately this positively affects how I relate to other people as well as my environment by keeping me relaxed and focused. In essence, it is what is often called a balancing of yin and yang. Whatever one cares to call it, it had a positive effect on my competitive years to the degree that I was the first Ed Parker Kenpo stylist to make the national top ten according to *Karate Illustrated* magazine in 1980. While I thought this was a substantial accomplishment, I could not have done it without the help I received from Mike Sanders and Ed Parker, and a couple years later from Huk Planas and Frank Trejo.

Although Kenpo is the foundation of my martial arts journey, I have studied many other systems and styles, including internal Kung Fu systems, Wing Chun, Escrima, Kali, grappling, Ta'i Chi Chaun, and others. Moreover, I have had personal experiences with the internal energy the Chinese call ch'i. In fact, I've seen a lot of strange things that I wouldn't expect anybody to believe unless they'd seen it themselves. I believe that ch'i exists. I believe that Einstein quantified it earlier in the twentieth century when he said there is a subatomic field that binds everything together, which to me is a clear and concise definition of ch'i. Furthermore, I believe we all actively have it – whether it is what the Chinese call ch'i or the Japanese call Ki or the people in India call Prana – and to that end I do not agree with people who say you've either got it or you don't. The reason is simple. Ch'i is the life force, and if I didn't have it, I would be dead. And obviously I'm not dead. So the question isn't whether or not Ch'i exists, but how we can find better ways to cultivate it.

Through the years I have found that my extensive cross training in other arts has helped me because it gave me the ability to evaluate and compare methods of motion of other systems. Ultimately I became convinced that Ed Parker's American Kenpo is like a Rosetta stone or a mother system that gives the practitioner the ability to decode other systems and read what they're doing and understand it better, sometimes even better than the students who are studying those systems.

What Kenpo has given me is the ability to

*Taken at an exhibition fight with Bill Wallace in 1980-81.*

make complex things simple by applying a method of thinking that Ed Parker taught through his principles and concepts. It is an invaluable learning tool that reminds me of something that my father told me when I first went off to college. He said, "Son, at college they aren't going to teach you what to think but how to think." This is what Ed Parker did for me.

Since I was a child I wanted to be a pilot, but my interest in flying really began to heighten when I was in high school. When I was in my thirties I had an apartment that was down the street from a small airport. One day I walked into the place and took the introductory lesson and I was hooked.

Having a solid knowledge of Kenpo proved to be immensely helpful in my learning how to fly. This was because learning to fly is really a process of learning a lot of little prearranged sequences, which is much like the forms. It really is like learning a lot of little katas for the airplane. You've got to turn this way, and then you have to put the flaps down at a certain time and speed, and next you have to put the carburetor heat on, and so on and so forth. After awhile, flying a plane is much like performing kata in that it becomes natural and almost instinctive. Not surprisingly, I learned to fly in the same way I learned martial arts – one logical step at a time

*Above, flying a Citation III as a First Officer. Middle, flying Air combat with "K-9." Below, never crashed either my helicopter or my bike!*

and simply continued to stick with it. Today I am an instrument multiengine flight instructor with an Airline Transport Pilot rating.

As with my Kenpo, flying has brought me great joy and has at times been a spiritual experience. On any given day I would fly along the Chicago skyline at dusk just as the city lights were coming on. And I'd look out my side window at my wing tips that were about even with the top of the Hancock Building or the Sears Tower. It is difficult to describe the experience of flying up there in the moonlight between the clouds. It is breathtakingly beautiful. Besides helping me to realize my lifelong dream to become a pilot, the martial arts gave me the nerve to jump out of airplanes and rappel down the side of a mountain and a whole lot more.

When I first began to study the martial arts as a young man, I was insecure and shy and would do anything to avoid being responsible for anybody else. I knew these things about myself when I came into the martial arts, although I had little or no understanding as to why I felt the way I did. My study of Kenpo has truly helped me to understand the deeper inner workings of myself. One of the things that learning Kenpo has shown me is that I am by nature a loner. And the way I discovered this is that through my study of Kenpo I learned that I am my own best teacher. This is not to say that I'm smarter than my teachers or even that I'm a better teacher than any of them have been. What I have learned about myself is that I am the only one who has enough patience

*Above, at the Byudo Inn on the island of Oahu in Hawaii.*
*Middle, with a Bengal tiger in California.*
*Below, with my niece Serena and my sister Mary in Florida, 2000.*

to tolerate the degree of perfectionism I demand of myself. This is the reason why as my martial arts training progressed and became increasingly more difficult, I gradually began spending more and more time training alone because I had chosen to work with teachers who were increasingly more distant. When I first began taking judo in Chicago, I could walk there. Then when my family moved to the suburbs there was nowhere to train within walking distance, and it was a couple of years before I got a car that I could drive to my first Kenpo school. After I left there, I began driving 120 miles in each direction to train with Michael Sanders. After Mike was killed in a motorcycle accident in 1979, I soon began training with Mr. Parker and starting flying 4,000 miles round trip in order to train in California. I trained with Ed Parker continuously and was promoted by him to sixth-degree in November 1990, just one month before his tragic and untimely death. The day he promoted me was the last time I ever saw him alive. Even today I live in Fort Myers, Florida, and my instructor, Richard Planas, lives out of state in New Orleans.

It has taken me many years to come to realize that I am not only my own best teacher but also my own best friend, and that throughout this entire journey Kenpo has been my lifeline to myself. This is why out of necessity I have remained a loner and "at all costs avoided taking responsibility for others." It has been about my perfectionism, which is a wonderful gift that can result in shining achievement. But until you find a satisfactory and workable outlet for perfectionism, it can make your life miserable, not to mention the lives of those around you. This is why I have all these years had such a passion for the forms, because they afford the practitioner little or no allowance for error. In this regard, forms are unlike self-defense techniques or freestyle. Ultimately Kenpo has provided me with a wonderful and profound vehicle of self-expression while at the same time allowing me a boundless creative outlet. For this I have Mr. Parker to thank for giving me the learning tools that have enabled me to work with my own gifts of self exploration and expression.

In my early years of my martial arts journey I relied on the Kenpo brotherhood and fellowship to give me a sense of family. And while I lived out of a suitcase while competing and traveling far and wide to learn more about the intricacies of the art I have come to love. I have begun to see that phase of my journey coming to a close.

Today my focal point is that of a teacher, and those with whom I feel a sense of family are closer to my heart and my spirit. One of those very special people is my niece Serena who lives here in Florida. Serena lost her father from a heart attack when she was a year old. When she reached the age of four, she began training in Kenpo at my school in Fort Myers. She's continued with her training for six years and is a first-degree brown belt and one day will make an exceptional black belt.

It's good for me to be able to be a part of her life and be there for her. This has been a tremendous plus for me. As I enter into the second half of my life, these bonds and needs are stronger than before. Kenpo has taught me a great deal about myself.

# Bob Liles
## 8th Degree

*If American Kenpo has a counterpart to Miyamoto Musashi, Bob Liles might well get a majority vote. Like Mushashi, in his early years Bob consistently put his head on the chopping block, only to then retreat to what many in Kenpo fondly refer to as "Bob Liles's cave." But while Musashi spent his later years painting and drawing impressive works of art, Bob followed a spiritual path, devoting years to intense reading, studying, and soul searching. With a life that spans from the local YMCA to the California State Capitol, from the full-contact fighting ring to Sacramento rooftops to repair swamp coolers in 120-degree heat, this Honoree's journey has been far and remarkably diversified. Known in Kenpo circles as a man that teaches like a Marine drill instructor, in 2001 Bob traveled to Europe where he assisted a team of instructors at an IKKA-supported seminar. With the energy of five men his age, he pushes himself to stay in top physical condition, and like many of the "old timers" is a strong advocate for regular cardiovascular workouts. Mr. Liles is associated with the United Kenpo Systems. He lives in Sacramento, California where he has taught Kenpo for over three decades.*

*Young Bob Liles.*

I n 1963 at the age of sixteen, I was a young-and-dumb junior at McClatchy High School in Sacramento. I was the classic string bean and a prime target for the local bully looking to kick sand in someone's face. I lived in a tough part of town and, because of an undesirable home life, began running the streets. It wasn't long before I was in trouble with the law.

In school I spent most of my time running the track. At six-foot-one and weighing 150 pounds, I was a natural for the high jump, although what I much preferred was long distance running. Mile after mile I could drift into my own world and forget about the shambles my teenage life had become.

Around that time the only reference I had of karate was when I

*Bob Liles at his first school in 1963*

saw the movie "The Manchurian Candidate" in which Frank Sinatra chopped through a table. I also remember seeing the first Billy Jack film and thought he was pretty amazing. Although there was a judo school somewhere in Sacramento, there wasn't anyplace that taught karate.

One afternoon I was riding home on the bus through seedy downtown Sacramento when I happened to pass by a storefront that had a display sign that read KARATE. The building was located only four blocks from my house, and so the next day I wandered into the place. There were no students on the mats and from what I could tell not much of a school. A lone man sitting at a desk shuffling papers looked up and asked if I wanted to do karate.

"How much?" I replied curiously.

"Ten bucks a month," the man said.

That was it. I signed up and returned that same evening.

Initially, karate classes were a godsend because they got me out of the house and allowed me to focus on something positive. It wasn't long before I truly began to look forward to lessons and ran down to the school every night after I finished my homework.

My dedication and discipline paid off, and after six months I was made junior instructor and helped teach the beginner's class. This really helped me get focused and, best of all, took me off the streets and forced me to start acting in a more mature manner. Because I was teaching adults, I couldn't walk out there as a soupy little kid with a smirk on my face. I had to command their respect.

Back then we didn't have many techniques and I honed in on basics. Although I was slender, I did have height, and it wasn't long before I started applying the principles of torque and began to generate a good deal of wallop.

Emotionally I started feeling more confident. I was empowered with this art that at that time in Sacramento very few had. We were definitely an exclusive club, and looking back I feel that our first group got a little too cocky and brazen with our newfound ability.

Today I shun the macho image of the karate man. As a contemporary style of self-defense, American Kenpo is as much a philosophy as it is karate chops to the neck. The media hasn't helped. Movies and television tend to glorify the whacking aspect, but the true spirit of the art is in knowing when not to whack.

Unfortunately, all too often money has gone hand-in-hand with the acquiring of a black belt. To me this has always been a moot issue. Sooner or later every chameleon lands on a plaid blanket. In the case of those who don a black belt, eventually everyone comes to know whether that individual has the physical and mental abilities to back it up. True black belts never concern themselves with this. For me, ultimately I had to put what was tough and what was bad into perspective. What karate did for me was to elevate my confidence to a level where I no longer had to think of myself as bad and instead focused on becoming good. This isn't that I envision myself as a guru-on-the-mountain martial arts expert. I just like to see myself as a regular guy with a special talent.

I had no way of knowing in the summer of 1963 that my curiosity about karate would result

*Bob Liles at his first Karate class in 1963*

in not only a hobby, but also a living. Back then, friends thought I was wasting my time, and for years even my own family members would ask, "When are you going to get a real job?"

"I have a real job," I would constantly reply. "I teach real people."

I spent twenty-one years teaching at the downtown YMCA, but very few outside the martial arts considered what I was doing work until in 1990 I built a beautiful mountain cabin with the earnings I had saved. It was around that time that I also began receiving various civic awards from local youth groups, law enforcement agencies, and even high government officials. Not long after that, family and friends began thinking that maybe I really did have a job, but for all those years I was pounding it out on the mats and in the competitive arenas I might as well been an aerobics instructor. Thankfully, this is now changing, and the public is beginning to accept martial arts as an honest profession.

There was a period when I did consider a career as an attorney. I attended two city colleges and Sacramento State University and received two degrees in law enforcement. Not long after I began my master's program, I entered Lincoln Law School and then transferred to McGeorge Law School. I completed almost two years and found myself dreaming about chocolate cake and ice cream and karate.

At one point I realized that attorneys take on other people's burdens and problems, and the job didn't end when you left the office. Besides, there was a lot of defeat and rejection in the practice of law. Not everyone turns out to be a Perry Mason or a Johnny Cochran, and in many cases law is a thankless job. Long after the case is resolved, at least in civil law, all the parties have made up and now share a common bond that they hate all the lawyers. My biggest problem was that I only owned one tie. There were a lot of things I loved about law, but owning several racks of suits and a hundred ties wasn't on the list.

Then one day it occurred to me that I already owned a three-piece suit in my karate uniform. I mean, I had a gi top and a nice pair of gi

*After karate, no more kicking sand in this guy's face*

pants, and I wore a black belt tied in a nice knot that looked as good as any half-Windsor I'd seen. Best of all I got to go to work barefoot. I didn't know any lawyer who was walking up the courthouse steps shoeless. And if my main function as a lawyer was to take on other people's burdens and problems, then martial arts fit the bill because there truly is no greater burdens than fear and low self confidence, especially when it becomes internalized as a way of life. As a martial arts instructor, I came to see that I helped alleviate fear in people by giving them an art that would allow them to exist with a sense of well being and security. So I had already found an honorable profes-

sion. It just took me a little while to realize it.

At several crossroads in my journey I had the opportunity to expand my martial arts endeavors into a much larger commercial success. Like many others in this profession I had hob-knobbed with my share of beautiful people with large bank accounts and a leaning toward generosity. Yet I remained faithfully at the downtown YMCA, which was my core for twenty-one years. That old building and the people that ran it fit me like an old easy chair. I started with a class of ten people in 1970, and by 1974 the Sacramento area Kenpo Karate program had grown to more than 400 students, making it one of the largest in northern California. Most important, I began to feel an obligation to my art and that was to continue teaching it to those who might not have the opportunity to get the help elsewhere.

At some point I knew I was never going to get rich teaching martial arts, but thus far I've enjoyed a comfortable life. The martial arts profession is a good life for those well-intentioned people who follow the path, and I highly recommend it.

I continued to teach and train through the sixties and also competed in a variety of exhibitions, including taking up the brutal sport of knockout karate in 1976 where my claim to fame was helping a Sacramento contingent beat Chuck Norris's All-Stars.

Almost as quickly as my ring career began, it was over. You couldn't pay me to get back in there

*Ed Parker with Bob Liles at the "Y" in 1972*

again. Prior to my first fight I endured three months of intensive physical and mental training that consumed nearly all of my time, and in the final month I literally couldn't sleep. Besides the training, the fight itself resulted in severe punishment to my body. The overall effect on my personal life was equally devastating, and around this time my girlfriend of five years left me. I paid a heavy price on many levels. There are times that as martial artists we can learn as much from having taken the wrong path as we do traveling along the right path. Eventually most of us get back onto the main road.

I would not be entirely truthful about my retirement from competition if I did not mention the summer of 1986. I had not fought competitively for a decade and, for whatever reason, decided to enter the International Karate Championships in Long Beach. Unlike my previous years of intensive preparatory training, on this particular weekend I entered on a whim and perhaps for no other reason than to stir up the competitive juices that had been dormant for ten years.

When I walked into the Long Beach Sports Arena that weekend, it was immediately apparent that I had become a virtual unknown. I entered the master's division and was hoping to get away

## Sacramento Gladiators Team

Larry Poore, Steve Guzman, Andre Sims, Anthony Avalos, Bob Liles and Mike Shintako.

**LARRY "SUGAR BEAR" POORE**
Kyokushinkai Style — Shodan Rank
Trained mainly under Sensei Don Bock
Four Years in Martial Arts
Side kick and power
6' 0"   185 lbs.

**STEVE GUZMAN**
Class - Lt. Weight  Blackbelt
Six years training
Known for power punches and strikes
5' 6"   135 lbs.  Age 20

**ANDRE "SPIDERMAN" SIMS**
Kenpo Style
Trained under Sensei Bob Liles
Four years in Martial Arts
Aggressive, quick hands and feet, likes to get
opponent tangled in web to finish him off.
6' 0"   162 lbs.

**ANTHONY "JUNIOR" AVALOS**
Shurin Ryu Style
Trained under Sensei Richard Dirham
Five years in Martial Arts
A thinker
5' 7"   135 lbs.

**BOB "BOURBON" LILES**
Kenpo Style 3rd Degree Black Belt
Trained under Mr. Steve Fox
Thirteen years in Martial Arts
6' 1"   180 lbs.

**MIKE SHINTAKO**
Tang Soo Do Style
Trained under Mariano Estoioko
Nine years in the Arts
Known for his beautiful kicking technique
5' 10"   155 lbs.

*Northern California full contact team (note: poster in error, should
have read that Bob was in 1976 a 2nd Degree black belt).*

with my limbs intact.

I came away with my limbs and a first place trophy. I was astounded, blown away. It was truly a high point in my journey. At that particular moment I had been viewed as one of the best in the country at what I did, and I may have been the third most honored man in a self-defense system that at that time included 25,000 members.

But on Monday I was back at the Y, carrying on with my classes and training in relative obscurity. It was good to be home. The Y was what I wanted to do and where my mountaintop was at that time.

I often talk to students about the composition of the mind and explain to them the benefits of knowing that they can do anything they desire to do in life – that they possess the strength and the capability. It took me many years to discover that a large percentage of the martial arts is fought

with the mind. My experience has shown that a successful martial artist is he who faces his demons head-on rather than leaping over or succumbing to them. The physical aspect of the martial art is merely an extension that is to used only when there is no other choice.

On the afternoon I tested for my fifth-degree, I felt I was probably prepared physically, but I knew I was prepared mentally. I arrived at the Santa Monica school and was told that Jeff Speakman would be my partner. The place was packed. I mean standing room only. In all my life I had never seen so many black belts assembled at one school. In addition there was a crush of media present, including reporters and photographers of *Black Belt* and *Inside Kung-fu* magazines.

When it came time for me to test, all I saw was Jeff. Literally. I locked in on him and focused on him. To me, he was the only individual present

*Promoted to third-degree black in 1982*

*United Kenpo Systems Sacramento 1996*

on the mat. I was oblivious to everyone else. Looking back on my test for fifth-degree, so much of the intensity was mental, and that day it was my focus that made the difference.

I am often asked what advice I would offer new students to the martial arts. Awhile back I was in my doctor's office getting my knee injected with cortisone. Prior to seeing the doctor, I picked up a copy of *Sports Illustrated.* There was a picture on the cover of football Hall of Fame star quarterback Johnny Unitas, and inside were the stories of two dozen great football players and the life-crippling injuries they have endured. The theme of the article was "Play now, pay later." One player can't move his right hand, and so-and-so has a disease in his disc, and so-and-so can't walk.

Martial artists tend to incur the same list of injuries as do many amateur and professional athletes. On a personal level, I have suffered a wide range of injuries, everything from a torn biceps that had to be sewn back on, to a bad knee, to a hip replacement, and on and on. So today I really stress practicing martial arts with a high priority for safety and protection of one's body.

Many martial artists come to feel that because they are young, they are infallible. There may be some truth to that belief, but make no

mistake, somewhere down the road if the martial artist continues to neglect protecting his body, particularly his bone joints, he will be presented with an enormous bill. I like to equate it to owing the Internal Revenue Service. The taxpayer who ignores the IRS sooner or later receives a bill in the mail. The original back tax may have been less than $500, but years later interest and penalties have driven up the bill to the value of his house.

So my advice in two words – Train Smart. Take the time to do a proper warm-up and use all the protective equipment available. And if you're nursing an injury, there is no shame or dishonor in resting. The greatest generals in history knew the wisdom of resting their troops.

Unquestionably my most treasured gift that I have received from my study of the martial arts is the ability to discipline myself. When I first came to the art as a sixteen-year-old kid, I had little discipline. And without discipline there can be no enduring focus. It was my Kenpo training that got me through college, and it was my Kenpo that enabled me to climb onto rooftops and work on swamp coolers in hundred degree plus temperatures. The discipline I have acquired through the martial arts is the driving force that today organizes and runs my life. And when one's discipline is

*At the California State Capitol. From left: Andre Sims, Clarence Craig, John Sepulveda, Ed Parker, Dian Tanaka, and me.*

in place, the doors to unlimited exploration and self-improvement begin to open.

Following my hip replacement, I felt the need to reevaluate my life. For many years one of my banner slogans was "party-hardy." And I did just that, for years and to great excess. Those who attended the Long Beach Internationals year after year can attest to that. Now I felt I was paying the price, and I wanted to close that account before I became seriously overdrawn.

My initial plan was to take a couple months off to spend time alone with myself. Six months turned into six of the most productive and insightful years of my life. Many of my friends and family saw me as having taken up the life of a sequestered monk. Others talked about Bob Liles having gone back to the cave era. Whatever it was, those years allowed me the time to read and to reflect on my life. As my focus became centered, it occurred to me that the three things I have in this life that are of value are Kenpo, my health, and time. And when I thought further about this, I

realized that all three are interchangeable and interdependent upon each other.

My expression of Kenpo belongs solely to me and to no one else. It is my art. No one can steal it from me. No one can purchase it from me. They can't even borrow it. The only way they can experience Kenpo is to walk a similar path paved with blood, sweat, and tears of joy and sorrow. Like every other martial artist, my art now flows in my arteries and veins as my very lifeblood. I depend upon it for my support of life, and amazingly enough it also depends on me for its existence. For without me to perform its wonderment, it has neither identity nor life within me.

Thankfully, I have had help along my spiritual path of Kenpo. Fourteen years ago I began teaching Kenpo to a priest, who had had some prior martial arts training. In a remarkable way, we both helped each other, and I shall be forever indebted for his kindness and caring. Most important, he was instrumental in getting me to accept the fact that I needed to make some major

262

changes in my life. He explained to me that as a higher-ranking black belt I am viewed by my students as a leader and therefore am obligated to set a good example. He further pointed out that I could count on a number of my students keying off the image I was portraying and that many would, in fact, want to emulate me. I had never thought of it in that way, but I came to realize the truth of his words. My many discussions with this priest helped me to start walking along a new path of my journey. I still have a long way to go, but the road feels good on the soles of my feet.

I'm often asked where I think American Kenpo is headed. When Ed Parker was alive, the IKKA was pretty much all there was. Since his passing there are probably over 100 Kenpo organizations, and everybody wants to be a grandmaster. That said, I think Kenpo is more than expanding. I think it's evolving. Something I often refer to in volume five of the Infinite Insights is the section in chapter seven that talks about the formula equations (p.97-100), but specifically the footnote on page100. I think this is one of the greatest statements Ed Parker ever made, and he gave us the answer to it in the manuals in the "what ifs?" Basically it says that when seeking to discover new ranges of motion not yet envisioned, ultimately the seeker will find that the number of new ranges of motion contained within Kenpo is infinite.

Realizing this, I tell my students to count the stars in the sky, and that will tell them how many variables there are in Kenpo. And this is a roundabout way of expressing where I see Kenpo headed. I think that over time it is going to go in as many directions as there are stars in the sky.

There are so many gifted and talented kenpoists who continue to carry the torch. Dian Tanaka has been a trusted friend for twenty years and is an icon who freely gives her time to promote the art to anyone who asks. My good friend Steve LaBounty inspires the spirit of the warrior and was truly forged in an iron mill. I have chosen Bryan Hawkins as my Kenpo teacher because of the man he has become. He is a prime example of a kenpoist who leads by example. I always personally felt that Frank Trejo is the consummate martial artist. Mike Pick has taken Kenpo beyond the thunder dome. They both move without effort, and it's my only hope to one day be as good as they are. Skip Hancock is another whose vast knowledge is truly impressive. Huk Planas is in a league by himself. I've always compared Huk to the Energizer Bunny. I've been to his seminars, and they never end when they're supposed to. He just keeps going and going. Ed Parker Jr. is one in our ranks who has a whole lot of knowledge that none of us has because he lived with our founder for all those years. And speaking of black belts that have been around for the whole ride, there's Chuck Sullivan. He was the first black belt since Mr. Parker's infamous split with Jimmy Woo. God only knows what Chuck Sullivan must know, and he's still working out as strong as ever at the young age of seventy. There are so many others, and all of them can teach me something. It is an honor to be a part of this book. When I look at the names of the other honorees and realize how much Kenpo knowledge is there and how many years on the mats they have collectively – it's impressive.

Ed Parker often said, "It's not who's right that matters, it's who's left." He would say this with regard to a fight, and in my mind I would extend that to all of life. So one of the things that I want to do is make sure I'm healthy enough to see my life evolve for as long as I can. If I work at keeping my body healthy, then my art thrives, and vice versa. And if these two things are in place, then I am given more time. In a sense, these three elements – my Kenpo, my health, and time – represent the strength of my Kenpo triangle. Surely this is why today I am more focused on health than ever before.

From time to time I have wondered what life would have been like had I not embarked upon this journey and chosen a normal existence of a nine-to-five job, wife and kids, the gold watch and pension. Yet when I reflect back on my life, I see that in hard times when all else had left, my art stayed with me. Kenpo has remained with me from the first lesson and like a true friend is still with me to this day. Had it not been for Kenpo, I probably would have spent my life running from shadows. Forty years later my conviction is a byproduct of my karate, and I revel in sharing my lifeblood with others.

# Vic LeRoux
## 9th Degree

*In the mid-1960s at the age of thirteen, Vic LeRoux was the youngest student to join the ranks of the legendary Crenshaw school that was located in South West Los Angeles. Little did he know at the time that three decades later he would go into partnership with the head instructor of that school, Chuck Sullivan. In the ensuing years, Vic frequently trained at many of Ed Parker's Kenpo schools and was a charter member of the Black Karate Federation (BKF). Fueled with the physical and mental energy of five people, Vic is a doer who puts his own spin on Elvis Presley's slogan "Take Care of Business - In a Flash!" Over the years he has been a school manager, instructor, tournament promoter, association co-founder, and still found enough time to serve in the California National Guard, build limousines, and customize Harleys! Often outspoken and opinionated, he is also one who practices in life what Ed Parker often said - that a kenpoist's two best weapons are his smile and his handshake. Vic lives in Seal Beach, California where he spends the majority of his time teaching Kenpo and actively helping the run The Karate Connection.*

*Vic LeRoux around the age of four*

A s a child I was a feisty kid who used to fight all the time. It was for that reason that my mother wisely chose not to enroll me in public school where I was sure to be thrown out for fighting.

I can still remember being in second grade in catholic school and working my tiny knuckles on my desk. Daily disputes were common on the playground and I wanted the kids to know from looking at my knuckles that I was a karate guy. There was a kid in school who knew a couple wristlocks, and I followed him around until he taught me. Not long after that, we put together a playground skit in which I'd do a wristlock and he'd do a front flip to get out of it. At a young age I liked the attention I got from my

267

*Vic LeRoux, Chuck Sullivan, John Conwar Sr. (deceased) and "Crazy George" Quinones*

banged up knuckles and martial arts prowess.

Sometime in the early sixties, when I was around the age of twelve, I saw my first example of karate on television. In looking back, I believe it might have been an episode of the "I Spy" series with Bill Cosby and Robert Culp. Poor Robert Culp had to fight a guy in what I remember as a cave. The boss calls in this heavy, who steps out from the shadows and stares Culp down while circling him slowly. Culp finally decides to attack. Big mistake, because the heavy did things I had never seen before. He was a blur of kicks and punches, and he was yelling and grunting. With blinding speed and within a few seconds he had laid Culp out and returned to the shadows. This topped all those magazine and comic book ads I'd been reading. This guy was a for real karate guy, and whatever it was he did, I wanted to learn it!

My mom and dad agreed that I could take karate lessons at thirteen. There were very few schools back then, and they'd found a karate school located in South West Los Angeles, just outside Inglewood where I lived and enrolled me for lessons a week after my thirteenth birthday.

The school didn't have a children's class but accepted me into the adult basics class that met in the early evening. The first person I ran into was "Crazy George" Quinones, who was the basics instructor and had hair all over him like a gorilla.

George about scared me half to death, and I thought he was going to kill me on the first night. My first lesson was learning how to block, and twenty minutes after I learned the inward and outward blocks, Crazy George said to the class, "Okay, now you people all know how to block, right?"

I could hardly speak, so I nodded my head along with the others, and the next thing I knew he was punching as hard as he could within a quarter-inch from my nose, and I had to stop him. Worst of all it was clear that I was going to spend the rest of my life in that class until I could block this instructor's potentially lethal punches. It was almost like a basic training frightening experience with Crazy George. I can still remember my mother picking me up and wanting to scream at her, "You left me in the school? You left me with that maniac!" But I was afraid if I did, she wouldn't let me go back.

I loved it. Eventually I became one of George's top students, and we became good friends. George is the strongest man I've ever known. I had a drawer in my dad's workbench. It was full of files, and my dad often told me that if I ever dropped it, I would lose my feet. The drawer was so heavy that it took both of us to pull it out. On the day I moved out of my parents' house, George not only single-handedly removed that drawer, but also stacked three other drawers on top and skipped down the driveway with my dad running alongside him.

After graduating from the basics class, I suddenly became a full-fledged member of the school. It was weird. One day I was watching it, and the next thing I knew I was a part of it and training right alongside Crazy George. Our instructor was Chuck Sullivan, who two decades later became my partner in the Karate Connection.

From day one I knew the name Ed Parker because the school I was training in had his name on the front window, but I had never met him or even seen him. Then one evening he walked in. It took a moment for me to make the connection, and when I did, I could hardly contain myself. Ed Parker was the same guy I saw battle Robert Culp in the "I Spy" show! And here I was training at his school, and he was our head instructor!

When my parents first enrolled me in karate, I just wanted to become a good fighter and for good reason. I was raised in Inglewood, which right around the time I began karate was thick with smoke from the neighboring Watts riots. I fought daily in school where being tough was a necessity, if not a way of life. This was the mindset I brought with me to karate class. I was a hard kid and often bullheaded. My parents and teachers had trouble controlling me, and I respected no one's authority.

This all changed after a short time into my karate training, and the reason was that I totally respected my karate instructors, primarily Chuck Sullivan. From the beginning, whatever he wanted me to do, or asked me to do, I did it because I knew that if I challenged his authority I was going to be out of the school. He simply made it clear from the first moment I met him that he was not going to tolerate disobedience in his class. At the same time, he was caring and consistent. Most of

*Vic a year after high school*

all he was fair. What this all meant to me is for the first time I found someone whom I wanted to like me.

I wanted what my karate seniors had. Unlike the attitude I first brought to karate class, these men displayed a control of their environment that was enviable. They had established boundaries and worked well within them. Later when I reached adulthood, I came to realize that boundaries were what I lacked as a child and, ironically, so desperately needed. Chuck Sullivan, his school and his teaching, gave me these boundaries that, once established, brought a sense of security to my static world. As the months unfolded, I became increasingly aware that outside the karate school I was a representative of that school and its members, including its instructors. This meant a great deal to me and helped tremendously to make me take personal responsibility for my actions and my character.

Back in the sixties Kenpo karate was a lot simpler than it is in today's mainstream. A typical class began with a rigorous five-minute warm-up that was followed by twenty-five minutes of basics

269

*Ed Parker kicking me for my fifth-degree. Chuck Sullivan in f.g. George Quinones middle, and Bernie Bernheim (deceased) to right of Parker.*

drill. A half-hour into the class, if your gi wasn't drenched with sweat, you weren't participating. The remaining half-hour was spent in learning new material, running the technique line, and ended with sparring. Those who stayed got consistently stronger and faster, and we proudly and respectfully believed that we could hold our own against anyone.

After class and on weekends we often socialized and came to know each other off the mats. This element of family and brotherhood was an enormous attraction to me and still is to this day.

The moment finally arrived that I was to receive my brown belt, and my proud mother had a front row seat. Back then being awarded a brown belt was akin to receiving a black belt today. On the night of the promotion a dozen kenpoists, each weighing over 200 lb. and whom I had never seen before, walked into the school

primarily to give me the ceremonial kick. Come to think of it, my reputation might have preceded me, even then.

When Mr. Parker's turn arrived, he measured me off, then delivered a front step-through ball kick, followed by a front cross unwinding heel palm and bounced me off the wall. Later my mother told me that she had attended her last promotion, that they were too real for her.

Shortly after receiving my brown belt, I graduated from high school and enrolled in junior college. The year was 1968 and amid the increasing civil unrest stemming from the Vietnam War, I soon rebelled and dropped out of school. Having lost my student deferment, I enlisted in the National Guard and spent six months in boot camp at Camp Roberts in northern California.

Upon my return to Los Angeles, I wanted more than ever to teach Kenpo full-time and

*Vic in the National Guard 1968*

*Vic kicking at the BKF. Note the platform shoes popular in the '70s.*

resumed my training at the Inglewood school, which is where Chuck and Mr. Parker had moved the Crenshaw school. My training was short-lived. Just prior to getting my black belt, they closed the school and Chuck started teaching evening classes for Ed Parker at the Santa Monica school.

Steve (Sanders) Muhammad had obtained his black belt from Chuck Sullivan and made quite a name for himself on the tournament circuit. Around the time Chuck closed the Crenshaw school, Steve (along with several others) founded the Black Karate Federation, and I began to work out there. Steve Muhammad and I were, and still are, good friends, and I knew many of the guys working out at the BKF. I stayed with them for three years and am considered a charter member.

I was a brown belt the first night I showed

up at the Black Karate Federation to work out, and they promoted me to first-degree black belt that same night. Two weeks later when I went to train at the West Los Angeles school, Ed Parker awarded me my black belt.

Receiving my first-degree black was one of the most memorable moments of my life. It was absolutely wonderful. I had worked and trained so hard for so long, and my heart and soul had been in it from the very first day. Like most other kenpoists, I truly felt inside that I had paid my dues by enduring great hardship. I mean, every gi I owned had at least one sleeve torn off and a few had both. When some of those animals at the Crenshaw and Inglewood schools got hold of you, you'd actually try to help them take the sleeve. It was better than letting them hang onto you and

271

*Vic the "Candy Man"*

beat your head in, but they were great teachers and pretty soon I was hanging onto their gi sleeves until they got torn off.

I didn't take off my black belt for a week. I showered with it and even wore it to bed and slept alongside my girlfriend. I honestly believe it meant as much or more to me than receiving my ninth degree in 1999.

The BKF was mainly a fighting school. Tournament fighting was what they did, and they did it well. This was a simpler Kenpo format than was being instituted over at the West Los Angeles school where the first round of teaching manuals were just starting to surface and there was talk about an instructor program.

In late 1970 I was routinely working out at the WLA school in the Tuesday evening advanced class that focused mainly on sparring. One evening Ed Parker walked in and asked me if I'd like to manage the school. I thought it over for about a half second, and he handed me the keys to the front door and told me to open up first thing in the morning, which I did for the next four years.

Looking back, these four years collectively represent one of the most explosive learning periods of my Kenpo journey. At the time I began managing the WLA school, Ed Parker's Kenpo was undergoing a revolutionary change in its curriculum. This was the period when the new

teaching manuals came into the system, including a high volume of new terminology, creeds, sets, and names of techniques. I could not have been in a better place, and I say this for two reasons. The first is because I was the manager of the school and was teaching all the private lessons, it was imperative that I learn all this material and that I learn it backwards and forwards. Secondly, the financial arrangement was such that a portion of my salary would be paid in private lessons with Ed Parker. In light of all this new material, I eagerly agreed to such a proposal and for obvious reasons.

It was a great four-year journey that eventually ended on a sour note. The approach of the mid-seventies marked a period of financial chaos for the Kenpo community, and the West Los Angeles and Pasadena schools were both in danger of closing. I stayed on as long as I could as manager of the WLA school and then resigned and went into business on my own.

With my departure, Larry Tatum was brought in from Pasadena in the hope of keeping the school from going under. At the time Larry was a brown belt, and he surely had his work cut out for him. Perhaps I better than most knew what Larry was up against, and in retrospect I commend him for the incredible job that he did in breathing life back into the ailing school.

Upon leaving my position as manager of the WLA school, I opened up a Harley shop and was painting custom cars and motorcycles. I was the number one custom painter in southern California. Those who remember the custom 20-colored rainbow-flamed Corvettes that were twelve feet deep in candy, well back then I was known as the Candy Man. During the day I painted cars and bikes and at night trained in karate. Because I no longer had an official home, I became a vagabond with my gi slung over my shoulder. Almost without fail, I continued to train in the WLA Tuesday night advanced class, and on

*Chuck Sullivan, Ed Parker Jr., and Vic LeRoux at Karate Connection tournament in 2001.*

*Vic with Chuck Sullivan and Jerry Poteet, Vic's JKD instructor*

other nights would drop in on some great dojos like Eddie Booze's Long Beach school, the Pasadena school and, of course, the BKF. I hit them all.

In 1980 Chuck Sullivan and I opened a school in Hawthorne, California, which we called the Karate Connection. A decade later the Karate Connection became prominent in the martial arts community as the first karate organization to teach through its extensive video correspondence course.

Such an enormous undertaking did not come easy. The main problem that plagued Kenpo had to do with the large volume of material. This would not have been an issue back in the sixties had there been the abundance of VCRs and camcorders that are prevalent today because back then there was only one-tenth the material that is contained in present day Kenpo.

Discovering a solution to this problem has unquestionably been the highlight of my Kenpo journey. The task, which I embarked on with Chuck Sullivan was how can the entire American Kenpo system be taught all over the world and at the same time, in light of the voluminous material base, be both cost and time effective? The resolution of this seemingly insurmountable problem came from scrutinizing the definition of American Kenpo with regard to its completeness.

At the outset I asked myself how I would define the "whole system"? As a general overview, I define the whole system as all the basics, all the

principles and concepts, all the forms and sets, all the techniques and their endings – everything Mr. Parker was teaching up to the time of his death.

My second question was do I know the whole system? And the answer was yes, I do. Mr. Parker taught it to me over the four-year period I was managing the WLA school, when all the new material first surfaced, and right up to the time of his death. He also taught it to a number of others, including Chuck Sullivan.

That said, I began to wonder if any of us "really" knows the whole system? The reason I ask is because since Mr. Parker's passing, there has been considerable rumor of additional material. New forms, more extensions to the techniques – even highly guarded technology with shades of the ninjitsu. This got me to thinking that if I somehow wasn't privy to any part of this material that may have been sequestered in Mr. Parker's attaché case or his computer, then I by strict definition don't know the whole system. Clearly this first step leads to nothing more than an exercise for fools. The other rude awakening came when I saw some of this new material and found it to be old material.

*Old Timers Mike O'Terry, Vic LeRoux, George Quinones, Chuck Sullivan, Albert Cornejo, Tyron Tarvin, and Addison Randall*

Kenpo is a process that comes full circle. I began with an empty cup and then filled it until it overflowed, at which time I again began to empty it. Bruce Lee said that in the beginning a punch is just a punch, and in the end a punch is again just a punch. The confusion lies in what happens in between the beginning and the end. My experience is that most high-ranking belts in Kenpo agree that the final process of Kenpo is not about piling on but tailoring down. To me this is what Mr. Parker meant when he said, "I'd rather have ten techniques that I can fight with than a hundred techniques that fight me." When viewed in this light, it seems clear that effective Economy of Motion is based on Economy of Kenpo.

In order for the system to be taught effectively through video, it was absolutely imperative that the voluminous curriculum be pared down. When I set out with Chuck Sullivan to find a solution to this problem, I came face-to-face with

what I suspected all along but never thoroughly investigated. And that was that much of what is contained in the whole system of Kenpo is redundant, while other material is to a lesser degree so exotic as to be impractical. The good news is that the whole system of Kenpo is its simplicity and is contained within the whole system of Kenpo and its complexity.

This is reminiscent of the old saying about the oyster, wherein the hungry man wants the oyster while the rich man desires the pearl. Throughout the early and middle stages of my Kenpo journey I was so hungry for knowledge that I was focused on the oyster rather than the pearl. Perhaps this is what Bruce Lee was saying in his classic message about the finger pointing at the moon.

If one's definition of the whole system includes the entirety of all the moves and sets and forms and techniques and all their extensions dating

274

back to Year One, then today I neither teach nor practice the whole system of Ed Parker's American Kenpo.

Alternatively, what I do teach through the Karate Connection is the whole system of Ed Parker's American Kenpo as defined by its simplistic complete structure that includes all the basic stances, strikes, and footwork, as well as the principles and concepts. I'm not teaching the moves and all the techniques in order, and I'm not teaching the forms. This really boils down to practicality that I equate to the Eskimos definition of ice. In the language of the Eskimos they literally have eight different definitions for ice. The reason is that in their part of the world ice is a vital element, and the existence and interplay between these different kinds of ice with regard to melting and inner structure and other key variables could mean the difference between life and death.

Where I live in California, however, I don't need eight definitions of ice. My single practical definition of ice is that it looks pretty much the same in cubes or crushed and it cools drinks on hot days. Similarly I feel the same way about my Kenpo. I don't live in an environment where multiple extensions of an endless string of techniques are of great value. Nor do I have a need to practice all those techniques strung together as katas, many of which exceed a couple hundred moves.

Instead, what I train in today is the whole system of American Kenpo in its simplistic form rather than its complex form, which under close scrutiny are really one and the same and are both expressions of the basic language of motion taught by Mr. Parker.

This is what I also teach my students. I give them the keys that will open all the doors rather than make them learn all the material behind the doors. I want this to be the new modern day path to obtaining a degree of Kenpo mastery. Put another way, I see no sense in telling my students to shuck oysters for twenty or thirty years when I can give them a pearl that I hold in my hand.

I am often asked where is the hands-on reality base of karate through video? First come the basics, then comes combining the basics, then comes the ability to use the combinations, which by that time are termed techniques, against random attacks from all angles and directions. We achieve this through a combination of drills, such as being grabbed from behind without warning or knowing beforehand what the grab or lock will be and having to do a workable technique to get out of it and away from it while doing serious damage to the opponent. Or being attacked from one of five different angles from a semi-circle of attackers not knowing which one will be attacking or with which hand or foot. And finally, it's being able to use these techniques to strike actual targets with accuracy, speed, and all the power you can have on a life-size dummy for the entire world to see.

There is no substitute for these drills and working with a full-size dummy as a partner is extremely realistic, and I encourage all my students to build one or invest in one. Perhaps the most valuable asset the student acquires from working with a dummy is precision accuracy, which to me is a more precise definition of control.

I'm a stickler about control because I feel it is a key aspect to mastery of Kenpo. To me there are four main elements to an effective martial art. First is knowledge. The student has to have a basic knowledge that includes movement, principles, and concepts. Once he has knowledge, in order to be effective, he must acquire speed, power, and accuracy. If he's missing any of those three, chances are he will not prevail against a formidable opponent.

It is clear to see how accuracy fits into the equation. A martial artist can be fast and powerful, but if he can't hit the target, then, without luck, he's ineffective.

So working with dummies is a major part of what I teach with regard to a reality base. And it is through training on a life-size dummy that the student learns precision control.

Mr. Parker was a firm believer in control and often said, "If you can hit, you can miss." And to me, a target is a target. Whether I'm hitting a target in a point in space or whether I'm hitting the actual target – a target's a target. I'll sometimes walk a student over to a dummy and hit the dummy in the head – POW! And then I'll come up and whip the punch within a fraction of an inch of the dummy's face – WHAP! Then I'll ask the student, "Now which of those two strikes was a hit?" And the answer is both. Maybe. Depending on my intention. If my intention was to strike the dummy in the face and did, that's a hit. If my intention was to come within a fraction of an inch of the dummy's face with the same speed and power, and I did, that's also a hit. Control is all about intention combined with accuracy. Teaching power and speed are often far easier to teach than control. But control, or accuracy, is often the deciding factor in a real confrontation. You can strike the heavily muscled parts of a body several times without doing any significant damage, but when the front teeth go, it's a real attention getter.

I am often asked about belt rank, almost always from a student whose primary obsession is obtaining rank. While I understand the importance of rank as it relates to goal setting and the feeling of self worth that comes with it, I try to encourage my students not to set their primary focus on rank itself. Instead, I suggest to them that they simply try to make a name for themselves in the martial arts. Bruce Lee never wore a belt or held any rank, but when he walked into a room everybody knew who he was and knew of his incredible proficiency.

Although not always the case, my experience has shown me that those who do not have a valid background in the martial arts almost always end up shopping lineage or rank. If you have a solid background and pay your dues putting in the necessary time, the rank will come, but your name is the most important thing of all. When Ed Parker and Bruce Lee were alive, few people cared one iota about who they trained under. So I tell my students to focus on making a name for themselves, and that if they'll do that, everything else will fall into place.

I strongly recommend the martial arts for children, especially kids who are having difficulty focusing and establishing boundaries in their lives. In prior years I ran a sizeable Youth Outreach program throughout California, and I saw firsthand how valuable and effective martial arts training was to a child who had wandered off the path. In my particular case, as a young child my life was chaotic and unpredictable until the day my mother signed me up for karate lessons at Chuck Sullivan's school a week after my thirteenth birthday. Within the school I found mentors and role models who had balance in their lives. For their many years of continued help, guidance and council I shall be forever indebted and grateful.

# Jeff Speakman
## 6th Degree

*Jeff Speakman may be one of the most recognizable Kenpoists in the world. An athletic youth who excelled in diving and swimming, he began his study of the martial arts with Goju-ryu during his college years. His first instructor was Lou Angel, who promoted him to third-degree (Nidan) black belt before sending him to California to study with Ed Parker. At Ed Parker's WLA studio, he was encouraged to pursue an acting career. This culminated in his first movie, "The Perfect Weapon," which showcased the American Kenpo system. Unfortunately, Ed Parker, who served as the technical advisor on the film, passed away three months before its release, although the film is dedicated to his memory. In his annual Las Vegas Seminar Camp, Mr. Speakman brings together a variety of respected instructors from within and from outside of the Kenpo system to provide a broad spectrum of instruction. In 1993 he was recognized as Instructor of the Year by Black Belt magazine for his attempts to promote Kenpo unity. He is also the founder of the "The Jeff Speakman's Champions Foundation" that teaches American Kenpo to orphaned children and problematic kids housed in locked-down facilities.*

I was born in the city of Chicago, the youngest of three. When I was in the second grade my family moved to the northwest suburbs where I grew up in a place called Arlington Heights. During my youth my father owned a popular restaurant with huge banquet facilities in downtown Chicago where I worked for years bussing tables and working in the hectic-paced kitchen.

My interest in athletics started with gymnastics when I was very young. Later in high school I competed in springboard diving and was a member of the swim team. Every morning in the icy winters of Chicago, I'd stand in the snow outside my house at five-thirty, waiting for the bus to pick me up and take me to the neighboring high school swimming pool because our school didn't have one. So our team would use theirs in the early morning and then be bussed to our own school for studies. This was a routine I did every day for four years.

In my junior year I broke several records in the conference and in the district. Many felt this was extraordinary because not only did our team not have a pool, but also didn't have a diving coach. The way I learned to dive was by watching other divers. I'd pick up their motion and imitate it and then advance from there. It proved to be a sound training method. In my senior year in 1975 I earned the status of All-American. Looking back on my early years, I feel that the athletics and the restaurant work added tremendously to what I consider today to be one of my strengths: a strong work ethic.

Because my parents were away from the house working long hours at the restaurant, I gravitated toward the two things that gave me joy and a feeling of accomplishment – gymnastics and springboard diving.

I was very small and very much a late bloomer. There's a picture of me on the high school swim team that shows me at five-foot-eight, 135 pounds, and not much muscle. So the older students who couldn't reconcile my small stature with the fact that I was breaking records in diving pushed me around quite a bit. Because I didn't have a strong physical presence or a clue about how to fight, I wasn't very good at defending myself and realized that at some point I needed to do something to correct this.

Because of my love for physical movement, when I began college I knew that eventually I was going to become either a professional dancer or pursue the martial arts. The reason was because dancing and the martial arts are structured around precise physical movement, which is what for many years had attracted me to gymnastics and diving. In essence, the expression of physical movement – primarily movement that measures excellence by degrees of precision – had long since become both my passion and obsession.

My original fascination with the martial arts began with the "Kung-Fu" television series that starred David Carradine. What really turned me toward the martial arts was the idea so brilliantly expressed in that television show, which was that there is a source of knowledge that transcends superstitious mumbo-jumbo. What truly appealed to me was that there could be a type of self-actualized knowledge and self-discovery combined with

physical expression that would ultimately lead to learning about myself and my place in the world.

When I left home in 1976, I had almost flunked out of high school. I was such a right hemisphere kid to a ridiculous extent that I tended to ignore academics in favor of athletics, but I eventually graduated. I had a friend who lived in southwest Missouri, and he invited me to live with him and suggested that I apply to his college. Considering my terrible SAT scores, it was probably the only school in the entire United States that would accept me.

I had been an art major in high school and continued to pursue that during the years that I attended Missouri State College in Joplin, Missouri. I worked my way through college at a wide range of jobs. I sold toys in a toy store, pounded nails on many a construction site, and tended bar. Because I had to take time off to save enough money to pay tuition, it took six years for me to obtain my undergraduate degree in psychology.

My first step of my martial arts journey occurred in 1979 when one day a friend casually mentioned that he was a black belt in karate. I was surprised because he had concealed it so well. I said, "Oh my God, this is amazing! I've been wondering about this."

I asked him to introduce me to his instructor, who turned out to be the night sergeant at the Web City Police Department. His name was Lou Angel, and he had quite an impressive background. In 1963 and 1964 he lived on the second floor of Gogen Yamaguchi's house in Tokyo, Japan, and received his sandan (third-degree) in Goju-ryu directly from Yamaguchi. Angel was only one of a couple of Caucasians over there. The only student that preceded him was Peter Urban from New York. Urban later brought Goju-ryu to the United States and opened the second karate school in the states called the Chinatown Dojo. Mr. Angel received his black belt from Peter Urban.

When I was first introduced to Lou Angel, he had retired from teaching. We sat in the coffee room of the Web City Police Department,

*Lou Angel with Gogen Yamaguchi in Japan, 1963.*

and I told him that I really wanted to study karate. I think he could feel both my sincerity and intensity.

"Okay," he said. "Start coming here twice a week."

We trained in the basement jail cell area of the Web City Police Department. Abandoned years ago, the place more resembled a dungeon with its rusted pipes, moldy walls, concrete floors, and one light hanging ominously from a tattered wire in the middle of the ceiling. The place felt haunted and reminded me of the ghost town of Alcatraz Island. It was a heck of a place to start my karate journey, but that was where I took my first steps.

After many months of working out together in that jail cell, Lou Angel's passion for karate was renewed and he opened a dojo called the Academy of Self Defense, which is still open today. It was at this school that my passion for the

martial arts really intensified. I trained religiously and without fail. There could be a severe ice storm and somehow I would wind up at the dojo waiting for my lesson. In addition to my personal training, I eventually began teaching for Lou Angel.

At first, the training was nothing like I thought it would be. It was all physical, and it was grueling and challenging. This made sense because my instructor was this night sergeant with these great big rock iron fists. When there was trouble in Joplin, he was the one who went out and got into it every night on the street, and he was, and is today, incredibly tough. We did knuckle pushups on concrete and worked the makiwara board. Japanese karate is highly disciplined and relatively basic compared to Kenpo, but it's extremely vicious. And the discipline is strict. Twice during my testing I failed. Mr. Angel's requirements for testing were unbelievably stringent. For example, there's a tension style of breathing in Japanese Goju-ryu called ibuke breathing that's done in a couple of traditional forms, one of the most famous being the sanchin form. If your breathing was either too soft or too loud, Mr. Angel would fail you. Your movements could be perfect, your fighting amazing, but if there was one little thing wrong, he would fail you.

Once during one of his tests, a student made first-degree black belt. After passing the test, the student walked out to his car and returned wearing a black belt. Mr. Angel took it off the student's waist and made him test a year later because the student was so arrogant to assume he would pass his test that he went out and purchased a black belt first. That's the kind of thing I came up against that was quite different from the classic mainstream martial arts environment.

Lou Angel taught me how to be a man. He was what he said he was. There was no ambiguity; there was no hypocrisy; he walked the walk, he lived in his dojo; he lived in Japan; he fought everybody. And whether I stayed with him or not, he didn't give a damn because he was going to stay true to his art and his life. This is something I truly admired in Lou Angel.

I place tremendous value in the process of a boy passing into manhood. What it is to be a man – the definition of what it is to be a man – is something that a boy is taught by a man. There is a passing of the gauntlet, so to speak, that defines or signals the boy's right of passage. There are rights of passage into manhood that are still recognized in what we would call barbaric cultures, but it's still very prevalent. I believe there is something inherent in the right of passage that is often overlooked in America, and I think that ignoring it in our culture is part of the emasculation of the American male. We are what we are. We are evolved, yet we are still part animal. And there is an urge to dominance that's part of being male. We want to have that primal urge gratified in a socially acceptable way.

Unfortunately, in the United States more so than in other countries we've squashed that. We

*As a black belt under Lou Angel.*

somehow see that as demeaning. We don't value it as an actual part of developmental health of our young men. I feel this is one of the things that the martial arts provide its practitioners. There's something subtle and intelligent and curious going on here. Even those who come from well-adjusted families still find the need to pursue this level of right of passage.

I stayed with Lou Angel up to the time that I moved to California. When I graduated in 1983,

*Larry Tatum delivers the ceremonial kick for my third-degree black.*

he told me that if I was moving to California and wanted to make martial arts my life, then I should study Kenpo from Ed Parker because he was the best in the world. Moving to Los Angeles was a culture shock to say the least. It was a time of great excitement and wonder and exploration and discovery. But it was also very difficult.

I came to California in 1983 and made my way to the Ed Parker's International Karate Championships. There was a huge turnout. I walked into the Long Beach Sports Arena from a little place in Missouri, and it was just gargantuan. I was taken aback to say the least. As I was meandering through the place, I was immediately drawn to somebody in a black karate uniform doing a form onstage, and I sat there and I couldn't believe what I was seeing. It was amazing. I was looking at it through the eyes of someone who lived in motion and coordination. I stopped

some other karate guy, pointed at the guy on the stage, and asked, "What does that crest on his karate uniform mean?" I'm thinking whatever that was, that's what I'm doing.

The guy looked at me like I was crazy and said, "That's Ed Parker's Kenpo."

And at that moment I knew why Lou Angel had sent me there. Not only did I understand why he wanted me to study Kenpo, but also at that moment something else struck me: the difference between a karate teacher and a master teacher. Lou Angel took his closest student – not his top student, but I was very close to him – and saw my potential. Keep in mind I'm coming from a very traditional martial art to a very non-traditional martial art. Mr. Angel was a master teacher who put me on a path that was completely divergent from his own. To me, it appeared that my benefit and my evolution were the most important things to him. That sacrifice was extraordinary, and it showed me the difference between just karate and a true martial art. And that's why I can say that Lou Angel taught me to be a man.

I found Mr. Parker, gave him a deep bow of respect and handed him a letter of introduction that Lou Angel had given to me. Mr. Parker opened the letter and after reading it said, "Oh, my God, from my old friend Lou Angel."

Following Mr. Parker's suggestion I began my study of Kenpo at the WLA school that in 1983 was run by Larry Tatum. The change from traditional Goju-ryu to Kenpo was difficult and demanding. I had no idea how big the difference was. But I caught on fairly quickly.

During that era of the WLA school, practically everybody was six-two, six-three, a few people six-five; and most weighed 200-230 pounds. I thought, 'Oh my God,' but kept coming in and training with determination. Not surprisingly, I got creamed every single night because those guys knew the philosophy of Japanese stylists and how they moved. And so they would immediately go to my weaknesses. My saving grace was that Lou Angel had instilled in me really strong basics, although the stances are radically different. Eventually after years of long arduous study, I was

*Ed Parker choreographing a fight sequence for "The Perfect Weapon"*

awarded the rank of third-degree black belt.

During my training at the WLA school, an individual who was involved in the Hollywood film industry was taking his child there for private lessons and one day, after watching me teach and work out, said, "You should take your skill and go study acting and go for it because this is really extraordinary."

At that time I really didn't want to get into acting. It wasn't my world. This guy kept bringing his child in and kept encouraging me to study acting. Finally one day he just handed me the address of a prominent acting school and told me to go and watch.

That week I went and observed this acting class and felt that acting fit me because it was another way of exploring myself. Over the years, I've found that studying acting is very much like psychology. The parallels are staggering.

Coincidentally, at that time Claude Van Damme's first movie came out called "Blood Sport," and I went to a local theater one afternoon to see it. When I left, I remember thinking, 'If they like what he does, wait until they see Kenpo!' And I made up my mind right then and there that I was going to pursue that dream and began studying acting in earnest.

Meanwhile, I still had to make a living. A fellow kenpoist and friend, Bryan Hawkins, had a dream of starting his own limousine business because he had been driving for a limousine company for many months. He got me a job on the weekends, working for the same company. After he went into business for himself, I drove limousines for him for a short while in order to pay bills.

In addition, I waited tables and worked as an eviction and collection agent for a company that owned second and third mortgages on mobile homes in Palmdale. Once the sheriff served the eviction notice, by law the tenant had thirty days to vacate. During those thirty days holders of the mortgage would take the paneling and the light fixtures, everything. To say that the atmosphere was tense is an vast understatement. I'd go out there to either get the money or get them out. I was quite successful at it until one day I pulled into a mobile home park that had the same dirt road that was the only way in and out. I drove in and found hordes of bikers everywhere. And they looked anything but friendly.

Wearing a tweed sports coat, I walked onto the porch and knocked on the door. An angry woman answered, and I told her that I was there for the money. She started giving me a hard time, and I stepped inside. In the middle of the filthy living room were three bikers sitting on a broken down couch, glaring back at me. It was a horrible situation and I felt like I had been set up. One guy stood up from the couch, and I hit him with everything I had and bolted through the front door and peeled rubber down that dirt road. Fifteen minutes later I walked into the office of the mortgage company and quit.

Martial arts has given me something to be totally and completely immersed in. There has never been a time in twenty-four years that I wanted to quit or did quit. All I have ever wanted regarding the martial arts is to be thought of, known, and prove myself as a real American martial artist. Over the years I have been judged strictly on my own behavior and my own dedication and the amount of work and pain, and whatever I was willing to endure. Thankfully, there was Lou Angel who stood up and said, "Here is black and white. Here is clarity in a world of confusion. You want to be a man, this is what it takes."

And I ate that up. I would put up with whatever it took; I would fight anybody; I would get my ass kicked, and I would come right back for more. Reflecting back on my forty-three years of living, I can honestly say that the martial arts has been without fail a positive thing for me. There has never been a time that it has let me down.

I wouldn't be anywhere in the movie business today if it weren't for the martial arts, and specifically Kenpo. When you go in for audition after audition for a leading role and you get a hundred call backs, and you think you're right there, and you walk in the next week and there's still a dozen guys in that room. What is it that separates them? The only reason I've been able to work in film and have had a degree of success is because I have a unique skill that is far more than American Kenpo Karate – it's the way Ed Parker individually tailored by Kenpo to fit me personally.

After only five years of studying, I landed a contract to make "The Perfect Weapon." For awhile I was the most resented guy in my acting workshop. In the eyes of those studying there, I had fallen from the back of a turnip wagon. And it's true. I was probably the last guy in the door of what those in the film industry refer to as the old studio system where a producer drags a guy in off the street and teaches him this and that and puts him under contract.

Ed Parker was really excited about the possibility of exposing Kenpo to a wide viewing audience. He knew from his decades of being a master instructor how many lives he had turned around and how many lives his students had turned around. If that could be done on an even bigger scale, the changes in our world and our society could be staggering. In addition, Mr. Parker and I thought that tough street kids would identify with the lead character in "The Perfect Weapon," as they had earlier in films like "Dirty Harry" and "Enter the Dragon," and be drawn into the discipline of the martial arts. So my job was to take this art to film – to bring those numbers and those masses to the table. Ed Parker was such a man of inclusion, which is why he often said that if people could only see what we do in Kenpo, then they will come to us.

The making of "The Perfect Weapon" fulfilled one of Ed Parker's life-long dreams to take his beloved art of Kenpo to the world through film. Sadly, he died three months before the film's debut. While the movie has served as a milestone in my personal life, it is still extremely difficult for me to watch because the emotional ties and memories are still so profound. What is particularly meaningful to me is something that many people do not know, and that is that in the film the actor who played my instructor wore Mr. Parker's first black belt. For this reason, and others, there is truly a large part of him in "The Perfect Weapon."

Because of the public visibility I have received from starring in "The Perfect Weapon," I have been able to put together an organization called "The Jeff Speakman's Champions Foundation." Funded by corporate donations, my foundation is able to teach American Kenpo to children in orphanages and problematic kids housed in locked-down facilities. In my opinion, if we don't as a responsible society do something to target these troubled kids, in fifty years we will find ourselves in big trouble.

I started the Champions program in 2000 in Mexico and currently have two locations in the United States – one in Lake Arrowhead and the other in San Dimas at the McKinley's Children Center, which is a locked facility for troubled kids who have been removed from their parents. Essentially my program is a combination of the world of American Kenpo, which teaches respect and discipline, coupled with a very sound behavior modification program. The result is that this program is changing the lives of these once troubled and problematic children, and I look forward to many years of continuing success stories.

The art for me has served as a lifeline to sanity and often has been the only clarity in a world of confusion. Because of the martial arts being so rooted in my inner being, I have a sense and a feeling that there's always a place for me to go no matter what happens in life. It's a non-physical location. It is the internal dimension I created based on my experiences in the martial arts. It's my sanctuary. I'm not a religious person. I'm not an icon kind of a guy. I think for myself and develop my own philosophies and things based on a wide variety of readings from divergent sources. My martial art is the one place I can go and feel good about myself because I am never measured against other people. That's the great thing about it. It isn't a team sport; actually for me it's not a sport at all. Rather, it is something I can achieve and nobody can take that away from me. No matter what happens in my life, I will always be a black belt. In my heart if I have walked the walk and earned my belt, this is the one thing that no one can tarnish.

To me, the strength of character that it takes to be a black belt is very difficult and stringent. It's a lifestyle of a high level of intelligence and spirituality; the pursuit of one's own inner being to become self-actualizing. It also means having a workable relationship with the world of health and fitness. The martial arts is not about how many people the practitioner can beat up and how much they can drink and how many trophies they have. Those are all measurements of how much that individual has, or could have, hurt other people. The world of martial arts isn't about whom we can hurt but about whom we can help. So the more people that I reach out to and help in whatever way so that they can have a better life, it exponentially makes me a better martial artist.

The most valuable aspect of my journey has been that besides teaching me the martial arts, Ed Parker taught me how to teach Kenpo. The way that I teach is based on the concept that a good martial arts teacher is one who allows his or her students to discover themselves. In the only article that Ed Parker wrote about me in *Black Belt* magazine he said, "I never taught Jeff Speakman how to be good, I taught him to discover how to make himself good."

I think that is very rare, and I am very grateful to Ed Parker for taking the time and caring enough to instill this in me.

# Bishop
# Donnie Williams
## 10th Degree

*Recently Ed Parker Jr. said, "I was walking through town and suddenly I heard someone call out my name. And I knew right away it had to be Donnie Williams; he has such a distinct voice." It was that same voice that in the early 1970s boomed onto the mats of a Los Angeles karate school with, "I'm Donnie Williams and I know I can whup any black belt in the place!" While luckily the moment turned into a round of raucous laughter, Donnie soon threw down the gauntlet on the tournament circuit and over the next ten years won every major tournament there was to win. And when he was finished winning in the U.S., he traveled abroad, often in the company of Steve (Sanders) Muhammad, to throw down the gauntlet on foreign soil. During that time he was one of several individuals who helped form the Black Karate Federation. Just before winning the biggest and most important match of his career, he found himself having a conversation with God, which years later led to him taking up a much greater challenge in his life by pastoring a ministry in Monrovia, California, and serving God.*

I was born in Savanna, Georgia and lived there with my mother and brother until the age of eight. We were what people called dirt poor. We lived in a one-bedroom shack that had a dirt floor. Later we moved up to what we felt was the big time to a house built on stilts. It was in a flood area by the railroad tracks, so when the rains came, the area got flooded out and our house had to be built on stilts to keep us safe from the flooding. As kids we actually looked forward to the flooding because we had a swimming pool during the rainy season and would dive off our front porch into the water.

From birth I've never seen my biological father. He left when my mom was pregnant with me. He was a whiskey

*My father Joe Williams.*

maker during prohibition and had his own still back in the woods where he made moonshine. I've got a one-by-two picture of him that my mom had tucked away somewhere, and when I found it she told me it was him. I've saved that picture all these years.

My mom worked for the school district cleaning the schoolrooms and later worked in the kitchen as a cook. She was a devout Apostolic Pentecostal Christian and her faith in God was stronger than any obstacle she ever faced throughout her life. I had a very happy childhood. Even though we didn't have a lot of the physical things, we had a lot of love and care, and I felt secure with mom. I didn't even know I was poor until I got into high school.

When I was around the age of six my mom married a white man. Living in the south, this created an enormous problem for our entire fami-

ly, and I didn't want to live there anymore and we soon moved to Monrovia, California.

I was a happy kid, but I wanted to be in the local gang, and the gang didn't like white people. I wasn't really a racist. I just had to become a racist in order to be in the gang. Of course, my mom had married a white man, and so I didn't like him because the gang members didn't like him. These were kids back then. We weren't like the gangs are today. We were more like cub scouts. Besides being a racist, the other prerequisite to being in the gang was that members had to be tough, and they wouldn't let me in because I couldn't fight.

This is how I got the idea that martial arts could be like my gun. I had a friend that was taking some form of Tai Chi or a soft style of Kung Fu in the mid-60s. When I first saw him doing all this hand waving and slow leg extensions, I thought it was some kind of weird dance. But

*Left, teenager Donnie Williams*

290

then I saw him fight, and that's when I decided that might work for me.

That weekend I hooked up with a gentleman who taught martial arts in his backyard. It wasn't a formal school by any stretch of the imagination, and we worked out in jeans and Levi's. It wasn't the quick fix that I thought it would be. I had a similar reaction to taking piano lessons. I didn't want to learn the scales; I just wanted to play at Carnegie Hall. Anyway, this guy wanted to charge me two dollars a week, and I just couldn't afford it. So I trained with him once or twice and that was it.

The following Monday I split to the streets. I had already figured out that I had taken my two lessons and that I was the now the king of the martial arts. I mean these were two lessons that nobody else had taken, so I could do what I want and people should fear me. That's what I had in my mind but not inside. In fact, I felt that if somebody were to call me out, I'd have to take off running. But I acted like I was tough, and with kids this is 90 percent of the game.

It worked for awhile and I began hanging out with the gang at the Frosters Freeze in Monrovia. We threw bricks at the cars and tried to snatch purses and stuff out of vehicles. In the late afternoon we'd go to the local pool hall and cause trouble. We were too young to be in the hall because they served beer there, but we were so rowdy nobody said anything. Back then had I really known the martial arts I probably would not have been such a troublemaker. But I faked it and acted like I was tough because that was the only way I knew to gain the respect of my peers.

It wasn't long before I got into a fight and got beat up. After that I went looking for a real karate school. There was a guy in Monrovia named Donald Griffith who had a Shotokan school on Foothill Boulevard. There were other karate schools in the area, but Griffith was a black instructor, and that attracted me.

Unlike the backyard Kung Fu teacher, Griffith ran formal school. He was a tough disciplinarian with roots back to Fumio Demura, and as a result I was afraid to get out of line. There

was no more working out in T-shirts and Levi's. I wore a gi and bowed when getting on and off the mats, which made me feel that I had something to prove. I trained at this school for about five months and never paid dues. I think Griff took me under his wing because he thought I had potential and thought that he could funnel all that anger I had into a positive direction. Anyway, I guess one could say that this was my first real step in my martial arts journey. When I left, I really don't think I knew anything – probably just enough to get me into trouble, which soon happened.

In 1963 when I was a month away from my eighteenth birthday, I lied about my age and joined the military. Although I officially joined the navy, I was attached to the 3rd Marine Division that was sent to Vietnam. No sooner had I reported for duty than I got jumped by five white guys, which heavily reinforced my desire to continue learning the martial arts.

While in the military I heard of many of the top people in the martial arts, including Ed Parker. I bought all the karate magazines and read them so I could familiarize myself with all the top names, although I had no idea who they were or how well any of them could fight.

Although I had a great desire to continue with what little martial arts training I had begun in Monrovia, there were no black teachers. Then while going through boot camp in Kingsville, Texas, I found a karate school that was run by a Kenpo teacher by the name of Jerry Atkins. The fact that it was a Kenpo school meant little to me. I just wanted to learn how to kick and punch.

Atkins was a white guy and there were no blacks in the school. But I wanted to train so badly that I decided to join. When I went in the school for the first time, one of the guys actually said, "Are we going to let the nigger train here?"

They accepted me and charged me higher dues than anyone else. But I paid it so that I could train and become good enough to whup everybody in that school. That was my goal and my motivator.

I trained with Jerry Atkins for about eight months and then was sent off to Vietnam. That's where I met up with Steve Muhammad, who was then Steve Sanders. I had heard about him, although I didn't know anything about his style. There were other great martial artists in my midst, like Byong Yu, who was with the Tiger Division. And of course by now my life is backdropped by an ongoing hot war, and so there are war drums beating all around me.

I trained for about a year, but I didn't train with anyone serious. I called it jailhouse karate. We just got a bunch of guys together in back of the barracks, and we'd kick and punch and do pushups and sit-ups, anything we could to develop ourselves. It was all self-training, mainly in basics. Thinking back, I may have worked out with Steve Sanders in Vietnam and didn't know it. He was not a personal friend of mine when we were in Vietnam, and I had no relationship with him. But he did have quite a name over there.

After my last two years of military service, I trained fanatically in Haywood, California in Tae Kwon Do with Byong Yu and actually stayed in his house for a couple of months before moving into the dojo.

Later I returned to Los Angeles and went looking for a school. I finally found one that was run by someone named Dave or John; I can't recall the last name. By this time I'm ready to make a name for myself, so I went into the school and said, "I can whup any black belt in this school. Any!"

There was about ten or twelve guys in the place, all suited up in gis. One of the kids broke the silence and asked, "Who are you?"

"I'm Donnie Williams," I replied, stretching to my full height. "And I know I can whup any of y'all."

Again there was silence that was finally broken by the same kid. "Well, can you whup Steve Sanders?"

I followed his eyes to a corner of the room where Steve stood, observing me in silence. I wasted no time in answering.

"Me and Steve Sanders can whup all of you!"

Steve laughed so hard that the tension was

*Ed Parker, Donnie Williams, and Curtis Wong*

shattered. He thought it was hysterical because I had come in all serious and ready like a man with a gun tucked away. You see, I wanted them to challenge me, and I figured if I could beat them, I'd be in. I wanted to show them I was tough like the days at the Froster Freeze. But Steve didn't even take it as a threat. He laughed and laughed, and I finally went over and we started talking. Somehow we just clicked, and over time we developed a very good relationship.

This was in 1967, and Steve and I soon began training together. Steve was training in

*Donnie Williams battling John Natividad*

Kenpo under Chuck Sullivan at the Inglewood school. I went down to the school several times, but I couldn't afford to train. I was really afraid of Chuck. To me he was the baddest thing that ever walked the streets. As tough as I was, he wasn't one I wanted to challenge. It was like Ed Parker, who to me was a legend in the martial arts. It wasn't because he was tough or bad, which he was, but rather because people made me afraid of him by the way they talked. They'd say, "Awe man, this guy's so fast and he's so powerful!" It was the same thing with Bruce Lee and everybody would ask, "Could you beat Bruce Lee?" Back in those days it was you never would be able to whup Ed Parker, or you'd never be able to whup Mr. Sullivan. Those names in Kenpo were the top names.

Over the next several years I trained under Steve and eventually was awarded my black belt from him in American Kenpo. It was around this

time that Muhammad began introducing me to prominent people in the martial arts and told me I should start fighting in tournaments. For me, initially the going was anything but smooth sailing. I'd go to tournaments, but because I didn't have a whole lot of representation in my corner, I mean no one to argue for me, I'd always get kicked out. This did not set well with my already confrontational and paranoid attitude, and I was quick to take everything personally. As far as I was concerned, everyone was cheating me, and I had no qualms about voicing that opinion – often loudly. None of the white people wanted me to win. No matter what I did, I couldn't win. Everyone was wrong but me. I was a hothead boiling over with the poor me syndrome.

By 1968, a group of us that included Steve Muhammad, Ron Chapel, a few others, and myself decided that we needed representation in tournaments. So one afternoon at the park we all decided to establish a karate organization for black people. That is when the Black Karate Federation was put together, which over the years became well known as a formidable fighting school and still is to this day.

Ed Parker to me was the single most prominent figure of Kenpo and surely was called the godfather of Kenpo for a reason. I first met him face-to-face just after Elvis Presley died. Because Elvis was one of our Kenpo brothers, Ed Parker had arranged for a small tribute to him at the Pasadena school that included a display of the bejeweled cape that Elvis had worn in his Hawaii concert. Anyway, word was all over town, so I drove over there to meet Ed Parker personally and attend the tribute to Elvis. That was the first time we met and had a conversation.

Not long after that I began dropping by the Pasadena school and Ed Parker's house. I was not a student at the Pasadena school. Let me make that clear. But I went there on and off to train with some of Ed Parker's top fighters like Frank Trejo.

As time went on I began helping with the Internationals and in 1977 was actually the tournament director. As for working out with Mr.

Parker, I was literally afraid to let him use me as a person to demo on. It wasn't so much that I was afraid of getting hurt. It was just that he made me look so physically inept. He would do hands, and even up to the year he died, he was a little out of breath, but man he was still fast. Those who were not fortunate to have witnessed Ed Parker in his prime can only imagine and still fall short. I mean the man hit like thunder. He was terrifying. I don't know of a better word to describe him. His speed was awesome. In fact, I attribute Steve Muhammad's speed to Ed Parker's techniques. Parker's execution of his techniques like Five Swords could put the fear of God into you in a hurry. Like everyone else around him, I was in total awe of the man. As time went by, I lost that because I began to see him as human. But when I first met him, he was a martial arts icon. Time and growth always change a man's perspective and the level of a playing field is forever changing.

Throughout the entire decade of the seventies, I traveled with Muhammad in the tournament circuits. To Japan, Hawaii, Jamaica, Mexico – if there was a major karate tournament handing out entry forms, I made sure that my name was on one. By the time my fighting career ended, I had won every major tournament that there was to win, and I would credit Steve Muhammad for this. When I'd make a mistake, he'd show me what to do to correct it. He was the one who made the difference in my tournament fighting. It was through many of the principles and concepts that he had learned in American Kenpo that he was able to make the difference in my tournament fighting.

My martial arts journey has had its moments of frustration and dejection. There were times during my training when I thought I was better than my teacher was, and that wasn't being acknowledged. This happened with several of my instructors, and Steve Sanders was one of them. I did challenge Steve once because I thought that my technique was a little bit better. I just told him that I thought I would whup him with a particular move, which caused him and me to go into a little scuffle that when it was over I had a little

*With Harold Borens and Isaac Hayes.*

more respect for him than I ever had. Then there were times when I'd go to tournaments and I didn't feel that I had performed at my best when I fought different people. I ended up despondent and angry with myself and wanted to quit. But

*Actor Donnie Williams*

295

you just have to suck it up and report in the next day. You can't have every tournament and every day go in your favor. I don't think life would be very exciting if that was the case, but I didn't think that way back then.

Today I am no longer angry at the world, and I credit the martial arts for changing me. This happened over time and through a simple process. The better I became as a fighter, the calmer I became and the more I respected other people because I wasn't afraid of them. As a result, I think that people began treating me differently because I was acting differently.

On a physical, more practical level, the martial arts taught me discipline. By discipline I mean the discipline to train, not the discipline that someone has over me. As an invaluable byproduct to this training, the martial arts has given me a life of robust health and energy for which I am grateful.

From a teaching perspective, the greatest thing that the martial arts can offer is not how to fight, but martial arts will teach you when to fight. Too many people are training how to fight and not everybody knows when to fight. There are reasons and times you should not fight. You should not fight a person because they insulted you. You should not fight a person because they've threatened you. You should not fight a person just because they make faces or gestures at you. Those are situations when you should not fight.

Alternatively, there are times when you may have to fight. If someone attacks your immediate family or places your family in danger, you have to fight; or if anyone presents some kind of weapon toward any loved one, you have to fight.

And it doesn't matter if it's a broom handle or a .357 magnum. There are no exceptions in that area. Also, I never fight to subdue someone. I always fight to hurt. I never fight to control. I fight to totally relieve the person of any anger they may have, which literally takes the fight out of them. Lastly, to the new student to martial arts, and even those who have been studying for some time, I would say to first train your body, and then secondly your spirit. And when your body and your spirit become disciplined, then you can control yourself. You can't control yourself if your spirit or your body is out of control.

My greatest moment in my martial arts journey occurred at the 1977 International Karate Championships in Long Beach, and it was what happened that day that later led me to establish my ministry and devote my life to God.

I did not go to the Internationals that year to fight. Instead, I was one of the tournament judges. Early in the first day of the fighting eliminations a guy called me a liar and said that I had cheated his student. I told him that not only did I not cheat his student, but that I could whup him and his momma and everybody else he could name. The idea was to anger him and it worked. He told me that he wasn't going to fight me in the street but that I should go get a gi and enter the tournament and that he would meet me there. And I said fine.

I went and got a gi and started fighting my way through the ranks. Keep in mind, I wasn't fighting to win the tournament. I was only fighting to get to him. He was my motivation. And the only way to get to him was to keep winning. By the end of the day the two of us were set to fight for the grand championship. And here's where the moment occurred that changed my life.

For me martial arts have always been spiritual from the beginning. Even when I used to go down to Chuck Sullivan's school and they used to kneel. Meditate they'd call it. I remember one time he just told his students to think – just think for awhile when he didn't want to deal with someone. I don't know what the principles were, but when I went to Ed Parker's school it was the same

thing. I'd go watch other styles and they were all meditating. Some of them have different representations such as BudoKwon and Tai Kwon Do, which is of the Buddhist faith. I didn't realize the importance of the spiritual part of my training until I was talking to Byong Yu one time and he was telling me how he has a relationship with the Buddha god, which is BudoKwon Tae Kwon Do.

Then there were people who used to ask me how I could be a Christian and train in the martial arts when the martial arts is everything against Christianity? Anyway, the more I began to try to get my spiritual side together, the more I began to be condemned.

This all came to a head on that particular weekend of the 1977 Internationals. Before fighting that guy who had called me a liar earlier that day, I went into the bathroom that evening before the final match, and I prayed to God. Remember my mom raised me up in the church, so I knew about God but I didn't know how to place Him in my training. So I said, "God, if you'll help me whup this guy, I'll actually serve you." I wasn't asking God to let me win the tournament because I wasn't interested in winning the championship. I was only interested in defending my pride. I said, if you let me win I will definitely be a good person and serve you. Well, unbeknownst to me I walked away with the grand championship.

Once I prayed and I was the champion, I didn't think about God after that and parked him like an old Buick. I went on with my life and my life began to open up. I started making movies. I did "Breaker, Breaker" with Chuck Norris, and then after that I did "Black Belt Jones" with Jim Kelly. I just started doing one movie after the next and totally forgot my relationship with God.

Then one day my church asked me to do a march against drugs, and the LA Times news reporter asked me about my martial arts and about God. I told him about how I had gone to the bathroom at the Internationals and prayed and from that point on I felt a need to truly keep my word with God. And then I suddenly remembered that I had never kept the promise I had made to God that night at the Internationals. I remember the news reporter talking to me and seeing his mouth move, and somehow I was answering, but my heart and spirit were elsewhere.

The next day I put everything on hold and stopped training so that I could do whatever was necessary to balance my spirituality. I studied the Bible and I began to see how the spiritual part of me was out of balance and that I needed to balance my spiritual body with my physical body. That is how I came to establish my ministry. I had made a promise to God that night at the Internationals, asking Him to help me get back my pride. After that, I found my way back to the God my mom had so caringly instilled in me. So that's how it all became – I made a promise to God by way of prayer and didn't keep it. Now that I'm back with God, I love the martial arts and work out and teach regularly.

When I think back to my lineage to American Kenpo, I think back to the time when Steve Muhammad and I opened a school together in 1969. I didn't have a job, and I lived at his house for a whole year and all I did was train and fight in tournaments, and he worked a job and took care of me. This is what the love of the martial arts is all about. These three men – Ed Parker, Chuck Sullivan, and Steve Muhammad – have helped me throughout my life and have contributed something to me and enriched my life immeasurably by way of the martial arts. Most importantly, I thank God, as the eternal part of Kenpo, for bringing these three men into my life.

# Rainer Schulte
## 6th Degree

*Born in Germany, Rainer Schulte traveled to the United States where he was raised in Santa Monica, California. As a young man he began taking flying lessons at Santa Monica Airport and obtained his pilot's license in July 1963. "All I wanted to do was fly," Rainer later lamented. But following his first meeting with Ed Parker, he devoted himself to Kenpo and obtained his black belt in 1970. Because of his expertise in martial arts and fluency in German, Rainer was offered a job with the U.S. Consulate in Germany and given anti-terrorism training courses. While working undercover in a variety of government security jobs, he continued to return to the States to train with Ed Parker. At Ed Parker's suggestion, Rainer opened a Kenpo studio in Dusseldorf and soon established a wing of the International Kenpo Karate Association in Europe. As a result, the popularity and growth of Kenpo in Europe is due largely to Rainer's efforts. Almost single-handedly he established Kenpo in Germany, Jersey, England, Ireland, Holland and Spain. Rainer and his wife Brigitte live in Florida where they enjoy cruising the Homosassa River and the Gulf of Mexico in their 22' pontoon boat.*

I was born in Dusseldorf, Germany at the outbreak of World War II. At that time everyone worked for the government in one form or another, and my father's job was arranging transportation for the wounded and homeless. Even today I still remember racing into underground bunkers at the sound of approaching Allied bombers. Food was scarce. With my friends I scrounged lumps of coal that fell from trains and stole potatoes from the farmer's fields.

When the war ended with Germany's defeat, I was six years old. My parents sent me to live in upstate New York with some friends of theirs when I was fourteen. For the first time in my life my stomach was full, and I looked at airplanes flying overhead with excitement, not fear.

By the time I was sixteen I was fluent in English. Soon after my birthday I joined the Merchant Marines and began my real education in the school of hard knocks.

Life was tougher in the Merchant Marines than in the navy because as a sailor you had a uniform to protect you, but we wore civvies. For example, I might wake up one morning on a ship flying the British flag, and with my German accent I'd ask the Brits to listen to American jazz music. It was certain I'd be in a fight before breakfast.

I was twenty-five years old when I left the Merchant Marines and was living on my own in Los Angeles. While in a bar one night I watched a very unassuming young man try unsuccessfully to verbally avoid a physical confrontation with a bigger man who was trying to pick a fight. One thing led to another, and the two men ended up outside, preparing to square off. As the bigger man opened with a sizzling haymaker, his smaller opponent effortlessly slipped inside, struck his opponent in the ribs and took him to the ground. Before anyone knew it, the fight was over, and the bully walked away, thankful his opponent had shown a degree of restraint, if not mercy. After the crowd dispersed, I walked over to the victor and asked him where he had learned to fight like that.

"It's martial arts," he replied calmly.

I vaguely recalled hearing about the martial arts when I was in the service and asked the man to explain further. He gave me a more thorough description and wrote down an address.

The next day I walked into a Tae Kwon Do school in Los Angeles and asked the Korean instructor what I could learn. Without warning, he jumped up and kicked an imaginary target a foot above my head, then landed with a punch and closed with a spinning kick that snapped his gi pants. Impressed, I thanked him and left. As far as I was concerned that wasn't something I could do, and my time in the Merchant Marine had taught me that in a real fight one doesn't have time to jump around.

I consulted the phone book and drove across town to a Japanese karate school. I was invited to

*On the set of "The Golden Goose"*

observe a beginner's class and soon found myself watching two dozen karate students moving back and forth on a hardwood floor, shouting a deafening yell as they executed deadly kicks and punches. It looked effective, but for my temperament it was too static.

There was one other school on my list. All I had written down was the word "Kenpo" and an address on Santa Monica Boulevard in West Los Angeles. I drove over the following day and was greeted by a somewhat shy Filipino man who, when asked what he taught, said in a mild mannered voice, "We teach self defense."

Sensing my naiveté, he summoned a young student to assist him. Moments later the instructor demonstrated an escape technique designed to be used against a rear bear hug. He executed each move slowly so that I could see what he was doing. The technique looked effective and simple to learn. What I liked best was that this instructor did not attempt to intimidate or impress me with his speed or power, although it was clear to me that he had both. Little did I know at that time that this man would go on to become world renowned for his incredible martial arts expertise

and his gentle, peaceful demeanor. The instructor who so impressed me that day was the legendary Dan Inosanto. I signed up and can still recall leaving the school that day and thinking that any common stranger I met on the street could easily have been one of these deadly black belts.

During my first week of training I met the man who through his example and his teachings would have a tremendous impact on my life. His name was Ed Parker, and I was working out in a crowded class when he entered the school through the main entrance. He acknowledged his black belts with a subtle grin and piercing eyes as he headed for the office. It seems odd now, but the truth is I was scared by the look on his face coupled with the way he walked. All that weight that swept gracefully along the mats like a tidal wave. What I remember most was the intensity of his eyes. I never met a man who was so in tune to his total environment and yet at the same time could rivet his attention on the head of a pin.

Later that evening he was introduced to the class, and when he smiled and began talking, I knew instantly that this art, which was his creation, was what I wanted to do for the rest of my

*With Ed Parker in a fight scene from "The Golden Goose"*

never had this level of mutual respect in my life before my study of the martial arts. The practice of routinely exchanging bows to my instructors and fellow students became of tremendous value in my life.

A year into my training Paul Dalton asked if I could help with a demonstration that was being given at a neighboring college university. I accepted and upon my arrival at the campus was both amazed and honored to discover that the third martial artist taking part in the demonstration was the world champion karate fighter Joe Lewis.

It was a fantastic experience to witness firsthand Joe's incredible speed and power. What impressed me most was his control. Over the years I have known talented martial arts instructors who either don't have the ability to control their strikes or don't care – or both. Like many others, I have had the disquieting and troubling experience of offering my body to another so that he may use me to demonstrate his art, only to have him selfishly inflict injury and pain to a stationary human target who had no intention of defending himself. Joe Lewis truly impressed me that day as one who not only cared about his art, but also cared for his fellow martial artists regardless of rank or notoriety.

One of the highlights of my personal journey was the day that Larry Hartsell introduced me to the incomparable Bruce Lee. Not long after our introduction I began studying at Lee's Kung-Fu school in downtown Los Angeles. I continued my study with Bruce for six months and learned a great deal, particularly with regard to simplicity and realism. To me Bruce Lee's Jeet Kune Do was the ultimate in cross training, but after awhile I came to feel that in order to make Bruce's art work, I would have to have Bruce

life. I can't explain it, but many of those who read this book will understand what I felt that night. I was looking at a true master.

In 1963 I obtained my pilot's license and was pursuing a career as a commercial pilot. But my study of Kenpo changed all that, and I began spending every free minute at the school. Over time, I began to eat, drink, and sleep Kenpo karate. I even took a job as a bouncer so that I could hone my Kenpo skills in a real time setting.

Although I was never a great kicker, the upper body movements in Kenpo came easy. All around me I saw a variety of students of all sizes, shapes, ages, and degrees of ability making Kenpo work for them. This was it. This was what I wanted to do, and I began to train five days a week to accelerate my learning.

Over time, my skills improved dramatically, and I began to enjoy a new level of self-confidence. Equally important was that I truly began to value the discipline and respect that was being demanded of me, as well as others. It felt good – even right – to bow on and off the mat. I had

*With world champion fighter Joe Lewis*

Lee's unprecedented and unique talents. I did not find this to be true with Kenpo, which offers the ability to adapt to the student, not the student to the teacher. Ed Parker never taught Rainer Schulte to fight like Ed Parker. Instead, Ed Parker taught Rainer Schulte to fight like Rainer Schulte. It was for that reason alone that I decided to devote 100 percent of my time and energy to my study of Kenpo, but I will never forget the time I spent with Bruce Lee, who was truly a master in his own right.

In September of 1970, Mr. Parker awarded me my first-degree black belt. For as long as I live I shall never forget the promotional ceremony. There were seven black belts on the board and every one of them kicked me. The first six I endured with a degree of luck, prior planning, and finesse. But when Mr. Parker positioned himself in front of me, I sensed immediately that something was wrong. I had heard tales of others

being catapulted, if not launched, into the wall behind them, and I had even witnessed a few of the unfortunates. But for me, I never felt the wall behind me. Mr. Parker's kick landed dead center, and I didn't go backwards; I went straight down. It literally took everything out of me, although I must say I enjoyed every second of it.

In the summer of 1972 I was summoned to the U.S. State Department in Washington and offered a job with the U.S. Consulate in Germany.

Two things had caught the attention of the Consulate – first, my ability to speak fluent German and, second, my martial arts expertise. What they needed was someone in security matters, and within a week I was flown to Germany and put through an antiterrorism training. At the completion of my training, I worked undercover for the U.S. Consulate for about a year until I got burned, which meant that I became too well

*Training security personnel at the U.S. Embassy in Germany*

known to be effective.

Throughout my undercover work, Kenpo proved to be invaluable and on more than one occasion saved my life, as well as the lives of others. Where I found Kenpo to be most effective was in my ability to quickly read my environment, including the people in it. Everything from

*My 50th birthday party with my German students.*

sensing the very ground I walked on to knowing where the nearest garbage can was located.

While I was in Germany, Mr. Parker suggested I start a Kenpo karate club on my own. At that time most martial arts enthusiasts in Germany were studying the traditional arts such as Shotokan, Tai Kwon Do, and Kung-Fu. Suddenly from out of nowhere this Kenpo instructor appears with flashy hands and scientific fighting principles.

At first, these established clubs simply refused to recognize me, but I wasn't about to go away. In fact, I redoubled my efforts and began putting on demonstrations and holding small seminars. I was alone over there and a sitting duck, really. I didn't have the troops waiting in the wings that many instructors had in the United States. I had definitely walked into a hornet's nest with a fly swatter. But I had total confidence in my personal art of Kenpo, as well as its ability to stand on its own. By that I mean that not only was I carrying an important overseas letter, but also I knew I had the ability to deliver it. To me, in the world of martial arts Ed Parker wasn't running for sheriff – he already was the sheriff!

I started out with only four students and

*Rainer kicking student Gary Ellis*

boring countries where Kenpo schools had been formed by black belt instructors who had a difficult time explaining their lineage. In an effort to put a stop to this, I came up with the idea of a passbook, which would keep track of a student's progression through the art. The way this worked was that the student would be given a numbered passbook at his very first lesson, and from that point forward an ongoing record of his Kenpo training would be kept in that book. This would include every promotion he received, every tournament he entered, and every seminar he attended. This passbook was to be similar in design to a passport, and its intention was to insure credibility

within a few months I had over a hundred. One Friday I failed a guy in his orange belt test, and he was so frustrated that he went to a tournament that weekend and kicked the crap out of everyone. On Monday I received a call from an instructor of a traditional school. He was not in a good mood.

"Mr. Schulte, just what do you think you're doing sending that shill to my tournament wearing a yellow belt when he beat my best brown?"

"I have some bad news for you," I said calmly. "If you're suggesting that I give that student a brown, it isn't going to happen. I just failed him on his orange belt test last Friday."

Not long after that incident, I received a letter from Mr. Parker, stating that word had filtered back to him that I had been ruffling some feathers in my neck of the woods. I replied that I had heard of a young Hawaiian who ruffled a lot of feathers in the U.S. during the late fifties and early sixties. His reply came promptly. I could actually read his smile on the page.

In 1974 Ed Parker's American Kenpo had become so popular in Germany that I began extending the IKKA throughout Europe. Within the first month I realized I had a serious problem. Over the several years I had been teaching Kenpo in Germany, the knowledge had traveled to neigh-

*Rainer with Angelo Dundee*

to the rapidly expanding European Kenpo community. Mr. Parker really liked the idea and wanted to incorporate this passbook throughout the United States as well. For whatever reasons, this never came about, either in Europe or the United States.

With the enormous popularity of Mr. Parker's American Kenpo, greater demands were made on his time. As a result, I (as I know were others) sometimes felt that I was being overlooked, when in reality the fact was that Mr. Parker was only one man faced with the impossible task of satisfying the insurmountable needs of his many thousands of students.

Following the weekend of the 1976 International Karate Championships in Long Beach, I was in a low mood. I had worked hard the previous weekend at the Long Beach Sports Arena to help make the event a success and was feeling sorry for myself because I felt I had not received the attention from Mr. Parker that I

deserved. Faced with a long return flight to Germany, I was walking through the packed LAX terminal, heading for customs, when I suddenly noticed movement in the crowd. I stopped and looked up to see Mr. Parker and his wife standing in front of me. Mr. Parker had a big smile on his face and was holding a trophy. Tears formed in my eyes when I realized that he had come all the way from Pasadena to see me off and to present me with the IKC Sportsmanship award. That moment of caring from a man who I loved and respected as a father was enough to last a lifetime.

My martial arts training was responsible for my getting an assignment handling security for the U.S. State Department, which in turn gave me the opportunity to work with police officers from the famous GSG9, as well as a number of SWAT teams.

By the mid-80s, American Kenpo had developed throughout Europe such a formidable reputation of its effectiveness that at Mr. Parker's sug-

*Rainer with fighter Lenney Lewis.*

*With Michael Buffer at center ring*

gestion I was holding seminars that specialized in hands-on self-defense for law enforcement.

I soon realized that too many of my students were getting hurt on the mat, and I needed protective equipment especially designed for martial artists. I went to a local sporting goods company and struck up a friendship with Brigitte, the company's secretary. After a brief courtship, Brigitte and I were married. When the company's owner got ready to retire, I acquired the company, and with Brigitte we turned it into a successful manufacturer of martial arts and boxing equipment. We soon developed a reputation for making first-class boxing gear for many of the top profes-

sional fighters.

I also formed my own security company specializing in protecting high profile diplomats and celebrities. We were hired to handle protection for Paul McCartney's world tour in 1989.

That summer I returned to Los Angeles to train again with Ed Parker, who promoted me to sixth-degree black belt. Soon after I returned to Germany I learned of Ed's tragic death. I was devastated but unable to return to the States for his funeral because I was on assignment in Europe. I mourned his passing in private.

After several months, I began asking myself what I was I going to do now that my master was gone? Like others in Kenpo, I became aware of the increases in black belt rank and was asked to join a number of Kenpo organizations. Several of these offers included belt promotion, and perhaps it was for that reason alone that I respectfully declined. The day I learned of Ed Parker's death I vowed never to put on another stripe.

To me personally, the stripes on a black belt hold a different meaning than they do to many others. When I look back on my Kenpo journey, the night I received my black belt was the greatest moment thus far. When a student first straps on a black belt, that belt is the blackest it will ever be. From that moment on, it continues to lighten, and if the student wears it long enough, the belt will lose all its color and become white. This to me is symbolic of the full circle of the martial arts. Regardless of style or system, every martial art eventually completes a full circle, from simplicity through complexity and returning to simplicity. And so in this regard stripes to me are in a sense representative of less knowledge, not necessarily greater knowledge. It is one of the wonderful ironies of the martial arts.

As to my personal Kenpo, with Mr. Parker's death I had grown depressed. After considerable thought, I reached the conclusion that perhaps what would reawaken my fighting spirit would be to look into cross training. I had not ventured outside the Kenpo circle since I had decades ago trained with Bruce Lee at his school in downtown Los Angeles.

In 1991 at the age of fifty-one, I joined a local boxing gym in Duesseldorf and got a trainer. It wasn't long before I realized that the art of boxing actually had been a part of my Kenpo journey all along. I just never realized it. Things that Ed Parker had taught me, which I didn't completely understand at the time, suddenly became meaningful. I seemed to know instinctively what my boxing trainer was talking about, and I think that both amazed and impressed him. When Ed Parker had shown me the same moves years ago, I hadn't completely grasped it. Back then I couldn't understand how boxing was interrelated with Kenpo. But they are interchangeable, particularly with regard to motion skills. A lot of the basic techniques in boxing are variations of what I was taught in Kenpo. Unquestionably, cross training in boxing has added appreciably to my personal Kenpo.

I am convinced that Mr. Parker's teachings and wisdom laid out the path upon which for me to walk, and I attribute my successes to living a life based on personal honesty and respect for others. I thoroughly enjoyed every minute I spent with Mr. Parker and feel I owe a debt to him that I can never repay.

As my journey continues, I am still looking for answers to many questions. I am confident that I will find those answers if I but continue to recall the words of Mr. Parker, who often said, "Don't be like the man at the bottom of the well who thinks all of heaven is what he sees."

# Elvis Presley 8th Degree

## "Warriors we must be"

### by Dr. Stevan Walton D. C.

The Entertainer of the Century, with 31 movies! The Artist of the Century, with 131 gold and platinum records! The King of Rock 'n' Roll! And . . . *Pioneer of American Karate?* Elvis's legendary accomplishments as an entertainer tend to eclipse his achievements in his "second love," the martial arts. A key to understanding Elvis as a man and as a performer is in realizing that from his early days in the army until the later years of his life, he was a dedicated martial artist who would draw upon the arts for *inner strength.* But Elvis didn't just *draw power* from the arts he loved, he also *gave back* generously: he was one of the earliest, most consistent and most visible promoters of the martial arts in America. In a single 1973 satellite broadcast he exposed American Kenpo to 1.5 billion people!

Even as a child Elvis had something special. He won his first talent contest when he was eleven. From the Chinese perspective, Elvis was blessed with a double portion of personal power, *jing/essence,* an extra measure of vitality or *"ch'i."*

Perhaps this is related to the fact that his older twin brother, Jesse Garon, was stillborn, and Elvis was raised an only child. In Chinese thought, a human birth is considered special because human beings are the link between heaven and earth. "Heaven's mandate" is the literal translation of the Chinese character for "destiny." *Jing/essence* is the reservoir that fuels the *ch'i* (aka *ki, prana,* internal energy) and is what allows man to actualize his potential and realize his destiny. Strong *ch'i* is manifested as a powerful spirit.

Early in life, as a child and as an adolescent in the Pentecostal church, then later as a young man when he embraced the martial arts, Elvis learned to reach deep within, release his strong spirit and tap into his abundance of vitality *(ch'i).* As a result he became acknowledged as the single greatest entertainer of the 20th Century!

Elvis's strong spirit was brought up in the First Assemblies of God Church in Tupelo, Mississippi. He received the "baptism of the Holy Spirit" at age nine, the primary evidence of which is "speaking in tongues," spontaneous vocal utterances directed toward God. Other manifestations of the Spirit would be involuntary physical movements, even falling to the ground, accounting for the label "holy rollers."

Being "different" in high school can bring unwanted attention from ones peers. Elvis's flashy clothes and long, duck tail sideburn hairstyle made him a target of bullies. Once, three jocks had Elvis cornered in the restroom, menacing him and threatening to cut his hair. Bobby "Red" West happened onto the scene and rescued Elvis. This was in 1952; a few years later, after Elvis's first record, Red West became his first bodyguard.

After a few small recordings, in 1955 Elvis signed with promoter Colonel Tom Parker, contracted with RCA and was booked for six TV appearances on the nationally-broadcast Dorsey brothers Saturday night "Stage Show." *Blue Suede Shoes* and *Heartbreak Hotel* made him a national celebrity.

Elvis's Pentecostal upbringing came out in his performances. He would later recall, " . . . the preachers . . . they cut-up all over the place, jumpin' on the piano, movin' ever' which way. I guess I learned a lot from them." During his electrifying performances, he would sometimes seem to be trembling in the grip of some greater force. From a 1956 TIME magazine review: " . . . his entire body takes on a frantic quiver, as if he had swallowed a jack-hammer." When Elvis tapped into his *source*, his *spirit* was contagious and audiences went wild!

Elvis had a very spiritual viewpoint on life. He often asked, "Why me? Why am I here? Why was I selected to be 'Elvis Presley'? Why do I receive all the attention, acclaim, love, and rewards?" He was unable to explain his own fame and popularity in any way other than to acknowledge that it was a gift from God. He was "chosen" in the sense that he was "gifted." He had a sense of destiny and the *power* to pursue it.

Throughout his career Elvis remained a devout Christian and found in Gospel music a constant source of comfort and inspiration, and a way to keep in touch with his spiritual roots. In fact, although he was often nominated for Grammy awards, the only three he won were for Gospel recordings (in 1967 and 1974 for "*How*

*Great Thou Art*," and in 1972 for the album "*He Touched Me*").

As the first rock and roll superstar, Elvis had no paradigm for dealing with the downside of fame. He rocketed to celebrity in America at a time when the atmosphere surrounding the famous was taking a dark turn. Elvis's career was bracketed between two telling events. The first: a 1944 concert at New York's Paramount theater where Frank Sinatra required 450 police officers to control his unruly fans. During Sinatra's performance a young man named Alexander Dorogokupetz threw an egg that hit Sinatra in the face. After his arrest, Dorogokupetz commented, "I vowed to put an end to this monotony of two years of consecutive swooning. It felt good." The second event: a generation later in December 1980, Mark David Chapman sought publicity by shooting and killing Beatle John Lennon.

In this atmosphere of rebellious American iconoclasm, fame through violence, and distrust of royalty, the "King of Rock and Roll" became a much bigger target than he was at Humes High School. In 1956, he pulled his Lincoln Continental into a Memphis gas station and asked the attendant to check his air conditioner. Fans spotted Elvis and surrounded him for autographs. This attention irked the 6'4" attendant, Ed Hopper, who asked Elvis to move. When Elvis replied, "OK man, just give me a minute," the attendant slapped him and said, "I said, move it!" Elvis decked him, giving him a cut and a black eye. Another attendant, Aubrey Brown, jumped in, and Elvis handled him, too. All three were arrested, and in court the two station attendants were fined (and fired) and the assault charges against Elvis were dropped. Elvis's girlfriend at the time, June Juanico, said, "The guys wanted to knock the crap out of this pretty boy."

A few months later Elvis was attacked at the Commodore Perry Hotel in Toledo. A nineteen-year-old sheet metal worker named Louis Balint, Jr. blamed the break-up of his marriage on his wife's love for Elvis. Balint took out a few of Elvis's entourage, then took a swing at Elvis. Again, the police intervened and Elvis was exonerated in court. Balint was unable to pay the $19.60 fine and spent three weeks in jail until his father finally bailed him out.

By 1956 Elvis required a flying wedge of National Guardsmen, state troopers, or police officers to run interference for him at his concerts. Clearly, he had strong motivation for developing self-defense skills. Elvis had already emphatically demonstrated that he possessed both the will and the ability to effectively defend himself *prior* to any formal training.

That year Elvis took an even bigger step into the spotlight by going to Hollywood, saying, "Singers come and go, but if you're a good actor you can last a long time." His first film, *Love Me Tender*, was not a starring role, but his presence made the film a box-office success. During filming Elvis became friends with actor Nick Adams, who would within a few years become one of Ed Parker's early celebrity Kenpo students. The story of Elvis's third film, *Jailhouse Rock* (1957), had art partially imitating life: his character, Vince, accidentally kills a man in a bar fight with a lethal punch, and is sentenced to jail. During the filming of his fourth movie, *King Creole*, in 1958, Elvis's arm was cut by knife-wielding actor Vic Morrow; ironic, because Vic Morrow was experienced in the blade-oriented Filipino martial arts.

Like the energy in his concert performances, the free swinging fight scenes in his early films were wild and undisciplined. Elvis's raw energy glowed from the screen.

The fame generated by the success of these first four films made Elvis even more recognizable, and the gilded cage that would envelope him for the rest of his life began to take form. He couldn't go anywhere without being mobbed. He was becoming a prisoner of his own fame.

In 1958, just as he finished filming *King Creole* and at the pinnacle of his blossoming career, Elvis was drafted into the United States Army.

Like American martial art pioneers Robert Trias and Chuck Norris, Elvis received his first exposure to the Asian fighting arts in the military. During basic training he witnessed a judo demonstration, but he didn't begin studying martial arts until he was shipped to Germany to serve in the 32$^{nd}$ Tank Battalion. In December, a few months after arriving in Germany, he attended a karate demonstration with fellow recruit Rex Mansfield, from Tennessee. The demonstration was by Jürgen

Seidel, a former judo man who had recently introduced Shotokan karate to Germany. Karate, a mind/body exercise focusing on life and death confrontations, greatly appealed to both the physical and spiritual sides of Elvis, and he was hooked. Spiritually, the mirror of mortality helped to sharpen his focus. Physically, he had already been the target of jealous boyfriends and assorted rednecks. Although he had already shown that he could handle himself in a fight, he felt that additional self-defense skills could be useful.

Elvis and Mansfield began lessons at sensei Seidel's Bad Homburg dojo, and when they were not in class, they spent hours practicing with each other. Elvis was a quick learner. He was so dedicated that when on leave in Paris in January 1960, he spent his time training with Murakami Tetsuji, another Shotokan sensei who came highly recommended by Seidel. Murakami was a traditionalist who taught, "Karate does not have competition as the objective, rather the liberation of body and spirit." In Japan, sensei Murakami had studied Shotokan for ten years, as well as Aikido and Kendo. Elvis worked hard and earned his brown belt under the watchful eye of the strict sensei. The following week Elvis was promoted to Sergeant.

After a year and a half in Germany, Elvis was sent back to the U.S. in early March 1960. On the trip back, he would play around and demonstrate karate with Rex Mansfield, causing Colonel Parker to comment, "If he ever loses his voice, we could make money with his wrestling!" Elvis offered his army buddy and karate training partner Mansfield a job, but Mansfield declined. After Mansfield wooed and married Elvis's secretary Elisabeth Stefaniak, the Mansfields and Elvis drifted apart.

When Elvis was discharged at McGuire Air Force Base, he remarked, "The Army made a man of me. I was glad for the experience, glad no one can now say that I had it made." He wrote to his karate teacher, Jürgen Seidel, "I want to thank you from the bottom of my heart for taking the time to teach me the basic steps of 'karate.' You have been very patient in teaching me and I want you to know that I have learned a lot and that I am very satisfied." He signed it "Elvis Presley, 3rd cue (sic) Karate."

On his return home, Elvis intensified his karate practice. Under Chito-ryu instructor Henry "Hank" Slemansky, an early teacher of Dan Inosanto, he was awarded his black belt on March 21, 1960.

His first post-army film was appropriately titled *G.I Blues*. Elvis kept up his karate practice, giving demonstrations between takes and breaking boards and tiles for the amusement of the crew. Apparently something went wrong and he damaged his hand during one of his demos. His swollen hand is visible in one of the film's scenes and on the album cover for the film's soundtrack. The board-breaking practice disciplined Elvis to focus and project his energy with an unwavering spirit, fueling even greater self-confidence.

During shooting on his next film, *Flaming Star*, Elvis broke Red West's arm during a fight scene. He also wrote another letter to his first karate teacher, Jürgen Seidel. He told Seidel of his plan to promote karate in film, "I want you to know how much I appreciate everything you're doing for me, and I hope I can repay you with the movies and records I'm making now . . . May God Bless you."

While shooting his final film of the year, *Wild in the Country*, Elvis stayed at Los Angeles's Beverly Wilshire Hotel where a convention of orthopedic surgeons was meeting. Terry Robinson, personal trainer to Mario Lanza, arranged for a demonstration to show the doctors how a skilled karate man could do amazing things without damaging his hands. The demonstrator was Kenpo Karate expert Edmund Kealoha Parker. Elvis learned of the demonstration through a notice in the lobby. Parker later recalled the event, "The demonstration was exceptional. Energy flowed with all of the intensity of a life or death combat."

Elvis's trained eye immediately appreciated the difference between his rigid, traditional training and Parker's creative, innovative approach. Parker's flamboyant and functional system featured fluid rapid-fire combinations. His non-traditional approach to teaching and his flair for showmanship, as well as his vision for Americanizing the art, struck a deep, responsive chord in Elvis. In addition, Elvis recognized in Parker that same special energy, or *presence*, that he himself radiated. After the demonstration, Parker was impressed by Elvis's humility as he introduced himself, "I don't know if you have heard of me, but my name is Elvis Presley . . . You seem to be a rebel in your field as I am in mine." Elvis told Parker of his love for the martial arts, and Parker offered to train him. However, at the time, Elvis's schedule of shooting two or three films a year precluded regular study with Parker.

Elvis began to surround himself with karate-trained bodyguards, who acquired the "Memphis Mafia" label. The first members were Red West and his cousin, Delbert "Sonny" West.

In March 1961, Elvis left for Kauai to film *Blue Hawaii*. He kept up his karate by sparring with Red West and breaking boards on the beach. By the time the film shoot was finished, the beach was strewn with shattered wood. A decade before Bruce Lee and David Carradine brought martial arts to the big and small screens, Elvis recognized that using karate added a unique element to his onscreen presence. Elvis's use of karate skills in his films, instead of the more typical standing exchange of John Wayne haymakers, helped to popularize the martial arts during their infancy in America.

*Blue Hawaii* opened at the end of 1961, at about the same time that the first issue of *Black Belt* magazine was published. By this time Elvis's friend Ed Parker was teaching film stars and scriptwriters, causing Kenpo Karate to be written into many screenplays of the 1960s. Parker was featured in that first issue, teaching Elvis's old friend, actor Nick Adams who starred in the TV series *The Rebel*.

During Elvis's next film, *Follow That Dream*, he would continue to practice between takes, applying joint locks to his cousin, Billy Smith, or practicing takedowns on his bodyguard Red West. He also penned another letter to his first sensei, Jürgen Seidel, dated February 5, 1962, "I have just arrived home in Memphis and found your book of Karate waiting for me. It was very thoughtful of you to send me a copy and it appears to be a very excellent book. I have attained my first-degree black belt. When time allows I practice as much as possible."

In preparation for his next role in *Kid Galahad*, Elvis was coached by boxing trainer

Mushy Callahan, who commented that Elvis's early streetfights and karate training made him a natural fighter.

Most of the films during this period were designed primarily to sell records, and the roles were not challenging. But, even the two-dimensional parts could not dim Elvis's incandescent aura of energy as it blazed from the screen bigger than life.

Elvis featured karate in many of his films during the sixties; this scene, from 1964's *Roustabout,* is typical: Elvis has just finished singing the song "*Poison Ivy League,*" irritating some frat boys. Outside, as he gets ready to leave on his Honda motorcycle, the frat boys surround him, giving him lip about his bike, "What's the matter — aren't American 'cycles good enough for you?"

Elvis replies, "You don't dig world trade, college boy, after all the economics they've tried to shove into you?"

Jock # 1 says, "Get off, buddy."

As Elvis dismounts, the big guy throws a right, Elvis parries and handswords his arm, then drops him with a strike to the face. Jock # 2 rushes in, is heel-palmed and then dropped with another handsword to the back of his neck. Elvis then turns to Jock # 3 and says, "Come on, come on!"

Jock # 3, "No! No – that's *KARATE!*"

Elvis says, "That goes with the 'cycle. Come on!"

The Jock flees, and Elvis eventually does some jail time for breaking his assailant's arm.

Elvis continued to practice karate at home and on the set, giving spontaneous demonstrations to friends and visitors. He loved what he perceived to be masculine endeavors. Karate was integrated into his life and became part of his macho image.

On May 1, 1967 Elvis married Priscilla Ann Beaulieu in a private Las Vegas ceremony attended by a group of fourteen family and friends. Their daughter, Lisa Marie, was born in February 1968.

The grind of churning out financially successful but formulaic films was stifling Elvis's creative spirit. He wanted recognition as a serious actor, but Colonel Parker refused to let him deviate from the shallow sure-thing film formula.

Elvis's new responsibilities as husband and father combined with his stagnant career to motivate him to seek a new direction.

After 1963 Elvis's record sales began to decline. The "British Invasion" had begun and groups like the Beatles and the Rolling Stones topped the charts. In the late 1950s Elvis was at the leading edge of rebellious youth culture. But now singers like Bob Dylan and Joan Baez were more in tune with the new counter-culture of psychedelic love-ins, flower power, and dope-smoking hippies that were "turning on, tuning in, and dropping out." How would a patriotic Elvis be received in the era of anti-war protest? Was he irrelevant and out of touch?

These questions nagged Elvis, and as he prepared to return to concert performances, he intensified his karate and spiritual practices.

In May 1968, he and Priscilla flew to Hawaii for some R&R. While there, he attended Ed Parker's 1st Hawaii vs. Mainland Team Tournament that was held in Honolulu. The Mainland team was composed of Chuck Norris, Steve (Muhammad) Sanders, and Mike Stone, the winner of Parker's 1964 Long Beach International Karate Championships.

Reunited with charismatic Kenpo master Ed Parker, Elvis arranged for private lessons in Parker's dynamic, expressive system at his West Los Angeles studio. Kenpo helped Elvis *tap in* to his special reservoir of *inner power*, that *jing/essence* source that fueled his *ch'i* and gave him the energy and courage to achieve the seemingly impossible.

Elvis was returning to the public spotlight at a dangerous time. On April 4, 1968, the Reverend Martin Luther King, Jr. was assassinated in Elvis's home town of Memphis, Tennessee, unleashing violence in more than 100 cities. Then, two months later on June 4, 1968, Bobby Kennedy was assassinated in Elvis's adopted hometown of Los Angeles, while campaigning for President of the United States.

Elvis also received threats of assassination. After the Kennedy and King assassinations, Elvis developed a theory that the assassins were seeking notoriety. He ordered his bodyguards to make sure that any assassin would not survive to enjoy publicity at his expense. The threats were all taken seriously, but Elvis wasn't going to allow fear to deter him from his path. In the margin of one of his books, Elvis wrote: "The only people who are afraid of death are the people who are afraid of life . . . Warriors we must be!"

Colonel Tom Parker wanted Elvis's comeback to consist of Christmas songs, but Elvis had other ideas. He would do it his way for a change. His 1968 NBC television special, *Elvis,* was taped as a series of jam sessions and studio production numbers before a small live audience. The segments were edited, and the show was broadcast in December to rave reviews. "Mind-blowing! Astounding! Stellar!" Superlatives abounded, and Elvis had escaped the trap of Hollywood-induced mediocrity. He still had the "juice." A segment that showed a singing Elvis using his karate skills to dispatch multiple attackers was edited out of the broadcast but can be seen on current video releases.

The success of the 1968 "Comeback Special" encouraged Elvis to return to *live* performances. Boldly, he set his sights on Las Vegas! Years before, in 1956, he'd received a lukewarm reception in Vegas. He hadn't performed before a live audience in nine years. What better challenge? The Kenpo moves he had assimilated into his life provided a unique element to his films and NBC special, so why not his live performances? Parker, the veteran of countless explosive Kenpo demonstrations, offered suggestions on how to integrate Kenpo into his choreography. Elvis, the veteran of countless concert performances, went to work adding his own unique elements. He began to work out in earnest, wearing wrist and ankle weights while he rehearsed, and by the time he opened, he was in shape.

He did fifty-seven shows in four weeks at the new International Hotel and broke all previous records. The critics raved:

"He wore a dark blue variation on a karate suit, tastefully tapered and belled…It felt like getting hit in the face with a bucket of melted ice. He looked so timeless up there, so constant, and yet you knew he was 33 . . . and then you felt unnerved." *New York Times* 8/10/69.

"Suddenly a lithe figure in a black modified karate costume dashed onto the stage and ripped into 'Blue Suede Shoes.' Guess who? It was Pentecostal. We were cheering before we had fully comprehended what had happened." *The Village Voice* 9/4/69.

Over the next several years, the choreography of Elvis's live performances became a perfect blend of Elvis's two great passions, singing and martial arts. Both artistic avenues allowed him to access and express his incredible inner power. Elvis would drop into low horse stances, wide kneels, neutral and forward bows, or finish a song in a crane stance. He would sink into a low one-legged deep knee bend and side-stretch the other leg, singing all the way down, then pause and say, "I hope this suit don't rip!" His songs were punctuated with blocks, strikes, and punches. Front, round, and knife-edge kicks flew through the air. Flashy hand combinations, usually a variation of American Kenpo's *Five Swords* technique, provided extra flourish. A long kata-like sequence might flow at the end of a song, ("Suspicious Minds") to the accompaniment of a drum solo. When it all melded harmoniously, the synergistic effect created a dynamic whole greater than the sum of its parts. He loved it, and it showed!

"Presley has also designed his karate chops for better frequency, so that when he does give the moves, the effect is dynamite in topping off a rhythm tune." *Variety* 2/3/71.

"Presley has evidently been in training for the physical side of his art. He does some modern dance stretches that are most difficult to accomplish without much training and practice. The karate exercise are also a part of his movements to the point of a well-rehearsed demonstration at the close of one of his hit ballads, 'Suspicious Minds'." *Variety* 8/25/71.

"Crouching and karate chopping, he teased the audience into a perfectly controlled, orderly, well behaved hysteria." *Chicago Tribune* 6/17/72.

A generation of imitators and impersonators has demonstrated that Elvis had *something* beyond good looks, voice, choreography and costumes. Call it *presence.* Call it *charisma.* Whatever the label, Elvis had "it." High-level martial art masters have it, too. Bruce Lee had it, and so did Ed Parker. These men all had that magnetic aura that brought a room to a standstill when they entered. Martial artists call it "*ch'i.*" Elvis was born with an abundance of *vital power,* his gift from God. But, just having the power wasn't enough; it needed avenues of expression. His Pentecostal upbringing allowed him to spontaneously express his strong spirit through Gospel singing. Disciplined practice of the martial arts taught him to focus and project his *ch'i* at will. The *combined effect* of Pentecostal expressiveness and martial arts focus was dynamite!

Watching one of Elvis's performances during this period, a high-ranking Kenpo master remarked, "I realized one day while watching Elvis perform a live concert that Elvis was using his *ch'i* power while performing. He had total control over his voice, his movements, the orchestra, the backup singers, and about 30,000 audience members. He was using his *ch'i* to bring everything into perfect harmony in that auditorium."

Sometimes Elvis's impromptu practice could result in humorous results. In May 1971, during a break in a studio recording session, Elvis was practicing gun disarms against Red West (he liked to practice against real guns). He knocked the weapon out of West's hand so hard that it smashed into Chip Young's custom guitar.

In 1972, having just separated from his wife, Elvis began to further intensify his training. A constant stream of threats made it prudent to have a more continuous karate presence, and in 1972 Elvis asked Ed Parker to work for him. However, Parker was at the height of his Kenpo-studio franchising efforts and suggested Dave Hebler as a replacement. Hebler was one of Parker's oldest and most skilled Kenpo black belts and had served as head instructor at Parker's Pasadena studio for seven years. He was amply qualified to protect Elvis and to train him and the Wests in Kenpo. He joined the Memphis Mafia team.

Elvis's extreme celebrity status stripped him of public privacy. Stars like Frank Sinatra and Sammy Davis, Jr. could enjoy themselves in the Vegas casinos without much bother. Elvis tried it – once! He was besieged by fans and robbed of any chance to relax and enjoy himself. Regardless, Elvis genuinely loved his fans and always poured out his heart and soul to provide the best possible performance.

Once again Elvis immersed himself in his frantic schedule of Vegas engagements and concert tours. His famous jumpsuit costumes evolved from his karate gi (uniform). The tight-fitting

sequin and jewel encrusted costumes cost thousands of dollars and could weigh as much as twenty to forty pounds. Performing in the costume was a workout in itself. One kick could, and often did, tear and ruin the expensive outfits.

In the early 1970s the martial arts were increasing in popularity in America. David Carradine's *Kung-Fu* television series began in 1972, and the next year Bruce Lee's *Enter the Dragon* exploded onto the screen.

Privately, Elvis's Kenpo studies gave him an inner refuge and a source of inner strength; his martial art was a life raft of stability in stormy seas.

Publicly, Elvis began to promote Kenpo with renewed evangelistic fervor. He wanted to share with his fans something that he loved, something that he was proud of. He placed Ed Parker's tiger and dragon International Kenpo Karate Association crest conspicuously on his black Gibson guitars where they would remain for years (1972 through 1975). He also had the IKKA emblem sewn onto his clothes.

As the most famous man ever to don a karate gi, Elvis promoted Parker's Kenpo more than any other single person. As the most visible entertainer of the *century*, his public endorsement of American Kenpo was literally priceless!

Bubbling with new creative energy, in 1973 Elvis undertook his most ambitious project to date: the *first* worldwide live television satellite broadcast. Elvis once again threw himself into training and rehearsal. When he landed in Hawaii, he was a lean 165 pounds. He had a new, all white American eagle outfit made for the occasion, and gave his costume designers fits when, a few days before the broadcast, he gave the cape and belt to Ed Parker as a memento. *Elvis, Aloha from Hawaii* was budgeted at 2.5 million dollars. It was broadcast live from Honolulu on January 14, 1973 and was watched by 1.5-billion people in forty countries, the IKKA crest prominently displayed on Elvis's guitar. To put that in perspective, four years earlier a "mere" 600-million viewers had tuned in to watch the 1969 Apollo moon landing! The concert also raised $85,000 for the Kui Lee Cancer Fund, more than tripling the anticipated amount. (Elvis bought a ticket to his own show.)

Ed Parker promoted Elvis to eighth-degree black belt on September 5, 1974, making him the highest-ranking black belt in the Kenpo system, under Parker. On the same day, Tom Kelly was promoted to sixth-degree, and Dave Hebler to seventh-degree. Hebler, who filled out the certificates in his capacity as President of the IKKA, points out that the word "honorary" does not appear anywhere on Elvis's certificate.

Skepticism has been expressed about Elvis's higher ranks, but in most karate systems rank above fourth or fifth degree is given for citizenship, community service, and service to the art. Famous for his patriotism and philanthropy, Elvis certainly qualified on the first counts; exposing Kenpo to 1.5 *billion* people clearly suffices for the last.

Elvis continued his live concert tours and Vegas performances. He was still a target for death threats and bomb scares, but his bodyguards suppressed publicity to minimize the copycat phenomenon. However, during a February 18, 1973 performance at the Las Vegas Hilton, three men rushed the stage and a brawl ensued. Elvis and his men "took out" the three assailants; Red West dragged one offstage in a headlock as Elvis scolded another, "You want to shake my hand, that's one thing; but you want to get tough, I'll whup your ass!" The audience cheered Elvis as the assailants were dragged off. Later, the three men sued Elvis for a million dollars, and lost.

Another time, Elvis happened to cruise by a streetfight in his limousine. He had his driver pull over, and he got out and suggested to the stunned participants that they find a peaceful resolution to their problems.

Elvis had a way of being on the cutting edge of things. Awareness of acupuncture dawned in the United States when, during President Nixon's historic 1972 visit to China, American television viewers witnessed acupuncture anesthesia for abdominal surgery. Acupuncture works by balancing the flow of a patient's *ch'i,* or vital energy. By the time acupuncture made American headlines, Elvis's spiritual and martial arts interests had already intersected in a long-time fascination with *ch'i.*

In 1973 Elvis heard that Bill Wallace, whom he had met in Memphis, was suffering from a serious injury to his left leg. Wallace, known as "Superfoot" for his superior kicking skill, used his left leg almost exclusively. Months of conventional medical treatment had failed to help, and things were looking bleak for Wallace's stellar tournament career.

Elvis invited Wallace to Graceland. When Wallace arrived, he discovered that Elvis had flown in an acupuncturist from Los Angeles to treat him. Acupuncture was unlicensed in 1973. As Wallace tells it, the acupuncturist stuck eighteen needles into his leg and, "I'll swear on a stack of Bibles, fifteen minutes after he stuck those needles in there, you could kick me in that same leg and it wouldn't hurt!" The leg was completely healed, and Wallace was able to continue his career, becoming the first middleweight champion at the *full-contact* PKA World Professional Karate Championships! Wallace gives Elvis credit for rescuing his career. He also noted, " . . . a lot of people (studied karate) that normally wouldn't . . . They took notice because of who he was."

By now, Red and Sonny West had earned their Kenpo black belts from Dave Hebler. Bill Wallace was available at the same time that Red West wanted to open up a karate studio in Memphis. West opened the Tennessee Karate Institute with Elvis's financial backing, and ads for the studio featured West and Elvis over the banner, "The School where Elvis trains when he's in town." Wallace was brought in to do the day-to-day teaching. Many of the era's top fighters, like Joe Lewis and Dominique Valera, would train at the TKI.

Elvis now had his own dojo. He designed a special "TCB" gi patch, based on his motto, "Take Care of Business, in a Flash!" The round patch featured the TCB/Lightning bolt symbol, over a red circle, surrounded by seven stars and the words, "Faith, Spirit, Discipline." Like Parker's IKKA crest, there was deep symbolism in the design. The seven stars represented seven as the divine number of Biblical numerology, the seven colors of the rainbow (symbol of God's promise) and the seven days of the week. The red circle symbolized the planet Earth, washed clean by the blood of Jesus. The TKI closed down when West left Elvis in 1976 and moved to Hollywood, and Wallace left the following year to pursue his full-contact fighting and movie careers.

Later, in an assessment of Elvis's skills, Wallace said: "He was pretty good for his age and, for the amount of time he had to spend on training, he was extremely good. He was forty years old when I started working with him . . . He always wanted to be the baddest dude in the world."

Thanks to Bruce Lee and JKD, the 1970s were the era of newly-created eclectic martial arts identified by initials. Not to be outdone, Elvis considered the formation of his own American TCB system. During a flight on his private jet, the *Lisa Marie*, he jotted down some of his musings, but tossed them in the trash. They were retrieved and preserved, and are now known as the "TCB Oath:"

More self-respect, more respect for fellow man.
Respect for fellow students and instructors.
Respect for all styles and techniques.
Body conditioning, mental conditioning,
Meditation for calming and stilling of the mind
and body.
Sharpen your skills, increase mental awareness,
for all those that might choose a new outlook and
personal philosophy.
Freedom from [excessive tension]

TCB TECHNIQUE
All techniques into one.

Elvis Presley 8th,
Applying all techniques into one.

Strangely, although Elvis and Bruce Lee had common interests and shared Ed Parker's friendship, they never met. MGM did float the idea of Lee and Elvis co-starring in a film, but Lee died (July 1973) before it could happen. The mind boggles at the prospect of the King of Rock and Roll and the King of Kung Fu together!

After Elvis's *Aloha from Hawaii* world broadcast, there were few mountains left to conquer in the entertainment field. When Ed Parker approached him with an idea, Elvis was ready to listen. George Waite, an entrepreneur and another Parker Kenpo black belt, had approached Parker with a film concept. He proposed a documentary that, in contrast to the current crop of Kung-Fu

movies, would show the true discipline and excitement of Kenpo. The concept was to follow a group of fighters through their training and competition and to reveal other facets of the arts.

Elvis, the martial artist who had always wanted to be a serious actor, loved the idea. When he met with Waite, the project's producer, at the Vegas Hilton in early 1974, he offered to finance the project to the tune of $125,000. The idea was to form a "United States Championship Team" to fight European teams.

After they talked for a while, Waite told Elvis, "You'd be the man to draw attention from a general audience to the martial arts. I would like you to be in it. I'd like to show your katas, your techniques, and interlace that through the film, and have you do the narrating for it." The film would be called *The New Gladiators*.

Elvis was in! In addition to demonstrating his own karate skills, he agreed to narrate the film. He told Waite, "I wouldn't mind showing the world I'm in karate." When Waite recommended Elvis contact *Fighting Stars*, a magazine devoted to celebrities studying the martial arts, Elvis replied, "That's just for celebrities. I'm a karate man. I want to be on the cover of *Black Belt.*"

Unfortunately, Elvis's contributions to the marital arts world were not widely recognized during his lifetime.

The US team was composed of Darnell Garcia, Tom Kelly, Ron Marchini, John Natividad, and Benny Urquidez. Parker and Waite led the Team to Europe in late 1974, introducing the Europeans to North American free-style sparring. Fights against British and Belgian teams were filmed. Two additional tournaments were filmed in the States; the Western Pro/Am in Oakland, and the Urquidez Brother's Invitational in Beverly Hills.

Elvis wanted the US Team to look sharp, so he special-ordered eighteen custom-made red, white, and blue top-of-the-line Tokaido gis from Japan. Tokaido Japan worked overnight to make the gis and sent them on a specially-booked Pan-Am flight. They arrived in four days at a cost of $400 each (normal price $35).

Waite recalled, "(In September, 1974) . . . about a week after I had shown (Elvis) what we had filmed in Europe . . . (he) called me and asked me if I could get a film crew over there. He was very excited about it. I sent down two cameramen and they filmed the whole segment. I got two twenty-minute reels of Elvis performing karate."

Photographers from *People* magazine were also invited to shoot photos for inclusion in their January 1975 issue, commemorating Elvis's fortieth birthday. Ignored by *Black Belt*, Elvis would have to settle for the cover of *People* magazine (circulation, two million).

Those present saw a rare demonstration by Elvis captured on film. Besides the usual karate demonstration, (if any karate demonstration by Elvis could be labeled "usual"), Elvis showed his ability to withstand punishment by absorbing big Red West's gut punches. Then Elvis demonstrated his *ch'i kung* skills.

Martial artists believe that one's *ch'i* can not only be accumulated and released, it can also be directed to specific parts of the body. A singer's voice is a delicate instrument; consider that Julie Andrews had her singing career sidetracked by a routine surgery to remove a throat polyp. In addition, breath control is important to a singer – and to a martial artist. Elvis was both, and he used his ability to its fullest in both fields. Breathing exercises are also an integral part of *ch'i kung* energy cultivation. Ed Parker defined *ch'i* as the remarkable powers that result when an integrated mind (conscious + subconscious = *super*conscious) is synchronized with body and breath.

Elvis summoned his *ch'i* and then amazed everyone by absorbing West's strike to his *throat!* Then, with Red West's clenched fist jammed against the front of Elvis's neck and another large man bracing West from behind, Elvis used his million-dollar throat to literally shove the two big men back across the room! It must be noted that in later years, even when his health was declining, Elvis's voice *never* failed him.

In March 1975 Elvis saw the footage of his demo and was motivated to step up his training and lose weight. In a 1977 issue of *Inside Kung Fu* magazine, George Waite told interviewer John Corcoran, "The film is something that everybody told me Elvis wanted to do for years, ever since Germany. He wanted to do a film of him and the arts and what they were all about. A true film, not one of the Bruce Lee types with a lot of flash and a lot of high kicks and jumps. He wanted to show what it was like to be out on the mat . . . little things that maybe only black belts experience."

The *New Gladiators* was to be Elvis's gift to the karate world. Unfortunately, the project lost momentum and was never completed. The footage still exists, however, and is owned by Wayne Carman, author of the book, *Elvis's Karate Legacy*.

Elvis continued his live performances. During his 1974-1975 seasons, his passionate proselytizing of Kenpo reached even greater heights. He would often appear onstage in Vegas with a black Kenpo gi-top over his jumpsuit, sporting a full complement of Ed Parker's IKKA patches. In addition to the karate moves integral to his act, he would frequently pause to give a karate demonstration, occasionally lasting nearly a half-hour. He would take breaks during his performances to explain to the audience the significance of the oriental ideograms on his patches or belt, the philosophy and benefits of the karate way of life, and his life-long involvement in the art. One night he explained to his audience that his hand was swollen from brick breaking earlier that day.

Elvis was not always content with the limitations of his own stage. On September 3, 1974, after his own Vegas show had closed, he attended a Tom Jones concert. Elvis was nattily attired in a leather suit, covered by his black Kenpo gi top. When Jones introduced him, Elvis got up on stage and gave a 20-minute karate demo!

On the IKKA Kenpo crest the tiger symbolizes the physical, technical side of the art, and the dragon symbolizes the intangible, spiritual side of the art. Elvis had two spectacular new jumpsuits made, one covered with a tiger design, the other by an elaborate dragon design. Never known for his conservative dress code, Elvis might relax on his private jet while wearing his gi and black belt. He would even occasionally appear in public wearing one of his fancy gi tops. As usual, his performances weren't limited to Las Vegas.

On a cold New Year's Eve in 1975, Elvis performed at the Silverdome in Pontiac, Michigan before a record-breaking audience of 65,000. His entire performance was infused with martial arts. There are photos of him gesturing to the crowd with exotic Kenpo hand formations, including Parker's favorite, "twin dragons fighting for the pearl" (2-fingered claw). The entire audience was enthralled by the energy he radiated.

Through 1976 and up to the time of his death, Elvis continued to perform, although his performances were sometimes uneven as his health began to decline. But all reviewers agreed on one thing:

"Involuntarily, Elvis made It All Happen again. His voice is as subtle and supple as a mellotron, and his gospel numbers were glowingly rendered." *LA Herald-Examiner* 4/27/76.

"The saddest part of all this is that Presley's voice is as good as ever. It is still rich and full, still has that deeply sonorous sexiness that made high school girls swoon two decades ago." *The Washington Post* 6/28/76.

Ed Parker was the last martial artist to spend significant time with Elvis, who asked Parker to accompany him on tour. During his later years, Parker would frequently travel with Elvis as a friend, providing him with companionship, training, and security.

Parker would later say, "Elvis was a damn good black belt . . . by any standards. He had a lot of guts and pain didn't bother him. If he got hit while we were working out he took it like a man. In fact, if you did hit him he'd come right back after you. He was tough and had a lot of courage. (His eighth-degree) was no nomination of honor. He was a good black belt no matter how he's tested." Parker also noted that Elvis's razor-sharp memory enabled him to know the IKKA manual better than he did.

At a February 1988 Tribute held in honor of Grandmaster Parker, Parker reminisced, "Another important man in my life was the late Elvis Presley. And the reason I loved him was that when he saw all the fans come about he said, 'You know, my mother always told me, never forget my fans. And I don't know why my fans are all up in awe about me, because I put my pants on one leg at a time like anybody else.'"

In a soft voice, Parker said, "It's the way you do it, Elvis; that's what makes the difference."

When Elvis was in the "zone" and his energy was flowing, he was still capable of putting on a great show for his fans. On New Year's Eve 1976, Parker accompanied Elvis to Pittsburgh. Elvis gave another long, dynamic performance and finished with a flashy Kenpo demonstration. He rang in the New Year and the final months of his life.

Elvis's last concert was on June 26, 1977. By all accounts it was an energetic performance. His voice still had its unique power. Meanwhile, his health was deteriorating.

A weight on a spinning top, if it is centered, will enhance its stability at high speed. But let that same weight move slightly off-center and it induces a wobble. The more it wobbles, the more the weight drifts off center, until the oscillations become so great that all stability is lost. Elvis's great gift of *inner power* was like that weight at the center of his spinning life. When his *energy* was centered, he was capable of drawing from it to fuel amazing achievements. But, as his energy moved off-center, his physical and mental condition began to wildly fluctuate. Great energy can lend itself to great imbalances. Because his underlying problem was an imbalance of *ch'i*, strong medications would only exacerbate the problem: it would be like trying to pat down the surface of a body of water to make it become still. The harder one tries, the more turbulence one creates.

In the final weeks of his life, the mental and physical oscillations of Elvis's yin and yang *ch'i* became increasingly extreme. He seemed to intuit the nature of his problem; the day he died, he was reading several books, among them the Bible, and another book on how to manage psychic energy (*ch'i*). But, his reservoir had finally run dry. In Chinese thought, the wax body of a candle is analogous to one's reserve of *jing/essence*, the flame is analogous to one's *ch'i/activity*, and the light, the *purpose of it all*, is one's *shen/spirit*. It is said that the candle that burns twice as bright burns half as long. Elvis had tremendous *ch'i*. His Pentecostal roots allowed him to radiate energy like a beacon; his Kenpo discipline taught him to focus energy like a laser. His ability to tap into his inner strength made him stand out, not only in a crowded room, but also in a crowded *world!* But, at the end, his *jing/essence* was exhausted, his yin and yang *ch'i* separated and, sorrowfully, his flickering flame finally extinguished.

The very energy that rocketed Elvis into orbit, the *power* that made him the greatest entertainer of all time and the most famous exponent of American Kenpo, shot him prematurely back to earth like a meteor. Like the waxen wings of Icarus that melted too close to the Sun, the *gift* that allowed Elvis to soar so high was the very thing that caused him to fall so far and fast.

However, there is a Chinese proverb:

*"It is better to be a diamond with a flaw, than a pebble without one."*

*Full Salute*

*And*

**Thank You, Brother**